CONTENTS

199
NIGHTLIFE

From risqué hostess clubs to down-home pubs, with plenty of dancing and drinking in between, Hong Kong is blessed with a host of nighttime amusements. Here's a look at our favorites.

209
SHOPS

You name it, Hong Kong's got it, and generally at unbeatable prices. In fact, Hong Kong's array of retail shops is so mind-boggling that the visitor can become hopelessly overwhelmed. That's where Gault Millau comes in: our insider's guide to the crème de la crème—priceless antiques, high-tech electronics, custom tailors, factory outlets—will steer you straight to the best buys in this capital of consumerism.

265
SIGHTS

A tour of Hong Kong's must-sees. Gaze across Victoria Harbour from atop the Peak. Take a step back in time while drifting on a sampan in Aberdeen Harbour. Catch Hong Kong's racing fever at the Happy Valley Racetrack. And steam across the harbor on the world's most dramatic commuter system, the Star Ferry.

275
OUT OF HONG KONG

Hong Kong's environs are as intriguing as the city itself. We'll take you on a tour of casino-crazy Macau, the lovely beaches and sleepy towns of the outlying islands, and the fast-growing New Territories.

297
CITYLORE

An insightful look at the underlying importance of superstition and spirits that permeates virtually every aspect of Hong Kong life.

The Best Of

HONG KONG

ichelles @ the Fringe
877-4000
2 Lower Albert Rd.

Szechuan Lau
891-9027
466 Lockhart Rd

Editor
Colleen Dunn Bates

Contributing Editors
Ken Barrett, Barry Girling, Adil Iskaros, Lorris Murail, Sondra Rosenberg, Merrill Shindler, Stuart Silverman, Deborah Sroloff, David Standish

Assistant Editors
Jennifer Rylaarsdam, Margery L. Schwartz

Prentice Hall Travel Editor
Amit Shah

Silks
8450154

Operations
Alain Gayot

Directed by
André Gayot

PRENTICE HALL ▪ NEW YORK

Other Gault Millau Guides Available
from Prentice Hall Trade Division

The Best of Chicago
The Best of France
The Best of Italy
The Best of London
The Best of Los Angeles
The Best of New England
The Best of New York
The Best of San Francisco
The Best of Washington, D.C.

Published by Prentice Hall Trade Division
A Division of Simon & Schuster Inc.
15 Columbus Circle
New York, New York 10023

Please address all comments regarding The Best of Hong Kong to:
Gault Millau Inc.
P.O. Box 361144
Los Angeles, CA 90036

Library of Congress Cataloging-in-Publication Data
The Best of Hong Kong
Includes index.
1. Guide-books. I. Bates, Colleen Dunn. II. Barrett, Ken.
DS769.H73B47 1989 915.12504'5
89-15986

ISBN 0-13-082975-7

Special thanks to the staff of Prentice Hall Travel for their invaluable aid in producing
Printed in Hong Kong

HONG KONG

SPEED CITY

Hong Kong is like a pinball machine by the sea—all lights and action and buildings going up or down. It's arguably the fastest city on earth; it makes New York City seem rather slow in comparison. At first glance, Hong Kong looks like a strikingly beautiful compacted version of New York moved to San Francisco Bay, with lighting by Las Vegas. Its magnificent harbor is always busy. Ancient-looking red-sailed junks (immortalized for '50s teenagers by Pat Boone), suggesting butterflies alight on bits of floating wood, glide timelessly past huge modern container ships, *Love Boat* cruise ships, snazzy little yachts, rusty freighters and gray-painted naval vessels flying various national flags. Overhead is the *thwup thwup thwup* of helicopters carrying CEOs to work in Hong Kong's Central from Kai Tak International Airport, with its single landfill runway jutting out into the harbor. Like waterbugs on speed, hydrofoils full of high rollers head for the casinos of Portuguese Macau, while dark seagoing vultures called black kites cruise low over the water looking for scraps and opportunities—just like everyone else in Hong Kong.

Hong Kong hums like no place else. It is *the* business arena in this part of the world, a capitalistic boxing ring where the ambitious gather to slug it out. Founded 150 years ago on the solid rock of profit back during the Opium Wars, Hong Kong has remained true to its school, though over the years its economic base has shifted from warehouse *entrepôt* trade to the manufacture of cheap and/or designer-knockoff goods, and now it's moving toward becoming the major financial center of East Asia. Lots of those new buildings going up belong to banks, and the amount of money turned over daily in Hong Kong's investment markets places it third in the world, after New York and London.

The high-rises elbowing each other in a free-for-all scramble on the Hong Kong side are futurist and innovative. Hong Kong's skyline—

or rather, harborline—is more dramatic and changes faster than any other city's. Two gunmetal-gray buildings adorned with strange blipping and bleeping lights suggest great camshafts for the Starship *Enterprise*. A gold-windowed high-rise box visible east of the Star Ferry docks has reminded one English-speaking writer of a giant Dunhill lighter, while it is referred to by Hong Kong's Chinese as "the servant's tooth."

All of this is best seen, of course, from one of the many white-and-green Star Ferries on their seven-minute runs, plying sedately between Hong Kong Island and Kowloon—easily the cheapest (about 20 U.S. cents) and most wonderful short commute on the planet. The yin and yang of mainland Kowloon and Hong Kong Island, like parts of a broken coin, form a cozy parenthesis that makes Hong Kong one of the world's best and prettiest deep-water ports.

Victoria Harbour was the reason for Hong Kong's settlement in the 1830s, since it provided a safe anchorage for the British fleet, which was pounding on Canton 75 miles to the northwest during the first so-called Opium War. The British prime minister at the time thought that claiming Hong Kong in 1841 was a decidedly foolish move, calling it "a barren island with barely a house on it"—which was true. But Hong Kong proved to be more valuable than even the *taipans* ever dreamed.

Today it's a city of 5.6 million people crammed onto the "barren island" and Kowloon, which together constitute a major capitalist blister on the socialist body of mainland China. However, this wayward part of the ancient Celestial Kingdom will be reclaimed by China in 1997, at the expiration of the 99-year British lease on the New Territories. It should be interesting.

There is no more resolutely materialistic city on earth. Hong Kong exists purely for buying and selling, which is why it's a shopper's heaven, the Bloomingdale's of Asia. Nowhere else do profit and the bottom line mean more than in Hong Kong, which remains devoted to the free-market ideas that led to its founding; for better or worse, the flame of unfettered capitalism still burns brightly here. Even the new multimillion-dollar tunnel project is privately funded. There are no tariffs on most goods going in and out, and income taxes top out at 16 percent for both individuals and corporations. There are more millionaires and Rolls-Royces per capita in Hong Kong than anywhere else. More money is routinely bet on a single race at Happy Valley than is dropped at any other racetrack on the globe. In Hong Kong, first they look at the purse.

There also seem to be more counterfeit designer-label goods and ubiquitous imitation designer watches for sale in Hong Kong than anywhere else. Check out the nighttime open-air Temple Street Market for phony designer items of every sort, along with bootleg cassettes of albums by all the current stars. They ought to put *Caveat Emptor* on Hong Kong's flag. It's a place where you can pick up an antique Ming jade sculpture that's maybe two weeks old, or a bargain new "Sony" video camera made in some Kowloon basement; then again, it could be the real thing. It just depends on how sharp you are.

And yet, in seven years, the People's Republic of China will be taking over this economic amusement park. The Chinese have pledged to leave Hong Kong alone for at least 50 years, to make it another "Special Economic Zone." The Chinese are great pragmatists (they invented Taoism, didn't they?) and it seems in their interest to do just that, since Hong Kong remains China's primary business window on the world—much of everything going in or out of China still passes through Hong Kong. So they may indeed keep their hands-off promise, no matter that Hong Kong ideologically is a neon viper in China's bosom.

But given the upheavals in China during the last 75 years, you never know. As we go to press, yet another upheaval—this one spurred by students demonstrating for democracy, freedom of the press and such—is building in significance and violence. The government's crackdown on the demonstrators has more than a few Hong Kong companies concerned about their profit-seeking futures. But still, China seems to be meditating on its Marxism in inventive ways, absorbing and changing these ideas to suit China, so it's hard to say how it will handle the takeover of Hong Kong.

The betting is going both ways. Noticeable numbers of people who can afford it are bailing out to places like New York and Vancouver—to such an extent that Hong Kong is suffering a brain drain in its professional classes. There's also a labor shortage for the first time in Hong Kong's history.

But billions of dollars in investments are still pouring in. Architect I. M. Pei has just completed the new X-marks-the-spot Bank of China Building that, at 74 stories, is the tallest building in Asia (it looks like Chicago's Hancock Center in living color). The just-opened high-tech exposition center also on the Hong Kong side is a multimillion-dollar project, equipped with "lifts" that can hold semi trucks, auditoriums whose armrest headsets provide United Nations–style simultaneous translations of the goings-on into four languages, and a three-story glass-walled atrium overlooking Victoria Harbour. A second cross-harbor tunnel is nearing completion at huge expense. And even such a presumably careful American corporation as Ramada Inn seems to be betting things won't change much, having sunk quite a few million into the elegant new Ramada Renaissance on the Kowloon side, just up the hill from the venerable Peninsula hotel, Hong Kong's grande dame.

Regardless of what happens with China, Hong Kong is nevertheless zooming full-speed ahead toward the future, and in some regards it's already there. It's futuristic *Blade Runner* come to life, albeit with more warmth, appeal and good food.

But it is also, for all its first-blush futurist Westernization, a predominantly Chinese city—more than 95 percent of the population is Chinese—and so its contrasts, as we used to say in the '60s, are mind-blowing.

There is the exquisite Regent hotel right on Victoria Harbour, with a view that won't quit and service to match, a hotel consistently rated number one or number two in the world. But just a mile or so up the way is the Wan Loy Restaurant, where Chinese men bring their live birds in cages each morning, along with the six-packs of live grasshoppers they've just purchased on nearby Bird Street, to sit around in beat-up brown Naugahyde booths, smoking, having their morning tea, cutting up the grasshoppers to feed to their birds, which keep the place ringing with birdsong.

And in Hong Kong's Central, there's a standard-looking 7-Eleven, such as you might see in Doom, Georgia, where you can get a Pepsi and a Twinkie 24 hours a day. But occupying a scrap of space in the alley next to it are the pleasantly exotic smells and the steam of a Chinese open-air diner, an impromptu setup consisting of a cooking cart and a few banged-up folding chairs and card tables. Here the special of the day might be Princess Eel or Three Happiness Snake— the main ingredients purchased live and wriggling that morning from the snake shops in West Central, which keep a portion of their wares stacked in round wire cages in Medusa-like tangles on the sidewalk by way of advertising.

What's great about Hong Kong is that, like at Alice's Restaurant, you can get anything you want. You can shop your brains out and wear your credit cards thin, eat at some of the hundreds of excellent restaurants and sleep on ironed cotton sheets in a harbor-view suite at The Regent or The Peninsula. Or you can duck off onto some side street or neighborhood and suddenly be worlds away, encountering things and ideas thousands of miles and many years distant from your own life: outdoor barbers, herbal remedy shops, little streets where they sell only eggs or "chop blocks" (personalized imprints carved in stone to stamp on letters and such), institutions such as the Buddha Secretarial School, the Companion Reptile Company, Popeye Topless and Thin's Travel Appliance Store (he sells luggage).

Hong Kong, we promise, will ring your gong.

RESTAURANTS

INTRODUCTION

Nowhere does the old maxim, "Eat, drink and be merry," spring more readily to mind than in the densely populated, cosmopolitan community of Hong Kong. The sheer number of restaurants will instantly convince you that perhaps no other people in the world are as obsessed with food as the residents of Hong Kong. Dining out is not a rare, special-occasion treat, as it is for most people in the world—it is an integral part of everyday life.

Although many of the world's great cuisines (notably French) are well represented in the region, it is the art of Chinese cooking—and believe us, it is an art—that has been carefully honed in Hong Kong, indisputably the greatest center of Chinese cuisine in the world. It's certainly the largest in terms of numbers: it's estimated that this compact community is home to an astounding 30,000 restaurants—one for every 200 people—from street stalls to small neighborhood restaurants to monstrous Cantonese feeding halls to the elegant dining rooms in some of the world's most famous hotels.

They say that the Chinese, when confronted with the unknown, will first try to taste it. We haven't the slightest doubt that this is true. Throughout history, the Chinese have used a remarkable degree of imagination, perhaps unmatched in any other culture, to cook just about anything in every way imaginable. What they lacked in natural resources they made up for with native resourcefulness. Nothing is allowed to go to waste, and no animal is taboo. The result is a cuisine that is one of the most intriguing and flavorful in the world. It's also one of the healthiest. Shunning frozen foods, the Chinese in Hong Kong will often make as many as three daily trips to the market in search of the best and freshest foods.

Chinese dishes are prepared and served with careful thought given to balance and harmony, the yin and the yang. The incredible range of ingredients and cooking techniques provides this balance. Harmony also comes into play in the physical act of dining out: eating in Hong Kong is a communal experience, and a shared meal is considered to be the visible manifestation of the harmony that should exist between family and friends. To while away the hours over a meal is not considered a waste of time. On the contrary— time spent at the table is an honor to your guests, who consider the abundance and refinement of the feast to be a gauge of their host's esteem for them. On such occasions all manner of praise—the noisier the better—is welcome.

Since we brought up noise, we must warn you that first-time visitors to a Hong Kong dim sum restaurant for a weekend lunch will undoubtedly leave with a lasting impression of utter chaos: a cacophonous din of voices, whizzing trolleys and clattering dishes. The best way to deal with this is to jump right in and ask for a center table. If you're tucked away in the corner, you'll have a problem getting food from the trolleys. You may miss some of the subtle aromas of the mouth-watering dishes as they are wheeled by, and you'll lose out on an opportunity to sit among a sea of Hong Kong families talking and laughing, often with three or four generations at the same table. No intimate tête à têtes here, when relatives, friends and co-workers assemble for one of the great moments of a Chinese day.

Another word of warning: if you arrange to meet your lunch date in a Chinese restaurant, be prepared to scour dimly lit nooks and crannies and floor after floor crammed with tables of people absorbed in endless discussion (food often being a favorite topic). Dining rooms in many Chinese restaurants come in all shapes, sizes and colors, sometimes connecting, sometimes isolated, and you may have to explore many of them before you find the familiar face.

Once settled, don't let yourself be intimidated by the curt, quick waiter, who will not hesitate to interrupt conversations and who rarely takes time to smile. He is as efficient a waiter as exists, and he's just getting on with his job. Sit back and watch him for a few minutes, and you'll be amazed at the perfection of his dexterous and speedy service. Not even the size of the tip will slow him down.

Of course, you don't find only Chinese food in Hong Kong. As you'll discover in the reviews that follow, refined samples of other Asian and Western cuisines are served here. In fact, the spectrum of international cooking is more widely and completely represented in Hong Kong than in any other city we know. There are two reasons for this: Hong Kong is a booming international marketplace that's home to people from all over the world, and also because the Chinese have employed their collective enterprising spirit to satisfy the tastes of every visitor. If you can't find food you like in Hong Kong, then you don't like food.

A final note: we have done our best to ensure that the information in all our restaurant reviews is accurate. But Hong Kong's restaurants are notoriously volatile. For instance, we recently returned to a favorite Cantonese restaurant, an immensely popular place, to discover that it had suddenly and inexplicably vanished. So we advise you to call first, or check with your hotel concierge, before setting out for your meal.

A CHINESE SAMPLER

China is a vast country encompassing a remarkable variety of climates, agricultural methods and traditions. Consequently, there is an equal variety of culinary styles. Here's a brief introduction to China's most popular regional cuisines:

CANTONESE

Of all China's regional cuisines, Cantonese is generally recognized to be the finest—an old Chinese adage advises those seeking the ideal place to live, marry, die and, most importantly, eat, to move to Canton. The area is famous for its sweet-and-sour dishes, familiar to Americans, for its devotion to seafood, and for its dim sum, that beloved array of little tastes (dumplings, buns, meats, tiny pastries) served for lunch or afternoon tea. So popular is dim sum that you are well advised to arrive early for a dim sum lunch; the place will surely fill up fast.

Since Hong Kong borders the Canton province, most of its population, and therefore its restaurants, are Cantonese. The style of cooking is light, refined and delicate in flavor, favoring such things as steamed fish and crisp vegetables. So respected is this cuisine that Cantonese chefs ran the emperors' kitchens in Peking. The Cantonese are also fond of such exotic delicacies as snake, bird's nest, shark's fin, frogs' legs and turtle.

CHIU CHOW

Centered around the Swatow port area in the Canton province, Chiu Chow residents were strongly influenced by the Cantonese. They are a fishing people, which explains the heavy reliance on seafood, prepared in light styles akin to Cantonese cooking. Shark's fin is a particular Chiu Chow favorite. They're also big on dumplings, goose (sliced goose in fried blood) and such inexpensive foods as chicken liver, steamed eel and goose and chicken blood. Beware of their beloved Iron Buddha tea, served in thimble-size cups before and after a meal—there's enough caffeine in that thimbleful to keep you wired for days.

HAKKA

The cuisine of the Hakka people, who originated in northern China and then emigrated to the Canton and Fukien provinces, is simple, hearty and rather plain. To see them through the heavy winters, they used salt to preserve foods, which explains such common Hakka dishes as chicken in salt. Another distinguishing feature of this cuisine is the use of grains, rather than rice, as its staple food. Also popular is tofu (Hakka-stuffed tofu) and cabbage (pork with cabbage).

BEIJING

Once home to the Imperial Court of China, Beijing, the most important city in northern China, is famous for its Peking duck, the most glorious and celebrated of the Imperial offerings. Since Cantonese chefs manned the Imperial kitchens, the Cantonese style was a strong influence in the development of Pekingese cooking. Other influences were the cold weather and the need to impress the Imperial Court with fancy techniques and presentations. This led to such hearty, flamboyant dishes as the aforementioned Peking duck, beggar's chicken (baked in clay) and hotpots. Also common are mutton, barbecued meats, pan-fried onion cakes (a staple) and garlic-and-chili sauce.

SHANGHAI

The biggest city in China and its greatest port, Shanghai is near the magnificent Yangtze River and surrounded by a fertile countryside that produces a variety of fruits and vegetables. This fine produce explains why the area is noted for its vegetarian cuisine. It's also noted for its reliance on noodles instead of rice, for such cold dishes as drunken chicken (steamed in wine) and smoked fish, and for the rich, soy-based brown sauce that seems to accompany most of its dishes. The river and long coastline ensure a plentiful supply of fresh fish and shellfish, which go into the making of such Shanghainese favorites as eels in rice wine and garlic, and freshwater hairy crabs.

SZECHUAN

Very much influenced by central Asia, Szechuan cooking is distinguished by its reliance on strong flavorings and hot spices, particularly red chilis, Szechuan peppercorns, ginger, onion and garlic. Commonly used in Szechuan cooking are such foods as smoked duck, eggplant, spicy soups (such as hot-and-sour soup) and potent garlic-and-chili sauces. Although beloved by Westerners whose attitude is "the hotter the better," Szechuan cooking is considered "barbaric" and heavy-handed by the Cantonese, who prefer lighter, more delicate flavors.

A FEW WORDS OF ADVICE

• More than a passion, food is an obsession in Hong Kong, and good food is considered essential to good living. Just as an American asks in greeting, "How are you?" the universal Chinese greeting literally translates: "Have you eaten yet?"

• Beneath their reserved exteriors, the Chinese can be formidable social drinkers. If you are invited to a banquet, make up your mind before you start: either drink everyone under the table, or decide to stay sober. Once you have accepted that first toast, there is no turning back.

• Spitting one's bones directly onto the table is quite acceptable, and the tablecloth doubles as your napkin.

- "Face"—maintaining propriety—is immensely important to the Chinese. Paying a restaurant bill after eating with a Chinese friend is no easy feat. He will probably use every trick in the book to pick up the tab. This could include paying a week in advance, signaling to his wife to pay the bill en route to the ladies' room or even keeping a signed blank check on file at the restaurant.

- As we discuss in the Citylore chapter, superstition is an important part of Hong Kong life. For instance, carving a fish served at your table should be done without turning the fish upside down. It is believed that turning a fish upside down can bring bad luck, causing the boat to figuratively "capsize."

- Topics of dinner-table conversation can also be sensitive. Money and age are particular subjects that should be handled with care.

ABOUT THE REVIEWS

RATINGS

As in all Gault Millau guides, Hong Kong's restaurants are rated in the same manner that French students are graded: on a scale of one to twenty, twenty being unattainable perfection. The rankings reflect *only* the quality of the cooking; decor, service, reception and atmosphere are explicitly commented on within the reviews. Restaurants ranked thirteen and above are distinguished with toques (chef's hats), according to the following:

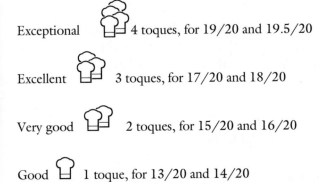

Exceptional   4 toques, for 19/20 and 19.5/20

Excellent   3 toques, for 17/20 and 18/20

Very good   2 toques, for 15/20 and 16/20

Good   1 toque, for 13/20 and 14/20

Keep in mind that we are comparing Hong Kong's restaurants to the finest in the world—just because the city's best restaurants don't get four toques doesn't mean they aren't exceptionally good. Also, these rankings are *relative*. One toque for 13/20 is not a very good ranking for a highly reputed (and very expensive) temple of fine dining, but it is quite complimentary for a small, unpretentious place.

PRICES

Unless otherwise noted, the prices given—*in Hong Kong dollars*—are for a complete dinner for two, including an appetizer, main course and dessert per person, as well as service and a bottle of wine. It is, naturally, difficult to estimate the cost of wine; for our purposes we've assumed it to be a modest bottle at a modest restaurant and a bit more expensive wine at a more serious place. Lovers of the great Burgundies and Bordeaux will find their bills higher than our estimates. At many of the humbler Asian restaurants, we quote the price for a dinner with beer.

Please note that it is also quite difficult to give an average price for a Chinese restaurant, since the prices of the individual dishes vary so dramatically. At many Cantonese restaurants, for instance, two can dine for about HK$200 (at the time of this writing, about US$25), if they stick to chicken, meat and simple seafood dishes. But if they indulge in such prized treats as shark's fin, bird's nest and abalone, their bill can double, triple or even quadruple. In general, our estimated prices do not include such costly dishes.

CREDIT CARDS

After the hours for each restaurant, we list the credit cards accepted, if any. "All major cards" includes all of the following: American Express, Carte Blanche, Diner's Club, MasterCard and Visa.

HOURS

The hours we have listed at the end of each review are the restaurant's official hours, but that doesn't necessarily mean they are open during those times. A place that claims to be open until midnight may well decide to close at 10:30 if business is slow. If you're planning to dine late, call first and have a backup restaurant in mind.

TIPPING

Many restaurants automatically add a service charge that ranges between 10 and 15 percent. But because this sort of enforced tipping isn't uniformly practiced, and since it's not always easy to figure out on a bill written entirely in Chinese, you should always check to see if the tip is indeed included. An additional modest gratuity is usually appropriate, unless your service was terrible. But terrible service is rare in Hong Kong; at the more elegant places, the staff usually bends over backward to please customers, and at the simpler Chinese places, the service generally makes up in speed and efficiency for what it lacks in warmth. In fact, we've often noticed that the grumpier the waiter, the faster the food arrives.

TOQUE TALLY

18/20

Lai Ching Heen *Kowloon*
Restaurant de France *Kowloon*

16/20

Hilton Grill *Hong Kong Island*
Plume *Kowloon*

15/20

Gaddi's *Kowloon*
Hunan Garden *Hong Kong Island*
Margaux *Kowloon*
Pierrot *Hong Kong Island*
La Rose Noire *Hong Kong Island*
Shang Palace *Kowloon*
Spring Moon *Kowloon*
Toh Lee *Kowloon*
The Verandah *Hong Kong Island*

14/20

Bentley's Seafood Restaurant and Oyster Bar *Hong Kong Island*
The Bloom *Hong Kong Island*
Bocarino's Grill *Hong Kong Island*
City Chiu Chow Restaurant *Kowloon*
Flourishing Restaurant *Kowloon*
Fook Lam Moon *Hong Kong Island*
Prince Court Szechuan *Kowloon*
Tai Pan *Kowloon*
Tao Yuan *Hong Kong Island*
Viceroy of India *Hong Kong Island*

13/20

Amigo *Hong Kong Island*
Arirang *Kowloon*
Baron's Table *Kowloon*
Chesa *Kowloon*
Cleveland Szechuan *Hong Kong Island*
Eagle's Nest *Hong Kong Island*
Excelsior Grill *Hong Kong Island*
Fat Siu Lau Seafood *Kowloon*
Flourishing Court *Kowloon*
Fung Lum Szechuan *Kowloon*
Ginza *Kowloon*
Golden Unicorn *Kowloon*
Great Shanghai *Kowloon*
Guangzhou Garden *Hong Kong Island*
Loong Yuen *Kowloon*
Lung Wah Hotel *New Territories & Outlying Islands*
Manhattan Restaurant *Hong Kong Island*
North Park *Kowloon*
Pak Loh *Hong Kong Island*
Pep 'n' Chilli *Hong Kong Island*
Perfume River *Hong Kong Island*
Red Pepper *Hong Kong Island*

Regal Seafood *Kowloon*
Sagano *Kowloon*
Sampan Dinners *Hong Kong Island*
Sawadee Thai Restaurant *Kowloon*
The Steak House *Kowloon*
Sun Tung Lok Shark's Fin Restaurant *Kowloon*
Sunning Unicorn *Hong Kong Island*
Tin Tin Hot Pot *Kowloon*
Tsui Hang Village *Kowloon*
Wan Loong Court *Kowloon*
Yung Kee *Hong Kong Island*

12/20

American Restaurant *Hong Kong Island*
Benkay Japanese *Hong Kong Island*
Bodhi Vegetarian Restaurant *Kowloon*
Bombay Palace *Hong Kong Island*
The Bostonian *Kowloon*
California *Hong Kong Island*
Chili Club *Hong Kong Island*
The Chinese Restaurant *Kowloon*
Chiuchow Garden *Kowloon*
East Ocean *Kowloon*
Flower Lounge *Hong Kong Island*
Fook Yuen Seafood *Hong Kong Island*
Gaylord *Kowloon*
Golden Island Bird's Nest *Kowloon*
Harbour View Seafood Restaurant *Kowloon*
Hugo's *Kowloon*
Jimmy's Kitchen *Hong Kong Island*
Kanetanaka *Hong Kong Island*
King Heung *Hong Kong Island*
Lalique *Kowloon*
Landau's *Hong Kong Island*
Lao Ching Hing *Hong Kong Island*
Mandarin Grill *Hong Kong Island*
Mistral *Kowloon*
Mozart Stub'n *Hong Kong Island*
Neptune Seafood *Hong Kong Island*
Oiman *New Territories & Outlying Islands*

Orchid Garden *Kowloon*
Palace Seafood *Hong Kong Island*
Peach Garden Seafood *New Territories & Outlying Islands*
Rangoon *Hong Kong Island*
Shanghai Garden *Hong Kong Island*
Silla Won *Hong Kong Island*
Spices *Hong Kong Island*
Spring Deer *Kowloon*
Sui Sha Ya *Hong Kong Island*
La Toison d'Or *Hong Kong Island*
Unicorn Szechuan *Kowloon*
Unkai *Kowloon*
Yue Kee Goose Restaurant *New Territories & Outlying Islands*

11/20

Au Trou Normand *Kowloon*
The Belvedere *Kowloon*
Café de Paris *Hong Kong Island*
Forum Restaurant *Hong Kong Island*
Fung Lum *Kowloon*
Golden Bull *Kowloon*
Golden Poppy *Hong Kong Island*
Inagiku *Kowloon*
Jade Garden *Hong Kong Island*
Java Rijsttafel *Kowloon*
Man Wah *Hong Kong Island*
Nadaman *Kowloon*
Parc 27 *Hong Kong Island*
Peking Garden *Hong Kong Island*
Pimelea *Hong Kong Island*
The Rotisserie *Hong Kong Island*
Stanley's French Restaurant *Hong Kong Island*
Tandoor Restaurant *Hong Kong Island*
Vegi Food Kitchen *Hong Kong Island*
West Villa *Hong Kong Island*
Woodlands *Kowloon*

10/20

Boil & Boil Wonderful *Hong Kong Island*
Casa Mexicana *Hong Kong Island*
City Hall Chinese *Hong Kong Island*
Five Continents *Kowloon*
Houston Chiu Chow *Kowloon*
Island *Hong Kong Island*
Jumbo Floating Restaurant *Hong Kong Island*
Leonardo *Kowloon*
Pattaya Fast Food *Hong Kong Island*
San Francisco Steak House *Kowloon*
Siu Siu *Hong Kong Island*
Tai Pak Floating Restaurant *Hong Kong Island*
La Taverna *Hong Kong Island*
Thai Delicacy *Hong Kong Island*
Treasure Pot *Hong Kong Island*
Valentino Ristorante *Kowloon*
Wu Kong Shanghai Restaurant *Kowloon*

9/20

Beverly Hills Deli *Kowloon*
Choi Kun Heung *Kowloon*
La Futura *Hong Kong Island*
Good Health *Hong Kong Island*
Luk Yu Tea House *Hong Kong Island*
Ocean City *Kowloon*
Po Lin Monastery *New Territories & Outlying Islands*
USA Deli & Restaurant *Hong Kong Island*

8/20

Ashoka *Hong Kong Island*
Glorious *Hong Kong Island*
Indian Curry Club *Kowloon*
Joe Bananas *Hong Kong Island*
Mad Dogs *Hong Kong Island*
Malaya *Kowloon*
Nineteen '97 *Hong Kong Island*
Sybilla *Kowloon*

7/20

Royal Thai *Hong Kong Island*

6/20

Hoi Tin Garden *Kowloon*
Lindy's *Kowloon*

5/20

Studio 123 *Kowloon*

HONG KONG ISLAND

American *Peking* Restaurant
20-24 Lockhart Rd., Wanchai
5-277277
PEKINGESE

12/20   527-
         1000

Despite the curious name, this is one of the more popular Pekingese restaurants on Hong Kong Island; it's filled day and night with fans of this spicy northern cuisine. We had one of our most interesting meals here when we arrived at the stroke of 11 a.m., just as the restaurant opened for business. We were the first customers, of course, so we were able to enjoy our complimentary appetizer of pickled cucumbers and salted peanuts in peace, while we watched the waiters lounge around near the kitchen, exchanging gossip and acting in a generally indolent manner. But at the stroke of noon, just as we finished an excellent order of Peking duck in mao tai wine soup and a plate of preserved pickled chicken, the whole world seemed to descend on the place, and the waiters suddenly turned into human dynamos. Where dishes had been emerging slowly from the kitchen, they suddenly started to fly out. And good-looking dishes they were, too: smoked pork "drumsticks," duck liver in wine sauce, a half dozen variations on Peking duck, ten preparations of shark's fin, marvelous cold spiced beef. And we found that we liked the taste of our food a bit more after the level of frenzy had increased—chaos may be one of the tastiest ingredients served by the Chinese kitchen. Dinner for two, with wine, costs about HK$220.
Open daily 11 a.m.-midnight. No cards.

Amigo
Amigo Mansion, 79A Wong Nei Chong Rd., Happy Valley
• 5-772202
FRENCH

Based on the name, you might expect to find a rowdy Mexican cantina, but this place is actually one of the most elegant and expensive restaurants in Hong Kong. And it's grown considerably in sophistication in the years since its days as Café d'Amigo at Causeway Bay. No one would dare call it a café today. Amigo is fit to arrive at in a limousine, and indeed many do, though more practical sorts drive their own Mercedeses and Rolls-Royces to the front door. Built on several floors, Amigo glitters with crystal and silver and glows with polished wood and equally polished service. Show up without a jacket (which, of course, you'd never dream of doing) and you'll be handed one. From tip to toe, this is one of Hong Kong's main centers of power dining—and yet, to us outsiders, the place left us strangely cold. Service is formal but so restrained that it made us feel a bit unwelcome, and the food is technically excellent but lacking spirit—all the right moves are being made, but without much passion. It's like watching a Russian gymnast at work—perfect but without fire. Still, the beluga caviar served in a baked potato has undeniable charm, as do the duxelles-stuffed deep-fried mushrooms in a crisp potato basket and the Scottish smoked salmon from Barnetts of London. This is the place to go for such classics as Dover sole, rack of lamb and medallions of lobster topped with a trio of caviar sauces. Strolling musicians provide the background music, and roses and cigars arrive compliments of the house, though you do, of course, ultimately pay for what you get. Dinner for two, with wine, will cost in the area of HK$800.

Open daily noon-3 p.m. & 6 p.m.-1 a.m. All major cards.

Ashoka
57-59 Wyndham St.,
Central
• 5-249623
INDIAN

8/20

It's hard to believe that even today Ashoka is considered one of the very best Indian restaurants in town. We found everything, from the bland decor and atmosphere to the cooking, pretty distressing. The chicken tikka was mushy and dull, the vegetable samosa was tough and smelled of cooking oil, the vegetable curry tasted as if it was prepared with either canned or frozen vegetables, and the naan bread was decidedly dreadful. For once, the least painful moment was that of the check—two can dine abundantly here, with wine, for hardly HK$250.

Open daily noon-2:30 p.m. & 6 p.m.-10:30 p.m. All major cards.

Benkay Japanese
The Landmark Bldg., Des
Voeux Rd., Central
• 5-213344
JAPANESE

12/20

One of the better Japanese restaurants in Hong Kong, situated in the basement of one of Central's largest shopping arcades, Benkay is the result of a collaboration between the ubiquitous Maxim's chain and Japan Airlines. Now that may not necessarily sound like the best of all possible culinary marriages, portending airline food served in a pleasantly generic setting. But the food is actually quite good, made with ingredients shipped in daily from Tokyo (via guess which airline). It's all served in a soothing setting that's notable for its use of light woods and understated panels. The most reasonable way to eat in this expensive place is to stick

to the fixed-price menus, which allow you to dine on sukiyaki and shabu-shabu at less-than-daunting prices. If you want to see your bill grow at a terrifying rate, order one of the set kaiseki dinners, ritualistic meals composed of lots of little tastes at not so little tabs. Sushi and sashimi, though well prepared, can also cost a shogun's ransom, and prized Kobe beef costs every bit as much as you've heard. It tastes good—but not that good. Service is pleasant and deferential, a nice change from the passive aggressiveness found in so many Chinese restaurants. An à la carte dinner for two, with sake, costs about HK$500; if you indulge in the kaiseki meals, you check can climb much higher.
Open daily noon-3 p.m. & 6 p.m.-10:30 p.m. All major cards.

Bentley's Seafood Restaurant and Oyster Bar
**Prince's Bldg.,
3 Des Voeux Rd., Central
• 5-8680881**
BRITISH/SEAFOOD

Hiding in the basement of an enormous building at the center of the business district, Bentley's is not easy to find. This terribly British branch of the Piccadilly restaurant in London is mainly an oyster bar that offers a choice of oysters from all over the world: superb Colchesters, Belons, Blue Points, varieties from New Zealand and Australia. . . . You can enjoy them with white wine or a local favorite, Black Velvet (Guinness and Champagne). Specials prepared by the very young English chef are served in the dining room: a surprising but delicious oyster pâté, Dover sole covered with a most satisfactory (if not particularly light and subtle) Mornay sauce (a béchamel with butter and cheese) and several typically British desserts—apple crumble, pudding and even Pavlova, a meringue with whipped cream and fresh fruit. The atmosphere is congenial and relaxed; Bentley's is said to require suit and tie for men, but that's not true. Prices are high but not excessive: about HK$600 for two, with wine.
Open Mon.-Sat. 11:30 a.m.-3 p.m. & 6 p.m.-midnight. Cards: AE, DC, MC, V.

Beverly Hills Deli
**2 Lan Kwai Fong, Central
• 5-265809**
AMERICAN/DELI

See Kowloon.

The Bloom

Pedder Bldg., 12 Pedder
St., Central
• 5-218421
CANTONESE

In the midst of the hubbub and near chaos of Central, The Bloom is a nearly perfect flower, blooming down in the basement of one of Hong Kong's oldest buildings. The room is one of the more elegant in Central and draws one of Hong Kong's more well-heeled crowds; a jacket and tie for men is more appropriate than not, even at lunchtime. But even though this is a place to see and be seen, the heart of The Bloom lies in the cooking, grounded in tradition yet including many flights of modernist fancy. This is one of the better places in town to order abalone, served braised and stewed, variously with Yunnan ham and black mushrooms, with oyster sauce or with bamboo stems. The Bloom is one of the few restaurants we've found that offers a choice of walma abalone and gibbun abalone—the latter a dense variety, almost like a thick foie gras. Specialties also include the fine roast lung kong chicken, served with skin as dark as polished wood covering a prized layer of yellowish fat and glistening white meat. Seafood abounds—try the roe crab if it's in season, and order the drunken shrimp flambé, a dish that has us reconsidering our bias against flamethrower cooking. The shrimp die a fiery death at tableside, so that we might better eat. Dinner for two, with wine, costs about HK$400.
Open daily 11 a.m.-midnight. All major cards.

Bocarino's Grill

Hotel Victoria
Shun Tak Centre,
200 Connaught Rd.,
Central
• 5-407228
CONTINENTAL/FRENCH

Should your fellow diners' schedules mesh perfectly, you can enjoy the unintentionally comic culinary cabaret that occurs when all the grill room's trollies are wheeled into action at the same time, as the trio of Filipino musicians wanders between the tables. Luckily for this pseudo-Mediterranean room (timber columns, whitewashed walls, invented Spanish-sounding names), the personable waiters, chef Egli's excellent menu and the contents of those trollies are worthy of respect, not giggles. You could live by the bread trolley alone: its dozen types of loaves are always fresh. Sparkling salads and countless condiments in giant glass jars sail past, followed by fine roast meats, dizzying decks of imaginative pastries and fresh fruit, and a floating brandy cellar. This cavalcade of trollies is parked near Bocarino's entrance, where the Stilton atop the wheeled cornucopia of cheeses wafts a greeting to all arrivals. Bemused by such grand gestures, we anticipated a cuisine so haute it would be ridiculous. Far from it—this cooking is admirably nouvelle and a good value to boot.

A steamed chicken breast is rolled around seaweed and wild-rice risotto, sliced sushi-style and bathed in a creamy leek sauce. Cheese-and-cream-sauced "yabbies" (baby lobsters imported from France, the knowledgeable waiters informed us) sail aboard a phyllo pastry boat, steered by a lobster tail, on a sea of bisque sauce (whose slightly burnt flavor barely diminished our enjoyment of the showpiece). The HK$95 multiple-choice fixed-price lunch is a bargain. We enjoyed one that began with sculpted "Greek-style eggplant," a dish that gave moussaka unexpected gourmet qualities, and continued with steak broiled over mesquite wood (maintained here when others abandoned the fad), as juicily good as its accompanying almond-coated potato croquettes and garnish of squash, tomato and cucumber pearls. The wine list is extensive and strong on Californians, and a wine machine dispenses glassfuls of such popular selections as Sancerre and Meursault for about HK$60 each. On our last visit, we had to wait fifteen minutes for menus, but service from then on was willing and knowledgeable. A haven for business people and gourmands, Bocarino's deserves a bigger audience. Dinner for two, with wine, will run about HK$600. The fixed-price menus are HK$95 for lunch, HK$240 for dinner and HK$165 for Sunday brunch.
Open daily noon-3 p.m. & 6:30 p.m.-midnight. All major cards.

Boil & Boil Wonderful

Food St., Causeway Bay
• 5-779788
CANTONESE

10/20

We're fond of this place, if for no other reason than for the name, which is either a very bad or very good translation of the Chinese characters (the name actually translates closer to "All Casseroles Are Good," which would also work as a good eccentric moniker). In either case, it has a nice zany ring that appeals to us. For that matter, so does the food, which, not surprisingly, is based around country-style casseroles, food that makes good sense during the winter but is a bit heavy come summer. Still, with the air conditioning cranked up to the maximum, Boil & Boil serves winter fare year-round. The choice of casserole ingredients is fairly encyclopedic, ranging from beef, chicken, pork, a multitude of seafood and a farmer's market worth of vegetables all the way up to more obscure hotpots made with such things as deep-fried garlic and eel, taro root and coconut, and bean curd and mutton. To eat here is to descend into a true Hong Kong feeding frenzy—even the room itself is boil & boil wonderful. Dinner

for two, with beer, comes to about HK$240.
Open daily 11 a.m.-3 p.m. & 5:30 p.m.-11 p.m. Cards: AE, DC, MC, V.

Bombay Palace
Far East Finance Centre,
16 Harcourt Rd.,
Admiralty
• 5-270115
INDIAN

12/20

One of the best-looking and best-tasting Indian restaurants in Hong Kong, Bombay Palace is the Far East branch of a chain that stretches from London to New York to Beverly Hills and ultimately to Hong Kong, where it sits on the ground floor of a newish building in the midst of many other newish buildings. Within, the peaceful setting is a refreshing change from the hurly-burly of the streets outside; for once, that maniacally repetitive sitar music sounds good to ears almost burst from the sound of too many car horns and too many jackhammers. The food, as at the other Bombay Palaces, is an educated cross section of the cooking of the subcontinent, though the choices here seem a bit more exotic—perhaps in deference to the local Indian population. Those familiar with the Indian food in England and America may be surprised to find dishes like roomali roti, translated literally as "handkerchief bread": as thin as linen and a good deal tastier. You'll also find a type of naan bread from Afghanistan filled with dried fruits; fish coated with a coriander and mint chutney, then steamed in a banana leaf; tandoor-cooked mutton; and rice cooked with milk, saffron and fruit. At the very least, the spices will revive a flagging spirit and ready you for another joust with Hong Kong's midday traffic. Dinner for two, with beer, costs a mere HK$180.
Open Mon.-Sat. noon-2:30 p.m. & 6:30 p.m.-11 p.m., Sun. 6:30 p.m.-11 p.m. Cards: AE, DC, MC, V.

Café de Paris
California Tower, 30-32
D'Aguilar St., Lan Kwai
Fong, Central
• 5-247521
FRENCH

11/20

Maurice Gardett was a radio star in France in the '60s, but the call of the wild has since drawn him to the end of the world and back. And throughout his lifetime, his many remarkable escapes have made him quite the daredevil. The SS shot him and left him for dead in World War II, but a surgeon removed him in extremis from the morgue. A few years ago, he arrived late at the airport and missed his flight—the fatal Korean Air flight shot down by the Russians. And the stories go on. The restaurant business being a dangerous one, it's not surprising that Gardett became a restaurateur. And he's met with success—at least financial. Business people from Central cram this bistro, which was hastily created out of a former supermarket, with all the charm you'd

expect of such a setting. A fresco and some posters over the bar attempt to suggest a Parisian atmosphere. The unbeatably priced fixed menu for HK$90 includes a salad of seasonal greens (but the season is European, since everything is flown in from Paris's Rungis market), rack of lamb that's copious but a bit too fatty, and a run-of-the-mill fruit salad. We also ventured into the à la carte menu, where we encountered sea scallops in Champagne competing with an avalanche of puréed potatoes and grated cheese, and an overcooked Mediterranean sea bass paired with a too-thick sauce invaded by anise. On the plus side, there's an interesting wine list with reasonable prices. The true attraction that keeps the crowds coming is Gardett himself, who puts on quite a show with his charming French accent. A fixed-price meal for two with a carafe of house wine will run HK$300; an à la carte dinner for two, with wine, will be considerably costlier at HK$700.
Open Mon.-Sat. noon-2:30 p.m. & 7 p.m.-11 p.m. All major cards.

California
Lan Kwai Fong, Central
• 5-211345
AMERICAN

12/20

When the urge to toss off the shackles of Szechuan and Shanghainese cuisine arises, when even Cantonese and Chiu Chow no longer entice us, and when Continental food just doesn't quite cut the mustard, it's good to come home in spirit to a funky '50s ambience and American burgers jammed against oodles of greasy fries. Big and meaty, the burgers may be ordered topped with avocado, cheese, chili, onions and the like. Fancier fare includes a seafood salad chock-full of sizable shrimp, creamy scallops and strips of paper-white calamari, and a dish of al dente pasta heavy with chunks of fresh tomato and enhanced by grated cheese. The hungry homesick will feel right at home with the nicely moist grilled and barbecued chicken, delicately poached salmon, hearty chili and cheddar-packed potato skins. Desserts, especially the first-rate carrot cake, are rich and flavorful rather than merely sweet. The place is crowded and full of kitschy Americana: a big bar, banks of TV sets playing old movies and videos, tones of pasty blues and pinks and a rear-wall mural playfully depicting America's love affair with the automobile. Benignly blinking real headlights, the car looks on while diners quaff draught beer or flamboyant tropical drinks that merit their own glossy menu. Dinner for two, with wine or beer, will run about HK$300.
Open daily noon-3 p.m. & 7 p.m.-11:30 p.m. All major cards.

Casa Mexicana

Victoria Centre, Watson
Rd., Causeway Bay East
• 5-665560
MEXICAN/CANTONESE

10/20

On a quiet street but with a grand entrance and a hostess who asks, "Do you want a table on the quiet side or the noisy side?" Casa Mexicana serves hearty, family-size portions of straightforward Mexican fare, with a few Chinese dishes thrown in for good measure. Hot sauce comes in three varieties, from weak to fiery. Apart from the dreadful tacos, the food is decent—we particularly liked such non-Mexican dishes as baked chicken in lotus leaves and chili king prawns. When we wandered over to inspect the "noisy side," we discovered the true point of Casa Mexicana: fun. The large room was filled with people wearing silly Mexican hats (provided by the restaurant), some of whom were dancing wildly to the Mexican music played by an orchestra, at a volume loud enough to blow the tacos right off your plate (which may not be such a bad idea). Sunday brings a Mexican buffet that's popular with families. Next door is the Texas Rib House, a steak-and-rib joint under the same management. Dinner for two, with wine, will run about HK$350.
Open daily noon-2:30 p.m. & 6 p.m.-midnight. All major cards.

Chili Club

~~68-70 Lockhart Rd.,~~
Wanchai
~~• 5-272872~~
THAI   *88 Lockhart*

12/20

527 2872

Claustrophobes and tender tongues, beware! The Thai cooks in this cheerfully crowded garret maintain the fiery authenticity that had chili addicts lining up on its narrow staircase when it opened in 1984. Reservations are still essential, because of and not despite increased competition—most of Hong Kong's 25-plus Thai restaurants are for timid taste buds. But chilis are alive and kicking here, starting with the spicy and sour soups, served in bigger (and more watery) portions than elsewhere. Sweet tooths forgo the popular tom yum kung (shrimp garnish) version, and instead ordering the tom kah kai, a chicken-and-coconut-milk soup so smoothly spicy that Cleopatra would bathe in it. Larb nuer (minced beef salad) is a culinary firebomb; minimize the magically moist meat's chili impact by chewing the accompanying hunk of raw cabbage. Rice is the better antidote, served steamed or, more exotically, fried and presented in a hollowed-out pineapple, a favorite dish of the tables of expatriates reliving youths spent in sweaty student bistros. Make space on your small café table for the showboat of pla pa sa, meaty "water" fish steaming festively with plum and ginger, garlanded with ribbons of chili, carrot, chive, lemon grass and coriander and served in a fish-shape "stove tray." When you finished the fish, spoon up the tangy fish stock. Starters include unusually sprightly chilied patties (tod mun pla) and deep-fried spring rolls (por pia tord) that were slightly burnt when we sampled them, though not enough to mar the tasty textures of seaweed, rice vermicelli and crunchy batter. Cheer the chilis with Thailand's Singha beer; iced Thai coffee is a cooling finish. At first glance the restaurant looks chaotic, but the waiters are happily harried, and dishes fly through the kitchen cubicle's hole-in-the-wall serving hatch in well-organized formations. Dinner for two, with beer, will run about HK$160.

Open daily noon-3 p.m. & 6 p.m.-11:30 p.m. Cards: AE, MC, V.

Chiuchow Garden

Hennessy Centre,
500 Hennessy Rd.,
Causeway Bay
• 5-773391
Connaught Centre, Central
• 5-258246
Vicwood Plaza,
Connaught Rd.,
Sheung Wan, Central
• 5-445199
CHIU CHOW

See Kowloon.

City Hall Chinese

City Hall Low Block,
Edinburgh Pl., Central
• 5-211303
CANTONESE

10/20

It's a fair gauge of the degree to which Hong Kong is food-obsessed to note that even the City Hall is home to a Cantonese restaurant, and not a bad one at that. Where most of the world's municipal buildings offer a sort of cafeteria cuisine that falls somewhere in between K-rations and hospital cooking, you can actually eat quite well in the Hong Kong City Hall, at a restaurant run by the ubiquitous Maxim's chain. If your image of a city hall restaurant involves a small, poorly lit room with steam tables and plastic trays, this one should come as a surprise. It holds 560 diners, and every one of those 560 seats is filled during lunchtime, when dim sum, served from rolling carts, is the dish of choice. When people speak of Hong Kong–style restaurants, meaning eateries as big as armories, this is exactly what they mean. The dim sum trolley service runs through all the standard items, along with a fair assortment of noodle and rice dishes and a variety of soups. Come evening, when the restaurant is considerably less busy, the menu shifts into standard Cantonese fare: try the chicken in lemon sauce, the crispy chicken and any of the whole steamed fish dishes. Expect the trademark brusque service—in the course of feeding so many people, the waiters have no interest in becoming your new best friends. Dinner for two, with beer, costs about HK$120.

Open daily 10 a.m.-midnight. All major cards.

Cleveland Szechuan

6 Cleveland St., Causeway Bay
• 5-763876
SZECHUAN

Up a flight of stairs, past alternating strips of marbled yellow vinyl and panel mirrors, past strings of enormous Chinese firecrackers, which look unnervingly like half-size sticks of dynamite, family groups rub shoulders amicably while ingesting family-size quantities of food: sliced pig's kidney with ginger sauce, beef tripe with hot chili, camphor-and-tea-smoked duck, a host of deep-fat fried fish dishes and such soups as carp and shredded turnip or salted vegetables, squid and pork in an earthen pot. We're partial to the gold carp in an unsurpassingly rich and garlicky vegetable sauce, which enhances rather than overpowers the rosy pink flesh of the fish. Not far behind are the pork-stuffed wheat dumplings, the dough worked to near translucency. Our group gave a mixed review to the frogs' legs with cashews and black pepper—some raved, some were indifferent. Good chicken with Szechuan hot chilis is a better choice than the texturally monotonous chicken blood and bean curd, a dish only partially redeemed by fragrant leeks. Steamed bread is moist, springy and moderately sweet. The sago (akin to tapioca) with honeydew and the mashed bean pancake are appealing desserts. The interior decor mixes mottled celadon-blue paper, appliqué wood-on-wood landscapes and black panels inset with jade-green calligraphic seals; the result is half kitsch, half elegance and reasonably comfortable. Dinner for two, with beer, shouldn't exceed HK$350 to HK$400.

Open Mon.-Fri. 11 a.m.-3 p.m. & 5:30 p.m.-midnight, Sat.-Sun. 11 a.m.-midnight. All major cards.

Eagle's Nest
Hong Kong Hilton
2 Queen's Rd., Central
• 5-233111
CANTONESE/PEKINGESE

For a rooftop restaurant whose orchestra, harbor views and readily available Western cutlery are the main attractions for many out-of-towners, the Eagle's Nest turns out surprisingly good Cantonese fare. Acceptable, too, now that there are citywide chuppie (that is, Chinese yuppie) standards, are the rarified atmosphere (glass-walled, with gray and lavender tones) and Western-style service (one dish at a time). You're even brought a complimentary appetizer, perhaps undistinguished deep-fried crisps served in a stylish yin-yang saucer. A sort of culinary cabaret is performed by white-gloved carvers of Peking duck (of which, helpfully for couples, half portions are usually available) and hammerers of clay-baked chicken, which is made more socially palatable here by being dubbed "vagabond" rather than "beggar's"). If expense-accounting is no object, order one of the finely prepared bird's nest or abalone selections, which will attract your waiter's attention. Otherwise, be prepared to hold them at bay to prevent them from serving your lemon-sauced boneless duckling beside your unfinished orange-flavored spareribs; mercifully, we were left to help ourselves to the "lotus" vegetable platter. Vegetarians have a wider choice here than elsewhere. So do solo diners: most soups can be served by the bowl (hot-and-sour and black mushroom with fish maw are both good), and the dinnertime "one price menu" is ideal for solitary diners. The dance floor is well used late in the evening; we suggest reserving a window table well away from it to minimize the impact of a seven-piece orchestra that hasn't yet decided whether it's classical or big band. Part supper club, part a Chinese Windows on the World, the Eagle's Nest is an old-style hotel haven that resolutely forbids jeans, shirtsleeves, shorts and sport shoes. The hotel assumes that its guests require a full wine list: it is wonderful and expensive. Lunchtime is less formal, and its dim sum and seasonal dishes are always fresh and flavorsome. Dinner for two, with wine, runs about HK$600; there are several fixed-price menus, including a four-person lunch for HK$320 to HK$350, a dim sum basket for HK$30 to HK$55 per person and a dinner for HK$245 per person.
Open daily noon-3 p.m. & 7 p.m.-11 p.m. All major cards.

East Ocean
Harbour Centre, 25
Harbour Rd., Central
• 5-8938887
CANTONESE

See Kowloon.

Excelsior Grill
Excelsior Hotel
Gloucester Rd., Causeway
Bay
• 5-767365
CONTINENTAL

This is the East as you might imagine it in the heyday of Kipling and the Raj, the East of Singapore, Manila and, of course, Hong Kong. Dark latticework panels trim the walls. The ceiling appears to be a billowing, canopied vault. Dull gold stripes upholster the banquettes and armchairs, which, if somewhat the worse for wear, remain comfortable. In the harbor, freighters wait to take on cargo, and behind them the blue Sony building and its gaudy sign loom against a backdrop of the mountains of the New Territories. Excelsior's famous salad bar isn't much by American standards, despite a half dozen distinctive dressings, but the cold table at the entrance displays snapper, crab, garoupa—whatever the market offers that morning—making an informed selection of seafood relatively easy. Presentations are unfailingly handsome. Barbary duck and wild mushroom terrine, for example, are served as overlapping triangles on Villeroy and Boch china. A boudin of scallops and turbot turned out to be a single sizable sausage on a red-pepper cream sauce base flanked by Chinese parsley and wild rice. The boudin might gain the zest it lacks with a touch of cilantro, but we suppose that could just as easily detract from its subtlety. Velouté of salmon, alas, did not come off as well, having been ingeniously relieved of any salmon flavor. Similarly, a shark's-fin-and-salmon consommé was neither offensive nor distinguished. But the other fish dishes can be trusted, especially the steamed snapper, mild with the faint edge of gaminess found in snapper. Julienne vegetables are bright and crisp. Lamb with green peppercorns is the sort of meat dish the Excelsior does well, along with jugged venison and blanquette of chicken breast, hearty and/or simple dishes that befit a grill. On the down side, the desserts are failures. They tend to be overly sweet (mocha cake with a boiled frosting) or hesitant (what should be a robust rhubarb pie dandified by custard and a good French pastry crust). The fixed-price dinner menus (HK$150 and HK$190), which include the likes of smoked duck liver, Scottish salmon filets in phyllo pastry and grappa-infused chocolate mousse, enable the near-impoverished to enjoy near-gourmet food at near-rock-bottom prices. However, to dine à la carte it's another story: Two will have to lay out HK$850 or more for dinner with wine.

Open daily noon-3 p.m. & 7 p.m.-midnight. All major cards.

Flower Lounge

Lockhart House, 441
Lockhart Rd., Wanchai
• 5-8937977
144-149 Gloucester Rd.,
Wanchai
• 5-8917019
CANTONESE

12/20

What drew us to this parent of the various Flower Lounges scattered throughout Hong Kong (see also Kowloon and New Territories) was word that here, more than at any of the other branches, wild game is served with great regularity. Wild game is actually found at many Cantonese restaurants in Hong Kong, but always in limited amounts. But at the Flower Lounges' flagship it's served frequently and with a remarkable variety that comes as a great surprise, even to the adventurous diner. When most of us think of wild game, we think elk, boar, deer and such. But at the Flower Lounge, a cluttered, busy restaurant in the midst of the fairly tourist-free Wanchai district, you'll find a menu offering owl, bear's paw, barbecued swan, cape buffalo filet, cray crane, wildcat, pangolin, water moccasin, spotted deer, diamond tortoise, wild hog, roebuck and so forth. Most of the game is served in hotpots, in stews so rich you might confuse the game meat for pork or mutton. As we often have with exotic game, we found the idea more appealing than the dishes themselves; all things considered, we'd rather see swans gliding in a lake in the park than be served their strangely fish-flavored flesh in a Wanchai restaurant. The rest of the menu offers a good selection of familiar Cantonese dishes, including some particularly good scallop and whelk creations. The kitchen also makes a terrific roast chicken, crisp and satisfying. Perhaps we've grown less carnivorous with age, but these days we'll gladly choose chicken over owl. Dinner for two, with wine, costs about HK$360.

Open daily 11 a.m.-midnight. All major cards.

Fook Lam Moon

~~459 Lockhart Rd., Wanchai~~
• 5-8912639
CANTONESE

35 Johnston
Road

(14)

In Courvoisier's *Book of the Best*, Chinese-food maven Ken Hom not only lists this Old-World restaurant as the best Chinese restaurant in Hong Kong, he also places it at number five on his list of the ten best restaurants in the world. Which is certainly going out on a limb, for though Fook Lam Moon is a fine Chinese restaurant, it doesn't hold a candle to The Regent's Lai Ching Heen. It's actually a pity that Hom has so glorified Fook Lam Moon for, consequently, you go there with the greatest anticipation, thereby setting yourself up for mild disappointment. Hyperbole aside, the food is excellent here, served in a setting that feels far more venerable than the restaurant's opening date of 1972 led us to expect. It's a big place, occupying all three stories of two connecting buildings. And it's a clear favorite among the business community; as is the custom at many Japanese restaurants, there are cases in which regulars store their bottles of Cognac. You enter Fook Lam Moon through a gallery of fish tanks that let you know that virtually every piscine dish you order will be breathtakingly fresh. The menu is a lesson in Cantonese cuisine, detailing innumerable—and unspeakably expensive—offerings made with shark's fin (available at many levels of quality and price), bird's nest and abalone. As to be expected, those dishes are significantly more expensive than anything else on the menu, which is actually only a little pricier than the average Cantonese bill of fare. More frugal sorts can do quite well with any of the crispy chicken variations, the sundry prawns (among the best we've found in Hong Kong) and the many types of whole fish. Perhaps recognizing Fook Lam Moon's position as one of the standard-bearers of fine Cantonese cuisine, the service is notably better than most Hong Kong restaurants—the waiters almost seem friendly. There's another location in Kowloon. Dinner for two, with wine, costs about HK$350. *Open daily 6:30 a.m.-11:30 p.m. Cards: AE, MC, V.*

Fook Yuen Seafood

Island Centre, 1 George St., Causeway Bay
• 5-766833
CANTONESE

12/20

"Seafood" in a Cantonese restaurant's name may be a culinary tautology (a Cantonese restaurant without fresh fish is akin to a pub without beer), but it is a public claim to special glory. So a successful chain like Fook Yuen (with two branches in Singapore and one in California's Millbrae) should present a better first impression than the small, skimpily populated, sickly looking aquaria stuffed into a corner of its elevator lobby. As in all good old-style Cantonese restaurants, however, customers ignore appearances, including the well-worn furnishings and stacks of chairs parked by the main entrance. And they ignore the standard menu, and instead pore over the table cards. On these are listed seven daily soups, "delicacies" (Japanese octopus, chicken's feet and duck's tongues) for the adventurous, along with such seasonal goodies as hotpot winter warmers and both home-style and nouvelle-chinoise specials. And, of course, seafood. A Chinese-reading companion is essential to discover the sparkling combo of shredded squid with bean sprouts and diced salted fish or the superbly tenderized sautéed beef (lacking any trace of MSG) with clam sauce and Chinese lettuce. Another lunchtime bargain (HK$25) is the tasty clay-pot chicken cooked with shallots and black beans. Also popular is the chili-flecked "elephant neck" clam slices, not so long ago a high-priced gourmet novelty but now a substitute for abalone (when, as it is here, the "cheap end" of the neck-shape mollusk is finely blanched). The only disappointment we've had at Fook Yuen came in the form of giant soup dumplings, a costly dim sum dish whose culinary magic had faded en route to our table. Service is brusquely efficient, and a few brand-name Western wines are available. Claustrophobes should avoid Island Centre at the lunch rush hour, when three "talking" elevators groan out floor numbers to the hordes invading the center's five floors of restaurant. A meal for two, with wine, can range anywhere from HK$200 to HK$500, depending on what you order. *Open Mon.-Sat. 11:30 a.m.-midnight, Sun. 10:30 a.m.-midnight. Cards: AE, MC, V.*

Forum Restaurant
485 Lockhart Rd.,
Causeway Bay
• 5-8912555
CANTONESE

11/20

Winding up with an astronomical bill is one of the risks you take when ordering the Forum's house specialty, abalone; the sea mollusk's cost is weighed by the tael (Chinese ounce), including its ear-shape shell. Abalone prices are seasonal (though as far as we can tell this delicacy never has an off-season), and seafood prices in general are high, even for the apparently humbler sea whelk, one of which provided us—for more than HK$600 (HK$80 per tael)—with four slim but succulent pan-fried slices, each a little larger than a 50-cent piece. Such wafers of delicacy should be savored with a near-religious fervor, which must be why Forum's chef/owner has created a new, appropriately opulent two-story marble mecca for the worshippers of abalone (and shark's fin, bird's nest and less esoteric fare). Putting a bit less of a strain on our budget was the fixed-price meal centered around good dried braised sea slug (elsewhere usually undercooked and euphemized as "sea cucumber" or "bêche de mer"), though its prawn's-seed garnish was unnecessarily fancy, as was the canapé-like dish of fried, mashed shrimp laid on slices of squid, far better than the usual toast. The select menu, fashionably embellished with color photographs of unidentified dishes, does have less exotic delights, such as Hakka-style salt-baked chicken, a special dinner-only item with a one-hour advance order time. Deep-fried crispy chicken, the lunchtime substitute, had lip-licking-good skin but dull, tired meat. We also tasted what seemed like inadequate quality control in the oily deep-fried vegetarian rolls and the molded mound of fried rice overfilled with cubes of ham and the flavor of lard. Dim sum items, chosen at random from small trays borne aloft by disinterested waitresses, were unexceptional. It appears that the gourmet paradise promised by the Forum's new marble magnificence is reserved for the happy few who can afford to be devotees of the mollusk family. You'll spend anywhere from between HK$500 and HK$1,200 for two, depending on how exotic the dishes are. *Open Mon.-Sat. 11:30 a.m.-11 p.m., Sun. 10:30 a.m.-11 p.m. All major cards.*

Fung Lum
20 Leighton Rd.,
Happy Valley
• 5-777669
CANTONESE

See Kowloon.

La Futura
California Entertainment
Bldg.,
34 D'Aguilar St., Central
• 5-227074
ITALIAN

9/20

Scruffily unpretentious, this tile-floored basement bistro is packed at lunchtime with Central office workers. Far from trendy, sporting a few framed prints and plastic vine leaves, the crowded cellar (with a big, ugly service bar) is a throwback to the late '70s and early '80s when a bandwagon of "Italian" cafés set out to exploit the younger generation's unexpected fancy for foreign noodles and garlic served on bread. (In fact, social theorists have agonized over the reason for Chinese youth's tradition-defying acceptance of cheese—albeit a processed version rather like bean curd.) La Futura fills a niche in the nightlife scene of the Lan Kwai Fong area of Central: its standard Italian dishes, pair of bearded Chinese waiters and casual style are a downscale contrast to its chichi neighboring

haunts of yuppies and chuppies (Café de Paris and Disco Disco). Pâté della casa really is homemade, fritto misto is properly deep-fried, there is a basic list of Italian table wines, and pasta dishes usually arrive al dente, like the firm fusilli spirals garnished with a pleasant tomato sauce and some green shreds (which the photocopied menu called spinach). Similarly colored shreds appeared in a potable creamed spinach soup. Like most of its clientele, La Futura lacks pretensions: few other Lan Kwai Fong spots cater to diners who do not expect to see or be seen. About HK$240 for dinner for two, with wine.
Open daily noon-2 p.m. & 6 p.m.-11 p.m. All major cards.

Glorious

East Town Bldg., 41
Lockhart Rd., Wanchai
• 5-281128
CANTONESE

8/20

Despite the shameless grandiosity (or perhaps it's wishful thinking) of the name, Glorious isn't very glorious at all. It is actually a down-home Wanchai dim sum and Cantonese restaurant notable more for its size than for its food. It holds an awesome 1,400 diners spread out over three floors, and come evening it even offers a nightclub (with all songs sung, of course, in Chinese). The dim sum assortment, which races by you on carts driven by a phalanx of dim sum ladies who would certainly do respectably if they powered their steaming vehicles around the Grand Prix de Monaco, runs to about 50 items a day, well beyond the far more modest assortment found at Luk Yu. Along with all the standard favorites—the shu mai and char sui bao, the miniature spareribs and shrimp dumplings—you'll find stuffed gourds, mushroom and yam cakes, pork in a sesame dressing and much more. Unfortunately, too many of the items suffer from an annoying oiliness. At night, all the standard Cantonese dishes abound, including a huge selection of duck preparations: braised duck, with mixed meat or with mixed vegetables, is one of the house specialties. This is a restaurant that rarely sees foreigners (the English-language menu is quite small); it provides a great opportunity to see how the natives eat, away from the bright lights of Central and Tsim-shatsui. Dinner for two, with beer, costs about HK$180.
Open daily 7 a.m.-midnight. Cards: MC, V.

Golden Poppy
Henan Bldg., Wanchai
• 5-283128
THAI

11/20

On a quiet street a block from the famous Suzie Wong Bar, this calm, relaxed Thai restaurant seems to be going through a bit of an identity crisis: when you enter you'll discover a Japanese-style pub. But head upstairs and you'll find what many consider to be a fine home of authentic Thai cooking. We did find the food to be fairly authentic—not exceptional, mind you, but fresh and pleasant. The seafood noodle dish was mushy and overcooked, but we were pleased with the spicy tom kha kai soup, loaded with fresh ginger, the appetizer of sashimi-like prawns, the chicken in leaf, the vegetarian curry, the aromatic Thai-style grilled fish and the mango with rice. The adventurous can try the chicken feet salad or the frogs' legs with garlic and pepper, and the sturdy of palate will be pleased to note the number of dishes marked with a red-pepper "hot" symbol. Dinner for two, with tea, will run about HK$250. *Open daily noon-3 p.m. & 6 p.m.-11 p.m. All major cards.*

Good Health
26 Leighton Rd.,
Causeway Bay
• 5-8901614, 8901673
CANTONESE/VEGETARIAN

9/20

A pleasant, brightly lit interior, white tablecloths, leafy ocher-on-white wallpaper and comfortable dark-wood chairs welcome you into this homey vegetarian restaurant. Frosted-glass ceiling fixtures, a chandelier with etched-glass sconces and a few pieces of decorative art add a soupçon of elegance. The food struggles to rise above the mediocre, but for the most part its struggles are in vain. Corn and white-fungus soup filled with crinkly fungi proved mucilaginous and inordinately salty—but there was plenty of it. Much better (which means it was only fair) was a shredded bean-and-olive casserole that tasted rather like overcooked Boston baked beans, laced with fine vermicelli and black mushrooms; it was savory, pungent and mildly cloying. "Mystery trio" refers to slices of bland taro roll, fried bean-paste fritters and deep-fat-fried custard balls—melon-flavored cream hidden in a thick, grease-laden batter. The mystery is why anyone would eat these creations. Stewed black mushrooms and sliced gluten dumplings on a bed of greens, savory and moderately salty, were the least misconceived of the dishes. The menu also lists meal-in-a-bowl congee (rice porridge) dishes, e-fu noodles with sliced squash and a seemingly endless litany of fungi. Passersby order sweet snacks from a booth opening onto the street. Alcohol is a no-no, so one must settle for sugarcane juice, soft drinks, Perrier or tea to wash down the food. A couple, whether confirmed vegetarians or adventurous omnivores, need spend no more than HK$200 for food and drink.

Open daily noon-3 p.m. & 5 p.m.-11 p.m. All major cards.

Guangzhou Garden
Exchange Square,
Connaught Rd., Central
• 5-251163, 253888
CANTONESE

Those who remember Jean-Luc Godard's futuristic movie *Alphaville* may get a shiver of déjà vu on their way to Guangzhou Garden, flitting along with the inevitable crowds under poured concrete overhangs that fan out from the Star Ferry wharf. One and Two Exchange Square rise like pistons suddenly and, as if tapping the crowd, draw a stream away from the walkways and into the atrium, where an escalator rises between parallel water screens made of loosely fitted cobblestones. The mezzanine restaurant looks out across a granite lobby (from which four trees improbably sprout) and beyond that across Victoria Harbour to Kowloon. The view inside isn't quite as dramatic, but it's nice enough: railings, immense barrel columns in chrome and pink carpets faintly marked with celadon diamonds. But enough looking at the setting—you came here to eat. Bypass the fairly obvious mixed hors d'oeuvres and cold-meat platters, and choose instead the roasted chicken liver and sliced pork, a harmony of pungent meat flavors played off against a fine textural contrast. Sliced smoked fish makes for a good second appetizer, or politely insist on fish cheeks with shredded meat, despite the waiter's good-natured attempts to dissuade Westerners from trying this somewhat exotic delicacy. A dusting of white pepper from the shaker on the table will enhance this blandly gamey peasant dish, with its fatty gobbets of fish and bits of duck floating in a thick brown stock. The mock goose turns out to be inch-wide slices of bean curd sheets rolled around stacks of thin carrot sticks and black mushrooms and baked. It resembles goose about as much as Prince resembles Prince Ranier, but the smoky flavor and slight crunchiness hold a modest charm of their own. If your palate cries out for stronger flavors, try sliced pork with hot garlic sauce, spicy pigs' knuckles or golden mushrooms with seafood. Other worthy dishes include the elegant baked sliced eel with honey sauce on a bed of wilted cabbage shreds, the appealing sautéed bamboo shoots with walnuts and the novel mixed seafood in winter melon. The adventurous ought to consider duck web with straw mushrooms, despite the occasional claw still attached to the soft, cartilaginous flap of skin. Iced sago cream flavored with honeydew melon, an Asian version of tapioca, makes for a refreshing dessert. Dinner for two, with wine, will come to about HK$450.

Open daily 11:30 a.m.-3 p.m. & 6 p.m.-midnight. All major cards.

Hilton Grill
Hong Kong Hilton
2 Queen's Rd., Central
• 5-8466833
CONTINENTAL/FRENCH

Hong Kong's crème de la crème fill this clubby, sedate, classic grill located off the Hilton's main lobby—look around and you'll see lots of prosperous international types drawn from the nearby financial district, U.S. Embassy and Foreign Correspondents' Club; such actors as Mel Gibson and Richard Gere also put in appearances when in town. In fact, at lunchtime this place is like a private club, with tables booked weeks in advance. The smell of good food is as strong as the aura of money and power. Under the young German chef, the Hilton Grill has been lifted from the ranks of a superb hotel grill to that of a superb restaurant—period. The restaurant's favorites are still much in evidence, and they're as good as ever: caviar and blini, fresh lobster, prime rib transported reverently in a silver cart, and an international selection of prime meats—New Zealand lamb, Angus beef—and seafood flown in from around the world. But now the kitchen has expanded its horizons, even absorbing a bit of Chinese flavor. What to try? Anything, really, but we do have a few favorites: steamed salmon, lobster and scallops in an Armagnac herb sauce, beef tenderloin wrapped in a rich leaf with a sauce of red vinegar and violas, and the most popular dish here, barbecued duck breast with five spices and Chinese cabbage. Dinner will easily run HK$1,000 for two, with wine, and lunch considerably less; the best buy is the six-course fixed-price meal for HK$300 per person.

Open Mon.-Sat. noon-3 p.m. & 6:30 p.m.-midnight, Sun. 6:30 p.m.-midnight. All major cards.

Hunan Garden
The Forum, Exchange
Square, Central
• 5-8682880
HUNAN

In a city so food obsessed, it comes as a surprise that until August 1988 Hunan cooking had gone unrepresented in Hong Kong. That's when Hunan Garden emerged to help plug the gap, which it has done in exemplary fashion. Just one building over from Guangzhou Garden, and under the same ownership, it is considerably more elegant and soignée than its companion operation, starting with the carpet, a handsome affair that suggests a brown lake on which pink lily pads and lotus blossoms float quietly. Etched-glass dividers and wall mirrors continue the lily pad motif, and brassy waterplants curl around massive copper pillars, which in turn rest on mottled green granite. Great sheets of the same granite form the walls of the two contiguous dining rooms. All this elegance would be a big bore, however, if the food was not equal to it. Thankfully, the cooking is completely worthy of the setting. The meal starts with a couple of snappy complimentary openers: dried bean curd and shrimp with cucumber swirled into a piquant, oily brown sauce. Next try finger-long duck tongues, a stack of a dozen or so under a velvety, delicately tangy mustard sauce. As for the soups, we prefer the conpoy (dried scallops) in chicken stock flecked with egg white over the mildly acrid shark's-fin soup steamed in bamboo with glass noodles and bits of rather tough chicken. A dish of fresh bamboo shoots with Shanghai cabbage, a colorful contrast of ivory yellow against dark green, is served under a pungent, fuschia-red preserved bean sauce. "Braised mutton paw" will warm the hearts of those fond of strong, cartilaginous meats cooked to falling-off-the-bone tenderness—it's smoky, indecently rich and splendidly filling. Fish dishes include braised freshwater eel, sea cucumber stuffed with crab meat and pan-fried spicy filets. Some pleasant surprises are found among the desserts, notably cassia cakes, flaky pastries filled with yellow bean paste, diced onion and scallion. Service is quick, as is generally true of Hong Kong restaurants, and smilingly responsive, which isn't always the case. Two can dine exceptionally well and in elegant comfort, with beer, for about HK$300.

Open daily 11:30 a.m.-3 p.m. & 6 p.m.-midnight. All major cards.

Island

Hotel Furama
Inter-Continental
1 Connaught Rd., Central
• 5-255111
CANTONESE

10/20

"Where's the crab?" we muttered. Island's "crabmeat egg foo yong" turned out to be merely a pleasant and expensive (HK$75) home-style ham omelet, the culinary equivalent of a haystack with a couple of crab needles. The restaurant itself and its select menu are similar disappointments, vainly promising adequate competition for the Chinese restaurants in Hong Kong's other major hotels. All is not lost, however: the deep-fried boneless duck had touches of finesse, with its crisp, strongly flavored, onion-cake-like "stuffing" of minced shrimp and water chestnuts, a welcome change from the ubiquitous mashed taro. And the duck slices are unusually generous. Either a self-conscious striving for gourmet delicacy or the hotel's desire to cater to tender tourist tongues may explain the mildness of the Szechuan-style eggplant with minced pork. Mild

by nature is bird's nest, the exotic delicacy culled from the coagulated nest-building saliva of special sea birds. It is presented here in a gentle broth enriched with minced partridge—pleasant enough, but lacking that indefinable extra touch needed to warrant its HK$180 tab. We found that extra touch wanting in the service, too. During our visit the headwaiter's attentiveness was marred by a junior's failure to respond to three requests for ice (which eventually appeared as welded lumps in a whisky glass with a spoon, when a sledge hammer was needed). The long, spacious (yet smallish) harborside dining room, a conversion of former banquet rooms, feels makeshift, though it is graced with attractive framed tapestries and pretty, boldly patterned tableware, counterpointed by overlarge common potted plants. The menu's "standard" portion sizes are designed for two to four diners. Lunchtime is devoted to dim sum, for which the place is always packed. Dinner for two, with wine, will drain your wallet of some HK$500, though that can vary either way depending on dishes selected.
Open Mon.-Fri. noon-3 p.m. & 6:30 p.m.-11 p.m., Sat.-Sun. 11:30 a.m.-3 p.m. & 6:30 p.m.-11 p.m. All major cards.

Jade Garden

Swire House, Connaught Rd., Central
• 5-239966
King's Theatre Entertainment Bldg., 30 Queen's Rd., Central
• 5-234071
Connaught Centre General Post Office, Central
• 5-238811
1 Hysan Ave., Causeway Bay
• 5-779332
53 Paterson St., Causeway Bay
• 5-778282
CANTONESE

11/20

Part and parcel of one of the biggest restaurant operations in Hong Kong, the Jade Garden chain is connected with the Peking Garden, Chiuchow Garden and Sichuan Garden chains; when you add them all together, you have one heck of a garden, and one of the dominant restaurant powers in Hong Kong: Maxim's. Unlike similar chains in America, for instance, each Jade Garden has its own personality and its own daily specials, though the standard menus remain the same. Also unlike similar chains abroad, the food never has that annoying cookie-cutter quality; if you didn't know the Jade Gardens were part of a chain, you'd have no reason to assume that was the case. We're particularly fond of Jade Garden at lunchtime, when a good portion of Central seems to descend upon the Connaught Road branch, filling it with the joyous noise of people eating good dim sum and washing it down with strong tea. The lunch dishes are notably light, and there's an entire menu of noodle and rice dishes. Dinner gets a bit more serious, with such offerings as salt-baked chicken, lemon-sauce sweet-and-sour pork (a quite distant relative of the Chinese-American abomination of the same name), even deep-fried sliced chicken with banana. Both the food and the settings tend to be comfortable at these establishments, easy on both the soul and the pocketbook. Other locations in Kowloon and the New Territories. Dinner for two, with beer, runs about HK$250.

Open daily 11:30 a.m.-11:30 p.m. All major cards.

Jimmy's Kitchen
South China Bldg., 1
Wyndham St., Central
• 5-265293
CONTINENTAL

12/20

This venerable Hong Kong institution dates back to 1928, when Jimmy Landau opened his first kitchen in Wanchai. The current two locations date back to only 1976 (this branch in Central) and 1969 (see Kowloon), but they look and feel as if they've been around since the late 1800s. And indeed, they're still run by the Landau family; son Leo took over the reins some years ago from father Jimmy. The two restaurants are as comfortable as an old shoe, as reliable as the sun and moon—and not half-bad places to eat, either. They're also excellent restaurants if you want to see how Hong Kong's Western half (or to be more precise, Western 2 percent) lives: at any given time, Jimmy's Kitchen is filled with a wide assortment of British expatriates, traveling business people and Hong Kong–born members of the British founding families. Jimmy's is a place to see and be seen. It's also a place to come home to the good solid cooking of the Continent, served in portions more suitable to the expansive dining habits of a half century ago. The menu is rife with such reliable standards as corned beef and cabbage, roast rack of lamb, baked onion soup, pickled herring and chicken cutlet Pojarski. The Swedish liver pâté, made with anchovies and ginger, is considered by some to be Jimmy's culinary sine qua non. It's hardly subtle food, but then this is hardly a subtle restaurant; it's a good place at which one eats well while millions of dollars are quite possibly being traded at the very next table. Dinner for two, with wine, costs about HK$300.

Open daily noon-midnight. Cards: AE, DC, MC, V.

Joe Bananas
23 Luard Rd., Wanchai
• 5-291811
AMERICAN

8/20

Joe Bananas is Hong Kong's answer to the Hard Rock Cafe, though in this case, it's a poor man's clone of the Hard Rock—the basic elements are there, but as in the case of most copies, the vibrancy of the original is missing. It's the perfect place for those who want to pretend that Hong Kong is Hollywood West, the sort of place where Sean Penn or Sting might drop by if they happened to be in the neighborhood. As you might expect, there's every manner of rock 'n' roll and movie memorabilia (including a Hard Rock poster), and a deejay keeps good American and British music blaring. But the pieces of this puzzle don't add up to the real thing. The food is functional, leaning heavily toward burgers, potato skins, salads and cheesecake. There's also quite a roster of nutty cocktails, bearing such names as the Danger Man (a ridiculous concoction of Bacardi, gin, Cointreau, banana liqueur and lemon juice), the Golden Cadillac and the African Rumble. The place is fairly moribund early in the evening; the scene doesn't really start shaking until after 11 p.m. Joe Bananas is a popular hangout for expatriate Westerners and visiting celebrities—management even claims heartthrob Mel Gibson as a fan. Dinner for two, with drinks, costs about HK$180.

Open Mon.-Thurs. 11:30 a.m.-2 a.m., Fri.-Sat. 11:30 a.m.-5 a.m., Sun. 9 p.m.-2 a.m. All major cards.

Jumbo Floating Restaurant
Shum Wan, Aberdeen
• 5-539111
CANTONESE

10/20

The chances are good that you'll spend so much time staring at the furnishings and decor in Hong Kong's most famous floating restaurant that you'll never actually get around to discovering that the food is mediocre at best. Fans of the place will most likely point out that the food certainly isn't the point of the Jumbo—this culinary Disneyland in the middle of Aberdeen's teeming harbor is such a feast for the eyes that the fact that it leaves the palate wanting seems almost irrelevant. Their point—and who are we to argue?—is that no trip to Hong Kong could possibly be complete without a visit to the Jumbo (or one of its nearby cousins). This is to Chinese restaurants what the Vatican is to churches: the grandest of them all. Everywhere you look, you're besieged by gilded dragons and phoenixes, often set against the brightest, most garish reds and greens. The place is complete with gift shops and people who will take photos of you dressed as the Last Emperor or Empress. The sheer size of aptly named Jumbo, which holds 3,000 diners on its three dining decks, overwhelms as it amazes. The kitchen offers a choice of more than 30 fresh fish, which we haven't found to be cooked with great skill—the battered items are heavy, the fish sometimes badly

overcooked. Deep-fried oysters were a particular disappointment, though the minced pigeon in lettuce cups was good enough. Otherwise, the food was unforgettable. In case you're curious, it takes more than 30,000 light bulbs to light the interior of the Jumbo. And contrary to the scene in *Noble House* in which a fire in the kitchen destroys a floating restaurant, the Jumbo's kitchen is on a separate boat, right next door. Dinner for two, with beer, costs about HK$250.
Open daily 7 a.m.-11 p.m. All major cards.

Kanetanaka
East Point Centre,
545-563 Hennessy Rd.,
Causeway Bay
• 5-8335617
JAPANESE

12/20

Surprised looks, rather than the traditional sing-song salutations, greet non-Japanese guests in this classically austere pine-and-paper aerie atop the Sogo Department Store. With no English name on its entry corridor, unhelpful and minimal transliterations on its à la carte menu and few English-speaking waiters, Kanetanaka appears perfectly content with its regular clientele of Hong Kong–based Japanese (and some Chinese businessmen). And it has reason to be content, since reservations are essential. At our last meal, rather than wait for a harbor-view table, we occupied stools at the nine-seat sushi counter and ignored the inadequately described à la carte "fixed" meals (HK$450 and beyond). We were happy to pass up even Kanetanaka's perfectly airy tempura and top-grade sukiyaki, choosing instead, once it had been translated for us, the HK$110 fixed-price sushi lunch on the handwritten menu insert. It is served on a tray, composed by the Japanese sushi chef and two assistants, and is the customary appetizing spectacle of unhurried craftsmanship. More than a dozen scored, rolled, molded, sculpted and sliced items are set in their prescribed positions or in individual ceramic containers. The various tastes and textures—too numerous to list—are as finely balanced as the visual collage. Side extras are a daily soup (perhaps delicate onion), ice cream and coffee or tea. Two of us successfully made a meal of one sushi tray, sharing everything and a large bottle of Sapporo beer, thus achieving a mission impossible of dining well and inexpensively in an upscale Japanese restaurant (whose formally polite staff masked their further surprise at such *gaijin* behavior). The fixed-price dinners normally offer the best values; for teppanyaki, go next door to the elegant, Tokyo-style Chitose steakhouse. Dinner for two, with beer, can easily approach the HK$1,000 mark, unless you are careful; lunch is the frugal gourmet's best bet. *Open daily noon-3 p.m. & 6:30 p.m.-11:30 p.m. All major cards.*

King Heung
59-65 Paterson St.,
Causeway Bay
• 5-771035
9 Kingston St.,
Causeway Bay
• 5-767899
PEKINGESE

12/20

Probably the premier restaurant in the often disappointing Food Street area (a sort of culinary mall near Causeway Bay that's taken on a sad, somewhat dejected aspect—it's almost as if the whole world of Chinese cuisine has been taken over by Burger King), King Heung serves very good Pekingese cooking in a distinctly elegant setting. Aside from the posh-hotel Chinese restaurants, this is one of the few Oriental restaurants in Hong Kong where a tie and jacket for men almost seem appropriate. At the heart of the rather limited menu is Peking duck, a nicely turned dish, carved with much pomp and circumstance—the major domo in charge of dissembling the duck wears white gloves to perform his sacred duty, no doubt to let you know that he's an artiste, not a duck-hacker. He does a good job of carving, too—the last time we ordered a duck here, the gloves were virtually spotless at the end of the carving session. Sizzling dishes are also a great favorite. We've noticed quite a few diners ordering an oversize sizzling herring dish, which may be positively delicious, though the intrinsic boniness of the herring has thus far put us off from sampling it ourselves. Hotpots are also a great favorite, and a dish we're fond of though, as we've noted, the weather in Hong Kong is rarely cold enough to justify a dish designed for the chilly Mongolian plains. Come the muggy summer months, cold appetizers and pickled vegetables do wonders to raise flagging spirits. As does a post-lunch walk through the nearby Daimaru supermarket, a little bit of Tokyo in Causeway Bay. Dinner for two, with wine, costs about HK$300.
Open daily 11 a.m.-midnight. Cards: AE, DC, MC, V.

Landau's

Sun Hung Kai Centre, 30
Harbour Rd., Wanchai
North
• 5-8912901
CONTINENTAL

12/20

Recently moved from its longtime home in Causeway Bay's Harbour View Mansion Bay to the more modern Sun Hung Kai Centre, this cousin of Jimmy's Kitchen seems to have maintained its old Hong Kong charm—no small trick, since the original Landau's only dates back to 1976. As with Jimmy's, both the setting and the menu are tailored to the needs of the many Europeans who find a home away from home at these Landau-family-run restaurants. Landau's is, as a rule, a slightly more formal place than Jimmy's, which means you'll see more men in ties in the former than the latter. The food is also a bit more serious, though not much: wienerschnitzel, tournedos Rossini, veal Cordon Bleu, pigs' knuckles (both boiled and baked), barbecued spareribs, knockwurst and so forth—filling food, well prepared, served by old pros who recognize that their job is to get the food to you with the greatest efficiency, not to chat you up. There are a few Indian dishes as well, and a reputable steak-and-kidney pie, and there's nary a Szechuan peppercorn in sight. Dinner for two, with wine, costs about HK$500.
Open daily 11 a.m.-midnight. Cards: AE, DC, MC, V.

Lao Ching Hing

6 Kai Chiu Rd., Causeway
Bay
• 5-8951781
SHANGHAINESE

12/20

Lao Ching Hing presents a choice. Cold Formica and stainless steel prevail downstairs, while one floor up, paneling in the chicken-bone grain famous from Ming furniture and a quartet of art deco light fixtures create a pleasanter, if stylistically confused, background. Yet another family-oriented Chinese restaurant, Lao Ching Hing boasts an immense menu: 344 items available in small (read *large*) or large (read *huge*) portions, most costing HK$20 to HK$110. Only a few seafood dishes—braised turtle, hilsa herring, freshwater shrimp—command higher prices. Three generations sitting at one table, digging into fairly oily and sometimes musty food with convivial abandon, is not an uncommon sight. The waiter first sets down dishes of redskin peanuts and pleasantly crunchy, soy-laced preserved vegetables for nibbling. These also provide a symbolic marker, a way of entering into the communal act of eating. At our last meal here, shredded pork with chives turned out to be pork with scallions, though whether the kitchen ran out of chives or the menu had been mistranslated we never could determine. A sourish fermented bean paste blanketed braised hilsa herring; sweet-flavored yet a touch muddy, the herring isn't for everyone. And, like all herrings, the fish are blessed with a maze of needle-sharp bones. As for the rest of the food, by Cantonese standards (and ours) it tended to be overcooked, as witnessed by the attractive but rather mushy Chinese cabbage with bean curd in flat ribbons. The thick, chewy, homemade Shanghai noodles in fermented brown-bean sauce with pork and onions neither rises above nor falls below average; more notable is the fried bread—lightly crisp outside and steamy inside, a superior performance. End your meal with the pancake with red-bean paste, a surprisingly satisfying dessert. The pancake is actually an eggy crêpe, the filling mildly pungent as well as sweet. Served sliced into chopstick-size bites, a portion can easily feed four. Dinner for two should run about HK$225, including beer.

Open daily 11 a.m.-11 p.m. Cards: V.

Luk Yu Tea House
24-26 Stanley St., Central
• 5-235463
CANTONESE

9/20

We rush off to Luk Yu for dim sum every time we're in Hong Kong. Yet we've been disappointed on every visit—often by the food, which is rarely better than average, but mostly by the service, which seems to have taken surliness to the point of becoming a blatant disregard for every imaginable creature comfort. There are eateries in the world, such as delis in New York, where surliness is part and parcel of the process of eating there; the surliness is ultimately amusing and the food is ultimately wonderful. But at Luk Yu, the waiters are partly surly and partly oblivious. You may find yourself wondering if you've suddenly turned invisible.

Nonetheless, you must visit Luk Yu at least once, simply because it is a historical monument to the way Hong Kong used to be, along with being one of the few remnants of old Hong Kong still standing. Its roots go back to 1925, though it has only been in its current location since 1975. Still, it was carefully reconstructed to look like it did in 1925, and no doubt many of the waiters have been with the place since day one. Luk Yu is constructed, as were many of Hong Kong's older restaurants, on many levels, with ceiling fans moving the turgid air within, spittoons on the floor, an assortment of private booths and a constant stream of laconic women carrying metal cases of various dim sum, reminiscent of the trays carried by prewar nightclub

cigarette girls. We've never found the dim sum to be exceptional, though the tea is some of the strongest we've ever tasted. In the evening, a basic selection of Cantonese dishes is served, along with the occasional oddity: perhaps sea turtle or crispy suckling duck. You must go to Luk Yu as a matter of simple ritual, just as you must ride on the Star Ferry. Thankfully, like the Star Ferry, the cost of this ritual is blessedly low. Dim sum for two, with tea, costs about HK$80.
Open daily 7 a.m.-10 p.m. No cards.

Mad Dogs
33 Wyndham St., Central
• 5-252383
BRITISH

8/20

We doubt that the witty and urbane Noël Coward would be much amused to discover that part of the title of his most famous song has been appropriated for this raucous, smoke-filled pub-away-from-home. Perhaps "smoke-filled" is too tame a term—the place looks as if someone lobs canisters of mustard gas into the dining room nightly. Crowded, hot and packed to the rafters, Mad Dogs is yet another expat outpost, where the drinkers laugh a little too loudly, the service is a little too rude, and the food is beside the point. You'll find the standard pub fare: club sandwiches, chips, shepherd's pie, remnants from the Raj, such as curried egg and cucumber, and, for some bizarre reason, a chicken Waldorf salad. But anything goes down pretty easily when you drink lots of silly coma-inducing cocktails—Grasshoppers, Chi Chis, Fluffy Ducks, Pussy Foots (does anyone actually drink these things?) and bottles of Guinness (the brew of choice). Dinner for two, with drinks, will run about HK$300, depending on the amount you drink.
Open Mon.-Thurs. & Sun. 11:30 a.m.-1 a.m., Fri.-Sat. 11:30 a.m.-2 a.m. All major cards.

Man Wah
Mandarin Oriental
5 Connaught Rd., Central
• 5-220111
CANTONESE

11/20

Some seventeen years ago, we experienced our first proper Chinese Imperial banquet at Man Wah, and it was truly a meal fit for the imperial palaces. Since then, the food has paled in quality, but we still love to come here to revel in the atmosphere. Situated on the top floor of the Mandarin Oriental hotel, Man Wah positively reeks of luxury, money and power lunching; it's a place that lays real ivory chopsticks next to solid silver cutlery. Around you (but not close enough to inhibit confidential merger talk) are some of the most important people in Hong Kong, from broadcasting tycoons to members of the legislative councils, all of whom are tended to attentively but not too fussily. The opulence is also reflected in the menu, which offers such luxuries as abalone for HK$1,000 a serving and a bottle of Château Lafite Rothschild for HK$21,880. Fortunately, both the menu and the wine list are well rounded, so you'll find plenty of more affordable dishes and drinks; bottles come from as far away as Chile, New Zealand and Washington State. The shortcomings of the food are made up for by the amiable atmosphere. Though we won't remember the fine but ordinary roast duck and the chicken with shrimp forever, we enjoyed them well enough while we soaked in the view and tried to eavesdrop on our neighbors. The sky's the limit on prices, but if you order carefully, two of you should be able to escape for about HK$700 for dinner with wine. *Open daily noon-3 p.m. & 6:30 p.m.-11 p.m. All major cards.*

Mandarin Grill
Mandarin Oriental
5 Connaught Rd., Central
• 5-220111
CONTINENTAL

12/20

Oh dear. When a restaurant charges HK$200 or more per main course, and trades on the old Mandarin name, greenhorn waiters who commit a dozen gaucheries are inexcusable. We can only hope the situation that we encountered recently was a temporary phenomenon during this time of speedy staff turnover in Hong Kong's booming hotel industry. The European head-waiter may be temporary, too, unless it is Mandarin policy to have allowed him to stand and chatter with his assistant instead of inspecting tables, and to turn a blind eye to a junior waiter having a long personal telephone call in full public view. At least the kitchen did what it has always done: grill top-grade meat to perfection, like our fourteen-ounce T-bone steak. But when the kitchen strays from the grill, it often disappointments. The steak's béarnaise sauce was okay, but the sour cream on the Idaho potato was unacceptably runny. Frightened away by the price of the mixed-grill platter, we ordered one of the nine "specialties": filet of turbot, "baked with an herb and almond crust, served with sautéed endives and a mild lime sauce," sounded like it might be worth its HK$198 price tag. But the "crust" was a dusting that did not flatter the naturally dryish fish; neither did the pungent, plummy sauce. The evening had begun well enough, though— while the resident duo (flute and Chinese mandolin) added pleasantly offbeat background music to the ter-raced, clubbish dining room with its brass and bottle-green decor, we enjoyed good appetizers: cream of pumpkin soup delicately flavored with sea shrimp and marjoram, and a sextet of al dente ravioli-like agnolotti pasta filled with ricotta and spinach in a sprightly basil-hued tomato sauce. Oh dear, again, though: does any other fine restaurant still dare to present house bread as a take-it-or-leave-it napkin-wrapped plate of cold, dry precut French slices and tired rolls? We sent it back; its clone replaced it. Would anyplace else train waiters to cut microscopic portions from a HK$65 cheese selection and forget to serve the biscuits? Our wine disaster, however, was our own fault. Overwhelmed by the menu prices and the list of rare and old vintage wines (mostly HK$3,000, going up to HK$21,880 for the 1895 Lafite-Rothschild), we chose a cheapie and wondered how such a nasty Spanish rosé got into the Mandarin's cellar. As for the total bill, *oh dear*: about HK$900 for two, with an extremely modest wine. *Open daily noon-3 p.m. & 6:30 p.m.-11 p.m. All major cards.*

Manhattan Restaurant
301 Hennessy Rd., Wanchai
• 5-742755
PEKINGESE

We've never bothered to look into the name, but it's curiously appropriate. This is the authentic, archetypal Chinese restaurant we remember from New York's Pell and Mott streets: unchanged over the past 30 years, covered with a patina of time-burnished scruff. Manhattan—the restaurant, not the island—occupies a half dozen rooms on the second and third floors of a Wanchai walk-up. Once a flourishing red-light district and good-time nightspot, Wanchai retains only glimmers of its former exuberance. These days, beggar's chicken, shredded beef and the like have to satisfy the appetites that rage convivially among its round tables and echo boisterously from its dingy walls. Clad in two and a half inches of dough (a convenient substitute for the traditional mud casing), beggar's chicken steams into a savory mellowness, its meat scented by the mushrooms, ham, golden needles and star anise with which the bird is stuffed. Manhattan also does a steady business in Peking duck, served in two courses: skin and meat sliced at the table and wrapped in wheat-flour pancakes, followed by soup made from a previous carcass. Among the best of the rest are yellow croaker soup, an egg-drop base chock-full of a sweet fish that tastes halfway between walleye pike and whiting; superb homemade noodles, chewily tender and richly oily, hiding cubes and strips of pork, bok choy and other flavorful tidbits; Tien Tsin cabbage with Yunnan ham, a salty, down-to-earth peasant dish; pan-fried onion

cakes; and aromatic braised sea cucumber with shrimp roe. Two will have a hard time spending more than HK$170, unless they order beggar's chicken or Peking duck (HK$140 and HK$120, respectively).
Open daily noon-10 p.m. Cards: MC, V.

Mozart Stub'n
8 Glenealy, Central
• 5-221763
AUSTRIAN/CONTINENTAL

12/20

Reservations are a must at this tiny *stub'n* (an Austrian farmhouse kitchen) hidden at the top of a steep windy road leading to Midlevel, near the Botanical Gardens and the Hong Kong Press Club. It's easy to see why the few tables are always filled: the wood-paneled dining room is wonderfully cozy, warmed with flowers, prints and soft candlelight. The Austrian/Continental fare is not dazzling, but it has its moments, particularly the admirable smoked swordfish, the delicious lentil soup and the memorable wienerschnitzel. The cucumber soup is also quite pleasant, and the cheese fondue is a house favorite. But the kitchen has its weak spots, as evidenced by the warm snails with an avocado sauce, which left us cold, the fried mushooms with tartar sauce and the garoupa, a normally tasty fish that was bland and overcooked here. Desserts are good but by no means irresistible; coffee aficionados will want to sample one of the dozen fancy coffee drinks, from the pharisher (dark rum and cream) to the fiaker (coffee with kirsch and cream). Dinner for two, with wine, will run about HK$500.
Open Mon.-Sat. noon-3 p.m. & 7 p.m.-10:30 p.m. All major cards.

Neptune Seafood
6 Tonnochy Rd., Wanchai
• 5-8932008
CANTONESE

12/20

This surprisingly elegant seafood house sits on the edge of one of Hong Kong Island's funkier neighborhoods. At one time, Wanchai was the down-and-dirty sailors' district, a teeming anthill of low dives and strip joints. But in recent years, the red lights of Wanchai have been replaced by neon and glitter, with nary a wild side left to take a walk on. Instead, Wanchai is steadily becoming an upscale neighborhood, home to such yuppified hangouts as Joe Bananas and such respectable Chinese restaurants as Neptune. All of which is a roundabout way of saying that instead of a dingy room lit by a single fly-blown 25-watt bulb hanging overhead, Neptune is an exceedingly fancy restaurant. In fact, Neptune was one of only 21 restaurants selected by the Hong Kong Tourist Association for its Gourmet Dining in Hong

Kong program, a part of the Hong Kong Food Festival. The winning dish here was Neptune's Petit Fours, a fine lazy Susan of carefully prepared little tastes, none of which are quite like anything else in town. Come here for such things as spiced chilled squid, a platter of prawns prepared a half a dozen ways and first-rate orders of crab, lobster, scallops and shark's fin. Given time, Neptune may become one of the best seafood restaurants in Hong Kong. It's still young; it has lots of room to grow. Dinner for two, with wine, costs about HK$300.
Open Mon.-Sat. 11 a.m.-10 p.m., Sun. 10 a.m.-10 p.m. All major cards.

Nineteen '97
9 Lan Kwai Fong, Central
• 5-260303
CONTINENTAL

8/20

With California and Beverly Hills Deli less than a block away, food isn't a problem hereabouts. As a result, the only reason we can find for patronizing this bastion of overly contrived food is to marvel at its pretensions. The name refers to the date when the Crown Colony reverts to China, and it's a bit of an expatriate British joke. The restaurant, up a steep flight of stairs from the canted street, plays host to local and visiting artists whose work is on sale. The minibar facing the staircase can manage a threesome if they're mannequin thin. A bilevel room beyond offers well-spaced tables, low ceilings, a somewhat cluttered area of lacquer-black woodwork giving way to the kitchen and, here and there, a lively patch of greenery. The food we tried here was outright awful, and not even attractively awful, as misconceived nouvelle cuisine can sometimes be. The famous cucumber soup and a special dish, carrot soup, were both bad, each in its own way. The cucumber soup had only the faintest vegetable flavor on a cream base, and the carrot soup would have been more aptly named "grated carrots in tepid water." Another signature dish, three homemade sausages, had us wishing for an honest hot dog. Its skin wrinkled like a badly fitted jacket, the pork-and-veal member of the wiener trio called to mind those boiled-to-oblivion frankfurters purveyed by the worst New York street stands. Homemade pasta has miraculously managed to be both mushy and undercooked at the same time, but it is nonetheless a popular item with the tables filled with sophisticates in the 18-to-25 age bracket. The homemade bread and fresh fish of the day are about the only palatable things at Nineteen '97. Desserts run to gooey sweets, such as nondescript mango ice cream on a raspberry purée.

Dinner with wine will set two back about HK$500.
Open daily 11 a.m.-3 p.m. & 7 p.m.-midnight. All major cards.

North Park
Lockhart Bldg., 440 Jaffe Rd., Causeway Bay
• 5-8912940
CANTONESE

See Kowloon.

Orchid Garden
481 Lockhart Rd., Causeway Bay
• 5-777151
Orchid Village, 339 Lockhart Rd., Wanchai
• 5-756891
CANTONESE

See Kowloon.

Pak Loh
23-25 Hysan Ave., Causeway Bay
• 5-768886
CHIU CHOW

If one Chiu Chow restaurant warrants a toque for heartily authentic tastiness, it is the consistent, old-fashioned Pak Loh, whose decorative modernizations (silver-patterned wallpaper, red-trim mirrors) coexist happily with ancient stone tile flooring, smoky wall shrines, a sidewalk roast-cooks' window and brilliantly washed old tableware. Pak Loh's kitchen proves the maxim that Chiu Chow cooks know best how to prepare and cook shark's fin: the HK$65 "Chiu Chow Special" soup has such tasty viscosity (the texture of the fin strands being both fine and firm) that the customary Chinese parsley garnish and thick brown vinegar sauce are almost redundant. Keep track of the constellation of saucers flying onto your table, and ask the waiters if you aren't sure what goes with which dish, since each has its appointed dietary role. So do thimble-size cups of powerful Iron Buddha tea, which are prescribed apéritifs and after-meal digestives (and one thimbleful is enough to give an elephant insomnia). A molasses-rich black-syrup dip does wonders for perfectly crisp and hot deep-fried prawn balls. Chiu Chow–style satay beef, our captain's wise extra choice from the menu's 154 items, arrived already bathed in a splendidly spicy sauce. Both that beef dish and our fried sliced pigeon had received tender loving care; the pigeon's pearl-leaf garnish was a crisp delicacy, as was the platter of standard bok choy greens, cooked and served at the moment of perfection. More exotic specialties include whelk, stewed freshwater eel, braised turtle soup and

frog. Fried rice noodles make for a fine filler. About HK$250 for two, with beer.
Open daily noon-1 a.m. No cards.

Palace Seafood
Elizabeth House, 250
Gloucester Rd.,
Causeway Bay
• 5-8336933
CANTONESE

12/20

When Elizabeth House's multistory parking structure was converted into a harbor-view restaurant space, Hong Kong's shoal of seafood lovers (virtually the entire population) found themselves with a choice: the showbizzyness of Tin Tin's open fish market or the more sedate atmosphere at Palace Seafood. They stream into both. Advance reservations are essential for lunchtime dim sum and dinner. Like its decor (marble, engraved glass, chandeliers resembling strings of pink jellyfish), the Palace serves mod Cantonese chow, with nouvelle menu touches. Traditionalists stride off to inspect the wall of aquaria: we turned our gaze from the waiter's pricey recommendation to a corral of seemingly cannibalistic "sesame" fish, one of which steamed handsomely. An à la carte novelty is "three-flavor shellfish": steamed double-decked scallops garnished with minced shrimp and a crab cream sauce, a combination of flavors that some of us considered to be a collision. For a taste of some culinary craftsmanship, savor the deep-fried duck slices "stuffed with" (meaning, laid under) mashed taro whose flaky fluffiness lacks any of the stodginess we've half-digested elsewhere. "West Temple" bean curd skins are deep-fried vegetarian delicacies, held together with tasty seaweed girdles. Make sure to ask for translations of the seasonal specials, written only in Chinese: a collection of "winter health" dishes proved to be a fascinating pharmacopeia attributed with various restorative values (who could resist a tonic of freshwater duck, preserved red plums and snow frog?). Upscale touches include flambéed prawns, an after-dinner tea trolley (stocked with fresh, individual brews) and restroom attendants to cope with the crowds. From HK$200 to HK$500 for dinner for two.
Open Mon.-Sat. 11 a.m.-midnight, Sun. 10 a.m.-midnight. All major cards.

Parc 27
Park Lane Radisson Hotel
310 Gloucester Rd.,
Causeway Bay
• 5-8903355
CONTINENTAL/FRENCH

11/20

Pity the chef who has to attract diners' attention away from the rooftop harbor panorama. Curse the interior designer who made the chef's task even harder by decking the open-plan, terraced restaurant with acres of mood-cooling marble. In the evenings, when the tinkle of a piano echoes in the cavernous space, and you need a magnifying glass to read the menu, the res-

taurant feels like a Romanesque observatory. The atmosphere warms when the waiters release aromas from the various rock-salt-baked "creations." Rock fragments tainted our vine-leaves-wrapped quail, a pigeon-size bird stuffed with chestnuts and goose liver (that tasted like chicken liver); the flavors battled with the plate's pepper sauce. Though the plate presentations are fanciful, the various foodstuffs tend to cool and curl by the time the plates reach the tables, obliging diners to eat quickly. We didn't mind quickly gobbling up two of the menu dégustation courses we tried there recently: succulent pan-fried sea scallops and tender morsels of sautéed, herbed lamb filet. But we picked at the mushy salmon terrine. The fish tasted like it had floundered in very different waters than those from which the fine smoked Scottish salmon leapt (but its three slivers—and HK$80 tab—warranted a grander garnish than four scraps of greenery). Colorfully saucy conceits surrounded our dessert's almost comical culinary collage of a fruit-filled, flaky-pastry confection. A muddled advance order spoiled our enjoyment of the house special soufflé, though the version we received, with unrequested Grand Marnier and bits of orange rind, was competent. Wines, showcased near the restaurant lobby's barn-like cocktail lounge, are the usual hotel-priced range, from the sublime (Lafite Rothschild at HK$1,500) to the ridiculous (China's brand-name bottles). Busy at lunchtime, when a marbled gallery boasts an above-average buffet (sushi, salmon, roast beef), Parc 27 appears to have an identity crisis in the evenings. As we went to press, the new chef was revising the menu, so perhaps the flaws will be corrected by the time you read this. Two will spend HK$700 or so for dinner with wine; fixed-price menus are HK$135 for lunch and HK$320 for dinner (per person).
Open daily noon-3 p.m. & 6 p.m.-midnight. All major cards.

Pattaya Fast Food
342 Shun Tak Centre, 200 Connaught Rd., Central
• 5-465800
THAI

10/20

One of Thailand's aristocrats (who is also Bangkok's top multimedia food publicist) displayed a shrewd knowledge of Hong Kong demographics when he invested in this homely, wood-and-mirror-paneled café in the Macau Ferry terminal. He knew there was enough of a passing trade in Thai tourists hydrofoiling over to Macau's casinos, and Thai masseuses returning

to their all-night labors in the Portuguese enclave. Inexpensive predeparture culinary sweat-outs also suit Hong Kong's gamblers, but few Thai food addicts would trek out to Pattaya for a bowl of the national dish, tom yum kung (a lime-and-spice shrimp soup) at a tab (HK$23) only marginally below that of Hong Kong's two dozen other, (mostly) more attractive Thai bistros. Ditto for tod mun pla, rubbery deep-fried fish cakes served with a satay-style cucumber-and-peanut sauce. But better bargains, both spicy and "No Chilly Hot," can be found on the 29-item laminated menu (complete with photo displays): khao tom mud, a glutinous rice dessert wrapped in a banana leaf, is a filling HK$3 takeout snack; another safe bet is either the Thai omelet rice platter, the fried pork on pepper and garlic, or the chicken-and-potato yellow Thai curry (whose yellow-skinned prik chili is the hottest devil in the entire chili species). There's also a cash-only order counter; customers line up for their numbers and await the fairly fast delivery of dishes. Ethnic authenticities include traditional tabletop condiments, a kitchen hand cleaning chilis at a café table and the lod chong cocktail made of jackfruit, green bean paste and coconut milk. Unfortunately, neither Thai beer nor whisky are available. About HK$120 for dinner for two.
Open daily 10 a.m.-11 p.m. No cards.

Peking Garden

Excelsior Hotel Shopping Arcade, Causeway Bay
• 5-777231
Alexandra House, Chater Rd., Central
• 5-266456
PEKINGESE

11/20

Owned by the massive Maxim's restaurant conglomeration, the various Peking Gardens do a commendable job of serving copious amounts of Pekingese cooking to a sizable number of loyal customers at eminently reasonable prices. Hotels often recommend the Peking Gardens to adventurous tourists who want to try "the real thing" without having to face the trademark brusque service found at so many Chinese restaurants. Here they can eat in a fairly pleasant environment without having to endure the shouts of either their waiters or their fellow diners; at the Peking Garden restaurants, everyone is on their best behavior. In the midst of all this is some undeniably good food, with heavy emphasis on Peking noodles spun before your eyes by a roaming noodle chef, whose antics are especially loved by small children (and rightly so—we still haven't figured out how he magically kneads and stretches the dough into noodels with his hands). Every

Pekingese favorite is served. Peking duck is suavely carved at your table; the banging of hammers is heard day and night, signifying the smashing open of the clay sarcophagi surrounding beggar's chicken; and scallion cakes and steamed Peking bread are found at practically every table, essential staples of any Peking Garden meal. Despite its popularity with Westerners (or perhaps because of it), the food is wholly authentic, from the redoubtable sizzling beef with scallions to the first-rate minced shrimp on toast to the excellent fried shredded eel. Specials vary a bit from branch to branch (there are also two Peking Gardens in Kowloon), but reliability is a constant. Dinner for two, with wine, costs about HK$260.

Open daily 11:30 a.m.-midnight. All major cards.

Pep 'n' Chilli
12-22 Blue Pool Rd.,
Happy Valley
• 5-738251
SZECHUAN

Hong Kong is blessed with a terrific collection of Szechuan eateries: Cleveland Szechuan, Price Court Szechuan, Fung Lum Szechuan and Red Pepper all well deserve the toque they've received in this book. Pep 'n' Chilli is the fifth worthy member of this spicy club. (We've noticed that these restaurants are more popular with pepper-obsessed Westerners than with the local Cantonese population, who prefer their flavors subtle rather than spicy.) In fact, Pep 'n' Chilli is related to the nearby Red Pepper; one of Pep's co-owners is the son of the Red Pepper's owners. What he and his partners have done here is take the homeyness of the Red Pepper and updated it for a younger, yuppie clientele. They've also modified the spices just a tad, toning down the fire a bit, a wise gambit that seems to have attracted more of a Cantonese crowd. And they've created a look in this split-level place that is decidedly non-Chinese. But the food will perfectly satisfy those in search of a strong Szechuan hit: hot-and-sour seafood soup (a dish that leaves you simultaneously laughing with joy and weeping with pain), excellent camphor-wood-and-tea-leaf-smoked duck, lobster with chili and hot garlic sauce, dry-fried shredded beef and genuinely wonderful braised eggplant with chunks of garlic and peppers. Like Lai Ching Heen, Pep 'n' Chilli is a Hong Kong restaurant of the future—*and* it's not a bad place to eat in today. Dinner for two, with wine, will run about HK$320.

Open daily noon-3 p.m. & 6 p.m.-11 p.m. All major cards.

Perfume River

89 Percival St., Causeway Bay
• 5-762240
VIETNAMESE

Every evening, shoppers and movie-goers visiting the adjacent Lee Theatre fill this bright, clean, green-and-cream Vietnamese bistro. A late lunch is our favorite meal here, enjoyed at a table on the ground floor, which we much prefer to the low-ceilinged converted-garret upper level. Get in the right Indo-Chinese frame of mind by quaffing a French "33 Extra Dry" or "Porter 39" beer (or brandy) while you thumb the index tabs that organize the dauntingly long menu. Saigon's entire repertoire is before you (printed in Vietnamese, English and Chinese), and it's all delicious: meaty pigeon cooked in fish sauce, king prawns cooked six ways, noodle and rice dishes, noodle and vermicelli soups (a page of each), a carnivore's carnival of "beef cooked in seven styles" (a multicourse feast for HK$85). That's just scratching the surface. There are 26 "Famous Vietnamese Food" representatives, 22 humbler "Vietnamese Dishes," bountiful curries and fine crab dishes (sold by the tael). French visitors and Indo-Chinese war veterans might choose frogs' legs fried in butter with lemon grass, peppermint and curry sauce; we were particularly fond of the mint leaves with succulent scallops enlivened by onion and red-pepper slices. Vietnamese charcuterie fills the assorted cold cuts dish with slices of deep-fried shrimp paste and Vietnamese-style salami and sausage, both of which are crude but tasty. Barbecued shrimp, blended and molded around sugarcane sticks, is a subtly sweet treat. Mild, too, are the satay and vinegar "pots" (cook-it-yourself dishes of meats dipped in boiling, gently sour stock). Vietnamese fish sauce, toned down to appeal to the locals, is served automatically, and platters of fresh lettuce and mint leaves accompany appropriate dishes. If only filter coffee was still available! A reasonable HK$200 for dinner for two, with beer.
Open daily noon-midnight. Cards: AE, MC, V.

Pierrot

Mandarin Oriental
5 Connaught Rd., Central
• 5-220111
FRENCH

Once an *homage vivant* to Picasso's masterly portrait of his son, Pierrot has undergone a face-lift. In the process, the Pierrot motif, myriad gaudy reproductions in vibrant red and gold, vanished. What replaced it resembles an Impressionist painting, perhaps a Monet floral. Crystal stemware and Noritake china complete as elegant an interior as any in town, and a window table, 25 stories up, adds a view that, clichés be damned, we must call breathtaking. Clearly Pierrot has set its sights on becoming *the* place for haute cuisine in Hong Kong. It has the decor and ambience to meet its goal,

along with flawless service. But that's only half of what's needed, and while the cuisine has plenty of ups, it suffers from a few downs as well. The salmon terrine with caviar is magnificent, a successful display of technical virtuosity and delicate flavor, and the crab velouté is marvelously tasty as well. Overcooked and ill-prepared, alas, the sweetbreads with truffles was distressing. The sea perch wasn't all that bad, but it really shouldn't have been "slightly smoked." If the lamb was decently prepared and cooked, the quality of the meat was wanting, as is so often the case in Hong Kong. And the coffee has been a touch burnt on occasion. On the up side, the rare pigeon in pastry on foie gras—Pierrot's budget for caviar, foie gras and truffles could probably retire the national debt—over a medley of green vegetables and leeks justified the extravagant expense. We also encountered a fairly good lime tart, a Gewürztraminer ice cream that was especially amusing and delicious, impeccable service and a splendid wine cellar. Unfortunately, the prices have been known to cause an abrupt loss of appetite: crab-and-mango soup for HK$64, magret of Barbary duck with lentils for HK$206, berries with honey and yogurt ice cream for HK$68. If you order from the fixed-price menu, two can eat for less than HK$800. But to eat à la carte with a good bottle of wine, be prepared to exit at least HK$1,100 poorer (and be warned that it can go higher). Men and women are required to dress appropriately; jacket and ties for men are essential.
Open Mon.-Fri. noon-3 p.m. & 7 p.m.-midnight, Sat.-Sun. 7 p.m.-midnight. Cards: AE, DC, MC, V.

Pimelea
Far East Financial Centre,
16 Harcourt Rd., Central
• 5-202212
CANTONESE

11/20

At this strikingly attractive, fairly new restaurant in the midst of Hong Kong Island's business heart, we were struck by the remarkable number of business people talking on portable phones while eating their lunch. It gave us the rather funny feeling that we had wandered into New York's Four Seasons or Los Angeles's Polo Lounge by mistake. Pimelea's business orientation is notable even in the business card you can pick up at the cash register—it's a calendar card, written in both English and Chinese. The food, as befits most of the Cantonese restaurants of Hong Kong, is seafood-intensive. We tried exceedingly crisp whole baked prawns in spicy salt; a fine order of small crabs, a couple of dozen of which would have been necessary to satisfy us; and a terrific whole steamed garoupa, one of several dozen fish the restaurant offers fresh at any given time.

Shark's-fin dishes abound, at prices that aren't astronomical. And despite the seafood bias, you can also do quite well here with chicken, beef and pork. Our only question is whether those businessmen really enjoy eating and talking on their phones at the same time; we've long considered the telephone to be the arch enemy of digestion. Dinner for two, with wine, costs about HK$260.

Open daily 11 a.m.-11 p.m. Cards: AE, CB, MC, V.

Rangoon
265 Gloucester Rd.,
Causeway Bay
• 5-8932281
BURMESE

12/20

Since htamin lethoke, ohn no khaukswe and kayanthee hnmutt are not among the world's best-known national dishes, it is a joy to discover that Hong Kong's only Burmese restaurant pampers diners with a menu of detailed descriptions (in English and Chinese), a labeled photo album of all the dishes and drinks, and a most helpful service staff. The menu makes for a long read, including two pages of spicy vegetarian delights and an introductory essay on Burmese cuisine's lethoke ("hand-mix") gourmet treats; your head aches after studying the album's parade of ethnic specialties and Thai, Indian and Chinese influences. Ask for "typical" recommendations and be piquantly pleased if you receive the Rangoon pork curry with mango (sweetly sensational), Burma hilsa herring (wholly edible, like a gigantic gourmet sardine) and Burmese satay (whose sauce boasts a soothing curried character). Rice or "bread" are also offered: order at least one griddled "hundred-layer pancake," a marvelous millefeuille-like paratha. Since local tastes are catered to by the various noodle, vermicelli and stir-fried dishes, the Sino-Burmese owners and their Burmese cooks have not had to modify Burma's national dishes. You'll taste authenticity (which can often be very oily) and distinctive ingredients: dried shrimp, coconut milk, ngapu (prawn paste sauce), tamarind, banana bark, long-simmered black glutinous rice and sugar (the last two forming a dessert congee with a blackberry-like flavor). But the café's setting is pure Hong Kong: a cozily bright coffee shop with rattan, marble, a chandelier and a TV set that's tuned to a Cantonese channel during dinner; sit well away from it if you want peace. And those three introductory tongue twisters? Lightly spiced tossed rice salad (htamin lethoke), curried noodles (ohn no khaukswe) and spicy stewed eggplant curry (kayanthee hnmutt)—they all deserve worldwide attention. Beer goes best with this cooking, but a few wines and all sorts

of cocktails are also available. An affordable HK$200 for two, with beer.
Open daily 11 a.m.-11 p.m. Cards: AE, MC, V.

Red Pepper
7 Lan Fong Rd., Causeway Bay
• 5-768046
SZECHUAN

577-3811

The name, of course, speaks volumes about the nature of the cuisine. This two-decades-old Szechuan favorite is a major hangout for the local ex-pat crowd on nights when they feel like breathing fire and drinking enough beers to put out the flames. The place is a jolly jumble of a room, with tables close together, lots of interaction between groups and a good sense of culinary bon-homie. You'll notice that Red Pepper's Chinese following is minimal at best, largely because Hong Kong's primarily Cantonese population finds the lack of subtlety in Szechuan cooking to be rather crude. But Brits and Americans love the stuff: heaping plates of pickled cabbage, eggplant with lots of garlic, sizzling chili-and-garlic prawns, eggplant with hot garlic sauce, smoked duck, yellowfish with sweet-and-sour sauce and so forth. Red Pepper is fun, inexpensive and decidedly memorable—who could forget a meal consisting of garlic with garlic, followed by more garlic? Dinner for two, with beer, costs about HK$300.
Open daily noon-midnight. All major cards.

La Rose Noire
8-13 Wo On Ln., Central
• 5-265965
FRENCH/CONTINENTAL

The signposted "French bistrot ambiance" awaits, near the end of one of Central's few remaining smelly, cat-infested, back-lane cul-de-sacs, up a tiny wrought-iron staircase next to a noodle shop. Clearly on the wrong side of trendy Lan Kwai Fong, this three-year-old black rose, the first French bistro in the area, has reblossomed like a lotus in a stagnant pond since Chris Hope became chef in 1988. He complements the bistro's blackness (black furniture, black bar, black silk roses, black piano) with his colorful feasts of flavor: subtly herbed and spiced orange-flavored fettuccine laced with fresh seafood; perfectly grilled sea bass topped with coconut crumbs and served with a tomato-and-tarragon-butter fondue; a melon-size veal mignon stuffed with goat cheese, pan-fried to magical moistness, garnished with spinach purée and laid in a raspberry and basil butter sauce. Hope treats his menu as a guideline, not a rule book: the coulis with the deep-fried Camembert wedges may be raspberry, not the promised cherry, or the sauce with the Norwegian salmon may revert from puréed snow peas in Cham-

pagne caviar to Cinzano grapefruit butter. Flavor combinations are as intriguing as the portion sizes are handsome: pan-fried goose liver in Pinot Noir, young roe deer with fresh figs, poached chicken breast with duck-liver mousse, banana parfait with an Amaretto sabayon (garnished, unexpectedly and gloriously, with coconut-coated deep-fried banana slices). Adventurous appetizers now include goat-cheese purses and snail ravioli; leave room for the house tiramisu, a culinary cumulus of hazelnut-topped chocolate-cream-cheese trifle cake set in a strawberry-rippled zabaglione. Wines, mostly French, are select and reasonably priced (like the perfectly chilled Pouilly Fumé for HK$190), and you can flatter each course separately with choices from the bar's Cruover wine machine (holding twenty varieties, from HK$33 to HK$110 per glass). Cozy and truly bistro-like, with net curtains (at least *these* are white), the long, mellow room swells with hum-a-long nostalgia every evening when the owners, chicly show-bizzy pianist Michel Emeric and his chanteuse wife, turn La Rose Noire into a natural setting for *La Vie en Rose*. Eat, drink and be merry: there is no need to speak French, and you can ignore the "Members Only" sign at the entrance. Dinner for two, with wine, costs about HK$550; fixed-price lunch menus are a bargain at HK$70 to HK$95.
Open Mon.-Sat. noon-3 p.m. & 6:30 p.m.-1 a.m., Sun. 6:30 p.m.-1 a.m. All major cards.

The Rotisserie

Hotel Furama
Inter-Continental
1 Connaught Rd., Central
• 5-255111
FRENCH/CONTINENTAL

11/20

One of the very few grill-style Hong Kong hotel restaurants that have barely changed their original design, the fifteen-year-old Rotisserie is a German-style château with a wooden ceiling, massive half-moon banquettes and a 1960s-vintage coziness. But the extra-long rotisserie counter is a redundancy; the short (30-item) menu lists only six grill dishes and features specialties enriched with Oriental flavors (ginger for monkfish, stuffed Chinese cabbage with Macau sole, lemon grass in crab consommé). An older-fashioned pleasure is the sweetbreads éclair with morels, matched with a garlic-tinged sherry sauce that's a mite too stimulating for delicate glands. Top-quality, perfectly cooked and handsomely garnished sweetbreads with a morel sauce also sometimes appear on the weekly changing seven-course fixed "gourmet dinner." It should perhaps cost more than its low HK$210, to avoid serving an appetizer of salmon that, thanks to either a poor piece of fish or a flawed marinade, had an off-putting aroma. Below par, too, was the dab of tired caviar dressing and a metallic-tasting chilled avocado soup. No fixed-price menu should serve a weak, watery mulligatawny to lead in to exquisite pan-fried slices of top-grade goose liver. The lemon in the lemon yogurt sauce was imperceptible, but salt was much too apparent in the chive cream sauce accompanying our otherwise perfect braised salmon wrapped in romaine lettuce. Pastries are a house specialty: almond ice parfait with white-chocolate sauce is superbly smooth, and the shortbread in the Austrian-style torte is delicious. Wines, displayed behind glass in the entry's characterless Wine Room lounge, are a standard mix. Full at lunchtime with Central's business people, the Rotisserie provides good service, and in the evening there's a pianist. Then, like old shoes or an aging spouse's embrace, it is a comfortable spot to slip into. About HK$600 for dinner for two, with wine. *Open Mon.-Sat. noon-3 p.m. & 7 p.m.-11 p.m., Sun. 6 p.m.-11 p.m. All major cards.*

Royal Thai

Elizabeth House, 250
Gloucester Rd., Causeway
Bay
• 5-8322111
THAI

7/20

It's unfortunate that Royal Thai chose to put so much care into its luxe decor and so little into its food. Light woods, muted blues, carved teak benches, giant brass flamingos and high-backed upholstered ebony chairs abound, leading you to naturally expect some substance to accompany the style. One tip-off is the service: during our last few visits, the staff acted indifferent and bored (which may have something to do with the serious shortage Hong Kong is experiencing of service-industry employees). We were not surprised that a kitchen hand was dispatched to bring us our black-beaned "spicy fried fresh clams"—the first and third adjectives were debatable. Be forewarned: you'll find very few authentically prepared Thai dishes here. Most have been considerably toned down for the locals, so if you like your food spicy, let this preference be known to your waiter. Otherwise you run the risk of encountering the mistakes we've made, including lifeless chicken filets wrapped in pandanus leaf and dull deep-fried Thai fish cakes. Some of the dishes aren't bad, though, such as the hot-and-sour soup with prawns, freshly flavored with lemon grass, the crab with vermicelli and black pepper, the chili crab in a tasty sauce and the fine charcoal-grilled chicken. At least the tab isn't too daunting: dinner for two should run about HK$220, without wine—not that you could order it anyway,

since alcoholic beverages aren't served.
Open daily 11 a.m.-3 p.m. & 6 p.m.-11:30 p.m. All major cards.

Sampan Dinners
Causeway Bay Typhoon Shelter, Causeway Bay
• No phone
CANTONESE

Our meal on a sampan in Hong Kong Harbour was without question one of the most unforgettable dining experiences we've ever had. It's not for the overly fastidious, and not for those who demand opulence or even ordinary creature comforts. But when it comes to great food in an amazing setting, there are few equals in the world. To get there, ask a cab to take you to the Typhoon Shelter next to the Royal Hong Kong Yacht Club. You'll know you're there when you find yourself assaulted by a small army of sampan ladies, all promising you the best of all possible meals aboard their little boats. As ever, you should bargain and haggle, and finally choose a boat that looks right to you—though if truth be told, they're probably all about the same. Most are no more than small, flat boats with a folding card table and some folding chairs; they often have a TV set on in a corner, for goodness knows what reason. After you're settled onto your sampan, you'll head out into the middle of the Typhoon Shelter, where a remarkable process will ensue. First, seafood and produce boats will float by, and with the help of your sampan lady you'll choose the raw ingredients for the evening's meal. Then cooking boats will arrive, and after some negotiation, your ingredients will be tossed into giant woks and cooked in a twinkling. Chances are good that the food will be served on plastic plates and eaten with chopsticks; paper towels will probably suffice as napkins. Beverage boats stop by, selling soft drinks and beer. And, ultimately, sing-song boats will drift by, allowing you to choose any number of badly sung Western favorites translated in peculiar ways. The last time we were out on a sampan, we feasted on crab, shrimp, two types of clams, lobster and whole fish. We ate seafood and drank beer till we thought we would burst. All around us, the lights of Hong Kong glowed. And in the distance, over mainland China, we could see a thundercloud flashing. It was, as they say, a peak moment. Dinner for two, with beer, costs about HK$400, depending on your ability to bargain. It's worth every penny.
Open daily sundown-midnight (hours may vary). No cards.

Shanghai Garden
Hutchison House, Murray
Rd., Central
• 5-248181
SHANGHAINESE

12/20

Although Great Shanghai is almost certainly our favorite spot in which to savor this highly eclectic cuisine (like Pekingese cooking, it seems to consist of a dish from here and a dish from there), Shanghai Garden, part of the ever-expanding Maxim's restaurant empire, is undeniably a pleasantly comfortable place to go for an excellent order of Shanghai dumplings (for a change, the vegetable-filled ones are even better than those made with meat) and a lovely plate of snow shrimp with Lungzhing tea leaves. Unlike many of the city's more typical Shanghainese restaurants, and probably due in part to the Maxim's people, Shanghai Garden is a handsome room, filled with casual items of chinoiserie: tea jars and drawings and that sort of thing. As at all Shanghainese restaurants, brown sauce is ubiquitous, though the menu is so large that all sorts of choices abound, including a somewhat unexpected roast duck with walnuts, and bêche de mer (sea cucumber) that's about as good as bêche de mer gets. The menu isn't actually strictly Shanghainese—it also holds dishes from Hangzhou, Yangzhou, Wuxi and other regions even more obscure. This place offers a minitour of China, conveniently located in the midst of Central. Dinner for two, with wine, costs about HK$340.
Open daily 11:30 a.m.-3 p.m. & 6 p.m.-midnight. Cards: AE, DC, MC, V.

Silla Won
Southland Bldg., 47
Connaught Rd., Central
(entrance on Jubilee St.)
• 5-458873
KOREAN

12/20

Walking advertisements for Silla Won's authenticity appear at noon sharp every weekday, when sober-suited Korean businessmen, newsmen and consular officials emerge from their offices in the western fringe of Central to take their regular places for early-lunch sessions in this compact harborside haven. The menu is printed in three languages, but tiny stickers explaining the daily "chef's recommendations" (HK$40 to HK$130) are handwritten only in Korean and (only sometimes) Chinese. Peer at the dishes being served to your fellow diners, and ask about those that intrigue you, as we did for a pair of handsomely grilled snipe fish, a regular menu item. Also on the regular menu is seaweed soup, sensationally smooth and garnished with a few mussels. More typically pungent peasant fare includes fried pork with kim chee (the national dish of garlic-rich, spicy pickled cabbage) and bean curd; the kim chee's strength and firm texture renders the pork almost absent to the palate. For the classic Korean barbecue experience, center-table metal plates, rather like colorful manhole covers, are lifted up to reveal the

built-in gas griddle. The do-it-yourself cooking of marinated meats is always convivial fun; here it is blessedly cooler than at other places, and they never forget to serve two sets of chopsticks (one for cooking, one for eating) and a spatula. Barbecued chicken slices, or any of the other top-quality meat choices, are amply portioned for two diners and are served with eight side bowls of standard accompaniments (bean sprouts, kim chee, dried silver fish and so on). Service is quietly efficient; evenings are less crowded. All meals end with the traditional Korean digestive and social aids: quartered oranges and ginseng chewing gum, which explains why sober-suited men can be seen thoughtfully chewing their way back to work after an early lunch session. Two small private rooms and a scattering of Korean artworks augment the clubbish air of this café. About HK$220 for two, with beer.
Open daily noon-11 p.m. All major cards.

Siu Siu
Highland Mansion, 8 Cleveland St., Causeway Bay
• 5-8902239
CANTONESE

10/20

In a way, Siu Siu is the perfect Food Street restaurant. This simple storefront is nothing much more complex than a Chinese grazing restaurant, specializing in small Cantonese dishes that work just fine for a light lunch, an afternoon snack or a casual (and inexpensive) dinner. Service is brisk, almost abrupt, but the food seems to be carefully and even generously prepared. The dim sum, served at all hours, can be nice, if not overly sophisticated. There's also a small yet select assortment of seafood dishes and a fair number of noodles. Unlike at the coffee shops that abound in Hong Kong, the food here is actually good—a rarity at places this easygoing and reasonably priced. Dinner for two, with beer, costs about HK$100.
Open Mon.-Sat. 11:30 a.m.-midnight, Sun. 10 a.m.-midnight. Cards: MC, V.

Spices
109 Repulse Bay Rd., Repulse Bay
• 5-8122711
PAN-ASIAN

12/20

Spices is well worth visiting, if for no other reason than its prime location on a hill above beautiful Repulse Bay, a name wrapped in history from Hong Kong's pirate-ridden past (it was named after HMS *Repulse*, a British man-of-war assigned to protect the colony during its pirate-beset infancy). It's worth visiting as well for its sense of the last days of the colonial Raj, reminiscent of the old restaurants of Singapore, in which history abounds in every sip of your Pimm's Cup, your gin, your bitters. This is a thoroughly tasteful restaurant, with a subdued tropical decor that makes you feel as if you should be wearing well-starched khakis and a properly peaked pith helmet. The food, as Pan-Asian implies, jumps all over the globe, with dishes ranging far beyond the confines of the Far East. Indeed, the cooking here begins in the Middle East, with such Arabic favorites as tabouli, hummus and pita bread. From there, it travels east, pausing in India for tandoori chicken, meat and fish; in Thailand for satay and salads; in the Philippines for pork adobo and garlic shrimp; in Japan for teriyaki; and in Korea for kim chee and bulkogi. With a menu this broad in range, you can't possibly expect everything to be good, but most of the dishes are better than expected. If we have any criticism of Spices, it's that the dishes are a bit underspiced. This is a restaurant that should take its name more seriously. Dinner, with wine, runs to about HK$500 for two. *Open daily 10:30 a.m.-10:30 p.m. All major cards.*

Stanley's French Restaurant

86-88 Stanley Main St., Stanley
• 5-8138873, 8139721
CREOLE/CAJUN/FRENCH

11/20

Save your postcards—despite the view of lovely Repulse Bay, Stanley's is no place to write home about. It is, however, just fine after a morning or afternoon of hard-core shopping. (Stanley Market, just down the street but a long bus ride from Hong Kong Central, repays dedicated shoppers with such bargains as silk Dior blouses for HK$30 to HK$40.) In keeping with Stanley's leanings toward Louisiana-style cooking, shrimp rémoulade and andouille-sausage gumbo appear alongside blackened prime rib and Cajun-style rice-stuffed bell peppers. But Stanley's also wears another hat, serving such Continental basics as salmon pâté, rack of lamb Provençal and cannelloni with pesto sauce. If you expect tolerable food instead of haute cuisine, you'll enjoy the place just fine. Three rooms upstairs flaunt shabby-genteel parquet floors, and complicated wooden moldings frame the ceiling. A genuine veranda provides a spot for a charming break; it's a delightful place to dally over a glass of wine or a cocktail or submit to the blandishments of bananas Foster, which is given a silken rum-and-Häagen-Dazs finish. Nautical oils line the staircase walls, and downstairs the snug lounge/restaurant and bar are decorated with pictures of Stanley's Chinese chef with Paul Prud'homme and lively cartoons depicting Creole/Cajun cooking and New Orleans jazz. Two will shell out about HK$500 for dinner with wine or beer. *Open daily noon-4 p.m. & 7 p.m.-midnight. All major cards.*

Sui Sha Ya

93-95A Leighton Rd.,
Causeway Bay
• 5-7953026
JAPANESE

12/20

Unlike most of the more formal (and more expensive) Japanese restaurants in Hong Kong, this one is of the three-ring circus school of Japanese cuisine. In the style that's also popular in the United States, everyone in the restaurant seems intent on making you feel welcome by making as much noise as is humanly possible. Drums bang all evening long, announcing the arrival of new diners. Chefs and waiters shout out things to one another and indulge in raucous laughter. And, as at Benihana, if a dish can be served with a show, it is. The food isn't particularly rarefied, as it is at restaurants specializing in kaiseki—this is just plain down-home Japanese cooking. But from the teppanyaki assortments to the shabu shabu (so called because that's the sound your slices of raw beef make when you dip them in hot broth), the sizzling tempura to the various sushi and sashimi assortments, it's good stuff. And after a few sakes, you'll probably find yourself bellowing out the occasional *"Domo arigato"*—something the staff will find unbelievably hilarious. Kowloon is home to another branch of Sui Sha Ya. Dinner for two, with sake, costs about HK$360.
Open daily noon-3 p.m. & 6 p.m.-6 a.m. All major cards accepted.

Sunning Unicorn

Sunning Plaza, 1 Sunning
Rd., Causeway Bay
• 5-776620, 7955009
CANTONESE

Prices tend to be steep at this handsome boîte, part of a chain of Unicorns that takes itself seriously, perhaps too seriously. The downstairs landing displays the *Nouvelle Cuisine Chinoise* cookbook, a coffee-table affair in four languages, with lovely color and 50 skimpy recipes, that parent company Unicorn Hong Kong put together. At HK$180, it's no bargain. Bargains, however, are not what the chic clientele wants. They settle in—against the art deco oyster-white-and-lavender walls alongside gold wall sconces or next to the mottled brown marble facings beside a balcony railing—and consume quantities of elaborate and expensive variations on classic Cantonese cuisine. The dim sum ranges from excellent to barely adequate. Among the best are sweet-and- pungent beef meatballs studded with diced water chestnuts and green onion, and steamed har gow dumplings, the dough fine and chewy, the filling a light sauté of spinach and ham. On the negative end are pedestrian egg rolls, greasy and slightly stale. Minced pork and cuttlefish, a flat oval pancake oozing aromatic juices, atones for many lapses, and the fried milk, a concoction of egg white, milk, crabmeat and vermicelli rice noodles, may be the best version in town; it's rather like fettuccine Alfredo or perfectly and lovingly scrambled eggs. Oily, strongly flavored pigeon can't compete with Hong Kong's best, however, and iced bean curd in sugar syrup has little except a chill sweetness to recommend it. Instead, end your meal with the mango pudding, banana bun with sesame or fairly pricey fresh-fruit plate. Avoid such extravagant ventures as bamboo pith with bird's nest (HK$480) or superior shark's-fin soup (HK$620), and two can sample upscale, finicky contemporary Cantonese fare for about HK$400, including beer.

Open daily noon-3 p.m. & 6 p.m.-midnight. Cards: AE, MC, V.

Tai Pak Floating Restaurant

Aberdeen Harbour, Aberdeen
• 5-526444
CANTONESE

10/20

There's quite a bit of competition between the trio of mammoth floating restaurants in Aberdeen Harbour, culinary Disneylands each and every one of them. Jumbo, because of its outlandish size and incredible garishness, is probably the best known of the lot. But old China hands say that if you must eat at any of them (these places are not taken very seriously by those with a serious commitment to haute Chinese cuisine), the one to visit is Tai Pak, which is the oldest and reputedly the best. We rather enjoy the fun and games of taking a double-decker bus from Central, up and around the Peak and down the winding, circuitous, potentially lethal coast road to Aberdeen, then taking one of the miniature ferries out to the floating restaurants. To say that Tai Pak is less ostentatious than the Jumbo is not to say that it's decorated in soothing tones of mauve and gray; it's still a chaotic world of writhing dragons, rising phoenixes and oceans of red. Tai Pak seems to attract more of a Chinese constituency than its neighbors, which doesn't necessarily mean the food is better. The selection of fish is awesome, though, and cooked in myriad ways. You can simply order a very large fish, for instance (brilliantly described on the menu as "One Big Fish"), cooked three different ways. For those who enjoy a bit of a "floor show" with their dinner, there's the ever-popular boiled jumping prawns, which do a bit of a jig when dropped into hot broth (you would, too).

Beyond that, the fish can be cooked every way imaginable: steamed, boiled, baked, fried, sautéed and sauced with a dozen combinations. After your meal, if it's lunchtime, consider a sampan ride through the floating villages of Aberdeen, past grand junks right out of the pages of *Taipan* and *Noble House*—life imitating art imitating life. Dinner for two, with wine, costs about HK$380.
Open daily noon-11 p.m. Cards: AE, MC, V.

Tandoor Restaurant
Carfield Commercial Bldg., 75-77 Wyndham St., Central
• 5-218363
INDIAN

11/20

Tandoor's reputation as one of Hong Kong's finest Indian eateries notwithstanding, we found the food to be second-rate at best. Among the less-than-commendable dishes we've tried were the mushy, somewhat watery tandoori chicken served on a bed of carrots, cucumber and onions that managed to be both soggy and tough; dry, saffron-deficient pullao rice studded with overcooked peas; and cooked-into-oblivion pakoras, vegetables encased in a thick batter. On the other hand, lamb with almond and dried fruit, though not quite "fit for a maharajah" as the menu claims, featured pleasantly grainy meat in a smooth, nutty, spinach-flecked sauce, and the glossy naan (tandoor-baked Indian bread), served plain or stuffed with meat, vegetables or cheese, was chewy and savory. These help counter the aforementioned culinary lapses. A dozen or so vegetable dishes complement the chicken and lamb offerings, and seafood aficionados will find several seasonal specialties, along with such regulars as chutney-stewed pomfret, marinated mackerel in a mildly spiced gravy and Goanese fish in coconut sauce. The usual assortment of Indian sweets, including dense kulfi (Indian ice cream) make up the dessert list. Masala tea, though properly heavy on milk and spices, is weak on tea flavor. Up one flight of narrow and ramshackle stairs, Tandoor is a cozy, dimly lit space; on the far end, a window to the kitchen affords a view of the chefs manning the tandoor oven. Comfortable upholstered benches and banquettes in muted pastel patterns line the right and left sides of the dining room; some etched-glass dividers, a few brass and tin teapots and an occasional piece of Indian pottery brighten up the almost-bare interior. Despite the acoustic tiles on the low ceiling, the noise level is high. Two can expect to spend about HK$250 for dinner with wine or beer. *Open daily 11 a.m.-3 p.m. & 6:30 p.m.-midnight. All major cards.*

Tao Yuan
Great Eagle Centre, 23
Harbour Rd., Wanchai
• 5-738080
CANTONESE

Packed with ambition but without false pretensions, this pink-and-gray-marbled harborside salon (with matching pink tablecloths and gray carpeting) sports a menu whose innovativeness illustrates the determination of the owner, the Shui On construction company, to establish itself as a leader in Hong Kong's restaurant industry. Those who don't read Chinese are put at ease immediately by the seasonal table cards written in both Chinese and English (without spelling blunders), a rarity outside of hotel restaurants. The exception, sadly, is the dim sum order form: during daylight hours, ask by name for melt-in-the-mouth har gow (shrimp dumplings), sweet, richly filled, light-as-air char siu bao (barbecued pork buns) and super-crisp spring rolls (unexpectedly, and deliciously, filled with Chinese sausage). When we arrived for our last meal here, we were considerately seated in the quiet side room (as non-Chinese visitors usually are), thereby avoiding the babel of the main dining area (whose sole wall decorations—four Chinese calligraphy masterworks—bless a much more refined evening scene). With more than 100 seasonal and lunch specialties to choose from, we selected some of the trendier dishes. Fried spareribs, a new Cantonese cooking fad served elsewhere with Champagne sauce, are graced here with a zesty orange marmalade sauce (complete with rind). The ribs are far from spare: often half of the eight pieces are meaty pork filets. Deep-fried stuffed bean curd in wafer packets is heavenly—shrimpmeat-coated bean curd cubes with chive and mushroom flecks and fine phyllo skins. The flair of the award-winning kitchen team is evident in both the traditional dishes (fresh seafood, barbecued meats, braised shark's fin with chicken) and the new-fangled local fads (drunken—steamed in wine—and flambéed prawns, double-boiled soups and casseroles with exotic ingredients, Portuguese sauces, Japanese scallops and teppanyaki tenderloin). Service is stylish, wines are offered, and coffee is readily available. Reservations are essential, but unfortunately they're not accepted for the wildly popular Sunday dim sum sessions. A meal here is an exceptionally good value at HK$300 for a feast for two; fixed-price lunches for groups of four

to eight are HK$120 to HK$140 per person.
Open Mon.-Sat. 11 a.m.-midnight, Sun. 10 a.m.-midnight. All major cards.

La Taverna
Shun Ho Tower, 24-30 Ice
House St., Central
• 5-238624
ITALIAN

10/20

In Central's dark age, La Taverna was one of the financial district's few bright spots at night. Founded in 1969 by two Italian brothers in the engineering business, it was a cheap and cheerful haven for resident expatriates who adored the cobbled, traffic-free, tree-decked hillside lane. Even when Lan Kwai Fong's goulash of trendy nightspots began catering to yuppified Central in the '80s, this Italian bistro kept its loyal following. Those followers are now forced to trek further uphill to reach the small, new office building in which La Taverna cloned itself. Italian-style nostalgia is still possible: jolly taped music (Tijuana Brass to Rimini pops) drown out the external traffic noise on the plastic-vine-leaved glass-walled terrace. Inside, the whitewashed walls are filled with the old place's grubby old pictures, the spiral iron staircase was re-erected (leading nowhere), and the age-blackened chandelier and zillion Chianti bottles were resettled, miraculously without disturbing their twenty years' accumulation of dust. Like the decor, the menu satisfies the old-timers. Their favorites include the alcoholic seafood soup, rosemary-rich tagliatelle and wide range of cold antipasti and hot "first plates." The extensive Italian wine list helps to lubricate the dry main courses, which seem to mutter heavily, "Never mind the quality, feel the weight," particularly the pair of mushy, capon-size minced-fish-stuffed squids and the stuffed balloon of a veal scallop (both of which are served with washed-out vegetables and dry croquettes). Even the "thin pancake" stuffed with spinach, ricotta and ham requires washing down (its dab of tomato sauce is minuscule); so do strands of fettuccine, whose skin gleams like plastic, whose sauce is a thick, cheesy cream and whose inspiration is supposedly Alfredo. There's no need to leave room for desserts: tiramisu is a dull sponge cake, and one's coupe runneth over with watery zabaglione. La Taverna has few gourmet pretensions and a sharp cappuccino. Dinner with wine will cost two about HK$360; fixed-price lunch menus are less than HK$100 per person.
Open Mon.-Sat. noon-3 p.m., Sun. 6:30 p.m.-11 p.m. All major cards.

81

Thai Delicacy
Hennessy Rd., Wanchai
• 5-272591
THAI

10/20

Less well known than the more high-profile Thai restaurants, such as Chili Club (Wanchai), Sawadee (Tsimshatsui) and Silks (Central), Thai Delicacy nonetheless produces some very satisfying Siamese dishes in a casual setting, an island of Thai food in the midst of a sea of what seems like hundreds of Chinese restaurants. As at most of the restaurants in Bangkok, don't expect to find the sweet fried noodle dish called mee krob here—it's ubiquitous at Thai restaurants in America, but the Thais say it is far too complex a dish to prepare properly in a restaurant setting. Instead, expect to find tasty chicken, beef and pork satays served with the sort of peanut-chili sauce you'd be proud to lick off your plate. Don't miss the more hot than sour chiang-mi cabbage or the yum king, a spicy prawn salad that's a refreshing change after a solid regimen of dim sum. If you've encountered one of Hong Kong's rare cold days, try one of the soups, especially the gai tom kah, chicken in a broth made of lemon-flavored coconut milk tinged with Siamese ginger—a soup to warm even the coldest of hearts. Dinner for two, with beer, costs about HK$200.
Open daily 11:30 a.m.-10 p.m. Cards: MC, V.

La Toison d'Or
147-149 Gloucester Rd.,
Wanchai
• 5-8383962
FRENCH

12/20

A lovely, brand-new facade at the foot of a dilapidated building located between two modern ones: La Toison d'Or is a striking example of the busy life of Hong Kong's buildings, which are perpetually in a state of transformation. The contemporary dining room is spacious, airy and pleasant, done in tones dominated by deep pink. La Toison d'Or is a new establishment owned by a Belgian, who is making his first foray into the restaurant business. There are some problems with the basic produce, a common problem in Hong Kong: the scallops and, especially, the lamb (from Tasmania) are of mediocre quality. An effort is being made, however, as evidenced by the exquisite shrimp served with a simple vinaigrette, and the kitchen staff deserves encouragement. If it can improve on the colorless, overly sweet chocolate mousse (quite a disappointment for fans of Belgian chocolate), they'll be on the right track. The reception is charming, but the wine list is in desperate need of expansion (though there's an excellent '82 Magence). Dinner for two, with wine, will run HK$650 to HK$700.
Open Mon.-Sat. 11:30 a.m.-3 p.m. & 6 p.m.-11 p.m., Sun. 6 p.m.-11 p.m. Cards: AE, DC, MC, V.

Treasure Pot
268 Jaffe Rd., Wanchai
• 5-748928
1 Sugar St., Causeway Bay
• 5-768680
CANTONESE

10/20

Hong Kong is a city of hidden restaurants. This plush Cantonese seafood restaurant is tucked away on a little-traveled thoroughfare in bustling Wanchai, a point that makes it seem even more worth tracking down; flavors somehow seem to intensify when you have to make an effort to find the place. And on several visits, we've found the service to be unusually attentive, as if the staff tries harder because they know you've stepped off the beaten path to get here—they seat you immediately and with a flourish, bring you menus in a twinkling and make sure dishes arrive in an instant. We've enjoyed some tasty crab dishes here, particularly whole crab in a deeply pungent garlic sauce, and an assortment of whole fish that you can see radiating steam as they travel from the kitchen to your table. The staff bones the fish in front of you with near surgical skill. This place also has a penchant for serving some of the biggest lobsters we've seen outside of the fishing villages of the New Territories: robust monsters whose meat seems to grow only more succulent the bigger they get. Beef and chicken dishes aren't prepared with the same skill as the seafood; the treasure at the Treasure Pot comes from the sea. Dinner for two, with wine, costs about HK$280.
Open daily 11:30 a.m.-11:30 p.m. Cards: AE, MC, V.

USA Deli & Restaurant
Hop Hing Centre, 8-12
Hennessy Rd., Wanchai
• 5-8653278
AMERICAN/DELI

9/20

Where the vaunted, high-profile Beverly Hills Deli entertains dreams of being New York's Carnegie Deli of Hong Kong, the USA Deli is nothing more than a neighborhood deli, serving perfectly decent sandwiches, meatloaf, chicken and a sizable selection of fish dishes. Neighborhood delis aren't a particularly unique phenomenon in, say, New York or Los Angeles, but in Hong Kong, they're culinary oddities. This small deli is located a few blocks from the Hong Kong Academy for the Performing Arts, across the street from the Marriott. It is immensely popular at lunchtime, when a small army of hungry workers descends on it from the office buildings of the nearby Admiralty district. The food here isn't about to set the Hong Kong culinary scene on fire, but the corned beef sandwiches are decent, the salads satisfying, the service brisk and the setting manic enough to satisfy anyone who misses the lunacy of a New York deli at noon. Dinner for two, with beer, costs about HK$100.
Open daily 11:30 a.m.-10 p.m. Cards: MC, V.

Vegi Food Kitchen

Highland Mansion, 8
Cleveland St., Daimaru
Household Square,
Causeway Bay
• 5-8906603
CANTONESE/VEGETARIAN

11/20

The business card for this cheerful, popular Food Street vegetarian restaurant says, simply, "Tasty Are Vegetables/Healthy Are Vegetarians." Unlike so many other Hong Kong vegetarian restaurants, which tend to be dreary places, Vegi Food Kitchen is the sort of place one actually looks forward to visiting, in order to clean out the system and give the body a rest for a day or so. It's notable that the crowd is fairly young—Hong Kong professionals trying to get away from meat for a while. The dishes follow the usual Buddhist culinary rules, which means they're made primarily of mushrooms and fungi, taro and bean curd. These trompe l'oeil bean curd dishes come closer to the real thing than most: the "pork" really looks and almost tastes like pork, and the faux scallops are remarkably close. As ever, though, it's the mushrooms that charm us—plump white and black mushrooms, small buttons, phallic little fungi that taste like fresh-mown grass. We wouldn't want to eat this stuff every day, but every now and again it's an undeniably healthy and satisfying change of pace. Dinner for two, with beer, runs about HK$120.
Open daily 11:30 a.m.-midnight. Cards: AE, MC, V.

The Verandah

109 Repulse Bay Rd.,
Repulse Bay
• 5-8122722
CONTINENTAL/FRENCH

During Hong Kong's last-but-one property boom, one of the Kadoorie family businesses (it also owns the Hongkong and Shanghai hotels) tore down the 1920-vintage Repulse Bay hotel, whose two eateries, the ocean-facing, fan-cooled Verandah restaurant and the Reading Room, home of popular fondue evenings, were colonial institutions. Heritage-conscious diners howled, and the Kadoories re-created the veranda-fronted main hotel building (not altruistically, but as an upscale dining and shopping center to serve the unsightly apartment towers they stuck up on the hotel site). Ceiling fans twirl again in The Verandah's long gallery—decoratively, since it is now air conditioned—and romantics have grudgingly accepted the fake historical building, which has been restocked with its original silverware, lamps and candelabra. And since mid-1988, gourmets have accepted it as well, ever since 30-year-old Stefan Herzog came here from The Peninsula, where he had been chef at Gaddi's for four years. One of our recent Verandah dinners here was extraordinarily memorable; another left us sorely disappointed. Clearly, consistency is a problem with young Herzog's kitchen, but his successes prove that he has it in him to become one of Hong Kong's finest chefs. Our out-

standing dinner began with a teasingly tangy chilled mango-and-crab soup, snails whose hazelnut-and-herb butter sauce was as light as a silky salad dressing, a flawlessly traditional Caesar salad, and Parma ham with an artichoke mousse whose flavor tickled the palate. Main courses were meaty perfection, each flattered by its accompaniments: veal steak with Armagnac sauce and preserved prunes, pigeon marinated in cinnamon and dressed with creamed asparagus. Our only slight disappointment was a nightly special, slightly underdone guinea-fowl wrapped in pâté. The desserts deserved unabashed raves: a poppy seed ice parfait with marinated black currants and chili-red orange rind; a collage of dark- and white-chocolate mousse shaped like the yin-yang symbol and set in a mango sauce; and excellent soufflés. So thrilled were we with this meal that we soon returned, only to be deflated by overcooked fish, shrimp as rubbery as they were gigantic and an émincé de veau that was a bit stuffy. This inconsistency forces us to lower the ranking we had intended to award. Nonetheless, we have confidence in Herzog, and we'll be watching his progress. The wine list offers rare good values: the 1980 Château Moulin-à-Vent, a delicately oaky Haut-Médoc priced at HK$240, is worth swimming in, unlike Repulse Bay itself. About HK$750 for dinner for two, with wine; breakfast runs HK$50 to HK$65 per person; high tea, HK$55.
Open daily noon-3 p.m. & 7 p.m.-11 p.m. All major cards.

Viceroy of India
Sun Hung Kai Centre,
Harbour Rd., Wanchai
• 5-727227
INDIAN

The glorious subtleties of Mogul cuisine were boldly showcased, and traditionalists were discomforted, when the Harilela family (Hong Kong's best-known brood of Indian multimillionaires) created this restaurant, which boasts absolutely no cushions, curtains or red velvet. So chic that it's stark, the spacious, pink-carpeted room with sloping harbor-view windows now needs refurbishing, but the spice-blending skills of the kitchen and the headwaiter's attentiveness remain faultless. Dishes baked in the clay tandoor oven, such as yogurt-marinated chicken, are visions of red-hued tenderness. Equally marvelous is the baigan bharta, a mishmash of eggplant, herbs and spices sautéed with onions and baked over an open flame. Of course, fiery curries, à la vindaloo or Madras, appear on the 100-item menu, but we prefer such delicacies as the fresh, flawlessly prepared prawn shahi. Appetizers set the kitchen's carefully measured tone: mutton samosa, subtly spiced

patties of perfect texture, and paneer pakora, a discreetly spiced "India-type" cheese (very mild) in a brilliant batter. Adding the homemade table condiments (mint sauce, mango chutney, spiced pickle, yogurt) to the refined main courses seems rather sacrilegious to us, like pouring ketchup on foie gras. On the other hand, these condiments are too good to pass up, so we use them as dips for any of the twelve breads—from the stuffed leavened naans to the lentil pappadums. Dessert brings a wholly wonderful trinity of choices: deep-frozen Indian milk ice cream (kulfi), rich Indian trifle (rasmalai) and gorgeously gooey sweetmeat balls (gulab jamun). Earl Canning, the first Viceroy of India, poses on the cover of the select wine list, and one wonders what he would think of this self-consciously Western-style Indian restaurant with low-key Indian background music. He would probably visit for lunch on Saturday, when this part of town is denuded of commuters, in order to sit in solitary viceregal splendor. About HK$250 for two, with wine; the weekday lunch buffet is HK$65 per person.
Open daily noon-3 p.m. & 6:30 p.m.-11 p.m. All major cards.

West Villa
Admiralty Centre, 18 Harcourt Rd., Admiralty
• **5-298333**
1-5 On Lan St., Central
• **5-212196**
CANTONESE

11/20

This curious chain of good Cantonese houses seems to be standing—decor-wise—with one foot in the past and one in the present. The branch in Central looks like a recently re-created warlord's palace, filled with vases, exposed beams and an excess of chinoiserie. The nearby branch in Admiralty is, if not downright modern, at least a great deal more streamlined. And the food varies as much as the decor. The dim sum lunch is usually wonderful, particularly the large assortment of noodle and rice dishes; dinner is a bit chancier, with an unexpected assortment of Szechuan dishes tossed in for good measure. They're well prepared but a little under-spiced for our taste—it's as if the Szechuan dishes were prepared with delicate Cantonese palates in mind. One can do well here with the beef in a chili-and-black-bean sauce, any of the plump, juicy prawn dishes and the fried chicken served in a luscious onion marinade. You'll even find a few dishes rooted in the Portuguese cooking of Macau, a twist not found in many Hong Kong restaurants; try them and save yourself a bumpy hour each way on the hydrofoil. There's another location in Kowloon. Dinner for two, with wine, will run about HK$300.
Open daily 11:30 a.m.-midnight. All major cards.

Yung Kee
32-40 Wellington St.,
Central
• 5-231562
CANTONESE

If a half dozen interior decorators were preserved cryogenically in the 1930s, defrosted in 1989, set loose in one large space, put to work in isolation and prevented from seeing one another's efforts, the result might be Yung Kee's interior. Gilt cube-shape light fixtures strut in parallel lines the length of the single long room. The ceiling glows with cinnabar on lime-washed beige, and the floors sport jaunty geometric tiles in black and bright Mandarin red. Gold wall tiles give way to a carved plaque depicting a tiger on a gnarled pine tree. On one side of the room are pink and gray marble walls; on the other, brown and white marble pillars. Perhaps a theory of discontinuous design was at work, or more likely the builder just ran out of marble halfway through. To all of this add an oversized illuminated **TAKE-AWAY** sign in English and Chinese, alcoves filled with hexagonal jars of herbal medicines, and several blue porcelain sages peering benignly down, and you'll have a fair idea of what to expect. Locals rate the food highly, more highly than we are inclined to do. That's not to say we don't like this food, because for the most part we do. The minced cuttlefish, for instance, is superb, bathed in a deep carmine sauce that mingles suggestions of sweet and bitter, pungent and acid. Eaten folded into lettuce leaves, it's a messy delight. Yung Kee's shark's-fin soup, served with a biting red-wine vinegar, also merits kudos, as does the prosaically named "stewed mixed vegetables," which turns out to be a veil of crunchy elm tree fungus over alternating broccoli and asparagus. And the homemade e-fu noodles with crab meat, shrimp with walnut and braised bean curd are easy to like and reasonably priced. But a few items have let us down, including one of the restaurant's signature dishes, goose—though moist and full-flavored, it has been somewhat tough. Served on a bed of pea beans that might easily be mistaken for Boston baked beans, it's not much better than average. Also avoid the fried rice, which tastes like it came from a Midwestern chop suey palace. And make sure to steer clear of the bizarre prize-winning dessert (if it's still being served): a pastry pear tinted a bilious shade of green, filled with a peanut paste with sesame seeds. If you choose your dishes carefully, two of you should be able to wine and dine well for HK$250 to HK$300.
Open daily 11 a.m.-11:30 p.m. Cards: AE, DC, V.

KOWLOON

Arirang

Sutton Ct., Harbour City,
Canton Rd., Tsimshatsui
• 3-696667
KOREAN

Korean cuisine, rarely presented in a stylish light in Hong Kong, has a casually smart, glass-fronted showplace in this newish Arirang flagship moored in the northernmost ground-floor bay of the Harbour City shopping complex (a maze whose upper levels no restaurant-seeking diner should enter without an emergency mobile phone). Tables are unusually spacious, separated by pine panels and sliding etched-glass partitions; they're equipped with pre-oiled, recessed gas barbecue griddles that are comfortably ventilated. The four-language menu (including Japanese) offers a full page of boolgogi barbecue dishes, including a fixed-price barbecue lunch (HK$27 to HK$50 a person). Cuttlefish slices, which arrive with a sparkling chili, chive and tomato sauce, curl up on the griddle with shivering excitement. Traditional side dishes include super-crisp small chow, served with kim chee that's milder than most and a sweetly subtle consommé. Hotpots are alternative feasts, and for unexpected gourmet elegance, try the deep-fried zucchini—large slim slices delicately stuffed with beef wafers and gently, quickly fried in egg batter. Lusciously chewy seasoned boiled beef muscle, garnished with strands of egg and chili, is another generous platter of surprising mildness. Garlic goodies do infest the longer-than-usual menu, but courtlier, more refined tastes (and prompt service) are Arirang's glory. Its only problem, at busy times, is its stone flooring: diners' conversations, reassuringly often Korean, ricochet off it—so you'll have to answer your mobile phone in the Seoul-style VIP phone booths. There are a few Western wines, après-dinner chewing gums are Wrigley's, and Korea's OB beer tastes German, but everything else in Arirang is an authentic delight. About HK$160 for dinner for two, without drinks.

Open daily noon-3 p.m. & 6 p.m.-11 p.m. All major cards.

Au Trou Normand

6 Carnarvon Rd.,
Tsimshatsui
• 3-668754
FRENCH

11/20

Au Trou Normand is a true institution in the colony, a place that has enjoyed some prestige in the past. Alas! The decor has been reduced to that of a somewhat ridiculous Norman cottage, complete with an imitation fireplace, imitation wood fire, imitation beams but authentic checkered tablecloths. The Norman sole, veal vallée d'Auge, warm Isigny tart and Norman crêpes complete the Normandy theme. Everything disappears under seas of rich crème fraîche and Calvados—though we waited in vain for the famous "trou normand," the glass of Calvados usually served halfway through the meal. But richness doesn't necessarily mean quality. The sauces have more calories than they do taste, and the quality of the meats is mediocre. As for the warm tart, it's merely adequate. The wine list, too, is disappointing, and the fact that the Chiroubles was served almost warm didn't improve our opinion any. Service is informal, sometimes high-spirited and often incompetent. All things considered, the HK$650 the two of us spent for dinner was a bit difficult to digest.
Open daily noon-3 p.m. & 6 p.m.-midnight. Cards: AE, DC, MC, V.

Baron's Table

Holiday Inn Golden Mile
50 Nathan Rd.,
Tsimshatsui
• 3-693111
GERMAN

This updated-German-style dining room is snug and comfortable, dark but not overly so, organized around a grill on which pieces of beef are cooked. The cuisine is more subtle and diverse than you might expect. Of course, you'll find the usual smoked cold meats, cabbage and pork cutlets, but you'll also find American beef, excellent game and a variety of fish and seafood, such as the ramekin of scallops, salmon and shrimp in a Champagne sauce—a well-prepared dish, served with vegetables cooked to perfection, which is so unusual in Hong Kong that it deserves a special mention. As for the smoked salmon, it is thick, tender and quite remarkable. Desserts are equally tasty, from the cheesecake to the impressive-looking cinnamon parfait with brandy sauce. Not surprisingly, the place is popular with pinstriped business types, often from Europe or America. The decor, the food and the smooth, consistently professional service put them immediately at ease. The wine list is both complete and expensive. About HK$800 for two, with wine.
Open daily noon-3 p.m. & 7 p.m.-midnight. Cards: AE, DC, MC, V.

The Belvedere
Holiday Inn Harbour View
70 Mody Rd., Tsimshatsui
East
• 3-7215161
FRENCH

11/20

Those familiar with the average Holiday Inn in the United States will be taken aback by the beauty of The Belvedere, a spacious yet intimate place with a decor of Chinese birds against a pastel background and a glass screen. The chairs are comfortable, the service is warm and attentive, and the large bay window provides a splendid view of the China Sea and Hong Kong Island. But those familiar with the average Holiday Inn will not be surprised by the disappointing cooking. The menu of consulting chef Alain Dutournier boasts that The Belvedere offers "authentic cuisine of the Landes." Actually, it's nothing of the kind. True, you may dine on foie gras and duck magret here, but as for the rest, neither the Landes region nor Dutournier seem to have left a lasting impression on the kitchen. We'd go so far as to say that we were quite disappointed. Our last meal consisted of meager portions of scallops and salmon carpaccio (though the quality of the products was perfect); leathery shrimp with fresh herbs in an unappetizing, greasy gravy; and cinnamon crème brûlée, hardly smooth (it tended to separate), that was prepared all too literally: instead of having a crunchy, caramelized topping, it was burnt on top—in short, a total disaster. We were somewhat mollified by the handsome, reasonably priced wine list. About HK$800 for dinner for two, with wine.
Open daily 7 a.m.-9:30 a.m., noon-3 p.m. & 7 p.m.-midnight. Cards: AE, DC, MC, V.

Beverly Hills Deli
New World Centre, Level
2, Salisbury Rd.,
Tsimshatsui
• 3-698695
AMERICAN/DELI

9/20

Like the proverbial talking dog, what's not so important is whether the Beverly Hills Deli does it well, just whether it does it at all. As the menu proclaims, this is, for better or worse, "The Only New York–Style Delicatessen in Hong Kong." So why it's called the Beverly Hills Deli rather than the more obvious New York Deli is something of a mystery. But there it is, in the midst of the imposing New World Centre, complete with a photo of the Three Stooges on its menu, serving chicken soup with matzoh balls, chopped chicken liver with crackers, gefilte fish and potato latkes. The food isn't about to put New York's legendary Carnegie Deli out of business, but for those who can't live another day without a Bel Air sandwich (hot corned beef and coleslaw on rye bread), this is definitely the place to go in Hong Kong. As observers of cultural collisions, we're quite fond of the way kreplach are described as "Jewish won tons," and we're utterly befuddled by the pizzas (in a deli?), topped variously with squid, chicken livers

and Texas chili. Only, we are sure, in Hong Kong. There's another branch in Central on Hong Kong Island. Dinner for two, with Dr. Brown's Cel-Ray Tonic, runs about HK$150.
Open daily 10 a.m.-10 p.m. Cards: AE, DC, MC, V.

Bodhi Vegetarian Restaurant
56 Cameron Rd.,
Tsimshatsui
• 3-7213561
CANTONESE/VEGETARIAN

12/20

The bright lights illuminate more than necessary in this no-frills eating establishment—worn carpeting, for example, and a dingy burlap wall covering—but the vegetarian food is tasty and varied. You can get a creditable and satisfying bean curd imitation of roast pork and other viands here. Nearly every dish on the more-than-100-item menu features some variety of fungus, fresh or dried, stewed or braised, steamed or fried. Saucing tends to be simple and sweet. Our favorite Bodhi dishes include fried eggplant accompanied by taro-stuffed mushrooms and chili peppers, chewy bamboo fungus whose delicate crunch is nicely offset by creamy, custardy bean curd, and thickly sliced gluten balls on a bed of broccoli surrounded by mushrooms. Desserts are not a strong point; stay away from the sweetened bean purée, which is reminiscent of Turkish coffee dregs. A wall telephone provides free calls for patrons, and therefore remains in constant use, mostly by giggling teenyboppers. Neither wine nor beer is served. Dinner for two will run about HK$250.
Open daily 11 a.m.-11 p.m. All major cards.

The Bostonian
Ramada Renaissance Hotel
8 Peking Rd., Tsimshatsui
• 3-3113311
AMERICAN/SEAFOOD

12/20

This self-proclaimed California-style seafood restaurant jocularly illustrates how to make a sow's ear out of a silk purse. Start with an elegant, two-floor dining salon and oyster bar (equipped with a grand wooden staircase, Rosenthal china and silverware). Next, add Hong Kong–raised Chinese-American chef Jonathan Choi's masterly celebration of American culinary triumphs. Then thoroughly sugar-coat with juvenile menu jokes and present a meal experience that many (including amazed Hong Kong–Chinese waiters) find cringingly embarrassing. By the end of our last meal here, our distaste for all the cutesiness was partly mollified thanks to a fine bottle of Stag's Leap Chardonnay. But even the Bostonian's magnificent long list of American wines is another excellence demeaned by the overly self-conscious concepts. Silliest of all are the pseudo-Parisian paper tablecloths (laid over a real cloth) on which the name of each table's host (the person presumably buying) is written, big enough for the whole room to

read, with an arrow to guide the waiter to the right person. That went down like the *Hindenburg* with the host of our neighboring table, who found her name, preceded by the designation "Mr.," pointing at the one man in the party. Even if this gaucherie and invasion of privacy were forgivable, the idea is still ridiculous, particularly when only one or two other tables are occupied. And why, at lunchtime, serve up quadrophonic disco music, whose decibel level is the same on both floors and which could/would not be lowered even after two appeals? Maybe diners are expected to be drunk, in which state they might appreciate the "jokes" that litter the one-page menu. If so, why serve such good food? Magically moist blackened catfish is superbly spiced, Cajun-style; remarkably tender Minnesota chicken breast is stuffed with succulent wild rice and topped garishly with mango and pineapple chutney. "Starters and other leftovers" make for filling snacks for bar-counter dining: we particularly like the spicy fried Creole-style calamari, chewily underdone battered squid balls presented handsomely on a thick tortilla shell. As for "fried alligator fritters (we're not kidding)," they must be: the marinated scraps are buried inside crisp dumplings of fish batter, the better, presumably, to camouflage their dull chicken-schnitzel flavor. Desserts, from the grasshopper mint pie to the chocolate-chip cheesecake, are quite fine—further reasons to pity a chef crafting all-American works of art for a freshman playground. At least The Bostonian dares to be different. So did we: we ripped up the tablecloth. About HK$400 for dinner for two, with wine.
Open daily noon-3 p.m. & 7 p.m.-11 p.m. All major cards.

Chesa
The Peninsula
Salisbury Rd., Tsimshatsui
• 3-666251
SWISS

Unprepossessing for The Peninsula, that grande dame of Hong Kong hostelries, this cozy simulacrum of a Swiss chalet hosts a surprisingly upbeat crowd. The rough-timbered dark walls, complete with knotholes, the mantelpiece replete with pewter plates and the double wall sconces that mimic candles capped by truncated red shades stare across the heads of embassy muckymucks, business people putting together multinational deals, and ultra-chic women taking a break from corporate in-fighting or the infinite pleasures of shopping in the Crown Colony. That they'll be scarfing down creamy-smooth fondue almost goes without saying, but they'll also sup elegantly on the likes of a feathery-light fish mousse (garoupa) on spinach, the whole enfolded by puff pastry; greaseless Rösti potatoes flecked with minced onion; émincé of veal; salmon or pomfret in a wine-laced cream sauce; or chicken breast, a dull gold contrasting with a deep green pool of puréed herbs. Soups are pleasant, if ordinary, except for the consommé of beef marrow and mushroom served under a pastry cover. Among the desserts—all good—the passion-fruit parfait of exceptional lightness stands out, though the intense chocolate crêpe stuffed with bananas runs a close second. Nice touches include the bottled water, discreetly cheery background music and complimentary mousse-light chocolate nougats with the dark-roast coffee. The wine list is extensive and expensive, but such Swiss bottlings as Vandois and Fendant are available by the glass and equally service-able with fish and light meats. Expect to spend HK$550 and up per couple, with a modest wine.

Open daily noon-3 p.m. & 6:30 p.m.-11 p.m. All major cards.

The Chinese Restaurant
Hyatt Regency Hong Kong
67 Nathan Rd.,
Tsimshatsui
• 3-3111234
CANTONESE

12/20

The name is puzzling, the restaurant being the equivalent of those generic products found in U.S. supermarkets, labeled simply "Breakfast Cereal" or "Carbonated Beverage." Well *of course* it's a Chinese restaurant—any fool can see that from looking at the menu. A slightly more elegant name certainly wouldn't hurt. Despite the functionality of the name, the room is pleasantly luxurious, as befits one of Hong Kong's better hotels. From the tumult of lower Nathan Road you climb to a room done in conservative grays and blacks, enlivened with the occasional art nouveau touch. We found the room a bit noisy, which isn't unusual in Chinese restaurants (indeed, a dull roar is usually expected)—but in Chinese restaurants of the elegant persuasion, noise is decidedly out of place. Service was also a bit remote; it took us quite a while to attract a waiter, most of whom seemed more concerned about tending to large tables of business people than a meager table of two. And groups are clearly part of the métier of this particular restaurant—the special Wild Game Menu offers two different dinners for groups, one of which (for twelve persons at HK$3,680) includes such delicacies as stew of civet cat, shark's-fin broth with five kinds of snake meat, and baked stuffed paddy sparrow. More prosaic dishes include deep-fried spareribs in a chili-pepper sauce, shredded roast duck with jellyfish and baked stuffed sea whelk. This has to be the most adventurous Hyatt Hotel menu in the world. Dinner for two, with wine, runs about HK$600. *Open daily noon-3 p.m. & 6:30 p.m.-11 p.m. All major cards.*

Chiuchow Garden

Tsimshatsui Centre,
66 Mody Rd.,
Tsimshatsui East
• 3-687266
Wong Tai Sin Shopping
Centre, Wong Tai Sin
• 3-3516368
CHIU CHOW

12/20

The cooking of the Chiu Chow people, fishing folk who come from the area around the seaport of Swatow, is sometimes indistinguishable to Western palates from the cooking of the Cantonese—and for good reason. Swatow is part of Canton Province, and hence the regional cuisine, which doesn't recognize the existence of borders drawn on maps, has blended thoroughly into the indigenous cooking of the Chiu Chow. The massive Chiuchow Garden chain, run by the ubiquitous Maxim's company, is an excellent place to come to an understanding of the subtle variations of Chiu Chow cuisine. That there's a strong reliance on seafood is obvious from the many fish tanks scattered about the dining room in any of the Garden restaurants—restaurants that you'll notice are (unlike Szechuan places) populated with far more Chinese than Westerners. Though many of the Chiu Chow restaurants in Hong Kong are small plain cafés that stay open well into the wee hours, Maxim's has cleverly tapped into an area of high culinary interest by making its Gardens fairly elegant, with a strong penchant for large groups; a table of two is an oddity at Chiuchow Garden. And for good reason—it's hard to order enough different dishes if you're only two. Some of the classic Chiu Chow dishes are highly flavored; just one bite of the steamed goose cooked with soy sauce should tell you you're eating food not quite like anything you've tasted before, flavored largely by another sauce of clotted goose blood. Dumplings, available at all hours, are perfect as an opening course. Shark's fin is also a Chiu Chow specialty, as are dishes made with eel and scallops. You'll know you're in a Chiu Chow restaurant if you're served tiny cups of fiercely strong Iron Buddha tea at the beginning and the end of each meal—tea so potent you'll feel your teeth chattering after a few glasses of the stuff. There are several other locations on Hong

Kong Island and in the New Territories. Dinner for two, with beer, costs about HK$250.
Open daily 11:30 a.m.-midnight. All major cards.

Choi Kun Heung
219E Nathan Rd.,
Tsimshatsui
• 3-667185
CANTONESE/VEGETARIAN

9/20

You're greeted with a sign reading, with no subtlety at all, **No Meat**, when you enter this pleasantly shabby Buddhist vegetarian restaurant on upper Nathan Road, at about the point where the tourists vanish and Hong Kong's real Chinese community begins. Eight pages of the menu are in Chinese, versus two in English, but those two pages offer enough vegetarian dishes (69 to be exact) to satisfy most cravings. We tend to gravitate toward the mushroom and other real vegetable dishes and away from the trompe l'oeil tofu dishes, in which tofu is made to look and taste like chicken or pork—if we want chicken and pork, we'll go to a restaurant that serves chicken and pork. We've had some reasonably satisfying orders here of fried dried mushrooms, sweet corn steamed with asparagus, fried noodles with (rather bland) white mushrooms, and congee (rice porridge) with bamboo fungus, which sounds much more exotic than it is. We enjoy the novelty of the cooking and the ease with which the food is digested, but this food isn't about to make us forswear our beloved liver and onions or the pleasures of a corned beef sandwich. Dinner for two, with beer, costs about HK$100.
Open daily 10 a.m.-10:30 p.m. No cards.

City Chiu Chow Restaurant
East Ocean Centre,
99 Granville Rd.,
Tsimshatsui East
• 3-7236226
CHIU CHOW

East Ocean Centre is not the same as the Ocean Centre next to Harbour City, a fact that took us two cab rides to learn. The restaurant, which covers one floor of the building, is a series of interrupted spaces that form open rooms in a horseshoe mezzanine around the escalator banks. Gold wallpaper with raised ideograms, pale-wood trim and brass-and-glass chandeliers create a glitter that stops just short of garishness, a lively, exuberant setting for some of the best Chiu Chow cooking in Hong Kong. Though the food is not very elaborate, it is filled with good flavors that work well together, resulting in dishes that are immensely satisfying. A general sense of abundance prevails: tables are large and portions huge. Goose with soy sauce, a Chiu Chow specialty, comes moist and meaty on a bed of thinly sliced bean curd, which soaks up the juices and winds up tasting like a full-flavored marrow custard. Savory mushroom caps filled with a briny fresh-shrimp mousse and accompanied by still-crunchy mustard greens is first-rate, as is shredded beef with jellyfish, the meat tangy-rare and tender, the jellyfish sweet and resilient. Much of Chiu Chow food is oily, but when it's done properly the oiliness imparts richness, not grease. Sautéed scallops and noodles with mixed meats are both properly oily, the latter chewy and pungent, the former delicately spiced in a ring of fried parsley. Mashed lotus seed surrounded by sago makes a sweet aromatic finish. Lilliputian servings of smoky, caffeine-loaded Iron Buddha tea begin and end the meal traditionally. Dinner for two, with beer, should cost no more than HK$250.

Open daily 11 a.m.-11 p.m. Cards: AE, MC, V.

East Ocean

East Ocean Centre, 99 Granville Rd., Tsimshatsui East
• 3-7238128
CANTONESE

12/20

After riding up and down the escalators in this rather grandiose shopping complex in the rapidly expanding Tsimshatsui East area (where old Kowloon seems to be turning into Los Angeles), we finally found East Ocean in the basement, which it appears to fill from one end to the other. It was also filled from end to end with a smartly dressed crowd, mostly in groups of eight or ten, eating immense portions of what we had been told is some of the best Cantonese seafood in this part of Hong Kong. Unfortunately, the service wasn't as good as the food—those large groups seemed to be eating up a good deal of the attention, and our small table was treated somewhat perfunctorily. But once the orders were taken, the food arrived with the speed of summer lightning. And if truth be told, the time we were given to study the extensive menu was well appreciated—it's a very pretty menu, printed on a background of ornate Chinese palace scenes (we kept looking for eunuchs and such but found only pomp and ceremony). The food was fine, particularly notable for the careful arrangements on each plate; East Ocean is clearly concerned with both form and function. Watch, in particular, for the seasonal specials, which are among the best items created in the kitchen: wonderfully sweet little Shanghai crabs; baby abalone with the taste and texture of the finest duck liver, served in a most subtle oyster sauce; shark's-fin soup dotted with crab roe. Despite East Ocean's Cantonese orientation, it makes a marvelous

Peking duck year-round. Dinner for two, with bee[
run HK$350 to HK$400.
Open daily 11 a.m.-11 p.m. Cards: AE, MC, V.

Fat Siu Lau
Seafood
Houston Centre,
Mody Rd.,
Tsimshatsui East
• 3-686291
CANTONESE

The first time we tried going to Fat Siu Lau, which we found (with some difficulty) on the third floor of the immensely convoluted Houston Centre shopping arcade, we made the mistake of showing up in the midst of lunch hour—and found what looked like at least 50 potential diners waiting anxiously at the front door for their names to be called for seating. Clearly, this is one of the more popular dim summeries in town, a restaurant that demands a certain amount of preplanning to secure a table. The next time we showed up we had a dinner reservation, and even on a weekday we found ourselves seated at one of the last available tables in this large T-shape room. It is for good reason that Fat Siu Lau is one of the most popular restaurants in Tsimshatsui East—it has a serious commitment to fresh seafood, its service is efficient and smart, and its setting, with its silk, its rosewood and its acres of chinoiserie, comfortably elegant. Along with Sun Tung Lok, this is one of the major shark's-fin restaurants in town, with a shark's-fin selection that is as encyclopedic as it is understandably expensive. We've rarely encountered plumper scallops or fatter prawns than these, most of which are best cooked in the simplest of ways; we prefer them sautéed rather than deep-fried, to bring out flavor at its best. We've also encountered some of the smallest pigeons we've ever seen, so delicate that they were more like ortolans than pigeons. Once again, this is a restaurant dominated by large parties, many of whom can be seen eating obscurely delicious dishes not described on the English section of the menu. If it looks good, point it out to your waiter; begrudgingly, he'll serve it to you, too. And expect the dish to cost accordingly. Dinner for two, with wine, will run about HK$360, if you stay away from shark's-fin delicacies.
Open daily 11:30 a.m.-midnight. All major cards.

Five Continents
Regal Airport Hotel
San Po Rd., Kowloon City
• 3-7180333
CONTINENTAL

10/20

When Hong Kong's airport hotel was managed by Meridien, its rooftop restaurant provided both culinary flair and a bird's-eye view of Kai Tak Airport's runway, both of which attracted downtown gourmets out to this shantytown district near Kowloon's infamous Walled City. The runway and harbor panorama, seen through a long wall of soundproofed sloping windows, is still an

attraction, but since the Meridien departed, the clientele in this casual (no dress code), pastel gallery now seems to be composed of hotel guests, airport transients and local couples. At our last meal here, our neighbors smooched between courses, which was understandable considering that the amplified melodies of the adjacent pianist makes conversation difficult. The menu is ambitious and large, but blandness rules this twelfth-floor nookery: "oven-baked" duck consommé lacks liquid taste and sports a flaccid puff-pastry crust, and the asparagus fricassée is a dull conceit of three tiny asparagus tips laid in a cheesy wine sauce garnished with five scallops and a scattering of truffles. "Trois filets aux trois poivres" sounds fun but is silly. The three meats are doused in yet another cheesy wine sauce (possibly the same sauce each time, varied only by its peppers) and taste identical; only their perfectly cooked spinach garnish is memorable. Filet of dry-as-usual turbot brings finer flavors, served with a cream sauce and caviar "pearls." The dessert trolley contains some edible confections; fresh fruit is as expensive as it is everywhere in Hong Kong (HK$35 for a small dish of strawberries). The menu is bottom-heavy with footnoted wine recommendations, but the wine list does not specify years, just asterisks for vintage wines. Most are too young, like the Château Haut-Madrac we ordered, which turned out to be a pricey, immature 1985. The willing waiters, who are also young, are learning that airline-cuisine standards (albeit those of first class) can now be learned on the ground at Kai Tak. Dinner for two, with wine, will set you back about HK$600. Fixed-price menus are HK$125 and HK$192 at lunch, and HK$215 at dinner.
Open daily noon-3 p.m. & 7 p.m.-11 p.m. All major cards.

Flourishing Court
Prudential Centre, 216
Nathan Rd., Tsimshatsui
• 3-7392308
CANTONESE

This large, unpretentious restaurant's pursuit of the discriminating mass market (not an oxymoron in Hong Kong, at least where Cantonese cuisine is concerned) has led to a sad consequence for visitors who cannot read Chinese: table cards are not translated, and the bilingual basic menu lists only standard staples. A Chinese-reading companion is essential, therefore, to discover such inexpensive seasonal specialties as drunken chicken (steamed in wine, then served cold) with scallions in a clay pot, various casseroles, a quartet of "American beef ribs" dishes (including one with black beans and garlic) and home-style platters (the savory steamed minced pork is a personal favorite). Approximate translations of the reasonable fixed-price menus (HK$208, HK$398 and HK$668, for two, four and six diners, respectively) are worth seeking from the casually friendly captains, and Peking duck (served in two courses here, with soup) is a good choice. And you can always resort to using sign language at the waterfall aquarium, where you point to the fish that looks good to you. We tried a lively member of the sea bream family, which was steamed to perfection. Perhaps out of consideration for foreign sensibilities, the "drunken" prawns we ordered were soused and boiled alive out of our sight, two tables away. These prawns, and the resultant rice-wine soup (offered automatically), were also perfect, as was the sealed elixir of double-boiled chicken and ginseng soup. Shark's-fin soups are another Flourishing Court bargain: the fins may not be top-grade, but their HK$55-to-HK$130 price range is tastily acceptable. One locally popular *nouvelle cuisine chinoise* dish should be ignored: lobster "salad," which comes with American-style mayonnaise. Popular rather than fashionable (and noisily popular for lunchtime dim sum), this three-year-old spot is wonderfully old-fashioned. Two will spend HK$300 to HK$400 for dinner with wine.

Open Mon.-Sat. 11 a.m.-midnight, Sun. & holidays 9:30 a.m.-midnight. All major cards.

Flourishing Restaurant

Shui Heng Yuen Apt.,
504-512 Canton Rd.,
Tsimshatsui
• 3-840358
CANTONESE

Not to be confused with Flourishing Court Restaurant, this sprawling establishment serves food on three floors: a small downstairs dining room that patrons share with tanks of live fish, and two upper floors, the first of which is moderately stylish, the topmost, pure cafeteria. We've never gone early enough to avoid being ushered to one of the Formica center tables or booths upstairs, where a few randomly distributed mirrors constitute the decor, but the food has never made us regret the visit. Start off with the generic fish soup, a dowdy-sounding Cinderella that turns out to be a shimmering bowl of delicately perfumed stock whose egg drops shelter pristine flakes of white fish, bits of chive and black mushroom, and loads of bean curd. Kai Sheki–style pigeon offers a crisp skin, pungent, molasses-winey meat and a clean, lingering aftertaste. Also tops on our list is a casserole of bitter melon stuffed with a seaweed-laced mousse of bean curd; the accompanying black-bean-paste sauce makes a heady foil for the bitter and sweet vegetables. Crab with broccoli needs a blast of chili paste to waken its flavors. The disappointing dim sum—fatty shu mai and scraggly buns filled with an anemic dab of pork—may be safely bypassed. Finger bowls are a godsend, especially if you order the pigeon, which demands at least an occasional hand-to-wing tussle to prize off the succulent morsels. Two hearty eaters should do quite well, with wine or beer, for HK$250. *Open daily noon-midnight. All major cards.*

Flower Lounge
3 Peace Ave., Mongkok
• 3-7156557
Royal Garden Hotel
69 Mody Rd.,
Tsimshatsui East
• 3-7221592
Harbour City, Tsimshatsui
• 3-699981
CANTONESE

See Hong Kong Island.

Fook Lam Moon
31 Mody Rd., Tsimshatsui
• 3-688755
CANTONESE

See Hong Kong Island.

Fung Lum
23 Granville Rd.,
Tsimshatsui
• 3-678919
CANTONESE

11/20

This chain, with branches in Taiwan and California (including what's reputed to be the largest Chinese restaurant in America, in Universal City near Los Angeles), began modestly with its Shatin (New Territories) branch, a restaurant noted for its bean curd preparations. Many speak reverently of the fried bean curd, roasted until brown on the outside but still nice and squishy within. We like it enough, but not enough to have us begging for seconds. The Fung Lums are high practitioners of the more-is-more school of Chinese restaurants—their menus go on forever and a day. Aside from the ever-popular bean curd dishes (which are still supposedly the best in Shatin), both locals and visitors flock to the various Fung Lums for the lemon chicken, the smoked duck and the baked shrimp with spicy salt, most of which are fine but none of which we find in any way memorable. Dinner for two, with beer, costs about HK$320.
Open daily 11 a.m.-11 p.m. Cards: AE, MC, V.

Fung Lum Szechuan

23 Granville Rd.,
Tsimshatsui
• 3-678919, 678686
SZECHUAN

Fung Lum Szechuan (not to be confused with Fung Lum's Cantonese restaurants) is one of Hong Kong's best Szechuan restaurants, right up there with Pep 'n' Chilli and Red Pepper. The exterior is basically an unassuming storefront; in fact, it resembles nothing as much as a New York neighborhood Chinese restaurant. The manager and waiters are very friendly to *gwai loh* (which we suppose is politic, since 75 percent of the patrons seem to be Occidentals), and they're happy to explain the menu. Every dish we've had here was terrific, starting with the special spareribs, one of the most popular dishes, which are moist, smoky and hot. You'll also encounter quite a selection of pickled and cold dishes, delicious smoked duck, a Szechuan-style steamed chicken that must be ordered in advance, lip-smacking frogs' legs in a kumquat-orange sauce, sweet honeyed ham and addictive vermicelli with chili and prawn balls. The kung pao chicken is a must, fabulous and fiery with chilis, peanuts, garlic and onions. And you must also order the pan-fried dumplings, their thin skins stuffed to bursting with a minced pork filling. You may laugh at the crystal chandeliers and bamboo-patterned wallpaper and cringe under the brain-surgery lighting, but you'll go back for the food. Dinner for two, with drinks, should run about HK$250.
Open daily noon-midnight. No cards.

Gaddi's

The Peninsula
Salisbury Rd., Tsimshatsui
• 3-666251
FRENCH

The most famous restaurant in Hong Kong is also located in the most famous hotel in Hong Kong. Years ago, Gaddi's was considered the best cuisine "east of Suez." What's left of it today? There's the opulence of the silverware, crystal and chandeliers, the beauty of the Belle Epoque dining room, the slightly stuffy atmosphere, the flawlessly attired clientele, the incredible magnificence of the fixed-price menus, and the legendary maître d', Rolf Heiniger, all of which cast an enchanting spell over the place. What about the cuisine? For the most part, its quality is still excellent: majestic, serious and classical. The meal begins on a positive note with a selection of fresh breads, including crusty, resilient rye. The grilled vegetable mix with an herb vinaigrette is an outstanding appetizer. The fish, of flawless quality, are perfectly fresh (we particularly like the sea perch with a ginger-spiked beurre blanc), though they can be a tad overcooked, at least to our (admittedly nouvelle) taste. You'll find all sorts of French cheeses and some delicious if unimaginative desserts, including passion-fruit soup, various sorbets, a nice crème caramel surrounded by cream-filled cornets, and pears belle Hélène topped with high-quality ice cream. Despite these good things, we're keeping Gaddi's ranking on the low side for now—after many superb meals we recently suffered through a mediocre one. Fortunately, we returned a short time later and found that the acclaimed quality had returned. But even an occasional slipup in a restaurant of this reputation— and price caliber—is cause for concern. The wine cellar is stupendous, containing bottles from all over the world, old ports and rare vintages—it has everything from a Latour '57 to a Coulée de Serrant. Men must wear jackets and ties. The attractive "discovery" fixed-price menu is worth mentioning (HK$820), since it includes a different wine with each course, and the HK$115 fixed-price lunch is a bargain. To dine à la carte with wine, two can easily part with HK$1,000—or more.

Open daily noon-3 p.m. & 7 p.m.-11 p.m. All major cards.

Gaylord
Hody Commercial Bldg., 6 Hart Ave., Tsimshatsui
• 3-7241001
INDIAN

12/20

Like Bombay Palace, Gaylord is part of a worldwide chain of Indian restaurants, whose appeal—in part— derives from its ability to be all things to all people. The food can be, as you wish, either very spicy or not spicy at all; either highly familiar and accessible or quite exotic. The settings, without fail, are comforting, reminiscent of the images the movies have given us of a maharajah's palace; you almost expect bejeweled elephants to wander out of the kitchen. After the chaos of so many Chinese restaurants, one does feel soothed at Gaylord, where the lights are low, the banquettes cozy, the noise muted by yards of fabric. Not long ago, Gaylord relocated from its old Chatham Road location to Hart Avenue, apparently changing little in the transition. The food is still quite often very good. The kitchen does a fine job with lamb and mutton dishes (mutton seems particularly well suited to Indian cooking—the spices and the gaminess blend elegantly). Try the mutton cooked in a lentil stew (dal), the exceedingly spicy lamb vindaloo or the minced lamb cooked with peas (keema mutter). Some excellent tandoori dishes also emerge from the kitchen: the chicken is crisp on the outside, tender on the inside, spicy but not overly so. And the kulfi, the traditional Indian ice cream, is the perfect palate-soother; it may be the best ice cream in Hong Kong. Dinner for two, with wine, costs about HK$350.

Open daily noon-2:30 p.m. & 6 p.m.-midnight. Cards: AE, DC, MC, V.

Ginza
The Regent Arcade
Salisbury Rd., Tsimshatsui
• 3-686138
JAPANESE

You can spend considerably more for a mediocre Japanese meal in Hong Kong than for an excellent Chinese meal. Many of Hong Kong's Japanese restaurants, in fact, seem to be trying their darndest to compete with their Tokyo counterparts in terms of price; we have particularly unpleasant recollections of spending a small fortune for a nondescript meal at Nadaman, wishing all the while that we were instead swallowing Szechuan shrimp at the Red Pepper instead. If you feel obliged to spend an evening (and a fortune) in a Japanese restaurant, one of the best of them is almost surely Ginza, situated in The Regent's exceedingly posh shopping arcade. As befits any operation connected with The Regent, Ginza glows with a fine sense of elegance and a superb view of the harbor, which led us to note how few Japanese restaurants have good views (the aforementioned Nadaman, for instance, is a windowless room in a hotel basement). Ginza offers the usual assortment of rooms, including a tatami room that holds up to twenty persons, and four teppanyaki rooms. We prefer the activity in the main room, where modern-day geishas deliver the food with casual haste. If money is no object, try the marvelous steamed abalone or the turtle soup made with turtles imported from Japan. The sushi is nicely turned and always fresh. Sukiyaki is prepared using Matsusaka beef, which is less well known than Kobe but considered by some to be superior. And expect a fair number of kaiseki dishes, refined small plates prepared seasonally depending on what's available. Expect the ingredients to be rarefied, with prices to match. Dinner for two, with sake, costs about HK$600, unless you splurge on the aforementioned abalone, turtle soup or kaiseki meals.

Open daily noon-3 p.m. & 6:30 p.m.-11 p.m. All major cards.

Golden Bull

New World Centre,
Salisbury Rd., Tsimshatsui
• 3-694617
VIETNAMESE

11/20

This unusual restaurant, whose main dining room is decorated in the style of a small bamboo village, is located in the shopping complex of the New World Centre. Authentic Vietnamese cuisine, catering to primarily Asian patrons, is served in a hectic, noisy atmosphere. The chef's specialty is a dish composed of seven products based on beef, but neither Vietnam's soups nor its variously prepared pigeon, chicken, pork and shrimp dishes are neglected. Compared with its Chinese cousins, this cuisine may seem a bit coarse to Western palates. What is hot is really hot. The pieces are cut large, the quality of the basic ingredients is mediocre, and the smells remind you of those drifting over Hong Kong's markets. You have to be an ace with the chopsticks to deal with chicken that's hardly precut at all. But the enthusiasm with which your table neighbors throw themselves upon this rustic food implies that it suits the Chinese tastes just fine. And in fact the food does make for satisfying eating. Marinated vegetables, their mouth-puckering acidity matched by a sugary sweetness, start dinner. They're served with a tea whose smoky pungency is not unlike tobacco. Chili-heads might avail themselves of the fiery oxtail casserole, a somewhat overwhelming portion crammed with red and green peppers as well as meat. An inexpensive and pleasant conclusion is the warm taro with lotus, the taro reminiscent of coconut pudding and the lotus seeds a bit like chickpeas. Golden Bull here is considered to be like a cantina for impecunious gastronomes. Count on about HK$350 for two, with beer.
Open daily noon-3 p.m. & 6 p.m.-11:30 p.m. All major cards.

Golden Island Bird's Nest

25-31 Carnarvon Rd.,
Tsimshatsui
• 3-695211
CHIU CHOW

12/20

The trick is finding the entrance, which is around the corner from the address, on Hanoi Street. The owners have found an innovative solution: they erected a gigantic neon sign emblazoned with the restaurant's name in yellow and red on Carnarvon Road to direct patrons to a somewhat smaller sign swaying over the Hanoi Street doorway. Upstairs, one large open space filled with tables, bright lights glaring through a latticework ceiling, plays host to extended families—often four generations crowded around one table—enjoying a few hours' respite from Hong Kong's pursuit of dollars, deutsch marks, dirhams and drachmas. When you're seated, diminutive saucers of astringent Iron Buddha tea make an immediate appearance, and they also end the meal, sending you out into the streets fortified with a potent

jolt of caffeine. Smiling waiters and waitresses plop steaming towels into your hands at every opportunity before, during and after each course. This is home-style Chiu Chow food, honest and well prepared. Crab in egg white reminds us of Cantonese lobster sauce: understated, sweetly briny and faintly pungent from its bed of steamed Chinese cabbage and straw mushrooms. Standouts among the dozens of seafood dishes are the steamed freshwater goby, a mildly flavored mackerel-like fish in a light soy sauce, and the Chiu Chow–style baby oyster omelet. That Chiu Chow standard, herb-roasted goose, is dark and glossy outside, but the meat inside can be a bit dry; make sure to dip it into the accompanying plum sauce. Dishes range from about HK$25 to HK$65, and three will feed two people amply. The captain, who hovers around the occasional foreigner, explaining and suggesting, accommodatingly ordered a half portion of crystal dumplings for us—six rather than twelve—and had half prepared with a molasses-intense black-bean paste and the remainder with a milder yellow-bean paste. Two should be able to pig out on this down-home cooking for about HK$200, including beer.
Open daily 11 a.m.-1 a.m. Cards: MC, V.

Golden Unicorn
Hongkong Hotel
3 Canton Rd., Tsimshatsui
• 3-7226565
CANTONESE

Despite competent-to-delicious food, Golden Unicorn ruffles our feathers. It seems unsure whether it's a chic boîte pirated from Manhattan's East 60s or a campy diner spray-painted to a fare-thee-well for the finale of a Busby Berkeley musical. Pushy waiters try to steer diners toward abalone dishes (at HK$260 to HK$1,200), serve single portions of soup reluctantly and urge the ordering of expensive and inappropriate wines. They also hover to refill dishes and whisk away plates, hustling diners along to promote rapid turnover. Still, at our insistence, our waiter presented the seafood soup in two bowls. Fine, seafood broth tangy with ginger held two chunks of garoupa, a couple of straw mushrooms and some bean curd—no bargain, however pleasant, at HK$70. Chili sauce helped to cut a fatty note in the otherwise moist and flavorful duck with taro. Novel and worth trying, the preserved egg with barbecued pork was rather like an Eastern version of a western omelet. A house specialty is drunken shrimp (steamed in wine), which is prepared in small batches, three or four cooking while the previous batch is consumed. Sliced conch with ham, fried shrimp with cashews and squid with chives are worthy dishes found on the reasonable end of the otherwise pricey seafood menu. For dessert, try the peony dumplings filled with sweet bean paste or the sago tapioca with lichee-like longan fruit. Two people choosing carefully will spend about HK$400 for dinner with beer or a modest wine. *Open daily 11:30 a.m.-11:30 p.m. All major cards.*

Great Shanghai

26-36 Prat Ave.,
Tsimshatsui
• 3-668158
SHANGHAINESE

In contrast to the several handfuls of Shanghainese cafés around town (like the multitude of Yat Pan Hongs), where the cooking is closer to late-night dim sum than full-scale meals, the hyperbolic Great Shanghai is indeed that: a great Shanghainese restaurant, both in terms of size and quality. With its 400-plus dishes, the menu can be a bit daunting. Many of the dishes, though, are fairly small—this is grazing cuisine, a cuisine based primarily on appetizers. This is also a noodle-intensive cuisine; it's not unusual to create a meal out of a half dozen different noodle dishes. When composing your meal, watch as well for the signature Shanghainese brown sauce: we once ordered too casually and wound up with a meal that was more brown sauce than anything else. It's a good sauce, but you don't want to build an entire meal around it. Service is unusually friendly, as it is at most Shanghainese restaurants; we once showed up for a meal at three in the afternoon, when this vast room was empty, and found ourselves treated with the utmost consideration. Don't miss the exceedingly crispy onion cakes, the cabbage stewed with abalone, the crispy eel in brown sauce or the Szechuan-style yellowfish soup. Dinner for two, with wine, costs no more than HK$300.
Open daily 11 a.m.-midnight. Cards: AE, MC, V.

Harbour View Seafood Restaurant

Tsimshatsui Centre, 66
Mody Rd., Tsimshatsui
East
• 3-72258888
CANTONESE

12/20

Another of the kingpins at the heart of the rapidly emerging Tsimshatsui East area, Harbour View is found on the third floor of the gigantic Tsimshatsui Centre. As its name promises, it offers an exceptional view of the harbor and Hong Kong Island beyond. One caveat: it's easy to get thoroughly lost trying to find Harbour View. Though its location on the center's third floor would seem to make it easily accessible, and though a number of signs point to it, we still went around and around in circles, until we discovered that it was reached via an elevator that takes you directly to it. And even after we figured that out, when we returned for another meal we got lost again, this time trying to find the elevator. The considerable number of people

in the restaurant seems to indicate that there's some secret to finding the Harbour View that we haven't yet deciphered. Geography aside, this is a handsome, polished place serving a broad selection of strikingly fresh seafood dishes. We had a particularly fine (and not overly expensive) lobster here, carefully chopped so that the crustacean looked whole when it arrived at our table but quickly fell into convenient chunks when we started pulling at its shell. Harbour View's crabs, if ordered at the right time of the year, can be bulging with bright orange coral. Whole fish, especially garoupa, are elegantly presented and carefully boned by skilled waiters. Interestingly, this is one of the few Chinese restaurants in town that offers a view; it's worth noting that with so much to look at, your dining pace seems to slow down, and the meal becomes almost leisurely. Dinner for two, with wine, costs about HK$350.
Open Mon.-Fri. 11 a.m.-midnight, Sat.-Sun. 9:30 a.m.-midnight. Cards: AE, MC, V.

Hoi Tin Garden
53-59 Praya Rd., Lei Yue Mun
• 3-481482
CANTONESE

6/20

The saving grace of tourist traps can be their entertainment value. That is the major reason for sailing into the murky waters off the Lei Yue Mun promontory on Victoria Harbour's northeastern tip (from which the Japanese launched their 1941 invasion of Hong Kong Island). Formerly a den of smugglers and now a popular seafood destination for locals, this cliffside shantytown is best reached circuitously, via the seven-minute harbor-crossing ferry from Hong Kong Island's Sai Wan Ho to Kowloon's Sam Ka Tsuen. There, a sampan ferry makes the two-minute journey across a polluted inlet. Planks lead into a maze of fish-market lanes, at the far end of which the high-ceilinged halls and open terraces of Hoi Tin Garden perch on shoreline boulders beneath the roar of jets on Kai Tak Airport's flight path. All of Lei Yue Mun restaurants are air conditioned, and all offer to procure fish for you. Hoi Tin Garden is the best-known of the lot, and its English-speaking staff seem helpful enough—but do-it-yourself fish purchasing is the name of Lei Yue Mun's game, so buyer beware! Some fish-mongering families still have piracy in their blood; rapacious rip-offs include rigged scales (the old-style bamboo-and-string), overcharging, excess water in the fish-weighing plastic bags, selling near-dead fish and more. Be prepared to bargain; even better, bring a streetwise, Cantonese-speaking companion with you. Ours was not streetwise: we overpaid HK$378 for an alleged *catty* (Chinese kilogram) of shrimp, eleven small abalones (we asked for ten) and a slippery fish whose ten-minute battle to avoid being netted was the evening's major delight. Hoi Tin charged a steep HK$110 to quick-steam the lot (unexceptionally, with ginger and Chinese onions), cooked a mediocre mixed-vegetable dish and added insult to injury by levying an unearned service charge *and* not presenting the HK$11 change due for the HK$189 bill. The waiters then hovered around, encouraging remaining tables to clear off. Enjoy Lei Yue Mun as a relic of ancient South China. A seafood meal will cost about HK$300 per person.

Open daily noon-11 p.m. All major cards.

Houston Chiu Chow

Houston Centre, Mody
Rd., Tsimshatsui East
• No phone
CHIU CHOW

10/20

We had gotten into Hong Kong late one night, but not so late that we didn't have time to throw our bags in our room and go dashing over to the Houston Centre in hope of snagging a late-night meal at the excellent Fat Siu Lau. Unfortunately, as is too often the case, Fat Siu Lau had decided to ignore its alleged midnight closing hour, instead shutting down at 10:45. (This is often the case—if business is slow, Chinese restaurants will close early. The hours listed are a good general guideline, but they are by no means carved in stone.) Feeling both weary and hungry, we wandered about the massive Houston Centre until we happened down into the basement, where we found Houston Chiu Chow not only open but quite busy. This is customary for many of Hong Kong's Chiu Chow restaurants, where the hours are late, the food inexpensive and the crowds inevitable. Because Chiu Chow cooking is a cousin of Cantonese cuisine, the city's dominant Cantonese community loves to flock to Chiu Chow restaurants in the wee hours for steaming plates of goose in soy sauce (probably the definitive Chiu Chow dish) and big bowls of shark's-fin and bird's-nest soup. Houston Chiu Chow stands out simply because of its design: unlike most Chiu Chow cafés around town, it sits in an attractive atrium, giving the place a spacious, airy feeling. The food is good but not exceptional, featuring an assortment of fresh seafood that may leave you somewhat confused—exactly what sort of fish is an eyebrough, a flagfish or a lum pown? As ever, you pay your money and make a choice. If you're a tad nervous about being confronted with a heaping platter of eyebrough (and who wouldn't be?), you can order the very good fried chicken in sesame-seed sauce, stewed Tientsin cabbage with minced chicken, and fine baked pigeon with spring onion sauce. Houston says it's open until two in the morning, but it's probably open until everyone goes home. Dinner for two, with beer, costs about HK$200.

Open daily 11:30 a.m.-2 a.m. Cards: AE, MC, V.

Hugo's
Hyatt Regency Hong Kong
67 Nathan Rd.,
Tsimshatsui
• 3-3111234
FRENCH/CONTINENTAL

12/20

How did the Hyatt ever come up with the idea of paying homage, through its hotel restaurant, to Hugo Ludwig Wilhelm von Glückenstein, a Bavarian innkeeper? It's more than a bit strange to find this Middle Ages setting, suitable for a bunch of Teutonic knights, smack in the middle of a super-high-tech Hong Kong hotel. And the decor was taken so seriously that walls are covered with actual stones, perhaps even extracted from the Black Forest. A squadron of waiters dress in uniforms that match the decor! The decor is quite cozy, gracefully but firmly enveloping you the moment you step into this castle. But the food is a bit more modern than look of the dining room. Though a bit heavy, the lobster ravioli with vanilla butter and a julienne of vegetables woke up our taste buds with its unusual vanilla zest. Other seafood dishes include the middle-of-the-road crab soufflé with crêpes and red pepper; the more interesting tiger prawns braised in a pepper sauce that the chef calls "subtle" (we'll leave him responsible for this description), served with a red-caviar pilaf; and the roasted sea bass with sea-urchin mousse, which was a tad overdone. Of course, venison would have to be served in such a setting, and surely it was no accident that it was the best dish we tried. The desserts are not worth the calories. While you dine, an excellent Filipino band will stop by to serenade your table, making conversation impossible, and they'll play their entire repertoire unless you threaten them with a tear-gas bomb. But everybody is so nice, so attentive, and all the details are perfect, including the cigar (complete with matches) offered to each gentlemen and the rose to each lady. In the end, in this German restaurant with its Chinese chef and French saucier, you can spend a rather agreeable evening, which you may enhance with a selection from the large, well-chosen list of German (of course), French and California wines. About HK$800 for dinner for two, with wine.

Open daily noon-3 p.m. & 7 p.m.-11 p.m. All major cards.

Inagiku

The Peninsula
West Wing, Salisbury Rd.,
Tsimshatsui
• 3-7391898
JAPANESE

11/20

Having stepped sedately across the sand garden's paving stones, and having swept up the duplex restaurant's grand staircase, you sit expectantly at an oak table, enjoying the rare (for Hong Kong) splendor of a gray, pink and purple gallery-like dining room. Sadly, some ingredients and the service do not live up to expectations heightened by such surroundings—and such prices. Sushi, tempura and teppanyaki are all specialties of a house originally established in Asakusa in 1866: devotees can sample them at individual lower-level counters, one for each culinary specialty. Though delicately battered, the assorted kiku tempura that we tried were dull. For HK$250, our assorted sashimi (mostly jet-fresh) contained too many rough textures. Neither platter was presented with flair; the meal's only aesthetic highlight was a sprig of buds garnishing the seasonal assorted appetizer of mixed tastes (perfect pork loin and dreadful dry fish). Another monthly seasonal choice, baby sea squid, was superb, unlike the prosaic crockery, sake vases and ragged bamboo containers. Doing our bit for world trade, we embargoed the HK$380 Kobe beef and chose its underrated—and top-grade—U.S. cousin, thereby saving HK$160 on our sukiyaki and stone-beef courses. A smiling, polite Japanese waitress started to demonstrate the traditional tabletop-cooking finesse, then handed the job over to a Cantonese woman who looked like she was agonizing with her costume and the volcanic grilling plate. Nevertheless, she grilled the meat and properly simmered the do-it-yourself sauce mixes, which flattered both courses; the miso soups were richly above average. An à la carte dinner for two, with sake, will set you back HK$1,100; per-person fixed-price meals range from

HK$100 to HK$200 for lunch, HK$300 to HK$700 for tempura/teppanyaki dinners, HK$480 to HK$600 for kaiseki dinners and HK$600 to HK$800 for full-blown gourmet feasts.
Open daily noon-3 p.m. & 6:30 p.m.-11 p.m. All major cards.

Indian Curry Club
Tsimshatsui Centre, 66 Mody Rd., Tsimshatsui East
• 3-7219873
INDIAN

8/20

The Indian Curry Club is a fun, unpretentious restaurant owned by Ranjan Dey, who recruits his chefs from all over India to come to Hong Kong. While the food's not fabulous, it makes up in quantity what it lacks in quality. The setting is attractive, and there's a very reasonably priced buffet table that features at least 30 different dishes a day. The food is quite authentic, and while some dishes are better than others, there are very good pappadums, chapati bread, various curried dishes, Sri Lankan string-hoppers and an Afghani chicken drumstick kebab marinated in yogurt and cashews. The rice pudding for dessert is pretty good, too. There's a full bar, so you can toast yourself for finding such a bargain—the buffet for two will set you back only about HK$100.
Open daily noon-2:30 p.m. & 6 p.m.-10 p.m. Cards: MC, V.

Jade Garden
Tung Ying Bldg., 36 Carnarvon Rd., Tsimshatsui
• 3-674041
Metropolitan Bank Bldg., 25 Carnarvon Rd., Tsimshatsui
• 3-698311
CANTONESE

See Hong Kong Island.

Java Rijsttafel
38 Hankow Rd., Tsimshatsui
• 3-671230
INDONESIAN

11/20

A genuine Dutch colonial rijsttafel (rice table) buffet would burst the walls of this 31-seat cubbyhole, in which batik-clothed side tables are about as wide as a single plate. Long an advance-order, weekend-only feast, the decimated version of rijsttafel at this homely, twenty-year-old café is now an ever-ready fixed-price dinner at HK$60 per person (minimum two diners). The good sampler of Indonesian staple dishes usually includes crisp shrimp crackers, spicy satay, chewy spiced Rendang beef and fish sambal, mild chicken curry, gado-gado (mixed- vegetable salad) and delicious des-

sert cakes, whose evocative Indonesian name is kue-kue: lurid green rolls that look like hand towels but are actually sweetly sensational coconut-filled pancakes. Even the coffee tastes truly Javanese. Other specialties on the 52-item menu include classic nasi padang and nasi rames rice platters, a fiery fried fish head in hot-and-sour gravy, Bali-style chili-sauced meats, Indonesia's fried spring rolls and hearty fried-potato cakes filled with minced beef. Red and white house wines are available by the carafe or glass, cold "es" drinks are well iced, and the inclusion of "Dutch gin" (Bols) on the menu is just one of the authentic touches that draw Dutch expatriates and tourists to this tiny corner of their imperial past. Ventilation is adequate, but jackets will need to come off if your neighbors are heating satay on the charcoal burners (for a change from beef, chicken or pork satay, ask the "seasonal" price for mutton, an expensive meat in Hong Kong). Smoking is frowned upon here. Dinner for two, with drinks, will cost two about HK$160.
Open daily noon-10:30 p.m. Cards: AE, MC, V.

Jimmy's Kitchen
Kowloon Centre, 29
Ashley Rd., Tsimshatsui
• 3-684027
CONTINENTAL

See Hong Kong Island.

Lai Ching Heen
The Regent
Salisbury Rd., Tsimshatsui
• 3-7211211
CANTONESE

The place settings alone speak volumes about the exceptional opulence at what many—including us—consider to be the best Chinese restaurant in Hong Kong (appropriately situated in what we consider to be the best hotel in Hong Kong). These place settings are rumored to cost $1,000 (that's U.S. dollars) each: ivory and silver chopsticks nestled in jade chopstick holders, buttressed by a jade-and-silver spoon and a solid jade serving plate. Between the breathtaking location at exactly the right spot on Hong Kong Harbour and the sheer beauty of the place settings and decor, the food seems almost redundant—and indeed, we wondered, how could it possibly compete with such grand physical beauty? It does, of course, and then some. This is Cantonese cooking raised to its apotheosis, a Platonic ideal; it is impossible to imagine Chinese cooking better than this. Order a dim sum assortment and you'll understand the meaning of perfection. You'll find yourself confronted with idyllic steamed shrimp dumplings, pan-fried vegetables wrapped in bean-curd sheets,

ime was when life's finer things such as Hine Cognac were the preserve of a privileged few.

Today, it is still the true connoisseur who appreciates the mature, mellow flavour of Hine.

The dictionary defines a connoisseur as "one who is an expert judge in matters of taste".

And who are we to argue.

HINE
MAISON FONDÉE EN 1763
COGNAC

BRASH, BOLD GUIDES
TO THE BEST OF THE VERY BEST

Also available:

steamed minced-beef dumplings, deep-[fr]
toast: small tastes of heaven that make all th[e]
sum you've eaten seem like the botched coo[king]
child. This is what knowledgeable Chinese food [lovers]
like to call Modern Chinese Cuisine, a giant step fro[m]
the chaotic cooking found on Hong Kong's back
streets. Here one does not eat, one dines: on deep-fried
lotus paste and sesame dumplings, elegant Shek Ki
pigeon simmered in oyster sauce, fried Japanese noodles with shredded beef in a mixed pepper and black-
bean sauce, the plumpest steamed scallops on earth,
steamed prawn balls subtly flavored with garlic, braised
lamb brisket with black mushrooms and bamboo
shoots, sautéed shredded turtle with bean sprouts and
green peppers. Dishes are served individually, elegantly
spooned onto your plate, so the smells can be savored,
the perfection admired. The price is high, but the
cooking is worth every penny. Dinner for two, with
wine, will run at least HK$600.
*Open daily 12:30 p.m.-3:30 p.m. & 6 p.m.-11:30 p.m.
All major cards.*

Lalique
Royal Garden Hotel
69 Mody Rd., Tsimshatsui
East
• 3-7215215
FRENCH

12/20

Lalique, unfortunately, is known primarily for its '20s
and '30s decor inspired, as you've guessed, by the great
glass designer René Lalique: vases, figurines, windows.
. . . It's exquisite, and the ride up in a glass-walled
elevator, which offers you a staggering view of the
hotel's lobby, with its basins and fountains, is breathtaking. However, the cuisine, prepared by a French-
Canadian chef, scarcely lives up to its promises. The
double truffle consommé en croûte, reminiscent of Paul
Bocuse's famed VGE soup, was quite a disappointment:
the truffles were savorless, and though it looked superb,
the feuilleté was undercooked. As for the beef with
walnut sauce and a julienne of green apple, it also
looked enticing—but this time the meat turned out to
be overcooked, so we had no idea of its quality, and the
sauce was rather run-of-the-mill. The slice of chocolate
with orange makes a decent, if not inspired, dessert. The
wine list is a bit meager, and the temperature of the
wines should be examined (it was surprising to be told
that our too-warm bottle of Bordeaux would cool in
the air-conditioned dining room!). About HK$1,000
for two, with wine.
*Open Mon.-Sat. noon-2:30 p.m. & 7 p.m.-midnight,
Sun. 7 p.m.-midnight. Cards: AE, DC, MC, V.*

Leonardo is a little bit of culture shock—a little Della Robbia wreath in the middle of hordes wielding cellular telephones. (It seems as though everyone in Hong Kong has a cellular telephone.) Although the restaurant is completely staffed by Chinese, there are no cross-cultural references here; both the menu and the decor are strictly Italian. The antipasto plate is more than decent, and while the insalata caprese (tomato, basil and mozzarella) suffered from rather tasteless mozzarella, it was otherwise quite nice. You can pass on the pizza—the crust we tasted seemed like it came straight from the frozen-food section of your supermarket—but the pastas, especially the fusilli with clams and artichokes in a cream sauce, are satisfyingly tasty. Leonardo also has an incredibly cheap fixed-price lunch special: three courses including a salad, an entrée or pasta and dessert for HK$48. Hong Kong may be one of the last places on earth you'd think of going out for Italian food, but Leonardo's corny checkered tablecloths, potted palms and Botticelli prints make for a kind of wacky alternative universe. Dinner for two, with drinks, will run about HK$200.

Open daily noon-midnight. All major cards.

Lindy's
57 Peking Rd., Tsimshatsui
• 3-671683
AMERICAN/DELI

6/20

We were drawn to Lindy's by memories of the good cheesecake served at the original branch in New York City, and by a review in a local guidebook praising the herring, the gefilte fish, the stuffed cabbage and the potato pancakes. Unfortunately, either the reviewer was writing about his or her New York experience, or Lindy's has gone through a significant change, for the surly waiter who dealt with us at this dreary second-floor restaurant brought us a menu that was certainly American and certainly not deli-like. We tried clam chowder as thick as glue, gummy lasagne, spiceless cioppino, a corned beef sandwich of embarrassing thinness on bread that would be run out of New York tarred, feathered and hung from a rail. The potato pancakes oozed oil. And if the food was bad, the service was worse. The pity was that we consumed joyless calories instead of indulging on a good Peking duck somewhere else. Dinner for two, with beer, costs about HK$150.

Open daily 8 a.m.-midnight. Cards: AE, DC, MC, V.

Loong Yuen

**Holiday Inn Golden Mile
50 Nathan Rd.,
Tsimshatsui**
• 3-7396268
CANTONESE

Though the basement of a Holiday Inn seems an unlikely site for a culinary mecca, Hong Kong makes a habit of such happy surprises. Loong Yuen's Cantonese cuisine explores a range of dishes that extends from goose web, abalone and bird's-nest soup with snow frog to sautéed bamboo pith with yellow fungus and winter melon stuffed with fish maw, ham and bamboo pith. Timid souls will be pleased to know, however, that Loong Yuen also purveys less exotic foodstuffs: sautéed shrimp with cashew nuts, lemon chicken, pork spareribs and pan-fried beef with assorted vegetables. Try the stuffed whelk, the meat extracted, chopped, mixed with onion, shrimp and pork, and repacked into the shell for baking. The overall effect is that of a pleasant briny pungency on a creamy-sweet base. Yellow fungi, resembling walnut kernels and having a slightly nutty flavor, go well with black mushrooms and Chinese greens. Steamed abalone and roast duckling, described on the menu as wrapped in sliced yam, turned out to have yam inside a thin layer of cucumber. Braised pigeon with hua tiao wine and Chinese broccoli is cooked and served in an earthenware pot; as with a great boeuf en daube or coq au vin, the slow cooking produces an orchestration of tastes and textures—black mushrooms, scallions, wine, bird and green vegetable—that haunts the palate afterward. Seafood and bean-curd soup is more like a duet for wind instruments: delicate shrimp, delicate bean curd and an undemonstrative, somewhat salty broth littered with egg drops. You'll be served a condiment of broad-bean paste that can add a lively note to dishes, but go easy—it may be overwhelming if not used in moderation. For dessert, try the thin, elastic dumplings stuffed with bean paste and rolled in sesame seeds, but skip the double-boiled papaya, a sickly concoction we suspect is valued more for medicinal than gustatory reasons. Two fish tanks and several pillars with gilt dragons curled around them are the extent of the decor. You'll see the waiters and waitresses carrying or wheeling dishes almost continuously into private rooms, yet somehow they also manage to serve the regular tables quickly and efficiently. Two of you can enjoy Cantonese food unlike any you're likely to get back home for about HK$400, including beer.
Open Mon.-Fri. 11 a.m.-3 p.m. & 6 p.m.-11:30 p.m., Sat. 6 p.m.-11:30 p.m., Sun. & holidays 10 a.m.-5 p.m. & 6 p.m.-11:30 p.m. All major cards.

Malaya
23A Granville Rd.,
Tsimshatsui
• 3-678550
MALAYSIAN

8/20

They don't make cafés like this any more. Luckily for budget-conscious locals and visitors seeking cheap, filling fare, several Malaya and New Malaya restaurants have survived from the '50s and '60s, when Chinese migrants from what is now Malaysia set up shop all over Hong Kong. This is one of the coziest, typically decorated with plastic-upholstered booths, slatted veneer wood, dim lighting and red-vested old waiters whose concept of fast food is plonking plates down quickly. Malaysian specials are listed first on the massive multiethnic menu, followed by Chinese and Western dishes. The priced photographs in the window illustrate the cooks' eclectic repertoire: chicken with rice (Hainan style), curried breast of beef with rice, sandwiches and pancakes (Fukien style), spring rolls (Singapore style) and, of course, satay. Cheap fixed-price meals include the four-course HK$45 "Special Malayan Dinner," whose curry soup (beef and vegetable), satay (four sticks with a watery sauce), sambal shrimp (four of them, with onion-rich curry sauce) and curry chicken and eggs with rice all taste similar, but pleasantly so. Soft bread rolls (always served warm) and coffee or tea complete these set bargains of food that is *not* Malaysian or even Straits Chinese. It's just filling grub. The economy-minded can also find the same fare and informality at the various cafés around town called Nam Wah or New Nam Wah. About HK$160 for two, with beer or wine.
Open daily 8 a.m.-1 a.m. No cards.

Margaux
Shangri-La
64 Mody Rd., Tsimshatsui East
• 3-7212111
FRENCH

The cuisine used to be nicely nouvelle in this 1981-vintage deluxe diner: duck breast flaunted Madagascar pepper and kiwi, and Margaux tried valiantly but in vain for the business that fully booked nearby Plume. Then in 1988, after East had met West at Plume and everywhere else, executive chef Mark Hellbach announced that Margaux was going to incorporate Eastern cooking influences. The duck breast (glazed Barbary) was calmed down with deep-fried eggplant and zucchini; saffron leaves and mangoes now garnished plates. To the relief of Margaux fans, however, nouvelle stylishness remains much more in evidence than Eastern elements, in both flavors and presentations. The chanterelle fricassée with millefeuille pastry shells has a delightful chive butter sauce. Partridge breast and a Savoy cabbage roulade are matched with a juniper-berry sauce, and sautéed, herbed and garlicked snails frolic on a parsley bed with tomato noodles.

Similarly rich (yet petitely portioned) are the medallions of roe deer in cranberry sauce. The flavor contrasts are dazzling, and all ingredients are first-rate, particularly the seafood, lamb and veal mignons. One of our rare disappointments here was otherwise excellent asparagus tips and fresh salmon, which was marred by slight oversalting. The sorbets (such as red-wine gratiné) sparkle, and the soufflés (if you'll pardon the pun) rise to the occasion. And the occasion is a grand one—full-length window niches, pastel tones, Wedgwood and Waterford, Viennese chandeliers, a private dining room. Unusual touches include personalized matchboxes, knowledgeable female sommeliers and a brilliant harpist. Service is superb: lids of dishes are lifted lovingly (though, for the teeny ones that cap pretentious silver butter stands, ludicrously). If only those lids could be laid over some diners' mobile phones, which are allowed to disturb the peace as well as the harpist. Margaux? Of course: 24 on the well-balanced wine list, from the Imperial-size 1983 at HK$22,000 to the 1980 at HK$1,350. We tasted its magic in the excellent house dessert, a Margaux-laced poached pear with sauce William and praline ice cream. About HK$800 for dinner for two, with wine—more if you indulge in the Margaux wines. Fixed-price meals are HK$98 for lunch, HK$248 for Sunday brunch and HK$348 for dinner.

Open Mon.-Sat. noon-3 p.m. & 7 p.m.-11:30 p.m., Sun. 11 a.m.-2:30 p.m. & 7 p.m.-11:30 p.m. All major cards.

Mistral
Holiday Inn Harbour View
70 Mody Rd., Tsimshatsui
East
• 3-7215161
CONTINENTAL

12/20

Though no odder than a bierstube in Los Angeles or a bodega in Canton, Ohio, this Mediterranean taverna in the sub-sub-basement of a Hong Kong Holiday Inn has an air of unreality about it, as if Kafka had taken to restaurant design. Cheery brown-and-white checked tablecloths, white stucco walls slashed by dark woodwork, wooden beams and brass chandeliers vie with hanging plants, a handsome tile floor, mirrored columns and hammered copper, a clutter of visual elements that is too self-conscious and bright to be authentic. But this setting is eminently suitable for a casual meal—which surprised us with its generally good flavors. Spanish fish soup, its tomato base aswirl with fresh, properly cooked squid, mussels and shrimp, still needed a bit of thyme or saffron to impart a regional character. Minestrone had thyme in abundance but lacked pasta and beans; it was more of an Italian-esque vegetable soup than a minestrone. A sprinkling of

Parmesan at the table helped boost it from acceptable to quite good. Homemade pasta includes lasagne verde, cannelloni with mushrooms and fettuccine in a cheese sauce. Though the latter's noodles and cheese sauce compared well with that of a stateside trattoria, ribbons of tasteless ham detracted from the overall effect. If you're in a seafood mood, the mussels mariniere may be a better bet than the salmon with pesto sauce, since the restaurant does better with hearty dishes than with those requiring finesse. Hence the admirably cooked osso buco: beautifully gelatinous and falling off the bone, it would have been wonderful were it not seasoned with soy sauce. Those homesick for cheese will find a goodly assortment of French and Italian to choose from. Coupe Sicilia, a pig-out treat involving glazed chestnuts, vanilla ice cream and whipped cream, is our favorite of the desserts, but the dessert trolley also provides a variety of pastries, notably fresh plums on a crumbly, slightly soggy tart base—but at HK$38 it's ridiculously overpriced. Bought from the takeout window in front, the same cakes and pies cost a mere HK$7. Picknickers can pick up baguettes of French bread for HK$6 and crusty whole grain bread for HK$8 to HK$15 at the same window. Two should be able to dine adequately with wine for HK$350 to HK$400.
Open daily 7:30 a.m.-3 p.m. & 7 p.m.-11:30 p.m. All major cards.

Nadaman
Shangri-La
64 Mody Rd., Tsimshatsui East
• 3-7213561
JAPANESE

11/20

For some reason we can't quite fathom—it may be a matter of culture—this first venture beyond Japanese shores of a century-and-a-half-old chain leaves us cold. Japanese visitors, however, especially expense-account businessmen in sharkskin suits, flock here for what Mr. Nadaman (Mansuke Nadaya) popularized in Osaka: Shijo-style cooking. It's supposed to be particularly delicate and subtle, but our Western tastes find it bland and unbalanced. And the prices are worthy of Tokyo, not Hong Kong—the fixed-price, per-person kaiseki dinners start at HK$260 for what the menu lists as "typical," including raw fish and steak; go up to HK$400 for a "refined" version; and top out at a whopping HK$500 for the no-holds-barred "deluxe" meal. Kobe beef sashimi, seven tangy, heavily marbled one-inch-square dabs of beef, served semifrozen, will set you back HK$150. The flavor of the tempura tsuki, batter-dipped fried sweet potato, lotus root, pepper, celery, shrimp, mushroom, fish and squid, crosses the line from delicate to elusive. Also bordering on the tasteless is the chawan mushi, a minibowl of Japanese egg custard studded with not fully rehydrated shiitake mushrooms, bits of chicken meat and a largish lump of chicken fat. Broiled Japanese mackerel, on the other hand, topped with a creamy-pungent soybean paste, made us wish there was more of it. The entrance mimics a section of a medieval Japanese castle, with roof tiles on top and a rock garden at the base. Inside, blond wood predominates on the ceilings, walls and cubicles, and a sushi bar in back looks like a Japanese wood-frame house with a gabled roof. Excellent green tea ends the meal on an upbeat note. With sake, this fairly lifeless dinner for two will cost a terrifying HK$800 to HK$1,000; prices are lower at lunch.

Open daily noon-3 p.m. & 6:30 p.m.-11 p.m. All major cards.

North Park

Tsimshatsui Centre, 66
Mody Rd., Tsimshatsui
East
• 3-697680
CANTONESE

Since 1979, North Park has been in the forefront of the new wave of Hong Kong's burgeoning world of upscale Cantonese restaurants. Where the average Hong Kong Cantonese eatery can be quite a down-home affair, the various North Parks are notable for their waterfalls, ornate ceilings, gala arches, rock gardens and burbling streams—they're anything but modest restaurants. They're also notable for their size: the branch in Tsimshatsui East holds an immodest 400 diners at any given time, not to mention the five banquet rooms decorated in a style that will overwhelm even the most jaded diners. For some, this is pure garishness incarnate; for others, it's fun Oriental kitsch; and no doubt there are also those who find the places quite pretty. We think they look like Cantonese miniature golf courses. Thankfully, the food served at the various North Parks is considerably less garish than the ambience. Despite the decor overkill, the menus are smaller than those found in many other Cantonese houses, and every dish seems to be well prepared and flavorful. The bird's-nest soup with crabmeat is fairly priced, perfectly done—and notable for being more a taste than a portion. If you've long wondered about goose web, the goose web casserole is more palatable than usual; the web, which we find rather fatty and a bit pointless, is just one element in a complex stew. At various times of the year, there are sundry wild game dishes as well: venison kebabs, turtle, civet cat, boar and so forth, all of which can be delicious, if the gaminess of the dishes doesn't scare you away. Some of the most elegant dim sum in town is

served during the day; expect to wait for a table at peak hours. Two other locations are found in Shatin, New Territories, and Causeway Bay, Hong Kong. Dinner for two, with wine, costs about HK$280.
Open daily 11 a.m.-midnight. Cards: AE, DC, MC, V.

Ocean City
New World Centre,
Salisbury Rd., Tsimshatsui
• 3-699688
CANTONESE/PEKINGESE

9/20

In a city where hyperbole is a way of life, for a change, this restaurant deals more in understatement than overstatement. Ocean City really is a city within a city; you can grow weary just walking through it. It's reputed to be the single largest culinary complex of any type in Asia, and though Guinness hasn't yet offered its imprimatur, we feel secure in suggesting that it's also probably the largest in the world. All told, Ocean City holds (give or take a few dozen) somewhere in the area of 8,000 revelers in its assortment of restaurants, massive nightclub (holding 1,500), various lounges, supper clubs, coffee shops and disco. The main restaurant is the Gallery Dining Room, with its impressive view of the harbor and its dim sum lunch. Actually, the view is a lot more impressive than the dim sum, which is far from the best we've had. In fact, many of the pieces either arrived cold or suffered from excess grease. With rare exceptions, as we've noticed in the past, the bigger the restaurant, the worse the food. And that maxim holds pretty true here. At best, the food we tasted in the Gallery was mediocre. It was a pleasant novelty to see what such a big restaurant looks like but not a pleasant experience to actually eat the food. The Ocean City Peking restaurant, which is blessedly smaller, offers a bit more in the way of good food, but there's still better Peking duck to be had in Hong Kong, notably at such reliable favorites as Spring Deer and King Heung. All told, big isn't better, it's just bigger. Dinner for two, with wine, costs about HK$360.
Open Mon.-Sat. 11 a.m.-11 p.m., Sun. 8 a.m.-11 p.m. (nightclub until 2 a.m.). All major cards.

Orchid Garden
37 Hankow Rd.,
Tsimshatsui
• 3-672126
CANTONESE

12/20

Luk Yu over in Central may be better known for dim sum, but old Hong Kong hands repeatedly say that the plain-as-a-brown-paper-bag Orchid Garden (which dates back to 1926) is the place to go for really fine dumplings and other tea snacks, and first-rate poultry and fish dishes at night, at some of the most reasonable prices in town. It's not for nothing that when *Newsweek*'s international edition did a feature called "Eating Asian Style" several years ago, the Hong Kong

restaurant it profiled was Orchid Garden. Unlike Luk Yu, where rudeness has become a high art form, Orchid Garden has servers who are actually friendly, often laughing good-naturedly at the befuddlement of their Western customers. The dim sum collection runs through all the basic dishes: shu mai, har gow, char siu bao and so forth, and delicious they all are, too. Wait long enough, and a cart carrying one of your favorites is sure to roll by. This is also a good place to try congee, the rice gruel that's sometimes called jook, which tastes much better than it sounds—it's hot breakfast cereal with a college education. Come the evening, the menu settles down to fried pigeon, lemon-sauce chicken, duck with stuffed minced shrimp and so forth. At prices like these, you can afford to order the whole menu at one fell swoop. Two other locations in Causeway Bay and Wanchai, Hong Kong. Dinner for two, with beer, costs about HK$150.
Open daily 8 a.m.-midnight. No cards.

Peking Garden
Star House, Star Ferry Pier, Tsimshatsui
• 3-698211
Empire Centre, Mody Rd., Tsimshatsui East
• 3-687879
PEKINGESE

See Hong Kong Island.

Plume
The Regent
Salisbury Rd., Tsimshatsui
• 3-7211211
FRENCH

Luxurious (yet not too stuffy) dining rooms provide a marvelous view of Hong Kong Island and the boats on the China Sea. Even better than that view is the walk-in wine cellar: behind its glass walls are thousands of bottles, some of them priceless treasures. In the past, Plume has been justifiably considered the best restaurant in town, and Gray Kunz, a disciple of Fredy Girardet, was truly an exceptional chef. But with Kunz gone, Plume is a bit of an orphan, and it's difficult to come to a judgment on the temporary Chinese chef, except to say that he has talent. But will he last? Indeed, as we go to press, he is the second Chinese man to have been placed in charge of the kitchen; it seems that Plume's management isn't quite sure what they'll do with the kitchen next. Despite one slightly disappointing recent meal (lobster and lamb of mediocre quality), Plume remains capable of serving grand dishes, such as the velouté of peas gourmands with truffles, and superb and imaginative creations, such as the passion-fruit soufflé served in a shell. The cheeses are superb, the service is as impeccable as ever, and, as we said, the wines are exceptional. Under Kunz, we would have awarded Plume an 18/20; for now, we're lowering it to 16/20. But since we've had so many wonderful meals here over the years, we are optimistic that by the time you visit, the kitchen will once again be on a steady and superb course. Strict dress code and a daunting tab: HK$1,200 and up for dinner for two, with wine.

Open nightly 7 p.m.-11:30 p.m. All major cards.

Prince Court Szechuan

115-6 Sutton Ct.,
Harbour City, Canton Rd.,
Tsimshatsui
• 3-663100
SZECHUAN

Getting there can be half the fun for those who make a late start. Harbour City can be a Daedalian maze through which increasingly famished souls wander in despair, and only the glibbest will prevail on Prince Court Szechuan to admit them if the hour is near 2:30 p.m. (at lunch) or 11:30 p.m. (at dinner). Happily, the effort is well worth making. Two satellite rooms for overflow crowds and/or private parties abut the main dining room, a handsome if somewhat severe place with dark gray walls, lacquer woodwork, pastel linens and the ubiquitous mirrors by which so many Hong Kong restaurants create an illusion of spaciousness. A cup of braised shark's fin offers the curious a relatively inexpensive chance to try that delicate specialty, and honey-braised eel, dark, tightly stacked chunks served on lustrous china, will convert even the squeamish to the joys of eel—its faintly floral sweetness overlays a crispy texture that's not unlike that of popcorn. Pungent, herbaceous whelk is spooned out of the shell it's baked in. Traditional garlic-and-chili-sauced eggplant can be overcooked, but only the most churlish could fault the magnificently aromatic and meaty tea-smoked duck. Beer or full-flavored jasmine tea accompany this food admirably, though die-hard oenophiles can choose from a respectable wine list. Two may dig into a varied and generous meal complete with wine or beer for about HK$350.

Open daily 11 a.m.-3 p.m. & 5:30 p.m.-midnight. All major cards.

Regal Seafood

**Regal Meridien Hotel
71 Mody Rd., Tsimshatsui
East
• 3-7238881**
CANTONESE

One of the better hotel Cantonese seafood houses, Regal Seafood is still new and growing, and it's just a step or two away from being on the same level as Spring Moon. In fact, Regal is probably already better than the Chinese Restaurant at the Hyatt. Regal's menu is unique, if for no other reason than it's trilingual: Chinese, English and Japanese. The look of the place is also unlike any other Chinese restaurant in town. In fact, there's some question whether Regal is a proper restaurant at all, or if it's really just a hotel lounge that happens to serve Chinese food; one is tempted to cozy up here with a Pimm's Cup for the evening. Though the name of the restaurant implies that it's seafood-intensive, fish and shellfish actually comprise a smaller part of the menu than one might expect. There are many fine shrimp and whelk dishes, but there's also lots of other dishes to choose from, including crisp roast Lhung Kong chicken, an exceptional sizzling chicken with black-bean sauce; a superb lemon chicken, perhaps the best we've ever tasted, a far cry from those dishes that taste like lemon meringue pie made with chicken instead of meringue; and quite a bit of game, if you get an uncontrollable craving for owl, ringdove, cray crane, bear paw or snake. Dinner for two, with wine, costs about HK$500.
Open daily 11 a.m.-midnight. All major cards.

Le Restaurant de France

**Regal Meridien Hotel
71 Mody Rd., Tsimshatsui
East
• 3-7221818**
FRENCH

For our money, this is the best Western cuisine the colony has to offer, the only place *consistently* in the same league as France's best. The young French chef, Jean-Yves Gueho, doesn't have at his disposal cooking equipment as sophisticated as that of his colleagues at Gaddi's and Pierrot. But this man from Brittany, who trained with Haeberlin, puts them to shame with his talent. His food is served in a remarkable fin-de-siècle setting—the dining room reminds us of a first-class restaurant on a great ship, say the *QEII*, or the fabled *Normandie*. Plate-glass windows afford the obligatory harbor view; velveteen wall benches and bentwood chairs in mauve fabric provide comfortable seating, tables are widely spaced, and flowers grace every table as a matter of course. Start, if you like, with the frogs'-leg salad dressed with balsamic vinegar, then continue with an exquisite ramekin of lobster with coriander. Gueho, who orders the fish from his native Brittany, will then serve you a superb grilled back of bass with Chinese chives. And if he offers the best seafood in Hong Kong, he is also gifted when it comes to meats and poultry: his pan-fried goose liver with candied vegetables is superb, and his squab cutlet with foie gras and truffles is a true masterpiece. He doesn't need much more to be a truly great cook—perhaps just a bit more inventiveness and audacity. His fresh, light desserts taste as if they were made by angels (warm rhubarb strudel with honey ice cream, a chocolate fantasy of mousse, cake and ice cream with chicory-laced coffee sauce, classic crêpes Suzette), and the service is unimpeachable. But why is it that Le Restaurant de France doesn't enjoy the same reputation or popularity as its prestigious competitors? Perhaps because its more relaxed atmosphere and its affordable prices don't attract the more clubby Hong Kong clientele: two can dine here with wine for less than HK$900, perhaps a bit more if they indulge in a noteworthy wine. As for the lunchtime fixed-price menus (HK$92 and HK$119 per person, excluding wine), they are probably the best deals on the planet. The wine list is engaging, but it needs to be expanded if it's to be a proper match for the cuisine. On the other hand, the liqueur and brandy cart shows depth and rarity, and humidor-fresh cigars are clipped and perfectly lighted for those who like to indulge at the end of a superlative meal.

Open Mon.-Fri. noon-3 p.m. & 7 p.m.-11 p.m., Sat.-Sun. 7 p.m.-11 p.m. All major cards.

Sagano
Hotel Nikko
72 Mody Rd., Tsimshatsui East
• 3-7391111
JAPANESE

Sagano, in the Japanese tradition, combines a spare, sober, blond-wood decor with a great variety of fixed-price menus offering good-quality dishes. The Shokado Traditional lunch menu brings you crispy jellyfish, clear soup with duck dumplings, seafood-taro stew, rice with shiso and a combination of delicacies; and the even more elaborate Zen lunch menu comprises mushrooms, clear soup, sashimi, chicken-taro stew, fried seafood with tofu, glazed scallops, steamed rice, miso and a pickle. Or try the Oai Monji Yake Sen: bamboo shoots, diced bean curd in clear soup, sashimi, beef plate, prawns, vegetables, salad and rice. These complete meals range from HK$80 up to HK$170 for the royal feast—a tremendous bargain. To make the place even more agreeable, Sagano provides quick service and a beautiful view of the harbor. For an à la carte dinner,

two of you should expect to pay about
wine.
Open daily 7 a.m.-10 a.m., noon-3 p.m
10:30 p.m. All major cards.

San Francisco Steak House

101 Barton Ct., Harbour
City, 9 Canton Rd.,
Tsimshatsui
• 3-7227576
STEAKHOUSE/AMERICAN

10/20

Gone are the days when a steakhouse was simple surf
'n' turf territory. Owner Joseph Velardi, who has run
this popular place since 1967, has expanded his market-
ing concepts and menu (the introductory essay on
"things done differently" here is a high-tech primer on
his purchasing and dietary policies—pasta recipes are
Sicilian, onions are "jumbos," coffee machines are special imports and so on). You also learn about the fat-free
trim of his "New York" beef, which may reassure diners
eyeing the rectangular slab for the first time. But the
twelve-ounce American Angus New York strip that we
tried (weighing the same as its specially bred companion
potato) looked like it might have been charcoal-broiled
processed beef substitute. It tasted that way, too: ordered medium rare, it revealed a juicy, rectangular-
shape pinkish middle surrounded by dry brown fibers.
The baked potato was okay, dressed with sweetly
smooth sour cream and stringy bacon bits. The calamari
were akin to crisply coated rubber bands, served with a
ketchup-like cocktail sauce; a better bet are the tasty,
freshly ground, half-pound "gourmet burgers"
(HK$37 to HK$43), found listed on the deli section of
the menu, which also includes monster sandwiches,
bagels and lox and the like, and which is offered until
5:30 p.m. The restaurant itself is a comfortably spacious
American/Victorian/Barbary Coast sort of place,
sporting wheeled chairs, painted-glass panels, red-flock
wallpaper, tanks displaying live Tasmanian lobsters,
oyster and clams and cases displaying the ballyhooed
beef. In true American fashion, the meats are aug-
mented by a well-stocked salad bar and a wine list strong
on Californians—*and* a TV lounge where American
football and basketball videos play (and framed
photographs show Frank Sinatra and Spiro Agnew
enjoying the owner's hospitality). The staff is attentive.
A steak dinner for two will run about HK$400, with
wine. Fixed-price lunch menus are HK$59 and
HK$77.
*Open daily noon-3 p.m. & 5:30 p.m.-midnight. All
major cards.*

...wadee Thai Restaurant

1 Hillwood Rd.,
Tsimshatsui
• 3-7225577
THAI

In Hong Kong, don't expect to find the spate of Thai eateries familiar coast-to-coast in the States. When locals want hot stuff, they think Szechuan; visitors naturally gravitate toward Hong Kong's culinary strong suit, Cantonese, or find the nearest thing to home, i.e., McDonald's. But Thai eateries do exist here, and of Hong Kong's collection of a half dozen or so, Sawadee may be the best and most authentic. Don't pass up the shrimp and lemon-grass soup, whose chili oil and cilantro compete for attention—it's chockablock with good shellfish and succulent straw mushrooms. Also excellent are the pungent chicken in coconut and the basil-perfumed red curry with crunchy Thai eggplant and a choice of meat. A variation of pad Thai—those beloved broad noodles—are woven with bits of omelet, chicken meat and strips of chicken gizzard. Though owing at least as much allegiance to Chinese as Thai cuisine, it's a satisfying dish. Tod mun pla, rubbery fish cakes, aren't bad, but the squid or green papaya salad are sprightlier openers. Sawadee, which means "hello," is a tunnel-like L-shape room whose Buddhas, geese and inlaid mirrors occupy scruffy alcoves set against scruffy walls. Gray and mauve upholstery, hanging lamps and areas of exposed brick make the overall effect pleasant, despite, on our last visit at least, the need for a vigorous dusting. Two strong appetites can sate themselves with good food and beer for a mere HK$200.
Open daily noon-3 p.m. & 6 p.m.-11 p.m. Cards: AE, V.

Shang Palace

Shangri-La Hotel
64 Mody Rd., Tsimshatsui
East
• 3-7212111
CANTONESE

Opulence is the operative term for this serious Chinese restaurant. Classical bird-and-flower ink paintings hang on Chinese red-lacquer walls. Gold damask upholstery, deep-pile carpeting and stylized calligraphic ideograms, again in red lacquer, also help create Shang Palace's unbroken sense of luxury. Service matches the decor: efficient yet courteous, whether you order double-boiled supreme bird's nest in coconut at HK$400 or barbecued pork loin at HK$43. And given the surroundings and the quality of the food, prices are remarkably reasonable. Even 'the chef's recommendations, which change month to month, include such bargains as barbecued duckling cooked in a casserole (HK$45) and braised squash filled with mixed seafood (HK$85). Huge portions, top-notch ingredients and seasoning that manages to be robust without becoming vulgar characterize the cooking. Dishes to try include the barbecued combination, a platter of juicy suckling pig, tough but succulent duck and tender, smoky-rich

chicken, all of which is bedded down on shredded jellyfish and embellished by an intense plum-and-ginger sauce. Firm, mild pan-fried garoupa, not unlike just-caught wall-eyed pike, is matched with oyster sauce and the contrasting texture and flavor of Chinese greens. Shrimp-stuffed bean curd also deserves kudos, as does mango pudding for dessert, a mousse-like custard that really tastes like fresh mango. As you leave, walking between a double row of massive pillars, the mirrored panel on the far wall reflects your image as you approach, like a doppelgänger, an appropriately exotic end to an enchanting meal. Dinner for two, with wine, should run about HK$400.
Open daily noon-11 p.m. All major cards.

Spring Deer
42 Mody Rd., Tsimshatsui
• 3-664012
PEKINGESE

12/20

After the floating restaurants of Aberdeen, this bustling, crowded, somewhat chaotic second-floor room in the midst of Tsimshatsui is probably the single most popular restaurant in town with out-of-town visitors. Which is not a point that should be held against Spring Deer, for despite the hordes of Americans, British and Japanese who flow through it daily, the food is actually quite good—this is a cuisine that only rarely concedes to Western tastes. Keep in mind that heading for Spring Deer without a dinner reservation is an act of self-torture—you may get in, but the wait will be nigh-on interminable. The specialty of the house—featured, in fact, on the postcards available at the cash register—is Peking duck, a dish that can be ordered with no advance notice, since the restaurant goes through hundreds of the birds every week. It's a classic duck, prepared as a single course (rather than the multicourse extravaganza found at other restaurants) and sometimes carved with a bit less care than we'd like, but it's usually full of flavor. As befits northern-style Chinese cooking, a fair amount of spice is found in many of the dishes: the prawns in chili sauce will do a good job of clearing your sinuses. If you have time to plan, order the beggar's chicken (which needs a day's advance notice); also consider the deep-fried mutton, a dish so savory it makes a usually questionable meat like mutton more than palatable. Also note that most dishes are available in three sizes—small, medium and large—which allows smaller groups to order more dishes. It's an excellent idea that more restaurants should consider adopting. Dinner for two, with beer, costs about HK$240.
Open daily noon-11 p.m. Cards: V.

Spring Moon

The Peninsula
Salisbury Rd., Tsimshatsui
• 3-666251
CANTONESE

As befits the premier Chinese restaurant in the exceedingly elegant, solidly old-money Peninsula hotel (where no matter how well dressed we are, we still feel underdressed), Spring Moon is a room of both commanding power and great delicacy, a dazzling meeting of yin and yang. The long large room, located deep within the folds of The Peninsula, is decorated with venerable vases, framed hunks of finely polished marble and one of the most beautiful carpets we've ever seen in a restaurant, a gala affair of flowers brightly woven onto a subtle gray background. As you'd expect, chopsticks are ivory (they tend, we've noticed, to be a bit slippery—elegance is rarely utilitarian). Like the hotel itself, Spring Moon's kitchen is deeply rooted in tradition; you won't find anything resembling nouvelle chinoise cooking here. Instead, this is one of the best venues in town to sample the great dishes of Cantonese cooking: exceptionally delicious (and exceptionally expensive) bird's-nest soup, available in a number of permutations that may seem a bit confusing to Westerners (how do you choose between braised superior bird's nest with crab cream and Kar Luen Lau superior bird's nest?). The abalone dishes, of which there are many, are reputed to be the best in the Crown Colony, a point we're not about to argue. For those who consider pigeon a meatless waste of time, the Shek Ki pigeons served here will put that belief to rest. And for a wonderful variation on a theme, try the Kar Luen Lau ("spring moon") chicken, which is a near cousin of Peking duck, only a good deal less fatty. Dinner for two, with wine, costs in the realm of HK$1,000—an extravagance, but one you won't regret.
Open daily 10:30 a.m.-10:30 p.m. All major cards.

The Steak House

The Regent
Salisbury Rd., Tsimshatsui
• 3-7211211
STEAKHOUSE/AMERICAN

Hidden on the lower floor of The Regent, The Steak House is Euroamerican in looks but Chinese in feel. All polished woods and glass, the large dining room has a spectacular view of the harbor (that view is just one of The Regent's aces in the hole), yet it manages to maintain a cozy feeling; at the tables is a veritable who's who of the rag trade. On the tables are fat, chewy rye breadsticks, and when one of our party ordered a Diet Coke, the waiter presented the can—nestled in a tiny silver ice bucket. We couldn't decide whether it was the classiest or the silliest thing we'd ever seen; in any event, it was the quintessence of upscale Hong Kong. The Steak House has a beautifully manicured salad bar (someone is constantly tending to it, wiping away any

stray drops of salad dressing and picking up any errant lettuce leaf that has dared wander too far afield) that can only be called discreet and tasteful, opting for restraint rather than Texas-size bowls of greens and other ingredients. There are at least five types of lettuce (including lamb's lettuce), radicchio and endive, along with the usual gang of salad-bar suspects, among them some of the best avocado we've tasted in years. This is no serve-yourself, all-you-can-eat pigathon—a white-jacketed gentleman mans the bar, genteelly doling out your selections with silver tongs. Main courses run to your basic grill fare: prime rib, filets, ten- and twelve-ounce sirloins, rib eyes, T-bones, lamb chops, squab and a toothsome veal steak. The noncarnivorous will find some critters from the sea: garoupa, salmon and excellent lobster-size prawns (lobsters are available as well, at market price). Each dinner comes with the salad bar, a baked potato, onion rings and herbed cherry tomatoes. And with the exception of the disappointing microwaved-tasting potato, the food is uniformly excellent. While the pastries are very pretty, they're nothing to fall in a fit over; opt instead for the fine selection of cheeses—Roquefort, Gouda, Brie, a variety of chèvres and Camembert—and fresh fruit. Last time we were in Hong Kong, we went to The Steak House on our last evening there—it is, after all, a comforting Western oasis for when you just can't look another bowl of rice in the face. And steakhouses back in the United States would do well to take a few lessons in service from The Steak House. Dinner for two, with drinks, should run about HK$975.
Open daily noon-2:30 p.m. & 6 p.m.-11:30 p.m. All major cards.

Studio 123
25-31 Carnarvon Rd.,
Tsimshatsui
• 3-7230303
AMERICAN/CANTONESE

5/20

Don't be fooled by the hip name and exterior—Studio 123 is a truly dismal restaurant. The good news is that it's open 24 hours a day; the bad news is that the food and atmosphere aren't even welcome at 3 a.m., when choices are slim indeed. We visited one morning at 8 a.m. for breakfast and encountered young waiters (we hope they were finishing off the night shift and not starting a new one) who were surly and in soiled clothes—their shirts and slacks were stained with food, which as we soon found out was probably the best place for it. The only other denizens at that hour were a couple of tables of adolescents (who appeared to be even surlier than the help) enjoying a healthy, stimulating morning meal of beer and scotch. The menu is split between American and Chinese coffee-shop fare, and in the true spirit of diplomacy, both cuisines are equally awful. There were steak and eggs, pancakes, French toast and omelets on the menu, but some sixth sense told one of our group to stick to toast—which arrived cold as a stone, and with about the same texture. Another in our group bravely opted for a Chinese breakfast of salted-meat-and-preserved-egg congee, pan-fried noodles and Oriental pasta, which was about as terrible as food can get and still be classified as such. Studio 123 can only be recommended to insomniacs or homesick expatriates desperate for a hit of Americana (the restaurant is decorated with American movie posters). The reproduction of the poster for *Jaws 3-D* on the place mats should be warning enough. Breakfast for two should run about HK$80, lunch a bit more. *Open daily 24 hours. All major cards.*

Sui Sha Ya
Hecny Tower, 9 Chatham Rd. South, Tsimshatsui
• 3-7225001
JAPANESE

See Hong Kong Island.

Sun Tung Lok Shark's Fin Restaurant
Phase 3, Harbour City, 25-27 Canton Rd., Tsimshatsui East
• 3-7220288
CANTONESE

Occupying a big chunk of pricey real estate with a glitter-and-glitz that has been frequently mistaken for elegance, Sun Tung Lok provides the expense-account set with suitably exorbitant and outlandish foodstuffs. Cravings for cockerel testicles, which are said to restore male vigor (though not in just one serving) or such seasonal, quasi-medicinal specialties as double-boiled civet-cat brains, the head and trotters of a munt-jac deer or snake broth with chrysanthemum petals can be satisfied here. Gigantic chandeliers, ten of them, each with hundreds of glass leaves dangling from massive brass rods, dominate the interior, but there's more. A wall of mirrored panels easily twenty-five feet high presents seemingly endless reflections of the chandeliers. Impressionistic seascapes in etched glass separate the two dining levels, and a checkerboard pattern of gold and earth-tone squares covers one long sweep of wall. The fringes of the room, however, also reveal worn spots in the carpet, dingy wallpaper and, toward the end of the day, pails of dirty water waiting to be disposed of. Shark's-fin dishes begin at HK$90, for which you get long, fibrous strands of meat in an acidic and pungent base, and go to HK$900, which buys you a whole fin of "superlative" quality, double boiled with chicken. More accessible to the taste and reasonable to the pocketbook are sautéed fatty pork with walnuts, savory sea cucumber braised with tangy blobs of shrimp roe, a soup of shredded chicken and fish maw, deep-fried crab claws seasoned with shrimp paste, and fresh mushrooms steamed with dried scallops. Stick to simple desserts—pass on the HK$150 boiled bird's nest with coconut in favor of the sago with honeydew melon (HK$20) or red beans with lotus seeds (HK$15). The fixed-price lunch menus are convenient, but they tend to cater to Western tastes. We suggest chancing the extensive à la carte menu but paying close attention to prices, which can add up with shocking rapidity. An interesting dinner for two, with beer or wine, needn't exceed HK$375 but can quite easily pass HK$1,200.

Open daily 11 a.m.-midnight. All major cards.

Sybilla
Franki Centre E26, 320 Junction Rd. (Kam Shing Rd.), Kowloon Tong • 3-366883
ITALIAN

8/20

Located in one of Kowloon's smaller (relatively speaking) shopping centers, in a part of town populated with more than a few no-tell motels, Sybilla is quite the posh place, and it's also the only Western eatery in the Franki Centre. Its black lacquered chairs, Roman columns and urns, golden lighting and sprays of baby orchids on each table give it an odd Sino-Italian look that somehow works. Sybilla is a major hangout for the media folk who slog away on nearby Broadcast Street, and while the food doesn't quite live up to the look, it is serviceable. The most popular dish is a godawful-sounding concoction, seafood rice in pineapple, which we recommend avoiding. Stick to the simple pastas and the salads and avoid the trickier dishes. Also worth ordering is the "Quick Lunch," which is simply a pasta and a cup of tea or coffee for less than HK$30—not a bad deal. Upstairs a coffee bar features three TV screens, though there's an unfortunate tendency to show the same few

music videos over and over and over again. Dinner for two, with drinks, should run about HK$300.
Open daily 11:30 a.m.-3 p.m. & 6 p.m.-midnight. All major cards.

Tai Pan
Omni Hongkong Hotel
Canton Rd., Tsimshatsui
• 3-7360088
CONTINENTAL/FRENCH

Born in the age when hotels, like cruise ships docked at the adjacent Ocean Terminal, had very distinct classes of dining, Tai Pan used to be an upper-deck "grill" complete with wandering minstrels. Now, a palm tree scrapes the ceiling of this flower-decked, L-shape harborside restaurant, whose 1969-vintage rotisserie is blatantly camouflaged by a half-moon black wall. A well-trained service staff and a dinnertime pianist now provide classy, low-decibel accompaniments for meals of grandly modest ambitions. Both gourmands and gourmets love the menu dégustation, whose samplings are virtually full-size. Salt-fresh French sea scallops are laid smartly in an orange sauce on a colorful collage of seasonal greens. Veils of eggplant wrap poached eggs in a tomato mousseline dusted with beluga caviar. The seafood is quite fine, cooked to the moment of firmly fibered perfection: notably the steamed John Dory filet flattered by a sprightly fennel and tomato butter sauce and the fresh, delicately roasted Atlantic skate. By comparison, the meat dishes we've tried were more pleasant than memorable. Tableside parades of clams, oysters, caviar and pâtés are tempting, but ask for prices before choosing: our fresh clam chowder, containing just one big beauty of a clam, cost HK$100 for barely two servings. Caesar salad is admired by those who like it oil-rich. Sherbets are okay, but desserts can vary: the terrine of white cheese with mangoes and a ginger sauce was scintillating, but the coconut ravioli turned out to be sextet of frigid brown things. Pass, too, on the complimentary starter, if it is the cold, coagulated goat-cheese omelet that we were offered. The wine list is comprehensive. About HK$900 for dinner for two, with wine. Fixed-price menus are HK$130 at lunch and HK$380 at dinner.
Open daily noon-3 p.m. & 7 p.m.-midnight. All major cards.

Tin Tin Hot Pot
16 Carnarvon Rd.,
Tsimshatsui
• 3-662332
TAIWANESE

In a city of lively, rollicking restaurants, Tin Tin Hot Pot is one of the more boisterous. The energy level is off the meter: bustling waiters, laughing, animated patrons and, as you'll see, animated food. The two dining rooms are found on the second and third floors of a building whose entrance beckons you with tanks of live—very live—seafood. The interior is clean, modern and quite Western-hip: marble and granite floors, pink and gray tile, glass bricks. As the name implies, a recessed burner sits in the middle of each table, into which your waiter sets a yin-and-yang bifurcated pot containing both beef and fish stocks, which are then brought to a rolling boil. You then select various items from the menu—beef, chicken, seafood and vegetables—and plunge them into the roiling liquid. We were a bit taken aback when one of our party realized that her plate of raw, skewered shrimp were wriggling around: they were disturbingly alive (in fact, one nearly leaped off the plate to freedom). If you're at all squeamish or have qualms about boiling creatures that are still breathing, pass on the shrimp. But we must tell you—these were some of the sweetest, most succulent crustaceans we have ever eaten. Tin Tin also provides a full complement of condiments on the table, such as chili and sesame oils, pickled ginger and scallion sauces, and the waiters are alert and full of quips. Two people can eat very well here for HK$150, including drinks.
Open daily 11:30 a.m.-midnight. All major cards.

Toh Lee
Hotel Nikko
72 Mody Rd., Tsimshatsui
East
• 3-73991111CANTONESE

You'll search long and hard for a Cantonese restaurant with a better view than Toh Lee's. Unfortunately, all that glass also allows a huge neon camera sign to seemingly loom over many of the tables; if possible, reserve a table that will keep your back to the sign. Otherwise, Toh Lee is comfortable and attractive, with high ceilings and an authentic Chinese interior design. As for the food, it is highly refined and eminently memorable. In fact, we had the best shark's-fin soup (the braised shark's fin with shredded chicken) we have ever had here. Other outstanding dishes include the steamed garoupa, crispy chicken, deep-fried crab rolls and sautéed scallops with fresh vegetables. The waiters are exceptionally discreet and attentive, and your fellow diners will be primarily Chinese. If you plan to visit at lunch, don't forget to make reservations. Dinner for two, with wine, will cost about HK$600.

Open daily noon-midnight. All major cards.

Tsui Hang Village
Miramar Hotel
132-134 Nathan Rd.,
Tsimshatsui
• 3-68111
CANTONESE

The guard downstairs will say, "Press 14: penthouse," and up you'll go through a transparent vertical tube looking out over the harbor. The view isn't much, the plastic being cracked and dusty, and when you emerge, this hotel restaurant looks like too many other hotel restaurants: blond-wood chairs looking dingy under a phalanx of overly bright chandeliers. But the food is another matter—this is classic Cantonese done with panache. If the market price isn't daunting, order a whole spiny lobster and cook it yourself, bite by bite, in savory broth at the table, or try the double-boiled shark's-fin soup. Less well-endowed wallets might explore the surprisingly mild shredded duck in fish-maw stock, the whole roasted pigeon, its skin just shy of crisp, its meat dark and aromatic, or the ocean scallops deep fried in a coating of creamy taro purée. For dessert, order the water- chestnut rolls, which are actually six rectangular fritters. The batter is frozen, sliced and deep-fried, so the crisp surface puffs around a slab of sweet jelly. Dinner for two, with beer, should cost about HK$300.

Open Mon.-Sat. 11:30 a.m.-midnight, Sun. 10 a.m.-midnight. All major cards.

Unicorn Szechuan
39A Broadway, Stage II,
Podium Fl., Mei Foo Sun
Chuen
• 3-7435888
SZECHUAN

12/20

"Are you sure that's where you want to go?" asked our driver when we climbed into his taxi near the Star Ferry Pier in Tsimshatsui. "Of course," we said, and off we went. For more than a half hour we traveled north, heading well off Hong Kong's well-trod culinary path until we were finally deposited in the midst of a market somewhere in northern Kowloon. When we asked the driver where Unicorn Szechuan was, he gestured vaguely and sped off. And for good reason—he clearly had no idea. Neither did anyone else, it turned out. But after another half hour of wandering around, we found it on the second floor of a plaza in the midst of what's supposed to be the largest private housing development in Asia. It's quite a trek getting to this Szechuan branch of the popular Cantonese Unicorn restaurant chain (with branches in Tsimshatsui, Causeway Bay and Food Street), but it's worth it for the adventure, even though better Szechuan food can be found at such popular venues as Cleveland, Pep 'n' Chilli and Red Pepper. They find Western visitors quite a novelty at Unicorn Szechuan, and they fed us marvelously spicy orders of duck's tongue in peppercorns, freshwater shrimp in hot chili sauce, dry-fried shredded beef with red peppers and eggplant in hot garlic sauce. We wouldn't go out of our way to eat here again, but if you're heading for nearby Sung Dynasty Village, you can't go wrong. Dinner for two, with wine, costs about HK$200. *Open daily 11:30 a.m.-midnight. Cards: AE, MC, V.*

Unkai
Sheraton Hong Kong Hotel and Towers 20 Nathan Rd., Tsimshatsui
• 3-691111
JAPANESE

12/20

A cross between a Japanese tearoom and a Western luncheonette, Unkai would be a useful lunch or dinner venue were its prices not so absurd. Stewed Japanese small potatoes of no great distinction cost HK$55, fixed-price kaiseki dinners range from HK$280 to HK$500, broiled fish begins at HK$60 (for Spanish mackerel), green-tea sherbet commands HK$30, and Japanese musk melon HK$100. A best buy at HK$150, the Fuji dinner includes lightly vinegared mushrooms, leeks, chicken and bean sprouts; stewed vegetables surrounding a chunk of fatty beef; miso soup; fair tempura; and rice. The sushi nigiri platter offers tough boiled shrimp, superlative scallops, fine flounder and salmon, overly salty salmon roe and good tuna wrapped in nori, sheets of crackly black seaweed. Smoky brown tea in pretty blue barrel-shape tumblers accompanies the meal, which ends with whisked green tea that lacks some of the intense, satisfying bitterness aficionados demand. Service in the celadon-gray and blond-wood room suffers when more than half the tables are filled. Private parties may request one of the tatami rooms in back past the sushi bar. Excellent sake or beer are the drinks of choice, despite an extensive wine list. Dinner

for two, with sake, will run upward of HK$700.
Open daily noon-2:30 p.m. & 6:30 p.m.-10:30 p.m. All major cards.

Valentino Ristorante
60 Cameron Rd.,
Tsimshatsui East
• 3-7216449
ITALIAN

10/20

Valentino is the sister (actually, brother is more appropriate) restaurant to Leonardo, albeit a more sophisticated sibling. Where Leonardo is country-style and family-oriented, Valentino is polished and intimate, though just as warm and cozy. The menu covers more territory as well, but, as at Leonardo, one is best advised to keep it simple. Pass on the snails in butter sauce (the menu here is more Continental than strictly Italian)— they're rather flavorless. The crabmeat-mushroom bisque and creamy clam soup are both fine, but the vegetable frittata makes a tastier starter. Be warned that the entrées lean toward the heavy side: rich, cream-clogged pastas, a rather awful filet baked with Gorgonzola cheese, pallid pizzas. But Valentino does well by its more simply prepared seafood dishes, notably the baked king prawns and scallops provençale and the zuppa de pesce. Try to ignore the fact that most main dishes are served with boiled potatoes and a vegetable, whether appropriate or not. But will somebody please explain why a most American baked Alaska is on the dessert menu? Dinner for two, with drinks, should run about HK$500.
Open daily noon-midnight. All major cards.

Wan Loong Court
Kowloon Hotel
19-21 Nathan Rd.,
Tsimshatsui
• 3-7392268
CANTONESE

Nestling in the marbled depths of a hotel shopping arcade, decorated with green and brown tones, a waterwheel, aquarium-flanked side booths and dragons etched on glass and mirror, Wan Loong is clearly a well-groomed member of The Peninsula hotel group's new stable of upscale restaurants (The Peninsula also owns the Kowloon Hotel). There are the inevitable abalone, shark's-fin and bird's-nest delicacies, all of top-grade pedigree and price. At HK$95, sliced whelk and scallops is a humbler good bet: a sweetly tender quartet of each shellfish served with a meal-size garnish of broccoli. Seafood is a specialty; steamed fish, squid baked with spiced salt and sea cucumber are all above average. So are the vegetables, particularly the platter of sautéed seasonal greens, which usually warrants its premium price. Westerners' favorites from the selection of competent fowl dishes include fried minced pigeon with lettuce puffs and lemon-sauced fried soft chicken. Less acceptable are some of the nouvelle-chinoise creations, such as the misconceived hybrid teppanyaki-cum-rissole concoction of fried sirloin rolls stuffed with onion, Chinese mushrooms and enoki (pin-headed, long-stemmed Japanese mushrooms)—the rolled beef slices were gristly and chewy. But the lunchtime dim sum selections are tasty, on a par with those served in The Peninsula's Spring Moon flagship (whose French-style, one-dish-at-a-time service is not aped here). The wine and cocktail lists are select and reasonably priced. An à la carte dinner for two will run HK$300 to HK$500; fixed-price menus are HK$165 to HK$230. *Open daily 11 a.m.-3 p.m. & 6 p.m.-midnight. All major cards.*

West Villa
South Villa, 58 Cameron Rd., Tsimshatsui
• 3-7215431
CANTONESE

See Hong Kong Island.

Woodlands
8 Minden Ave., Tsimshatsui
• 3-693718
INDIAN/VEGETARIAN

11/20

All things considered (if such a thing is possible), we much prefer Indian vegetarian cooking to Chinese vegetarian cooking. While very few mainstream Chinese dishes are built solely around vegetables, many of India's most basic dishes are vegetarian—so the food makes more sense from a vegetarian point of view. At Woodlands, a whimsical little restaurant on a cluttered Kowloon back street, Indian vegetarian cooking can be best sampled by ordering any of the prearranged thalis (the Hindi word for a large, round metal platter on which smaller bowls are placed). Both the Madras thali and the Punjab thali feature at least seven dishes: in the first case, sambar (a rich vegetable soup), rasam (an intensely hot tamarind-flavored soup), dal (a split-pea dip), a fried potato, yogurt, a quartet of purées, rice, a fried pappadum and a vegetable stew of the day; in the latter case, channa masala (spiced chickpeas), two vegetable curries (kurma and aloo mutter), bhaigan burtha (mashed eggplant), raita (yogurt and cucumber dip), dal, bread, rice and so forth. There's much, much more to choose from on the à la carte menu, at prices that make the food only a little more expensive than if it were free. Dinner for two, with saffron-flavored hot milk, costs about HK$80. *Open daily 11:30 a.m.-3:30 p.m. & 6 p.m.-11 p.m. Cards: MC, V.*

Wu Kong Shanghai Restaurant

27 Nathan Rd.,
Tsimshatsui
• 3-667244
SHANGHAINESE

10/20

One of the few Shanghai restaurants around, Wu Kong is a place to eat, not dine—a cavernous basement establishment whose bright lights glare relentlessly on dingy beige walls trimmed with green woodwork and a brownish-green carpet set off by pink-topped tables dotted with green napkins. Tables, mostly packed with lively, chattering families of eight, ten and even twelve, are close together, making entering and exiting awkward, and conversation all but impossible. As is typical of Shanghainese cuisine, the food here is oily and salty: a heavy, unrelieved dark-brown sameness pervades most of the dishes on the 150-item menu. Among the better dishes is cold spiced smoked fish, which is mild, sweet and plentifully supplied with bones. On our last visit, the crispy rice with sea cucumber, though chock-full of sea cucumber, pork and mushrooms, had almost no flavor, despite its thick, somewhat peppery brown sauce. The dish of assorted meats, which featured an overworked meatball, boiled fresh shrimp, smoked ham and chicken chunks, tasted intensely salty, as though someone forgot to say "when" on the soy sauce. Avoid the acrid, metallic winter-melon soup and go instead for the noodle dishes and steamed or fried breads. Wu Kong will prepare beggar's chicken, but it must be ordered in advance, which may require the intercession of a Chinese-speaking friend. Two need not spend more than HK$250 to HK$300 for dinner with beer.

Open daily 11:30 a.m.-11 p.m. All major cards.

NEW TERRITORIES & OUTLYING ISLANDS

Chiuchow Garden

Luk Yeung Sun Chuen
Shopping Arcade, Tsuen
Wan, New Territories
• 0-4983381
East Asia Commercial
Centre, Tsuen Wan, New
Territories
• 0-4143636
CHIU CHOW

See Kowloon.

Flower Lounge
New Town Plaza, Shatin,
New Territories
• 0-6981168
CANTONESE

See Hong Kong Island.

Fung Lum
45 Tsuen Nam Rd.,
Tai Wai, Shatin,
New Territories
• 0-621175
Siu Yat Bldg.,
Sai Kung New Town,
New Territories
• 3-2816623
CANTONESE

See Kowloon.

Jade Garden
East Asia Garden,
Texaco Rd., Tsuen Wan,
New Territories
• 0-463681
CANTONESE

See Hong Kong Island.

Lung Wah Hotel
Taipo Rd., Shatin Heights,
Shatin, New Territories
• 0-611793
CANTONESE

Families trek out here just for the salt-baked pigeon, and with good reason—it's outstanding. Presented first in a dough-swaddled casserole, the birds are then uncovered, sectioned and returned to the table on a platter, wine-rich and anise-scented. A group can also order a whole roasted suckling pig, the skin crisp and crackly, the meat juicy and aromatic. The extensive menu features such hearty and satisfying offerings as sweetly pungent honey-roasted ham, richly gelatinous goose feet and wings with mushrooms, and savory steamed eel with black-bean sauce. The more adventurous will be tempted by such combinations as stewed seafood and bone marrow or shrimp and kidney with celery. Despite its name, Lung Wah Hotel is a restaurant, not a hotel, and unlike most eating establishments in this crowded corner of the world, its grounds are spacious, if somewhat in need of sprucing up. On the grounds is an aviary, whose clattering cockatoos and macaws compete with the shrieks and laughter coming from the neighboring children's playground; an outdoor terrace looks onto these and a superhighway just beyond. Inside, two cheerfully gaudy medium-size rooms flaunt dark-wood walls and a potpourri of ink paintings, lacquer screens and decorative ceramic fish. A 25-minute ride from downtown

Kowloon, a meal here becomes an outing. Two people can dine sumptuously with beer for HK$250.
Open daily 9:30 a.m.-11:30 p.m. Cards: AE, MC, V.

North Park
North Park Palace, New Town Plaza, Shatin, New Territories
• 0-6066338
CANTONESE

See Kowloon.

Oiman
Seafood Market, Lau Fau Shan, New Territories
• No phone
CANTONESE

12/20

There are perhaps a dozen small, funky seafood restaurants in the two-block-long fishing village of Lau Fau Shan, a popular stop for tourists spending a day in the New Territories. From the end of the pier, one looks out across acres of oyster shells toward China, which is usually hidden in mist across the water. In Lau Fau Shan itself, you walk past fish shop after fish shop, many specializing in dried fish and abalone, which you can see hanging in the sun on wire fences. In Seafood Market itself, we saw the largest lobster we've ever encountered. He (or she) weighed close to 25 pounds, had feelers more than two feet long and seemed to have a malicious look on his (or her) face that told us to move along—that he (or she) wasn't about to become a meal for the likes of us. Near this lobster we found Oiman, which we had been told was one of the best (and, we noticed, one of the cleanest) seafood restaurants on the Lau Fau Shan waterfront. It's a small place with a handful of Formica-topped tables and brusque, abrupt service. But the seafood is, as you might expect, as fresh as could be. Come to Oiman for heaps of shrimp, served grilled in their shell, boiled, in spicy salt or steamed with peppery garnishes. Lobster comes baked with a soy sauce and chili dip. So does crab—a dip so good you'll be tempted to lick the bowl clean. This good food is served without a trace of pomp or circumstance: it emerges from the kitchen and lands on your plate. This cooking goes very well with beer and costs a fraction of what it would cost down in Kowloon: dinner for two, with beer, runs about HK$200.
Open daily 11 a.m.-10 p.m. No cards.

Peach Garden Seafood
11 Main St., Sok Kwu
Wan, Lamma Island
• 5-9828581
CANTONESE

12/20

Monetarists who admire laissez-faire Hong Kong will adore Sok Kwu Wan. The harborside village's response to the curtailed ferry services obeys the law of supply and demand: its dozen or so balconied, waterfront restaurants vie for the limited business by serving, with English-speaking friendliness, very fresh seafood and properly chilled wines. Rather Mediterranean in style, the restaurants are actually shop sites with roofed balconies separated by a pathway (Sok Kwu Wan's Main Street). Business booms for the three-unit Peach Garden and its neighbors only on sunny Sundays, when junkloads of weekend sailors are steered out of nearby Aberdeen's boat clubs and into this Lamma Island bay. Its waters are littered with fish farms, and the opposite coastline has been ravaged by quarrying, but Sok Kwu Wan is still many expatriates' idea of paradise, in which the healthy outdoor life consists of shucking fresh shrimp and sucking black-bean sauce off crabs. Appropriately, all of Main Street's restaurants sport large signs touting their wine; their cabinets are well stocked with Paul Masson, German whites and Portuguese vinho verde. To enjoy the best service, take the ferry on an uncrowded weekday (50 minutes from Central or Aberdeen). Choosing to work up an appetite, we arrived in the late afternoon, left our shopping bags at Peach Garden and hiked around the coastline of almost-uninhabited south Lamma. When we returned to eat, Peach Garden was completely uninhabited, and as the only customers, we reveled in a feast of inexpensive seafood and discreetly attentive service (including a reminder of our ferry's departure time). Most menu prices are seasonal (lobsters the priciest): fried prawns with a mild chili sauce were an excellent value at HK$45. "Small fish for two? About forty dollars?" suggested the lady of the house, who then produced a perfectly steamed fish with ginger, soy and spring onions. An assent to her "Good deep-fried squid with spiced salt?" gave us a generous "small" portion of zesty succulence for only HK$35. Perfect, too, was the locally grown choy sum (a green vegetable), washed down well with China's Tsingtao beer. All this cost the two of us only HK$168, which seemed shockingly reasonable (after being tourist-trapped in Lei Yue Mun). Sok Kwu Wan is a total, and totally delightful, travel experience. *Open daily 10 a.m.-9 p.m. All major cards.*

Po Lin Monastery
Lantau Island
• **No phone**
CANTONESE/BUDDHIST VEGETARIAN

9/20

Lantau Island is a beautiful, lushly overgrown isle just an hour away from Hong Kong by ferry but a world away in feeling. Dotted with rice paddies and surrounded by pristine beaches—and home to a couple of penal colonies as well—Lantau is a blessed respite from the hustle, bustle and noise level of Hong Kong. Right off the ferry, you hop on a bus for an hour's kidney-jostling ride up the rugged, verdant mountains of Lantau to the Po Lin Monastery (for some reason, taxis aren't allowed up, though you can hire a driver and private car if you don't feel like being shaken and stirred on public transportation). Ignore the tacky souvenir stands and wind your way through massive pots of bougainvillea in the main courtyard. Braziers of incense fume away on the pathways leading to the various temples and shrines; saffron-robed priests and adopted stray dogs pad quietly around the grounds. Lunch is served to the public every half hour on the half hour; you purchase a meal ticket to gain entry to the dining hall, an austere affair with round communal tables. For your first course, you take your bowl to the front of the room and serve yourself from huge kettles of soup, boiled vegetables, rice and rice gruel. These first dishes are definitely on the ascetic side, but don't despair—heaping platters are soon brought to the tables, family-style, and you'll find a few delicious dishes to dig into: flavorful stir-fried vegetables, heavy on the Chinese cabbage; a combination of about five different types of mushrooms in a musky, mellow sauce; and wonderfully crunchy veggie-stuffed spring rolls. Tea is served, or you can get a variety of canned soft drinks from the vending machine. This is hardly grand cuisine; rather, it's tasty vegetarian fare that will make you feel quite virtuous (and perhaps even a touch spiritual) for eating it. And the island is truly lovely (for the intrepid, the government-maintained hiking trails make Lantau a favorite of day-trippers). The tariff is virtuous, too: lunch for two is only HK$50. *Open daily 7:30 a.m.-8 a.m. & 11:30 a.m.-3:30 p.m. No cards.*

Yue Kee Goose Restaurant
Sham Tseng, New Territories
• No phone
CANTONESE/GOOSE

12/20

About a half hour out of Kowloon, heading northwest by west along the beach road, just on the other side of the road from Gemini Beach, you'll find a small town called Sham Tseng, which shares its particular little patch of the New Territories with a brewery. It's not the sort of town tourists would necessarily head for—except that Sham Tseng is the roast-goose capital of Hong Kong. Like Mealhada, the town in Portugal that consists of nothing but roast-pig restaurants, Sham Tseng boasts a main street lined solely with goose eateries. Yue Kee, which is set apart by its wonderful billboard on the highway, is typical of the goose restaurants: a small open room with a double handful of battered Formica-topped tables, a noisy kitchen and a lot of people eating goose. The menu is as limited as could be: heaping plates of goose, leaner than usual (more like duck, in fact), served with a sweet-and-sour dipping sauce, a spicy red sauce and pickles. There's also an assortment of simple noodle dishes and various steamed greens. We think a plate of steamed cabbage is the ideal foil to the goose's fattiness. It was a great snack, and not the sort of thing many foreigners know about. And the goose restaurants follow very well the old adage about how the best Chinese restaurants are the smallest—it's no more than three steps from the kitchen window to any table in Yue Kee. Dinner for two, with beer, costs about HK$100.
Open daily 11 a.m.-11 p.m. No cards.

RESTAURANT INDEXES

LATE-NIGHTERS

A word of warning: the places below are *officially* open late, but Hong Kong's restaurants, particularly its Chinese places, are lax about maintaining standardized hours. If business is slow, a restaurant that says it is open until midnight may just decide to close up at 10:30. So you are well advised to call before heading out for a late-night meal, or at least have a couple of back-up places in mind in case your destination turns out to be a bust.

OPEN AFTER MIDNIGHT

Amigo *Hong Kong Island*
Golden Island Bird's Nest *Kowloon*
Houston Chiu Chow *Kowloon*
Joe Bananas *Hong Kong Island*
Mad Dogs *Hong Kong Island*
Malaya *Kowloon*
Pak Loh *Hong Kong Island*
La Rose Noire *Hong Kong Island*
Studio 123 *Kowloon*
Sui Sha Ya *Hong Kong Island*

OPEN AFTER 11

American Restaurant *Hong Kong Island*
Au Trou Normand *Kowloon*
Baron's Table *Kowloon*
The Belvedere *Kowloon*
Bentley's Seafood Restaurant and Oyster Bar *Hong Kong Island*
The Bloom *Hong Kong Island*
Bocarino's Grill *Hong Kong Island*
California *Hong Kong Island*
Casa Mexicana *Hong Kong Island*
Chili Club *Hong Kong Island*
Chiuchow Garden *Hong Kong Island, Kowloon, New Territories*

City Hall Chinese *Hong Kong Island*
Cleveland Szechuan *Hong Kong Island*
Excelsior Grill *Hong Kong Island*
Fat Siu Lau Seafood *Kowloon*
Flourishing Court *Kowloon*
Flourishing Restaurant *Kowloon*
Flower Lounge *Hong Kong Island, Kowloon, New Territories*
Fook Lam Moon *Hong Kong Island, Kowloon*
Fook Yuen Seafood *Hong Kong Island*
Fung Lum Szechuan *Kowloon, New Territories*
Gaylord *Kowloon*
Glorious *Hong Kong Island*
Golden Bull *Kowloon*
Golden Unicorn *Kowloon*
Great Shanghai *Kowloon*
Guangzhou Garden *Hong Kong Island*
Harbour View Seafood Restaurant *Kowloon*
Hunan Garden *Hong Kong Island*
Jade Garden *Hong Kong Island, New Territories*
Jimmy's Kitchen *Hong Kong Island, Kowloon*
Kanetanaka *Hong Kong Island*
King Heung *Hong Kong Island*
Lai Ching Heen *Kowloon*
Lalique *Kowloon*
Landau's *Hong Kong Island*
Leonardo *Kowloon*
Lindy's *Kowloon*
Loong Yuen *Kowloon*
Lung Wah Hotel *New Territories*
Margaux *Kowloon*
Mistral *Kowloon*
Nineteen '97 *Hong Kong Island*
North Park *Hong Kong Island, Kowloon, New Territories*
Orchid Garden *Hong Kong Island, Kowloon*
Palace Seafood *Hong Kong Island*
Parc 27 *Hong Kong Island*
Peking Garden *Hong Kong Island, Kowloon*
Perfume River *Hong Kong Island*
Pierrot *Hong Kong Island*

Plume *Kowloon*
Prince Court Szechuan *Kowloon*
Red Pepper *Hong Kong Island*
Regal Seafood *Kowloon*
Royal Thai *Hong Kong Island*
Sampan Dinners *Hong Kong Island*
San Francisco Steak House *Kowloon*
Shanghai Garden *Hong Kong Island*
Siu Siu *Hong Kong Island*
Stanley's French Restaurant *Hong Kong Island*
The Steak House *Kowloon*
Sun Tung Lok Shark's Fin Restaurant *Kowloon*
Sunning Unicorn *Hong Kong Island*
Sybilla *Kowloon*
Tai Pan *Kowloon*
Tandoor Restaurant *Hong Kong Island*
Tao Yuan *Hong Kong Island*
Tin Tin Hot Pot *Kowloon*
Toh Lee *Kowloon*
Treasure Pot *Hong Kong Island*
Tsui Hang Village *Kowloon*
Unicorn Szechuan *Kowloon*
Valentino Ristorante *Kowloon*
Vegi Food Kitchen *Hong Kong Island*
Wan Loong Court *Kowloon*
West Villa *Hong Kong Island, Kowloon*
Yung Kee *Hong Kong Island*

BY NEIGHBORHOOD

ABERDEEN

Jumbo Floating Restaurant
Tai Pak Floating Restaurant

ADMIRALTY

Bombay Palace
West Villa

CAUSEWAY BAY

Boil & Boil Wonderful
Casa Mexicana
Chiuchow Garden
Cleveland Szechuan
Excelsior Grill
Fook Yuen Seafood
Forum Restaurant
Good Health
Jade Garden
Kanetanaka
King Heung
Lao Ching Hing
North Park
Orchid Garden
Pak Loh
Palace Seafood
Parc 27
Peking Garden
Perfume River
Rangoon
Red Pepper
Royal Thai
Sampan Dinners
Siu Siu
Sui Sha Ya
Sunning Unicorn
Treasure Pot
Vegi Food Kitchen

CENTRAL

Ashoka
Benkay Japanese
Bentley's Seafood Restaurant and Oyster Bar
Beverly Hills Deli
The Bloom
Bocarino's Grill
Café de Paris
California

Chiuchow Garden
City Hall Chinese
Eagle's Nest
East Ocean
La Futura
Guangzhou Garden
Hilton Grill
Hunan Garden
Island
Jade Garden
Jimmy's Kitchen
Luk Yu Tea House
Mad Dogs
Man Wah
Mandarin Grill
Mozart Stub'n
Nineteen '97
Pattaya Fast Food
Peking Garden
Pierrot
Pimelea
La Rose Noire
The Rotisserie
Shanghai Garden
Silla Won
Tandoor Restaurant
La Taverna
West Villa
Yung Kee

HAPPY VALLEY

Amigo
Fung Lum
Pep 'n' Chilli

KOWLOON CITY

Five Continents

KOWLOON TONG

Sybilla

LEI YUE MUN

Hoi Tin Garden

MEI FOO SUN CHUEN

Unicorn Szechuan

MONGKOK

Flower Lounge

NEW TERRITORIES

Chiuchow Garden
Flower Lounge
Fung Lum
Jade Garden
Lung Wah Hotel
North Park
Oiman
Yue Kee Goose Restaurant

OUTLYING ISLANDS

Peach Garden Seafood
Po Lin Monastery

REPULSE BAY

Spices
The Verandah

STANLEY

Stanley's French Restaurant

TSIMSHATSUI

Arirang
Au Trou Normand

Baron's Table
Beverly Hills Deli
Bodhi Vegetarian Restaurant
The Bostonian
Chesa
The Chinese Restaurant
Choi Kun Heung
Flourishing Court
Flourishing Restaurant
Flower Lounge
Fook Lam Moon
Fung Lum
Fung Lum Szechuan
Gaddi's
Gaylord
Ginza
Golden Bull
Golden Island Bird's Nest
Golden Unicorn
Great Shanghai
Hugo's
Inagiku
Jade Garden
Java Rijsttafel
Jimmy's Kitchen
Lai Ching Heen
Leonardo
Lindy's
Loong Yuen
Malaya
Ocean City
Orchid Garden
Peking Garden
Plume
Prince Court Szechuan
San Francisco Steak House
Sawadee Thai Restaurant
Spring Deer
Spring Moon
The Steak House

Studio 123
Sui Sha Ya
Tai Pan
Tin Tin Hot Pot
Tsui Hang Village
Unkai
Wan Loong Court
West Villa
Woodlands
Wu Kong Shanghai Restaurant

TSIMSHATSUI EAST

The Belvedere
Chiuchow Garden
City Chiu Chow Restaurant
East Ocean
Fat Siu Lau Seafood
Flower Lounge
Harbour View Seafood Restaurant
Houston Chiu Chow
Indian Curry Club
Lalique
Margaux
Mistral
Nadaman
North Park
Peking Garden
Regal Seafood
Le Restaurant de France
Sagano
Shang Palace
Sun Tung Lok Shark's Fin Restaurant
Toh Lee
Valentino Ristorante

WANCHAI

American Restaurant
Chili Club
Flower Lounge

Fook Lum Moon
Glorious
Golden Poppy
Joe Bananas
Landau's
Manhattan Restaurant
Orchid Garden
Tao Yuan
Thai Delicacy
La Toison d'Or
Treasure Pot
USA Deli & Restaurant
Viceroy of India

WONG TAI SIN

Chiuchow Garden

THE WORLD'S CUISINES

AMERICAN

Beverly Hills Deli *Kowloon*
The Bostonian *Kowloon*
California *Hong Kong Island*
Joe Bananas *Hong Kong Island*
Lindy's *Kowloon*
San Francisco Steak House *Kowloon*
The Steak House *Kowloon*
Studio 123 *Kowloon*
USA Deli & Restaurant *Hong Kong Island*

AUSTRIAN

Mozart Stub'n *Hong Kong Island*

BRITISH

Bentley's Seafood Restaurant and Oyster Bar *Hong Kong Island*
Mad Dogs *Hong Kong Island*

BUDDHIST VEGETARIAN

Po Lin Monastery *New Territories & Outlying Islands*

BURMESE

Rangoon, *Hong Kong Island*

CANTONESE

The Bloom *Hong Kong Island*
Bodhi Vegetarian Restaurant *Kowloon*
Boil & Boil Wonderful *Hong Kong Island*
The Chinese Restaurant *Kowloon*
Choi Kun Heung *Kowloon*
City Hall Chinese *Hong Kong Island*
East Ocean *Kowloon*
Eagle's Nest *Hong Kong Island*
Fat Siu Lau Seafood *Kowloon*
Flourishing Restaurant *Kowloon*
Flourishing Court *Kowloon*
Flower Lounge *Hong Kong Island*
Fook Lam Moon *Hong Kong Island*
Fook Yuen Seafood *Hong Kong Island*
Forum Restaurant *Hong Kong Island*
Fung Lum *Kowloon*
Glorious *Hong Kong Island*
Golden Unicorn *Kowloon*
Guangzhou Garden *Hong Kong Island*
Harbour View Seafood Restaurant *Kowloon*
Hoi Tin Garden *Kowloon*
Island *Hong Kong Island*
Jade Garden *Hong Kong Island*
Jumbo Floating Restaurant *Hong Kong Island*
Lai Ching Heen *Kowloon*
Loong Yuen *Kowloon*
Luk Yu Tea House *Hong Kong Island*
Lung Wah Hotel *New Territories & Outlying Islands*
Man Wah *Hong Kong Island*
Mistral *Kowloon*
Neptune Seafood *Hong Kong Island*
North Park *Kowloon*

Ocean City *Kowloon*
Oiman *New Territories & Outlying Islands*
Orchid Garden *Kowloon*
Palace Seafood *Hong Kong Island*
Peach Garden Seafood *New Territories & Outlying Islands*
Pimelea *Hong Kong Island*
Po Lin Monastery *New Territories & Outlying Islands*
Regal Seafood *Kowloon*
Sampan Dinners *Hong Kong Island*
Shang Palace *Kowloon*
Siu Siu *Hong Kong Island*
Spring Moon *Kowloon*
Studio 123 *Kowloon*
Sunning Unicorn *Hong Kong Island*
Sun Tung Lok Shark's Fin Restaurant *Kowloon*
Tai Pak Floating Restaurant *Hong Kong Island*
Tao Yuan *Hong Kong Island*
Toh Lee *Kowloon*
Treasure Pot *Hong Kong Island*
Tsui Hang Village *Kowloon*
Vegi Food Kitchen *Hong Kong Island*
Wan Loong Court *Kowloon*
West Villa *Hong Kong Island*
Yue Kee Goose Restaurant *New Territories & Outlying Islands*
Yung Kee *Hong Kong Island*

CHIU CHOW

Chiuchow Garden *Kowloon*
City Chiu Chow Restaurant *Kowloon*
Golden Island Bird's Nest *Kowloon*
Houston Chiu Chow *Kowloon*
Pak Loh *Hong Kong Island*

CONTINENTAL

Bocarino's Grill *Hong Kong Island*
Excelsior Grill *Hong Kong Island*
Five Continents *Kowloon*
Hilton Grill *Continental*
Hugo's *Kowloon*

Jimmy's Kitchen *Hong Kong Island*
Landau's *Hong Kong Island*
Mandarin Grill *Hong Kong Island*
Mozart Stub'n *Hong Kong Island*
Nineteen '97 *Hong Kong Island*
Parc 27 *Hong Kong Island*
La Rose Noire *Hong Kong Island*
The Rotisserie *Hong Kong Island*
Tai Pan *Kowloon*
The Verandah *Hong Kong Island*

CREOLE/CAJUN

Stanley's French Restaurant *Hong Kong Island*

DELI

Beverly Hills Deli *Kowloon*
Lindy's *Kowloon*
USA Deli & Restaurant *Hong Kong Island*

FRENCH

Amigo *Hong Kong Island*
Au Trou Normand *Kowloon*
The Belvedere *Kowloon*
Bocarino's Grill *Hong Kong Island*
Café de Paris *Hong Kong Island*
Gaddi's *Kowloon*
Hilton Grill
Hugo's *Kowloon*
Lalique *Kowloon*
Margaux *Kowloon*
Parc 27 *Hong Kong Island*
Pierrot *Hong Kong Island*
Plume *Kowloon*
Le Restaurant de France *Kowloon*
La Rose Noire *Hong Kong Island*
The Rotisserie *Hong Kong Island*

Stanley's French Restaurant *Hong Kong Island*
Tai Pan *Kowloon*
La Toison d'Or *Hong Kong Island*
The Verandah *Hong Kong Island*

GERMAN

Baron's Table *Kowloon*

HUNAN

Hunan Garden *Hong Kong Island*

INDIAN

Ashoka *Hong Kong Island*
Bombay Palace *Hong Kong Island*
Gaylord *Kowloon*
Indian Curry Club *Kowloon*
Tandoor Restaurant *Hong Kong Island*
Viceroy of India *Hong Kong Island*
Woodlands *Kowloon*

INDONESIAN

Java Rijsttafel *Kowloon*

ITALIAN

La Futura *Hong Kong Island*
Leonardo *Kowloon*
Sybilla *Kowloon*
La Taverna *Hong Kong Island*
Valentino Ristorante *Kowloon*

JAPANESE

Benkay Japanese *Hong Kong Island*
Ginza *Kowloon*
Inagiku *Kowloon*

Kanetanaka *Hong Kong Island*
Nadaman *Kowloon*
Sagano *Kowloon*
Sui Sha Ya *Hong Kong Island*
Unkai *Kowloon*

KOREAN

Arirang *Kowloon*
Silla Won *Hong Kong Island*

MALAYSIAN

Malaya *Kowloon*

MEXICAN

Casa Mexicana *Hong Kong Island*

PAN-ASIAN

Spices *Hong Kong Island*

PEKINGESE

American Restaurant *Hong Kong Island*
Eagle's Nest *Hong Kong Island*
King Heung *Hong Kong Island*
Manhattan Restaurant *Hong Kong Island*
Ocean City *Kowloon*
Peking Garden *Hong Kong Island*
Spring Deer *Kowloon*

SEAFOOD *CHINESE*

See Cantonese.

SEAFOOD *WESTERN*

Bentley's Seafood Restaurant and Oyster Bar *Hong Kong Island*
The Bostonian *Kowloon*

SHANGHAINESE

Great Shanghai *Kowloon*
Lao Ching Hing *Hong Kong Island*
Shanghai Garden *Hong Kong Island*
Wu Kong Shanghai Restaurant *Kowloon*

STEAKHOUSE

San Francisco Steak House *Kowloon*
The Steak House *Kowloon*

SWISS

Chesa *Kowloon*

SZECHUAN

Cleveland Szechuan *Hong Kong Island*
Fung Lum Szechuan *Kowloon*
Pep 'n' Chilli *Hong Kong Island*
Prince Court Szechuan *Kowloon*
Red Pepper *Hong Kong Island*
Unicorn Szechuan *Kowloon*

TAIWANESE

Tin Tin Hot Pot *Kowloon*

THAI

Chili Club *Hong Kong Island*
Golden Poppy *Hong Kong Island*
Pattaya Fast Food *Hong Kong Island*
Royal Thai *Hong Kong Island*
Sawadee Thai Restaurant *Kowloon*
Thai Delicacy *Hong Kong Island*

VEGETARIAN

Bodhi Vegetarian Restaurant *Kowloon*
Choi Kun Heung *Kowloon*

Good Health *Hong Kong Island*
Po Lin Monastery *New Territories & Outlying Islands*
Vegi Food Kitchen *Hong Kong Island*
Woodlands *Kowloon*

VIETNAMESE

Golden Bull *Kowloon*
Perfume River *Hong Kong Island*

QUICK BITES

INTRODUCTION

While Hong Kong is a restaurant city nonpareil, it is not strong on the sort of quick food so common in the West, particularly America, where burgers, barbecue, pizza, deli and diner chow so often feed people quickly, cheaply and well. However, as you'll discover below, Hong Kong does have some excellent-to-serviceable quick-refreshment spots, ranging from coffee shops (curiously popular here) and tearooms to pubs and good old mass-produced American fast food. (Sadly, the tremendous success in Hong Kong of such American imports as McDonald's, Pizza Hut and Kentucky Fried Chicken seems to have taken away business from the once-plentiful dim sum parlors, which are now entirely too rare.)

Take note that you won't find full-fledged restaurants serving dim sum—one of our favorite quick bites on the planet—in this chapter. To find the best of Hong Kong's many Cantonese dim sum places, see the Restaurants chapter. Also in that chapter are many modest Chinese restaurants that serve terrific food quickly, whether it's for lunch, dinner or an afternoon snack.

Street food is not as plentiful in Hong Kong as it is in other parts of Asia, notably Singapore and Hong Kong—people seem to confine their eating more to restaurants than street stalls. Food Street, in fact, is not what it sounds like at all, but rather a modern, shopping mall–like collection of restaurants. Those in search of good Chinese street food do, however, have a couple of areas to explore: see the listings for Poor Man's Nightclub and Shanghai Street in the Sights chapter.

CAFES & COFFEE SHOPS

A-1 Bakery
179-181 Hennessey Rd.,
Wanchai

Located in what was once Hong Kong's most notorious red-light district, A-1 Bakery has been around since 1948, so it's definitely seen some action. Although the district has now been gentrified, it remains quite colorful. This is a German bakery, with lots of pastries, cakes and breads for eating in the shop or taking out. A snack for two will cost about HK$20.
Open daily 7 a.m.-6 p.m. No cards.

Abe's Café
Ramada Inn Hong Kong
61-73 Lockhart Rd.,
Wanchai
• 5-8611000

Serving breakfast (including a buffet), lunch and dinner Abe's Café is a near clone of Café Society in the Ramada Inn Kowloon. You'll find some rather greasy, scary artificial-looking eggs and bacon (stick with the bread basket and fresh fruit); while the dim sum here is okay, it's not worth the calories. For lunch and dinner, most of the sandwiches and main courses (like the sandwich of Michigan sausage, baked beans and cheese) get a little bizarre; breakfast is what Abe's does best. Breakfast for two should run about HK$80.
Open daily 6 a.m.-midnight. All major cards.

The American Cafe
Queensway Plaza,
Admiralty, Queensway
• 5-294595

The American Cafe is a Denny's in disguise (it actually was a Denny's franchise at one time); it's your basic bus-terminal coffee shop (located above the Admiralty bus station). Fairly large, with the standard wood and plastic decor, it allows you to either eat the customary coffee shop fare at the counter or at a table. It's not a bad choice, though, if you're in the mood for a milk shake. About HK$80 for a snack for two.
Open daily 7 a.m.-11 p.m. No cards.

Apple Coffee Shop
Sheraton Hong Kong
Hotel and Towers
20 Nathan Rd.,
Tsimshatsui, Kowloon
• 3-691111

We think the Apple is more popular for its view of the folks strolling down Salisbury Road than for the food it serves, which elaborates on the usual coffee shop fare. The Western-style breakfasts are pretty straightforward and do just fine, but watch out for the overcomplicated, frequently inedible lunch and dinner dishes—like the seafood crêpe in Nantua sauce and the veal piccata. There are also hot dogs, pizzas, burgers, Reuben and club sandwiches, spaghetti and some Oriental dishes;

proceed with these at your own risk. About HK$150 for a quick lunch for two.
Open daily 7 a.m.-midnight. All major cards.

The Bahunia
Hongkong Hotel
3 Canton Rd.,
Tsimshatsui, Kowloon
• 3-676011

Although it can't be classified as a Quick Bite in the evening hours, the rather posh Bahunia (named for the city flower of Hong Kong) serves excellent Western breakfasts and lunches, including a lunchtime buffet with heaps and heaps of salads, cold and cooked dishes and desserts. About HK$120 for breakfast for two.
Open daily 7 a.m.-midnight. All major cards.

The Balcony
Royal Garden Hotel
69 Mody Rd., Tsimshatsui
East, Kowloon
• 3-7215215

The Royal Garden Hotel is quite beautiful, built around an atrium fairly dripping with greenery, complete with a pianist playing on an island in a triangular pool. The Balcony, basically the hotel's coffee shop, is a terrace lounge overlooking the ivory-tickler and the ornamental pools. The food is so-so, but it's so spectacularly displayed on a buffet table ornamented with rice-paper umbrellas and artfully arranged crates of fresh produce that its limitations don't seem to matter much at all. We will, however, advise that you stick with the salads or come here for early-evening cocktails. About HK$240 for lunch for two.
Open daily 11 a.m.-midnight. All major cards.

The Big Apple
Ruttonjee Centre, Unit
111, Duddell St., Central
• 5-8107103
116-118 Harbour Centre,
Harbour Rd., Wanchai

This is one of Hong Kong's several New York–style delis, and, like the others, it's a deli gone amok. Patrons of the world-renowned Carnegie Deli would swoon if they suddenly found a sushi bar installed in their favorite haunt—but why not? After all, lox is (sort of) raw fish, too. The popular lunch menu lists omelets, sandwiches, hot dogs, even Welsh rarebit. The Strudels and crêpes are only worth eating if you think you'll perish without a pastry; the cappuccino is good. About HK$120 for two.
Open daily 7:30 a.m.-10 p.m. Cards: MC.

The Bonbonnaire
Holiday Inn Harbour View
70 Mody Rd., Tsimshatsui
East, Kowloon
• 3-7215161

A terrific place for a rest and a little something sweet; this is simply a pastry and candy shop (everything is made on the premises), where you can eat in or take out. Perfect for parking your shopping bags and resting your shopping-weary feet to enjoy a fresh tartelette with a hot cup of coffee. About HK$80 for two.
Open daily 8 a.m.-7 p.m. All major cards.

La Brasserie

The Marco Polo
Harbour City, Canton Rd.,
Tsimshatsui, Kowloon
• 3-7215111

La Brasserie is a popular, upscale café, all in leather upholstery, wood and etched glass. While not exactly cheap, this well-appointed version of a French bistro does dish out some pretty good food. (The hotel is part of the Peninsula group, so quality control is high, and close attention is paid to detail.) Some dishes run to the froufrou (such as the vol au vent), but the earthier dishes, such as the bouillabaisse, pot au feu and the duck liver with endive salad, are notable. There's also a three-course business lunch, complete with a glass of wine, that costs a most reasonable HK$88. The dishes rotate on a seasonal basis. Lunch runs about HK$200 for two.
Open daily noon-midnight. All major cards.

Café Rendezvous

Holiday Inn Harbour View
70 Mody Rd., Tsimshatsui
East, Kowloon
• 3-7215161

Though it's a coffee shop, it's a classy coffee shop, decorated in rich colors in a sort of Regency-chinoiserie mode. You can face out and take advantage of the terrific view of the always mesmerizing harbor, or sit on the open terrace for lobby-watching. There's traditional tea trolley service, with a good selection of teas—that and the dessert trolley are the best things going here. If it's real food you want, you can order Asian dishes as well as hamburgers and steaks. About HK$200 for two.
Open daily 7 a.m.-1 a.m. All major cards.

Café Society

Ramada Inn Kowloon
73-75 Chatham Rd. South,
Tsimshatsui, Kowloon
• 3-3111100

We're sure legendary society columnist Cholly Knickerbocker would cringe over this upscale coffee shop being named Café Society, and while it has little to do with the old El Morocco and the Trocadero, this very pretty room has been done up to resemble a garden conservatory—spick and span, in shades of beiges and greens. There are various fixed-price breakfasts (Continental, American, Chinese and fitness) as well as à la carte items. The juices are all freshly squeezed, and, although we'd pass on the eggs, the assorted bread basket is excellent. The lunch and dinner menu offers a variety of salads, sandwiches, pastas and Chinese dishes; as ever, common wisdom suggests that you avoid the more involved plates (like the roast rack of lamb provençale with a vegetable soufflé) and stay with the simple. Lunch for two is about HK$200.
Open daily 6 a.m.-midnight. All major cards.

Cat Street
Hong Kong Hilton Hotel
2 Queen's Rd., Central
• 5-233111

This 25-year-old warhorse with its 1900s ambience is a hodgepodge all around: the decor is Westernized Chinese, and the food is all over the map. This usually leads to trouble, but the New Orleans chowder, Greek salad, Japanese tempura, Bronx bagel and Mexican taco were all better than we would ever have guessed. And there's even a roster of ice cream treats. Though this joint gets crowded, it remains comfy. About HK$150 for a simple lunch for two.
Open daily 6 a.m.-3 a.m. All major cards.

Coffee Garden
Shangri-La Hotel
64 Mody Rd., Tsimshatsui
East, Kowloon
• 3-7212111

Open almost round the clock, this grill-like room features yet another around-the-world-in-80-dishes menu. The deli section of this tome offers bagels, cream cheese and lox and matzo ball soup; you'll also find burgers, sandwiches and a house specialty, chilled fruit soup with hazelnuts. A sampling of Asian dishes are offered, too. In all, this is a fine place to while away the lunch hour or grab a late-night bite. About HK$225 for lunch for two.
Open daily 6 a.m.-2 a.m. All major cards.

The Coffee Shop
Hongkong Hotel
3 Canton Rd.,
Tsimshatsui, Kowloon
• 3-676011

Though four separate buffets are served throughout the day here, and there's a rather lengthy à la carte menu, The Coffee Shop serves its purpose best for breakfast or an afternoon snack. The food is more than serviceable, the waiters attentive, and the surroundings soothing. Snacks for two are about HK$130.
Open daily 6 a.m.-midnight. All major cards.

Food Street
Kingston St., Causeway Bay
• No phone

Unfortunately, Food Street sounds a lot more exotic than it is. We were expecting a twisting alleyway lined with aged vendors proffering strange and wondrous edibles, but apparently we've seen too many movies. Instead, Food Street is an ultra-modern arcade, well lit and gleaming white, with a center-strip pond lined with potted plants. There are twenty restaurants in the mall, some quite good, offering a variety of cuisines. While it lacked the mystery and funk we had hoped to find, it's nonetheless a fun place to snack and sample. Among the restaurants in Food Street (many of which you'll find reviewed in the Restaurants chapter): King Heung (Pekingese), 5-771035; Boil & Boil Wonderful (Cantonese), 5-779788; Riverside Restaurant (Cantonese),

5-779733; Cleveland Szechuan Restaurant (Szechuan), 5-763876; Paterson Vietnamese Restaurant (Vietnamese), 5-8908288; Siu Siu Restaurant (Cantonese), 5-8906096; Vegi Food Kitchen (Vegetarian), 5-8906603; and the better-than-it-sounds Dim Sum Burger (Shanghainese), 5-777199. Prices vary from restaurant to restaurant, but all are very reasonable. *Hours vary. Most restaurants do not accept credit cards.*

Gigi
Swire House, Connaught Rd., Central

Despite some snippy service from waitresses wearing tight, floor-length skirts slit up to here (a popular look in tearooms, we discovered), this cozy-on-the-edge-of-cloying room, decorated with tapestry-covered chairs, floral carpeting, travertine and mirrors, makes for a good refueling stop, during which you can contemplate how big your credit card bill will be from shopping in Swire's tony boutiques. The cappuccino and espresso at Gigi are actually quite good; you can also get sandwiches (club and pastrami among them), pastries and some wacky alcoholic coffee drinks (like a Coffee Fair Lady made with Cointreau) that seem to be very popular—even at 11:30 in the morning. The cappuccino is of a sort of do-it-yourself variety—you're brought an espresso with a small pitcher of steamed milk and a postage stamp–size square of yummy bittersweet chocolate. Gigi also encompasses a small gourmet shop that sells wines, cakes and other goodies. A snack for two is about HK$100.
Open daily 8 a.m.-6 p.m. All major cards.

Harbour View Coffee Shop
Holiday Inn Harbour View
70 Mody Rd., Tsimshatsui East, Kowloon
• 3-7215161

Though its view of the harbor is clearly the best thing in the room, the Harbour View serves workaday Western- and Oriental-style breakfasts in several ways: fixed-price, à la carte and buffet. While the buffet isn't exactly going to bankrupt you at HK$68, on our last visit, none of the hot dishes looked particularly appetizing; but then, steam-tray dishes often leave much to be desired. As is often the case in hotel coffee shops, cereals, yogurt, juices and breads are the way to go here. About HK$120 for breakfast for two.
Open daily 6 a.m.-midnight. All major cards.

Harbourside
The Regent
Salisbury Rd., Tsimshatsui, Kowloon
• 3-7211211

Harbourside is a real eye-popper—you can switch back and forth from staring at the dramatic view of the harbor through the wraparound picture windows, to looking at the denizens of the café, most of whom are involved in the rag trade, often wearing the "fashions" they manufacture. You'll find Hong Kong's best coffee shop fare here; in fact, it's almost not fair to classify it as such. The service is impeccable: snowy-white napery, quietly attentive waiters. The bread and pastry baskets are excellent, and even the lunch and dinner items (they do a great BLT sandwich and terrific french fries) are good. This is also a good late-evening dessert stop, with good selections from the pastry tray and a crackerjack hot fudge sundae. About HK$250 for lunch for two. *Open daily 6 a.m.-12:30 a.m. All major cards.*

The Lobby

The Peninsula
Salisbury Rd., Tsimshatsui,
Kowloon
• 3-666251

Nineteen ninety-seven may be fast approaching, but stepping into the quietly opulent lobby of the grand Peninsula Hotel feels like a trip back in time to the heyday of colonial Hong Kong. With its towering white plaster columns topped and woven with gold-leaf gods and angels, thick carpeting and the regal, sweeping staircase leading to the mezzanine, you feel special just being there. Though meals from breakfast through a midnight snack are served, the repast that's the sine qua non here is afternoon tea. From 2 to 4:30, a quartet sends music wafting throughout the room, and the most civilized ritual in the world begins. The waiters, gloved and in crisp whites, move quickly and silently. They present you with a choice of several teas, which are brought to the table in lovely silver pots enveloped in a white-linen cozy and accompanied by all the usual tea tidbits: the fresh scones are excellent, served with jams and Devonshire cream; the finger sandwiches are delicate; the small cookies perfection; and the selections from the pastry tray absolutely elegant. You may never see so much Chanel and Louis Vuitton in one place. We also noted that at practically every table at least one person was carrying one of those remote cellular telephones—quite an anachronism in this context. Afternoon tea at The Peninsula really isn't to be missed—it's both a glimpse of a time gone by and a look into the future. Tea for two is about HK$180. *Open daily 7 a.m.-1 a.m. All major cards.*

The Lobby Lounge

Hongkong Hotel
3 Canton Rd.,
Tsimshatsui, Kowloon
• 3-676011

Though both lunch and afternoon tea are served here, we'd skip the lunch (primarily soups, salads and sandwiches) and settle in for an afternoon snack after a hard day in the shopping mines. It's the standard British tea: fresh scones, finger sandwiches, pastries, cakes and, of course, tea. Although not nearly as good as the tea at The Peninsula, this one's quite passable, and the lounge is a very pretty setting. About HK$100 for two. *Open daily 11:30 a.m.-6 p.m. All major cards.*

Marimo
New World Centre, B1-43,
Salisbury Rd., Tsimshatsui,
Kowloon
• 3-697046

A decent pit stop while navigating the wilds of the vast New World Centre. Forget the pizzas and sandwiches; the coffee drinks, ice cream drinks and milk shakes are far more refreshing. About HK$50 for drinks for two. *Open daily 10:30 a.m.-8 p.m. No cards.*

Maxim's Boulevard Restaurant
Ocean Terminal, Canton
Rd., Tsimshatsui, Kowloon
• 3-673377

Maxim's has what has to be the nuttiest menu in all of Hong Kong. The food can only be characterized as Bizarro Americana, with such dishes as New Mexican beef, Kansas black pepper steak, Chicago spicy scallops and Golden State chicken salad. Try them if you're adventurous; we prefer to stop here for a refreshing cup of tea or a glass of wine instead, to collect ourselves before another assault on Ocean Terminal. About HK$150 for a snack for two.
Open daily 11:30 a.m.-9 p.m. All major cards.

The Mayfair Empress Hotel
17-19 Chatham Rd.,
Tsimshatsui, Kowloon
• 3-7218168

A nondescript café in a nondescript small hotel, The Mayfair serves the usual roster of Continental and Oriental coffee shop food: a tired bread basket, eggs and the rest for breakfast, soups, sandwiches and pallid main courses for dinner. Come here only if you're staying at the hotel and are too tired to go anywhere else. About HK$120 for breakfast for two.
Open daily 7 a.m.-midnight. All major cards.

Nuts
17-19 On Lan St., Central
• 5-261750

Not to be confused with the overwrought Barbra Streisand movie of the same name, Nuts is a European-style health food restaurant—in fact, it's Hong Kong's only Western vegetarian eatery. Not far from the Star Ferry terminal, the super-scrubbed, no-smoking-allowed Nuts serves lots of salads, quiches and good-for-you-but-still-fattening banana and carrot cakes. However, they're not unduly virtuous here: wine and beer are served. About HK$100 for a snack for two. *Open daily 11 a.m.-3:30 p.m. No cards.*

The Pâtisserie
Ocean Galleries, Shop 268,
Harbour City, Canton Rd.,
Kowloon
• 3-7215111

This garden-like tearoom, with its marble-topped tables, French doors and potted trees, is yet another spot where you can rest your tired tootsies while traversing this mall-to-end-all-malls. Afternoon tea is the main attraction, with waitresses dressed like maids from

'30s movies (short black dresses, starched white collars, aprons and cuffs) wheeling around carts bearing teas, pastries and sandwiches. About HK$100 for tea for two.
Open daily 11 a.m.-8 p.m. All major cards.

Sara's
Ocean Centre, Shop 249,
Canton Rd., Tsimshatsui,
Kowloon
• 3-3110992

This place can be a blessed oasis after you've gotten yourself completely lost in the Ocean Centre/Ocean Terminal/Harbor City complex. The sandwiches here are dreadful, but it's a good stop for ice cream, tea or cappuccino. Some of the pastries are tasty, too, notably the tarts. A snack for two is about HK$40.
Open daily 7 a.m.-7 p.m. No cards.

Seasons Bar & Café
17-19 On Lan St., Central
• 5-268429

The Italian-theme food at Seasons is far from great, but it's a fun hangout that caters mostly to Western expatriates and assorted trendoids. You'll find lots of pastas and fresh seafood; the specialty is a so-so cheese-and-spinach stuffed phyllo pie. But prices are reasonable, the waiters friendly and the atmosphere convivial. About HK$300 for a light meal for two.
Open daily 11 a.m.-3 p.m. & 5 p.m.-11 p.m. All major cards.

Spaghetti House
36 Cameron Rd.,
Tsimshatsui, Kowloon
• 3-688635

The Spaghetti House chain has been around since 1978, and, while the quality (particularly of the pizza) is better than at the ubiquitous Pizza Hut, the fare here is best suited for kids or unknowing Chinese who want a hit of Western food. In deference to the tastes of the local populace, the pizzas are light on the cheese, and the pastas have an Oriental touch (like spaghetti Hong Kong–style with clams). Steer clear of the greasy fried chicken and wan apple pie. There's also liquor for put-upon parents. Branches are scattered throughout Hong Kong and Kowloon. Dinner for two runs about HK$180.
Open daily 11:30 a.m.-2 a.m. No cards.

The Spice Market
Hongkong Hotel
3 Canton Rd.,
Tsimshatsui, Kowloon
• 3-676011

Decorated with palm trees, Indonesian wooden figures and huge glass canisters of exotic spices lining the buffet table, this better-than-average eatery serves all manner of pan-Asian food, along with a great view of Victoria Harbour. The Malaysian, Thai, Singaporean, Indian, Indonesian and Filipino food is available either à la carte or via the overladen buffet table (Chinese dishes are also offered à la carte). About HK$180 for two.
Open daily 11 a.m.-midnight. All major cards.

T & Tea Coffee Shop

Allied Plaza,
760 Nathan Rd.,
Tsimshatsui, Kowloon
• 3-972332

This is part of the terrific Tin Tin restaurant group, which is a pretty good recommendation in and of itself. Though T & Tea's specialty is catering, you can order good Chinese and American snacks (the Chinese ones are better), desserts (mango pudding, caramel custard, chocolate mousse) and even sushi. There's also a full bar if you need a quick quaff. About HK$120 for a tasty quick meal for two.

Open daily 11:30 a.m.-11 p.m. All major cards.

La Terrazza

Landmark Bldg.,
Pedder St., Central
• 5-264200

When you just can't try on another Armani at the Joyce Boutique here, shuffle your poor, tired body over to the atrium of the building for sustenance at La Terrazza. It's part of the mediocre chain of Maxim's coffee shops, but it's a pleasant, open space for people-watching. The fair dessert waffles are very popular; also worth trying are the ice cream sundaes and sodas. About HK$110 for a snack for two.

Open daily 8 a.m.-7 p.m. No cards.

The Verandah Grill

The Peninsula
Salisbury Rd., Tsimshatsui, Kowloon
• 3-666251

This recently remodeled Edwardian grill is The Peninsula's main dining room. There's a gorgeous copper grill at the center of its spacious two wings, and although the hotel's once-panoramic view of the harbor has been obscured by the creepy, windowless Space Museum across the street, there's still a wide-open feel about the place. It's technically a coffee shop, but what an elegant one! Both Continental and Oriental dishes are served here, along with breakfast and lunchtime buffets, fixed-price meals and à la carte dishes, running the gamut from dim sum to grilled salmon—and the food is good. Lunch is about HK$200 for two.

Open daily 7 a.m.-11 a.m., noon-3 p.m. & 6:30 p.m.-11 p.m.; the bar stays open until 2 a.m. All major cards.

FAST FOOD

Café de Coral
**Ocean Galleries, Shop
204-207, Star Ferry
Terminal, Tsimshatsui,
Kowloon**

This too brightly colored, plastic fast-food snack shop on the ground floor of the cavernous, ship-like Ocean Galleries serves hot dogs and sandwiches (the usual gang of suspects) as well as an assortment of more native bites (coconut split peas, for instance). It does make for a decent beverage stop: coffee, tea, sodas and more soothing infusions of Ovaltine and Horlicks. About HK$48 for two.
Open daily 9 a.m.-10 p.m. No cards.

McDonald's
**Star Center, 3 Salisbury
Rd., Tsimshatsui, Kowloon
• 3-7237727**

What can possibly be said about this place that hasn't been said already? Stepping into a McDonald's in Hong Kong is like stepping into a McDonald's in Anytown, USA. We can say that we're not surprised to have heard recently that the many McDonald's in Hong Kong do more business than any others in the world. Peopled just about equally with Asians and Occidentals (it makes you wonder about the future of the Chinese diet), the Salisbury Road branch is decorated in haute Hollywood, with movie posters, various other American iconography and marquee lights everywhere you look. And, truth be told, you really can't beat its french fries—they're a Proustian taste of home. Branches are found throughout Hong Kong. About HK$48 for two.
Open daily 7 a.m.-midnight. No cards.

Snap Foods
**Great Eagle Centre, Shop
101, Harbour Rd.,
Wanchai**

Snap Foods is a terrific little Indian fast-food outlet that's as inexpensive as it is tasty. You can get potato bhajis, pooris, delicious pappadums, samosas and curries. All are available individually or as part of a fixed-price lunch, which includes two meat curries, a pappadum, samosas, chapati bread and an iffy dessert called gulab jamun. Beware the rush at lunchtime. Snap Foods also does catering. Lunch for two is about HK$60.
Open daily 11 a.m.-6 p.m. No cards.

PUBS & WINE BARS

Brown's Winebar
104-206 Tower 2,
Exchange Sq., Central
• 5-237003

Real men may not eat quiche, but the financial types must, as evidenced by the lunchtime crowds at this agreeable little wine bar strategically located in Exchange Square. It would be best if you didn't mention the stock market crash here; instead, enjoy the good choice of wines and reasonable selection of foods. At lunchtime this place is full, but in the evenings it can be a little too quiet. (See also Bars in Nightlife.)
Open Mon.-Sat. 8 a.m.-midnight. All major cards.

**The Falcon Pub
and Discotheque**
Royal Garden Hotel
69 Mody Rd., Tsimshatsui
East, Kowloon
• 3-7215215

Located in the basement of the Royal Garden Hotel, the red-plush and darkly wooded faux-Victorian Falcon Pub serves lunch and dinner (it's big on roast beef). But the real deal here commences at the 5 o'clock happy hour, when a variety of bar sandwiches and salty snacks are served, and at 9 p.m., when, instead of turning into a pumpkin, The Falcon transmutes into a happening disco. Drinks and snacks for two will cost about HK$200.
Open daily 11:30 a.m.-2 a.m. All major cards.

The Gun Bar
Hongkong Hotel
3 Canton Rd.,
Tsimshatsui, Kowloon
• 3-676011

Despite its macho name, The Gun Bar is quite elegant, in a veddy British-Victorian fashion. Some bar snacks are served, but this is primarily an après–business meeting or après-shopping spot for patrons of the hotel and weary Harbour City shoppers, respectively. Snacks and drinks for two run about HK$150.
Open nightly 4 p.m.-2 a.m. All major cards.

The Kangaroo Pub
15 Chatham Rd.,
Tsimshatsui, Kowloon
• 3-7239439

An Aussie (and Brit and American) hangout, The Kangaroo offers the usual pub grub—chips and vinegar, sandwiches, meat pies—as well as steaks and other more hearty items. It's noisy and rowdy, and the food is really an afterthought—an excuse to order yet another pint of Foster's to wash it down with. The Kangaroo now boasts that it's currently serving breakfast (perhaps to the folks left over from the night before?). Drinks and snacks for two will cost about HK$200. (See also Bars in Nightlife.)
Open daily 8 a.m.-2 a.m. No cards.

The Tavern
Prince Hotel
Harbour City, Canton Rd.,
Tsimshatsui, Kowloon
• 3-7237788

As the name implies, The Tavern is a Brit-style pub, and the big deal here is the sandwich selection served at lunchtime. Though not state-of-the-art, they're not bad, and some of them are downright Dagwood-esque, such as the Gourmet's Surprise, which consists of smoked salmon, mushrooms, artichoke hearts and mozzarella cheese. One of the best, though, is the Tartar Broeth: steak tartare sprinkled with onions and capers on toast. Sandwiches and beverages for two should run about HK$100.
Open Mon.-Sat. 11 a.m.-11 p.m. All major cards.

White Stag Pub
72 Canton Rd.,
Tsimshatsui, Kowloon
• 3-661951

Just a hop, skip and jump away from Harbor City and set in the midst of a gaggle of hotels, the White Stag Pub is popular with both expatriates and visitors, due in no small part to the fact that it's open 24 hours a day. It's as smoky and abuzz as pubs are wont to be, and, as is usually the case, the drinks are better than the food. Hearty, basic sandwiches, meat pies, bangers and mash and salads are available—and the faces get ruddier and the voices get louder as the evening wears on. About HK$100 for a pub lunch for two.
Open daily 24 hours. No cards.

HOTELS

INTRODUCTION

The plain truth about Hong Kong's hotels is that they spoil you for life. Even if you're staying in a mid-price place, or even a link in the Holiday Inn/Marriott/Ramada chains, the hotels here are head and shoulders above those in just about any part of the world. With the possible exception of The Oriental in Bangkok, The Regent, on Hong Kong's Kowloon side of the harbor, is our absolute favorite hotel in the world. And from The Regent on down, you'll find the levels of service, decor and amenities to exceed your most wishful dreams. At the high-end hotels, guests are treated like royalty, and service is solicitous yet without being obsequious. And the quality of service doesn't dip all that much as you slide down the price range.

Make sure to take advantage of these services, particularly those offered by the concierges. They'll help you unravel the mysteries of Hong Kong's Byzantine back alleys, and they'll tell you where the best buys are. Need a massage (not *that* kind, though we're sure they're obtainable)? Poof, you've got one. Want a personal guide to the factory outlets? It's yours. Letters or documents translated? No problem at all. Never have we felt so pampered and well taken care of as in Hong Kong; it's a real shock to come home and turn back into the proverbial pumpkin again.

In recent years it seems like new hotels have been popping up as fast as mushrooms after a rainstorm; by the time you read these lines, at least a couple of new places are bound to have opened. The most promising hotel newcomer (still under construction as we go to press) is the Ritz-Carlton in Central. This large, opulent hotel promises a harbor view and the Ritz-Carlton's customary level of beauty, comfort and service.

Our reviews of Hong Kong's noteworthy hotels are divided into four price ranges based on starting rates for a single or double room: Top Dollar (HK$1,100 and up), Expensive (HK$750 to HK$1,099), Moderate (HK$500 to HK$749) and Inexpensive (less than HK$500). Please note that the four distinctions are based not on our evaluation of these establishments but only on how much they cost.

Our opinion of the comfort, service, decor and amenities of each hotel is expressed in a ranking system, as follows:

Exceptional

 Very good

 Average

 Modest

You'll note that just one of the hotels is distinguished with a red ranking symbol: The Regent. We have set The Regent apart because it is one of the world's two or three very best hotels. Its truly remarkable service, opulence, decor, views, cuisine and comfort earn The Regent a ranking above all others.

Keep the price range in mind when noting the ranking; a modest ranking is not good for a very expensive hostelry, but it's just fine for a budget place.

TOP DOLLAR

**Hong Kong
Hilton**
2 Queen's Rd., Central
• 5-233111

A Hilton is a Hilton is a Hilton, no matter where you are, but we must admit that the Hong Kong version is nicer than most. Quite large (758 rooms) and located near the Victoria Peak tramway, the Hong Kong Hilton is tastefully decorated, has an outdoor swimming pool (one of the few in Hong Kong), harbor views and five floors of Executive Rooms (which have their own reception desks), guests of which are served complimentary cocktails and breakfasts. The eight restaurants and bars serve Chinese, Continental, Italian, Japanese, Mediterranean and other international victuals; one of their number, the Hilton Grill, is fast becoming one of Hong Kong's very best restaurants (see Restaurants, Hong Kong Island). Service is ultra-professional and friendly.

Singles and doubles: HK$1,340-HK$1,680; suites: HK$1,900-HK$5,500.

Hotel Nikko

72 Mody Rd., Tsimshatsui
East, Kowloon
• 3-7391111

This new addition to the Nikko group, right next to the Holiday Inn Harbour View, may be a bit of a trek from the Star Ferry, but that's a small price to pay when you have such a panoramic view of Victoria Harbour. The Nikko, on the waterfront, is beautifully landscaped and extends excellent service. On the top two floors—the VIP Nikko Floors—all the suites feature Jacuzzis, and guests on these floors have access to a fully serviced business center, a fitness center and a rooftop swimming pool. French, Cantonese and Japanese restaurants (including the admirable Sagano; see Restaurants, Kowloon) are complemented by a coffee shop and lounge/bars.

Singles and doubles: HK$1,100-HK$1,950; suites: HK$2,800-HK$9,800.

Hyatt Regency

67 Nathan Rd.,
Tsimshatsui, Kowloon
• 3-662321

Just a few convenient steps from the Star Ferry, with its attendant shopping arcades and a subway station, is the theatrically glamorous Hyatt Regency, situated in the heart of the Nathan Road Golden Mile. Both the rooms and the hotel's lobby, slick and shiny with Italian and Spanish marble, are furnished in a sort of streamlined Chinese Moderne style. Large, with 723 rooms and suites on seventeen floors, the Hyatt Regency was one of the first hotels to offer business-class floors—in this case, two floors that comprise a sort of hotel within a hotel, accessible only by a keyed private elevator. These floors have their own concierge and the Regency Club Lounge (beautifully done in faux-bamboo woods and celadon upholstery), where you are served a complimentary Continental breakfast in the morning and gratis cocktails and hors d'oeuvres at night. The rooms are attractively decorated and have spacious marble bathrooms and computerized safes. There's also a recently renovated business center, four restaurants and two bars, and though there's no swimming pool or spa on the premises, complimentary use of nearby facilities can be arranged. But the rooms aren't cheap—especially considering the lack of the above-mentioned sports amenities.

Singles and doubles: HK$1,150-HK$1,350 (some "supersaver" rooms are available for HK$850 upon request); Regency Club floor rooms: HK$1,500-HK$5,000.

Mandarin Oriental
5 Connaught Rd., Central
• 5-220111

As international travelers and hotel cognoscenti well know, the Oriental Group of hotels (along with the Regent Group) are responsible for what are considered the best hotels in the world, consistently earning the highest ratings in various hotel surveys. The Mandarin Oriental is no exception. Designed in 1963 by a former movie-set designer (in fact, the ship's figurehead in the Clipper Lounge is a prop from *Billy Budd*), the Mandarin Oriental is lavishly yet tastefully beautiful, with rooms quietly decorated in neochinoiserie. The wonderful view of the harbor doesn't hurt either. But reputations are not made on looks alone. The staff is remarkable: attentive, even anticipatory, without being obsequious; they actually, as at The Regent, remember guests' names. You'll want for nothing here. There is also a remarkable array of amenities and services: a fully equipped business center, complete with computers, faxes, photocopiers and secretarial and translating services; a terrific health spa with a pool, sauna, whirlpools and masseuses; a tony shopping arcade; and some excellent restaurants and convivial bars. If you're planning a stay on the Hong Kong side, you can't do better than the Mandarin Oriental—it's pricey, but it's worth it. After all, how many times in your life will you be pampered like this?
Singles and doubles: HK$1,400-HK$2,200; suites: HK$3,300-HK$14,500.

The Peninsula
Salisbury Rd., Tsimshatsui, Kowloon
• 3-666251

The grande dame of Hong Kong hotels, The Peninsula is favored by diplomats, royalty and captains of industry. Established in 1841, it recently underwent a complete refurbishment. The lobby is truly grand, with soaring pillars, beautiful carpets and furnishings, a musical quartet playing on the mezzanine that overlooks the lobby, and the Lobby Lounge, which is *the* place to see and be seen for afternoon tea. The Peninsula's arcade of boutiques is home to the likes of Chanel, Kenzo, Louis Vuitton and Kent & Curwin as well as some excellent restaurants, including the legendary Gaddi's (see Restaurants, Kowloon). The rooms are large and the suites palatial, decorated in a country British–Raj style that's quite lovely, with such modern amenities as bedside TV and lighting controls, two-line telephones and powerful hair dryers. The suites come equipped with VCRs (videotapes are available from the hotel's library), and you can hire one of The Peninsula's Rolls-Royces on an hourly or daily basis. At this writing, the hotel had begun work on two new towers that will contain 425 rooms, business and fitness centers and a swimming pool. While The Peninsula lacks The Regent's spectacular harbor views (that blasted bowling ball called the Space Museum now blocks it), its superb amenities more than make up for this unfortunate loss.

Singles and doubles: HK$1,750-HK$2,500; suites: HK$3,400-HK$8,000.

Ramada Renaissance Hotel
8 Peking Rd., Tsimshatsui, Kowloon
• 3-3113311

The crown jewel of the three Hong Kong Ramadas, this large (501 rooms) hotel represents the Ramada chain's grab for the upscale guest in Hong Kong. This imposing structure is at the heart of Tsimshatsui's shopping and commercial district, and it boasts excellent conference and business facilities, including one room that proudly houses the only rear-projection audio-visual facility in Hong Kong. The service is crackerjack, and the six restaurants offer cuisines ranging from northern Italian to Californian; while not great, at least they represent a change from the usual gamut of hotel fare. The health club, at the top of the hotel (with great views, of course), has all the latest in exercise equipment—and even offers dietary counseling, certainly a first in the hostelry business.

Singles and doubles: HK$1,100-HK$1,600; suites: HK$2,200-HK$5,800.

The Regent
Salisbury Rd., Tsimshatsui, Kowloon
• 3-7211211

In almost any reputable survey of the world's great hotels, those in the Orient nearly always garner the highest ratings, with The Oriental in Bangkok and The Regent in Hong Kong often duking it out for first place. These two hotels will spoil you for life. While some pooh-pooh The Regent's ultra-modern looks, preferring The Peninsula's more stately grandeur, that's simply a matter of taste. In fact, the only fault we can find with The Regent is what we call The Last Mile—there's simply no dignified way to enter the hotel as a pedestrian. The fairly steep driveway is intended for automobiles, and maybe that's the point: patrons of such a posh establishment should disembark from posh automobiles—via foot is just too declassé. Toward that end, you can always rent a car from The Regent's fleet of Daimler-Benzes. Then revel in the sort of pampering that is near impossible to find these days. From the moment the young bellhops in their crisp, white uniforms and caps open the heavy glass doors for you, smiling and bidding you welcome, you feel like a pasha. The soaring lobby is beautifully furnished and burnished: all the woods, granite and glass are constantly being buffed to a high gloss. Elevators seem to arrive before you even ring for them (we've never had to wait more than five seconds for one), whisking you to your good-size room, tastefully decorated in muted colors and antiques. The bathrooms are luxurious: glassed-in stall showers big enough for two; deep, comfy tubs; toilets discreetly tucked away as adjacent chambers (complete with telephones, of course). Even the toiletries provided—full-size bars and bottles of Hermès soaps and shampoos, urns of aqua-blue bath salts, jars of cotton balls and swabs and a hair dryer—are first rate. Each floor is watched over by several butlers who attend to your every need. And in the evening, no paltry mint is placed on your pillow; instead, you'll find a plate of a dozen delicious chocolates from The Regent's own bonbonnaire. And if you're traveling on business, secretarial services are available, as well as computers and faxing facilities.

The Regent also houses some of Hong Kong's finest restaurants, including Plume, Lai Ching Heen and The Steak House (see Restaurants, Kowloon). And the luxurious spa is complete with saunas, whirlpool baths and masseuses. But it's not those amenities that keep us returning to The Regent: we're happy to just book a room with a view of the harbor, put on the fluffy terry robe and slippers provided and watch the ships sail by. Doubles: HK$1,400-HK$2,180; suites: HK$2,200-HK$13,000.

Shangri-La
64 Mody Rd., Tsimshatsui East, Kowloon
• 3-7212111

Opulent, expensive and wonderfully located (on the Kowloon waterfront, near the Star Ferry and many shopping possibilities), the Shangri-La recently became part of the worldwide Westin Hotel chain. Its seemingly ceilingless lobby is ringed with Chinese murals of epic proportions. But while this is most certainly a grand hotel, it doesn't have quite the same intimate feel that The Regent and The Peninsula, though also large, manage to accomplish. The spacious rooms are elegant if a little cold, and 24-hour in-house movies are gratis. At the nine international restaurants and lounges, as well as throughout the hotel, service is friendly and helpful—but, of course, you pay a hefty price for it. Other draws: some nonsmoking rooms, a complete business center, ten meeting rooms and a health club with an indoor pool.
Singles and doubles: HK$1,200-HK$2,100; suites: HK$2,200-HK$12,000.

EXPENSIVE

The Ambassador Hotel
4 Middle Rd., Tsimshatsui, Kowloon
• 3-666321

Location is certainly worth something, and with its terrific positioning directly off Nathan Road (and in between the Holiday Inn and Sheraton), the Ambassador is a fine, midprice place in which to lay your weary head. Moderate in size (313 rooms), the Ambassador boasts large, cheerful rooms with the customary amenities, and the youthful staff is eager and helpful. While there's not much in the way of frills to be found here, the hotel is comfortable and well priced for the location. The Cantonese restaurant serves dim sum daily; there's also a Continental eatery.
Singles and doubles: HK$880-HK$1,280; suites: HK$1,880-HK$2,880.

Excelsior
Gloucester Rd., Causeway Bay
• 5-767365

With a harbor view that peers down over the posh Royal Hong Kong Yacht Club, the mammoth (950-room) Excelsior, which underwent a sprucing-up a couple of years ago, can boast that it's constructed on the first piece of property auctioned off by the government following Hong Kong's colonization. But the Excelsior doesn't rest on its historical laurels. Its service is top-notch and its location excellent (near Causeway Bay's shopping and Wanchai's nightlife). For jocks, there are tennis courts, an in-house tennis pro and a driving range for golfers. There's also a fully equipped business center, the Talk of the Town disco and some fine cuisine at the Excelsior Grill. The hotel's Dickens Bar hosts live jazz on Sunday afternoons.
Singles and doubles: HK$900-HK$1,400; suites: HK$1,900-HK$5,000.

Furama Inter-Continental
1 Connaught Rd., Central
• 5-255111

The Furama was one of Hong Kong's first hotels specifically tailored to the business traveler, and for that purpose, it's very well stocked. There's a business center with private offices that can be rented by the day, secretarial services, translators, interpreters and staff members to assist in setting up local business appointments. And while the views are fabulous—panoramas of both the harbor and Victoria Peak (particularly breathtaking from La Ronda, the rooftop revolving restaurant)—the decor in the rooms is institutional, and the lobby is done in eye-popping shades of too-bright

oranges and golds. There are four restaurants, a bar, two shopping arcades and a friendly staff.
Singles and doubles: HK$1,000-HK$1,450; suites: HK$1,700-HK$5,000.

Holiday Inn Harbour View

70 Mody Rd., Tsimshatsui East, Kowloon
• 3-7215161

Basically a business person's hotel, the Harbour View is wonderfully located—hailing distance from the waterfront—with stunning views of the harbor. Though farthest from Central of any of the other area hotels, it's only a short cab ride (and not even a very long walk) to Kowloon's business and shopping centers, and the Harbour View has a pretty good shopping arcade of its own. The rooms are, well, Holiday Inn rooms—that is, functional, clean and formulaic. Like the Hyatt Regency, it has an "executive floor," which is reached by private elevator and which comes complete with a fully equipped business center offering secretarial and translation services, fax machines, typewriters, personal computers and a meeting room. Business sorts also appreciate the sauna and health spa, rooftop swimming pool and fitness room, five restaurants, the Golden Carp Bar, which features a live band and a small dance floor, the cake and confectionery shop and the Corner Delicatessen, a takeout spot that may have the best bread you'll find in Hong Kong.
Singles and doubles: HK$950-HK$1,650; suites: HK$2,500-HK$6,500.

Hongkong Hotel

3 Canton Rd., Tsimshatsui, Kowloon
• 3-676011

The Hongkong is a huge (789-room) link in the Marco Polo hotel chain. Slick and glitzy, the lobby is a popular meeting place for business people staying at the hotel, and its location—adjoining a maze of shopping malls, including Ocean Terminal and Harbour City, and just steps from the Star Ferry—makes it a magnet for those committed to serious shopping. Some of the quite pleasant, moderately priced rooms face the harbor, and others overlook a tropical roof garden and pool. Ten restaurants and bars are scattered about the Hongkong, ranging from the swanky Tai Pan to the Victorian-theme Gun Bar; also on the premises is a well-equipped health club. And if you so request, there are a limited number of nonsmoking rooms available—a rarity in Asia, where few seem to have gotten the message that smoking may be not only be hazardous to your health,

but hazardous to a room's aroma as well.
Singles and doubles: HK$950-HK$1,900; suites:
HK$1,550-HK$7,000.

Lee Gardens
Hysan Ave., Causeway Bay
• 5-8953311

While you won't drown in opulence here, the Lee
Gardens is a good journeyman's hotel. Though the lack
of a business center makes it an unwise choice for the
working traveler, its location, central to shopping and
with easy access to the MTR subway, has made this
hotel quite popular with tour groups (though it isn't
inexpensive). The Lee's rooftop restaurant, the Rainbow Room (considerably drabber than its Manhattan
namesake), serves excellent dim sum to accompany the
view, but the rest of its cuisine is dull; you'll fare better,
food-wise, at the Japanese restaurant in the basement.
Singles and doubles: HK$800-HK$1,200; suites:
HK$1,800-HK$2,500.

The Marco Polo
Harbour City, Canton Rd.,
Tsimshatsui, Kowloon
• 3-7215111

If you're a business traveler who doesn't want too many
distractions within your hotel, stay away from the
Marco Polo. This place is like the Grand Central Station
of Hong Kong. Located in the Harbour City mall, it
has a lobby that's crowded, noisy and cavernous, looking more like a futuristic transportation terminal than a
warm hotel lobby. However, the location is central to
transportation, shopping and business, and while the
rooms are nothing to swoon over, they are serviceable.
Extras include a business center, three so-so restaurants
and a bar. Although the Marco Polo offers neither a
pool nor health/spa facilities, guests have full access to
those at the nearby Hongkong Hotel.
Singles and doubles: HK$950-HK$1,050; suites:
HK$1,600-HK$4,500.

Miramar Hotel
130 Nathan Rd.,
Tsimshatsui, Kowloon
• 3-681111

Located in the Golden Mile, the Miramar was the first
hotel in Hong Kong to be designed in the ultra-con-
temporary International style, and it was all the rage
when it was built in the early '60s. It is still a quite
handsome place, though the gold-colored decor is a bit
much. However, it is in the midst of a major renovation,
so we are hopeful that by the time you read these lines
it will be toned down a tad. The Miramar caters to tour
groups and has no business center. But for the serious
consumer, there are four shopping-arcade floors and a
conference center. While the French, Cantonese and
Western-style restaurants won't thrill you, they're quite

serviceable.
Singles and doubles: HK$850-HK$1,250; suites: HK$3,000-HK$9,200.

Park Lane Radisson Hotel
310 Gloucester Rd.,
Causeway Bay
• 5-8903355

If you want to be smack dab in the middle of Hong Kong's shopping district, the Park Lane is perfectly located. Recently refurbished by Dale Keller, who is famed in this part of the world for hotel design, the Park Lane also overlooks Victoria Park. Its Parc 27 restaurant (see Restaurants, Hong Kong Island) boasts one of Hong Kong Island's best views. Business-center facilities are available.
Singles and doubles: HK$850-HK$1,450; suites: HK$2,200-HK$7,500.

Prince Hotel
Harbour City, Canton Rd.,
Tsimshatsui, Kowloon
• 3-7237788

If your lifelong dream has been to live smack in the middle of a shopping mall, you can make that dream come true with a stay at the Prince Hotel. Located in the aptly named Harbour City (more for the "city" part of the name than the "harbor" part) shopping metropolis, the Prince is midsize (401 rooms), has a rather glamorous white marble lobby and pleasant rooms featuring queen-size beds. A business-class hotel that is kin to the Hongkong Hotel and the Marco Polo, the Prince puts you right at the hub of Canton Road, shopping, the harbor, shopping, the ferry, shopping and, as a bonus, more shopping (as a matter of fact, this place would make an ideal recovery facility specializing in aversion therapy for shopaholics). There's no pool here, but patrons have access to the one at the Hongkong Hotel. And should you miss dining at the Prince's Western-style restaurant, don't worry, you're not missing a thing.
Singles and doubles: HK$950-HK$1,050; suites: HK$1,600.

Regal Airport Hotel
San Po Rd., Kowloon
• 3-7180333

It's doubtful that anyone's idea of a good time is staying at an airport hotel, but there are situations that necessitate such an action. And when it does, alas, it might be too late—the Regal Airport Hotel has become so wildly popular that it's usually booked to full occupancy. Not too long ago, when it was run by France's Meridien chain, this was rated the best airport hotel in the world by a business association (a dubious achievement, perhaps, but an achievement nonetheless). Now the Meridien is gone, as is its French cachet. Still and all, the rooms are fully soundproofed, airline information is available on your TV screen, and an air-conditioned conveyer-belt walkway leads directly to the airport (there's also a free shuttle service to the Star Ferry). Business center.

Singles and doubles: HK$750-HK$1,200; suites: HK$1,800-HK$5,000.

Regal Meridien Hotel

71 Mody Rd., Tsimshatsui East, Kowloon
• 3-7221818

Though at first glance the lobby appears to be a result of the Albert Speer school of architecture, the moderately priced Regal Meridien, which is partially owned by Air France, is actually quite attractive, neatly blending East and West in its decor. The rooms and suites are of a good size and decorated in muted tones and chintz, with attractive period furniture. Scattered about the place are a bar and four restaurants, including the superb Le Restaurant de France (see Restaurants, Kowloon), and the Regal Meridien often hosts visiting chefs from Europe. Nonsmoking rooms are available, as is a full-service business center. And, in a gesture that verifies that women are finally being taken seriously in the Asian business world, the Meridien has a women's-only gym and executive rooms for women. We've found the staff to be extremely helpful in setting up sight-seeing tours and trips into mainland China.

Singles and doubles: HK$900-HK$1,480; suites: HK$2,000-HK$6,500.

Royal Garden Hotel

69 Mody Rd., Tsimshatsui East, Kowloon
• 3-7215215

Located smack in the center of Kowloon, the Royal Garden is quite a dramatic sight to behold, built around a stunning atrium that features three levels of shops and soars upward for seven floors, with a lobby dotted with hanging and potted plants and ornamental pools. The hotel is also home to five restaurants, including the lavish art deco Lalique (see Restaurants, Kowloon); the Falcon Pub, which turns into a well-populated discotheque after 9 p.m.; and the terrific Fine Foods Delicatessen, a takeout shop that sells wines, pastries and other goodies. Another Royal Garden plus is the Business Centre on the third level, which provides secretarial, interpreting, research and photocopying services as well as a reference library and two private meeting rooms. When it's time to play, there's a health spa with sauna and massage facilities.

Singles and doubles: HK$950-HK$1,450; suites: HK$2,200-HK$4,500.

Royal Pacific Hotel and Towers
China Hong Kong City, 33 Canton Rd., Tsimshatsui, Kowloon
• 3-7361188

The recently opened Royal Pacific is part of the new Hong Kong–China/Macau Ferry Terminal megalopolis located on the Kowloon waterfront. And if you're looking for an intimate inn tucked away on a side street, this isn't the place for you. However, if you like being in the thick of things, you can't get much thicker than this. The rooms are quite nice, as is the service. The duplex tower rooms are luxurious, and there's a floor that boasts full butler service à la The Regent. Other Royal Pacific draws include: a full business center, Swiss- and international-style eateries (as well as a lounge and a faux-Parisian café) and a lovely landscaped area on the grounds that affords a commanding view of Victoria Harbour and Hong Kong Island.
Singles and doubles: HK$750-HK$1,600; suites: HK$2,220-HK$4,500.

Sheraton Hong Kong Hotel and Towers
20 Nathan Rd., Tsimshatsui, Kowloon
• 3-691111

Ultra-large (nearly 1,000 rooms) with an ultra-location (on the waterfront, at the corner of Nathan and Salisbury), the Sheraton is also ultra-swanky in an unfortunately ultra-Sheraton sort of manner: that is to say, the sum of all its parts doesn't quite add up to the elegance of The Regent or The Peninsula. The rooms, however, are surprisingly lovely, and there's a resort-like rooftop swimming pool, health-club facilities and a full business center. The arcade here houses 80 good-quality shops, and the two top floors, which make up the Sheraton Towers part of the name, offer such extras as complimentary breakfast, cocktails, personalized stationery and its own check-in area. You can take your pick among the Cantonese, Japanese and Western-style restaurants. After dinner, you can visit the cruise ship–style Pink Giraffe lounge on the eighteenth floor, which hosts wacky costume parties and theme nights for the not easily embarrassed.
Singles and doubles: HK$850-HK$1,700; suites: HK$1,800-HK$8,000.

Victoria Hotel
Shun Tak Centre, 200 Connaught Rd., Central
• 5-407228

Rather ultra-moderne, the Victoria's location in the Shun Tak Centre, which is part of the Macau Ferry Terminal, really places its guests where the action is. The hotel occupies the top fifteen floors of the center, and, of course, you never have to venture far to shop or dine—there are some 160 shops and restaurants in the complex. Prices are steep, but so's the view (an amazing one of Hong Kong Harbor). In addition to the business center, swimming pool and indoor tennis courts, the Victoria Club floor up on the 39th level, which comprises seven suites with access to roof gardens on the 40th, is popular with those who feel they deserve a splurge. The Western-style Bocarino's Grill serves commendable grilled dishes as its specialty (see Restaurants, Hong Kong Island), and the Dynasty offers above-average Cantonese food.

Singles and doubles: HK$1,000-HK$1,300; suites: HK$2,400.

MODERATE

Empress Hotel
17-19 Chatham Rd.,
Tsimshatsui, Kowloon
• 3-660211

Tucked away near Mody Road, yet still in the hub of activity (it's a short walk to upper Nathan Road), the European-style Empress is a simple yet charming hotel that, perhaps because of its location, is quite reasonably priced. Though not stacked with modern, luxury-standard amenities, the Empress does have a fair restaurant, the Mayfair, and many of its comfortable rooms have balconies with harbor views. The staff is friendly, and as we mentioned, the location is central to shopping, the business district, the Star Ferry and the subway.

Singles and doubles: HK$600-HK$950; suites: HK$1,500-HK$2,500.

Grand Hotel
14 Carnarvon Rd.,
Tsimshatsui, Kowloon
• 3-669331

About the best thing the Grand has going for it is location, off Nathan Road in the Golden Mile. The 1960s decor was updated a few years back, but it's still not going to win any design awards. However, the rooms are clean and cheery, and its main restaurant serves up quite a spread for its lunch and dinner buffets. And if you don't mind the lack of froufrou amenities (or the lack of a business center), the Grand provides good value for the money.

Singles and doubles: HK$520-HK$820; suites: HK$1,500.

Grand Plaza Hotel
2 Kornhill Rd., Quarry
Bay, Hong Kong
• 5-8860011

Another Hong Kong newcomer, the Grand Plaza is part of the Grand Hotel group, a glitzy contender in Hong Kong's ever-burgeoning hotel wars. The lobby is a vision of polished marble and white surfaces, with sweeping, circular lines, and the rooms are also quite handsome (there are 348 of them—moderately sized by Hong Kong standards—including the fully serviced apartment-style suites on the 18th through 22nd floors). The real attraction here, though, are the recreation facilities. On the ninth level is the Club Floor, which has a high-tech gym, an aerobics room, video-game room, four squash courts, heated indoor swimming pool, sauna, Jacuzzi and dual-purpose sports hall, which—get this—can be used as either a basketball court or a party room. And wait, there's more. The eleventh floor plays host to a mini–putting green and a jogging track, all landscaped with artificial turf. If you have any time to talk deals in between the sporting activities, there's also a business center. And when it's time to stop sweating and eat, you'll find Cantonese and Western-style restaurants, along with the Hideaway Bar, where you can get that Gatorade that you'll probably need after all that huffing and puffing. The Grand Plaza also provides a shuttle-bus service to Causeway Bay.
Singles and doubles: HK$680-HK$1,382; suites: HK$1,500-HK$2,800.

Guangdong Hotel
18 Prat Ave., Tsimshatsui,
Kowloon
• 3-7393311

Geared primarily toward Chinese travelers, the new, rather institutional-looking Guangdong Hotel is located within a few minutes' walking distance of the Star Ferry. The lobby is cavernous and rather cold, and the rooms on the lower floors tend to reverberate with street noise, so we suggest you ask for a room at the top. The restaurants here feature Japanese, Chinese and Western food, and there's a Chinese-language business center.
Singles and doubles: HK$600-HK$800; suites: HK$1,200-HK$1,700.

Holiday Inn Golden Mile
46-52 Nathan Rd.,
Tsimshatsui, Kowloon
• 3-693111

One of Hong Kong's busiest hotels, the Holiday Inn Golden Mile offers great location (right in the midst of shopping-intensive Nathan Road), terrific service and a lobby that, because it's so busy, is a great people-watching spot. The Golden Mile is also close to all manner of transportation—there's a subway entrance just steps away, the cross-harbor tunnel is nearby, and the Star Ferry is about a five-minute walk from the hotel. While it doesn't have its own business center, it does provide fitness facilities: the rooftop gym is complete with a sauna, exercise equipment and a pool, and the concierge has jogging maps if you feel like hitting the pavement (we did, by the way, and discovered Hong Kong to be a remarkable city at five in the morning: nightclubbers making their way home are joined on the streets by t'ai chi enthusiasts on their way to the many small parks). Though the hotel's restaurants (there are three of them, along with two bars) are mediocre, there's a branch of the Delicatessen Corner, which is actually quite good—tasty breads, sausages and sweets—and can provide the perfect sustenance for a picnic on one of the outlying islands.

Singles and doubles: HK$700-HK$1,280; suites: HK$2,300-HK$5,500.

Kowloon Hotel
19-21 Nathan Rd.,
Tsimshatsui, Kowloon
• 3-698698

New, glassy and modern, the Kowloon is operated by the same management as that of the venerable Peninsula and is, in fact, located directly behind The Pen. Conceived as a reasonably priced business traveler's hotel, the Kowloon features all the latest in high-tech hardware: each room has its own "telecenter," a sort of bastardized TV/computer that accesses preprogrammed files with airline, sight-seeing and tourist information—and it allows you to tap a key to get your phone messages. In addition, there's a fully equipped business center, a basement shopping arcade and fine Cantonese, Continental and Italian restaurants.

Singles and doubles: HK$590-HK$720; suites: HK$1,150-HK$1,400.

New World Hotel
New World Centre, 22
Salisbury Rd., Tsimshatsui,
Kowloon
• 3-694111

Though not nearly as luxe as its next-door neighbor, The Regent (but then, how many hotels are?), the New World does share many of the pleasures offered by its more affluent friend. It has the same breathtaking view, the same great location (on the harbor, close to shopping, the subway and the ferry), and, in fact, the two hotels are literally joined at the hip by the gargantuan New World Centre Plaza, home to some 400 shops, many of them quite au courant. This large (740 room) hotel also (surprisingly) encompasses a beautifully manicured 40,000-square-foot garden, complete with terraces and a rooftop pool. Other features include a business center, a couple of decent restaurants (the Continental Park Lane and the Panorama) and one of Hong Kong's most popular discos, Faces. So it's not

The Regent, but then neither are its rates, which are roughly half those of the monarch's.
Singles and doubles: HK$540-HK$1,450; suites: HK$1,300-HK$2,700.

Ramada Inn
73-75 Chatham Rd., South
Tsimshatsui, Kowloon
• 3-311100

This imposing, recently opened structure on busy Chatham Road is quite impressive: the lobby is lovely, filled with elegant furnishings and huge floral arrangements. And the staff bends over backward to assist guests. The rooms are decent in size, well appointed and tastefully decorated (though the bathrooms are rather cramped), and while not completely soundproofed, most of the ambient street noise—and it's considerable—is effectively filtered out. Of the eateries housed here, the garden-room coffee shop is the best. Business center.
Singles and doubles: HK$680-HK$960; suites: HK$1,600.

Windsor Hotel
39-43A Kimberley Rd.,
Tsimshatsui, Kowloon
• 3-7395665

This new hotel is the maiden hotel voyage of the China International Travel Service. Midsize (167 rooms) and midrange in price, the Windsor is close to Nathan Road, and while it lacks the more sybaritic amenities found in Hong Kong's fancier places, the rooms are pleasant, the service quite good, and there's a business center. While the Continental and Chinese cuisines served at the Windsor's restaurants are passable, they're more of a convenience than an attraction.
Singles and doubles: HK$700-HK$900.

ECONOMY

Bangkok Royal Hotel
2-12 Pilkem St., Yau Ma
Tei, Kowloon
• 3-679181

Cozy and tucked away on a side street, the Bangkok Royal is currently undergoing gradual renovation. Amazingly inexpensive and neat as a pin, its only real fault is its minuscule bathrooms. It's also noteworthy for the fact that it's home to one of Hong Kong's few Thai restaurants, which is quite popular. Helpful and friendly personnel.
Singles and doubles: HK$310-HK$580.

Caravelle Hotel
84-86 Morrison Hill Rd.,
Happy Valley
• 5-754455

About the most the Caravelle has going for it is its location just across the street from the Happy Valley Racetrack; if you play the ponies, you can't get much closer to them unless you sleep in the paddocks. Small (102 rooms) and utilitarian, with rooms in various scary shades of green, the Caravelle is inexpensive and has an attendant on each floor. And diehard racing enthusiasts will appreciate the rooms facing the track. We suggest passing on the hotel's Western-style restaurant—you're better off eating oats and lumps of sugar with the ponies.

Singles and doubles: HK$360-HK$420; suites: HK$450-HK$700.

Harbour Hotel
116-122 Gloucester Rd.,
Wanchai
• 5-748211

Well located (on the waterfront between Causeway Bay and Central), the Harbour Hotel is close to the Hong Kong Arts Centre, the Exhibition Centre and the Wanchai subway station. Popular with travel groups and Chinese businessmen, the Harbour is rather dull looking, despite a recent renovation, and after a while its small rooms can make you feel as though the walls are closing in on you. But the price is right for those who'd rather spend their dollars on duds than digs.

Singles, doubles and triples: HK$360-HK$720; suites: HK$900.

Harbour View International House
4 Harbour Rd., Wanchai
• 5-201111

Run by the YMCA, and rather chichi for a Y, the Harbour View occupies a plum spot right on the waterfront, next door to the Hong Kong Arts Centre. The rooms at this bargain-basement medium-size hotel are bright, clean and tasteful, and most face the harbor. Don't expect a lot of extraneous goodies here, but all the rooms are equipped with TVs, private bathrooms, radios and international direct-dial phones—just like a regular hotel. And the Western-style restaurant and coffee shop are quite adequate. If you're on a budget, but you want a room with a view, you could do a lot worse than this.

Singles and doubles: HK$385-HK$440; suites: HK$470-HK$560.

Imperial Hotel
30 Nathan Rd., Kowloon
• 3-662201

While beautifully located (on Nathan Road, within short walking distance of the Star Ferry and the Mass Transit Railway), the Imperial itself may lack glamour, but the tariffs are eminently reasonable and the spare yet comfortable rooms feature large bathrooms. Though the view actually offers more in the way of the

Ashcan School of Art than pastoral Turneresque vistas, we did get a taste of real life in Hong Kong by gazing through those windows and seeing laundry lines, people yammering in the streets and even picturesque stacks of trash. If you can reserve a room on one of the upper floors, however, you'll have a glimpse of the harbor. Western and Chinese restaurants.
Singles and doubles: HK$300-HK$780; suites: HK$1,000-HK$1,300.

Ritz Hotel
122 Austin Rd., Kowloon
• 3-692282

Although its location at the far edge of the Golden Mile isn't exactly prized by the sluggish (it's about a twenty-minute walk to the Star Ferry), the Ritz is a small, clean, well-lit hotel with just 60 rooms; it's has a loyal following of business people and value-conscious travelers. The personnel are friendly and helpful, and though the Ritz lacks glitzy accoutrements, all the basics are in place—and the tab is pleasantly low.
Singles and doubles: HK$290-HK$580.

Shamrock Hotel
223 Nathan Rd., Yau Ma Tei, Kowloon
• 3-662271

When the Lord decreed "Let there be light," the folks at the Shamrock took him quite literally. While this vintage '50s hotel is otherwise undistinguished, the lobby ceiling is encrusted with about two dozen chandeliers, making this place an ideal stop for those who fear darkness. Catering primarily to Asians, the rooms are small yet clean and comfortable. And prices are remarkably low. American- and Malaysian-style restaurants.
Singles and doubles: HK$350-HK$550; suites: HK$620-HK$670.

YMCA
41 Salisbury Rd., Tsimshatsui, Kowloon
• 3-692211

Don't laugh. The Hong Kong Y is situated on a prime piece of Kowloon real estate—on the waterfront, next door to The Peninsula–and it boasts a swimming pool, sauna, Jacuzzi, gym and tennis courts. The building itself is quite beautiful—it was built about the same time as The Peninsula and bears a more-than-passing resemblance to it. So it should come as no surprise to discover that the place is always packed; make your reservations at least a couple of months in advance. It may not be Hong Kong's most luxurious inn, but for the price and the unbeatable location, you can't do better.
Singles and doubles: HK$180-HK$330 (dormitory beds, for HK$65, are available but can't be booked in advance).

HOTELS BY REGION

HONG KONG ISLAND

Caravelle Hotel
Excelsior
Furama Inter-Continental
Grand Plaza Hotel
Harbour Hotel
Harbour View International House
Hong Kong Hilton
Lee Gardens
Mandarin Oriental
Park Lane Radisson Hotel
Victoria Hotel

KOWLOON

The Ambassador Hotel
Bangkok Royal Hotel
Empress Hotel
Grand Hotel
Guangdong Hotel
Holiday Inn Golden Mile
Holiday Inn Harbour View
Hongkong Hotel
Hotel Nikko
Hyatt Regency
Imperial Hotel
Kowloon Hotel
The Marco Polo
Miramar Hotel
New World Hotel
The Peninsula
Prince Hotel

Ramada Inn
Ramada Renaissance Hotel
Regal Airport Hotel
Regal Meridien Hotel
The Regent
Ritz Hotel
Royal Garden Hotel
Royal Pacific Hotel and Towers
Shamrock Hotel
Shangri-La
Sheraton Hong Kong Hotel and Towers
Windsor Hotel
YMCA

NIGHTLIFE

INTRODUCTION

After a frenetic day of work, there is nothing the citizenry of Hong Kong like more than a frenetic evening out, and this high-speed city happily obliges.

Unlike those in so many other lively cities, Hong Kong's hotels are attractions in their own right, especially after dark, when their restaurants, bars and nightclubs fill up with as many local residents as international visitors. Practically every hotel, from the modest to the world-class, has a popular nightspot of its own.

Outside of the hotels, Hong Kong is alive with every form of nightlife imaginable. Its colonial heritage means there are plenty of inviting English- and Australian-style pubs. Restaurants combining good dining and dancing or cabaret entertainment are somewhat rarer: the finest hotels are the places Americans and Europeans look to, because, although there are some excellent Chinese supper clubs with good food and music, these tend to appeal much more to the local taste.

The younger folk—Asian and Western—have a choice of discos, a few of which are favorites of the gay community, though Hong Kong's anti-homosexuality laws make these places a little furtive. Topless bars abound, but they are most often dreadfully tacky; the days of Suzie Wong are long gone, though there are a couple of bars in Wanchai named after her. At the top of the expense-account tree are the hostess clubs, some of which have their tables hooked up to a computer so that the women's time can tick away as if it were on a taxi meter.

For a casual evening stroll, the action takes place in Central around a network of roads known as Lan Kwai Fong. Numerous little restaurants have sprung up there in recent years, and there is a sprinkling of discos and folk-music clubs. Wanchai and Causeway Bay tend to provide the less-expensive forms of entertainment—everything from supper clubs to English pubs, pop-music concerts to girlie bars. Across the harbor, in Tsimshatsui, the tiny streets are also a joy to explore for just about any type of entertainment.

BARS & PUBS

The Blacksmith's Arms
16 Minden Ave.,
Tsimshatsui, Kowloon
• 3-696696

Nestled within the small network of streets running through Tsimshatsui, in the midst of some very pleasant little restaurants, stands one of the largest and, at the same time, most intimate of Hong Kong's English-style pubs. After entering through the heavy oak front door and negotiating some dangerous little steps, you'll find an odd, curving bar and numerous tiny tables, where you can enjoy drinks and hearty pub grub along with the many locals.
Open daily noon-1 a.m.

Bottoms Up Bar
14-16 Hankow Rd.,
Tsimshatsui, Kowloon
• 3-7214509

This basement place bills itself as having been featured in the James Bond adventure, *The Man with the Golden Gun*, and it's now so well established that it's actually become respectable. Topless girls sit at the small circular bars on high seats so that when they have to reach under the bar, the effect is pretty much as the name suggests. This is essentially a tourist spot, but the pricing is fair, and the place is tightly run by a very formidable lady.
Open nightly 4 p.m.-3 a.m.

Brown's Winebar
104-206 Tower 2,
Exchange Sq., Central
• 5-237003

Brown's well-rounded collection of wines and good, simple wine-bar food make it a good spot to know about when you're seeking an after-theater stop or a convenient meeting place. The atmosphere is quiet in the evenings, so it's a good place to talk.
Open Mon.-Sat. 8 a.m.-midnight.

Bull and Bear
Hutchison House, Murray Rd., Central
• 5-257436

In an unlikely location on the ground floor of a modern office building is this olde English pub with real Tudor wenches serving English draft beer, cider and good pub grub, such as bangers and steak-and-kidney pie. At lunchtime it's crowded with British expats doing things they would do at home—chatting up the waitresses and drinking too much beer. Evenings are a bit quieter, but still busy, with a lot of young Asians who were indoctrinated into pub culture while studying overseas.
Open Mon.-Sat. 11:30 a.m.-1:30 a.m.

Captain's Bar
Mandarin Oriental
5 Connaught Rd., Central
• 5-220111

Welcome to the wardroom. This is probably the only bar in town with a maître d'. But it's somehow appropriate in the Captain's Bar's plush, dark interior of old wood and leather. There's a terribly Mandarin atmosphere about the place (meaning superb, clubby service by the stiffly attentive captain and waiters, and the occasional *taipan* sipping at the bar).
Open daily 11 a.m.-2 a.m.

Chin Chin Bar
Hyatt Regency
67 Nathan Rd.,
Tsimshatsui, Kowloon
• 3-3111234

At lunchtime this spot is friendly and relaxed and presents a good buffet; evenings it is dark and full of tourists, business types and singles on the prowl. Chin Chin has only a vaguely Oriental feel—done in black leather, with occasional music playing. Although it's situated in the Hyatt's lobby, the bar feels totally independent of the hotel.
Open daily 11 a.m.-2 a.m.

Dickens Bar
Excelsior
281 Gloucester Rd.,
Causeway Bay
• 5-767365

This traditional meeting place for visiting business sorts has gone unchanged for many years. You'll find Dickensian prints on the walls and draft beer at the bar, which gets too crowded during happy hour. There is a large, overpopulated seating area, where Chinese waitresses—most of whom constitute more than a match for the ribald comments dished out from imbibing expats—serve the usual pub food. If you're lucky, you'll catch a jazz band playing. On weekends you can enjoy the popular curry buffet.
Open daily 11 a.m.-2 a.m.

Dragon Boat Bar
Hongkong Hilton
2 Queen's Rd., Central
• 5-233111

Many a daring scheme has been hatched, snatched or dispatched from the Dragon Boat. It's a hangout for American diplomats from up the hill, government types from down the hill, bankers from next door, journalists en route to or from the Foreign Correspondents Club, and the mournful ghosts of secret service agents. This bar is also an excellent primer for the venerable Grill Room next door.
Open daily 11 a.m.-1 a.m.

Godown
Admiralty Tower II,
Harcourt Rd., Central
• 5-8661166

Recently relocated after twenty years in the basement of a Central building that was actually demolished around it, Godown has changed its style from a murky but cozy jazz cellar into a modern-day London bar and chophouse. English-style beer and food are served to guests in comfy booths or at the long table in the center of the room, which is generally overhung by neckties that have collected there for some long-forgotten reason. The doorman, Mr. Chow, who spent twenty years standing at the head of the cellar steps in the original Godown, now has his Hitchcock-like profile on constant view cameo-style through the circular windows. You can hear live jazz on Wednesday nights starting at 9:30.

Open daily 9 a.m.-2 a.m.

Gun Bar
Hongkong Hotel
3 Canton Rd., Harbour
City, Tsimshatsui, Kowloon
• 3-676011

Come evening time, this is a business-person and tourist hangout, with comfortable seating, a small bar and colonial prints on the walls. It's a good launching point for a night out in Tsimshatsui. Outside, look out for sellers of brand-name knock-off watches.

Open daily 11 a.m.-2 a.m.

Harbour View Lounge
Holiday Inn Harbour View
70 Mody Rd., Tsimshatsui
East, Kowloon
• 3-7215161

The Harbour View Lounge serves as a cocktail lounge for the elegant Belvedere restaurant. And for anyone who thinks the Holiday Inn is only about butter sculptures and double beds, this place might change your mind. It's really pretty classy, with plenty of seating, a big bar and good singers. Informal yet respectable, it offers a wonderful view of the glowing harbor lights.

Open daily noon-3 p.m. & 5:30 p.m.-midnight.

Harlequin
Mandarin Oriental
5 Connaught Rd., Central
• 5-220111

At the top of the Mandarin Oriental, conveniently located next to the chic Pierrot restaurant, Harlequin offers a starry-eyed view of the harbor that is paralleled only by its sky-high prices. The pretty round bar serves a well-heeled crowd under intimate lighting.

Open daily 11 a.m.-1 a.m.

The Jockey
Swire House, 108A,
Connaught Rd., Central
• 5-261478

This comfortable English-style pub in the financial district has plenty of seating and a large bar. The decor is done in racing colors, with prints of horses on the walls; the ambience is enhanced by the occasional bray from watering stockbrokers. Good pub food is served; we were particularly impressed with the excellent pies, mounds of fries and draft beer. The Jockey is lively at lunchtime as well.

Open Mon.-Sat. 11 a.m.-11 p.m.

The Kangaroo Pub
115 Chatham Rd.,
Tsimshatsui,
Kowloon
• 3-7239439

If a real Aussie-style pub is what you're after, you've found it. The huge horseshoe-shape bar serves up plenty of Australian beers and hearty pub grub, including some decent steaks. (The same menu is available in the neighboring Windjammer restaurant as well.) Naturally, the clientele includes a hefty number from Down Under. Ask for beer by the schooner.
Open daily 10 a.m.-2 a.m.

Mad Dogs
33 Wyndham St., Central
• 5-252383

Outside, a huge bulldog sign invites you into this English-style pub on the fringe of fashionable Lan Kwai Fong. You'll get a real feel of a London hostelry in the small interior crammed with Victoriana and Edwardiana. Mad Dogs is populated with media and artsy types from the little publishing houses and design studios in the neighborhood. Draft beer and disappointing pub food await you.
Open Mon.-Thurs. 11:30 a.m.-1 a.m., Fri.-Sat. 11:30 a.m.-2 a.m., Sun. noon-1 a.m.

Someplace Else
Sheraton Hong Kong
Hotel and Towers
20 Nathan Rd.,
Tsimshatsui, Kowloon
• 3-7216151

This cozy Edwardian-style bar/restaurant is in the basement of the Sheraton, but it seems to have a life and identity of its own. The good, original dishes and low prices are especially popular with the younger set. The Chinese bartenders wear real English barrow-boy (street vendor) outfits.
Open Mon.-Thurs. & Sun. 11 a.m.-1 a.m., Fri.-Sat. 11 a.m.-2 a.m.

Yum Sing Bar
Lee Gardens
Hysan Ave., Causeway Bay
• 5-8953311

The dark, narrow, partitioned seating areas make this a nightmare of a place to meet someone, yet it still maintains its reputation of being a good Causeway Bay spot for friends to gather. A mixed clientele includes business people and a fair proportion of tourists staying at Lee Gardens hotel. Live music plays, and prices are fairly low.
Open daily 11 a.m.-2 a.m.

DISCOS

California
California Tower, 24-26
Lan Kwai Fong, Central
• 5-211345

This is the heart of the heart of Hong Kong's yuppiedom. A big bar at the entrance allows you to see and be seen; amid the clean white decor, TV sets show old movies, often with no sound. You can enjoy the dancing or order some bona-fide California-style salads or surf 'n' turf with a good California wine. The place is home to a modest sprinkling of gay clients and the smart Chinese set, many of whom were educated overseas. If you can't stand the hype, stay out of the kitschiness.
Open Mon.-Tues., Thurs. & Sun. 10 p.m.-1 a.m., Wed. & Fri.-Sat. 10 p.m.-4 a.m.

Canton
161-163 World Finance
Centre, North Tower, 19
Canton Rd., Harbour City,
Tsimshatsui, Kowloon
• 3-7210209

Canton's entrepreneurial owner has created a progressive disco that is one of the most successful of its kind. The dark, high-tech interior has mechanized objects hanging from the ceiling and dramatic dry-ice clouds on the floor. The crowd is primarily composed of the young Kowloon set. Prices are moderate.
Open Mon.-Thurs. & Sun. 9 p.m.-3 a.m., Fri.-Sat. 9 p.m.-4 a.m.

Disco Disco
38 D'Aguilar St., Central
• 5-235863

Old and established (in Hong Kong terms), Disco Disco was one of the first dance places in the Lan Kwai Fong area. It still attracts a mixed crowd: young folks favor it for its low prices, the local media/advertising crowd is also well represented, and it's a leading gay meeting place.
Open Mon.-Thurs. 9:30 p.m.-2 a.m., Fri.-Sat. 10 p.m.-closing varies, Sun. 9 p.m.-2 a.m.

Duddell's
1 Duddell St., Central
• 5-8452244

Duddell's keeps changing, but at our last examination the dimly lit, black leather–filled disco was downstairs in the basement, and there was a decent restaurant upstairs. The evening begins with financial types enjoy-

ing the long happy hour; then the small floor fills with dancers moving to the beat of live or recorded music.
Open Mon.-Sat. 11:30 a.m.-3 p.m. & 5:30 p.m.-2 a.m.

Faces
New World Hotel
22 Salisbury Rd.,
Tsimshatsui East, Kowloon
• 3-694111

This posh, trendy lobby disco attracts lots of socialites and media folks, yet it's surprisingly modest, money-wise. Public holidays are generally celebrated by pretty good deals on admittance and free drinks.
Open nightly 9 p.m.-3 a.m.

The Falcon Pub and Discotheque

See Quick Bites.

Starlight
Park Lane Radisson Hotel
310 Gloucester Rd.,
Causeway Bay
• 5-8903355

The hotel may have changed its name three times over the past couple of years, but Starlight just keeps on going as a popular nightspot. Lots of pretty lights dot the walls, and there's a quieter end where you can hear and be heard. The crowd tends toward the older, wealthier set.
Open nightly 5 p.m.-2 a.m.

HOSTESS CLUBS

China City Nightclub
Peninsula Centre, 67 Mody
Rd., Tsimshatsui East,
Kowloon
• 3-7233278

This blockbuster of a place has an art deco decor, good music and hundreds of women. For those seeking company and not minding how much time and money they spend (all tabs are computerized), this is the place. There are facilities for business gatherings, intimate parties, intimate anything. In fact, if you can't do it here, you can't do it anywhere—at least not without a credit card.
Open daily 6 p.m.-3 a.m.

Club Cabaret
New World Centre, 22
Salisbury Rd., Tsimshatsui
East, Kowloon
• 3-698431

Club Cabaret has more than 200 slinkily gowned hostesses of different nationalities, live dance bands and plush private rooms. A complete cross section of clientele is attracted to this classy place. Decent food is served.
Open nightly 6 p.m.-3 a.m.

Club Volvo

Mandarin Plaza, 14 Science Museum Rd., Tsimshatsui East, Kowloon
• 3-692883

Club Volvo is the most famous hostess club of them all, and it's easy to see why: a miniature Rolls-Royce transports the male guests to their tables, then countless (more than a thousand) females help them relax and spend their money after a hard day of earning it. Everything is on computer, from drinks to the number of minutes a woman spends with a customer. A large number of Japanese and local Chinese favor the club. *Open nightly 3 p.m.-4 a.m.*

New Tonnochy Nightclub

1-5 Tonnochy Rd., Wanchai
• 5-754376

A worn red carpet attached permanently to the pavement outside, and old-fashioned, solid Sikhs manning the door usher customers into a dark interior. It's nowhere near as flashy as some of the newer versions of hostess clubs, and it is frequented by an older, very Chinese clientele. But the place is well run, with lots of music and dancing and good Chinese food. *Open nightly 6 p.m.-3 a.m.*

NIGHTCLUBS

Casablanca

Marina Tower, Shum Wan Rd., Aberdeen
• 5-540044

On the south side of Hong Kong Island, overlooking Aberdeen Harbour, and a short distance from the floating restaurants, is this sumptuous nightclub. From the art deco elevators to the wide, sweeping staircase, ornate doors, Moorish windows and a huge sunburst design on the marble floor, everything speaks of style. Pink tablecloths adorn cozy seating alcoves with huge, decadent cushions. A good band plays to an eclectic crowd on the dance floor. Serving the predominantly grilled items from a limited menu are attentive, friendly waiters, who tend to be a bit gauche; they are inclined to giggle at minor mistakes—and so would you if you were wearing cute Arabian Nights pants and a bright little fez. Play it again, Chan. *Open nightly 7 p.m.-2 a.m.*

Eagle's Nest

Hong Kong Hilton
2 Queen's Rd., Central
• 5-233111

There's a terrific harbor view from this Chinese-restaurant-turned-nightclub. It's the place for Westerners who are a bit intimidated by the exoticism of some Chinese food. The restaurant is run very much along European lines, with engraved matchbooks and fine cutlery laying alongside chopsticks, and the food is

beautifully prepared and presented. A good place for a late supper or a view-enriched dance and drink.
Open Mon.-Thurs. & Sun. 10 p.m.-1 a.m., Fri.-Sat. 10 p.m.-2 a.m.

Ocean City Restaurant and Nightclub
New World Centre, 22 Salisbury Rd., Tsimshatsui, Kowloon
• 3-699688

Here you'll find one of the biggest and best of Hong Kong's traditional Chinese nightclubs. The interior is so dark you need a flashlight to find your seat. Once there, you can order from the good Cantonese menu, or, if it's just drinks you're after, you can order Black Label scotch or Cognac by the bottle and have it stored away, carefully marked, for your next visit (you can also order by the glass). The show features attractive Cantonese singers playing to a predominantly Hong Kong Chinese crowd, with the occasional Western tourist thrown in, also enjoying the music.
Open nightly 8 p.m.-2 a.m.

Ocean Palace Restaurant and Nightclub
Ocean Centre, 4th Fl., Canton Rd., Tsimshatsui, Kowloon
• 3-677111

Cabaret, Chinese classical dance and dancing to a live band are all on the bill at this huge and well-established spot near the Star Ferry terminal. You can order delicious Cantonese dishes, and there's no worry about a language barrier, since English is widely spoken here.
Open nightly 8:30 p.m.-2 a.m.

Pink Giraffe
Sheraton Hong Kong Hotel and Towers
20 Nathan Rd., Tsimshatsui, Kowloon
• 3-691111

From the moment you step into it, the Pink Giraffe has the feel of special occasion about it. Inside, a pink and blue decor with tiny lights set into the ceiling mirror the spectacular view of a sunset over Hong Kong's harbor. The food is award-winning, with a tendency toward nouvelle cuisine. The cabaret acts range from pleasant to raucous—the Pink Giraffe is often thought to stick its neck out just a little too far.
Open Mon.-Sat. 6:30 p.m.-1 a.m.

Talk of the Town
Excelsior
281 Gloucester Rd., Causeway Bay
• 5-767365

This upscale, high-priced, high-rise disco-turned-nightclub in the Excelsior hotel has a lovely view of the Causeway Bay Typhoon Shelter. It's the place to go for a couple of sunset cocktails accompanied by some nice piano music. Otherwise, the music varies from live bands to recorded music. You'll see an interesting erotic sculpture on the way in (watch how many guests turn around for a rear view).
Open nightly 5 p.m.-2 a.m.

SHOPS

INTRODUCTION

As is widely recognized, Hong Kong is the hard-core shopper's Valhalla, a legend among consumers—a legend in which reality actually dwarfs the tales spun around it. Perhaps the basic consumer lesson was learned from Hong Kong's genesis as an opium trader's port in the nineteenth century: give the people what they want, and they'll buy it in quantity.

Hong Kong is like a candy store for adults. Walking down Nathan Road, one is dazzled and seduced by window displays featuring heavy ropes of pearls, gleaming rows of Piaget and Patek Philippe watches, trays and trays of glittering emeralds and diamonds, and stereo equipment that could echo the sound of Gabriel's horn all the way to Madagascar. Wandering through the basement shopping arcade of The Peninsula hotel, you blithely pass in and out of such boutiques as Chanel, Prada and Louis Vuitton, boutiques that in cities like Paris and New York are forbidding but here in Hong Kong are somehow demystified.

Part of the psychology of shopping in Hong Kong (from the buyer's point of view) is that if there's so much of it, it must be cheap. Goods tend to be displayed en masse rather than treated like precious museum pieces. And this theory seems to work; someone who wouldn't dream of buying a Cartier Panther watch for US$4,000 in the United States thinks it's a steal in Hong Kong at US$3,500. And while you can purchase certain luxury goods for considerably less than you'd pay at home, it's easy to find yourself spending too much money on baubles and *schmattes* that under normal circumstances you'd never even consider. But that's the gestalt of Hong Kong. Something in the air fairly screams, "Buy! Buy! And buy some more!" And if you're at all susceptible to such exhortations, you may be in for a shock when your credit card bill comes.

You may be in for another shock if you come home and find that the amazingly low-priced string of pearls you bought is just a well-executed fake. We suggest you buy with caution and patronize shops that display the official Hong Kong Tourist Association (HKTA) sticker. These stores are recommended as "certified" by the tourist association and are trustworthy places to shop.

A note on Hong Kong's malls: they are not your garden-variety type, with two anchor stores and a couple of dozen boutiques. These are mutant malls from futuristic models that encompass hundreds and hundreds of stores, underground malls in which you could meander for days without seeing sunlight, malls that could make a marathon runner weep with exhaustion. But don't be daunted by such megalopolises as the Ocean Centre and the New World Centre—take them a section at a time. (In Hong Kong the true shopaholic is like a general mapping out his battle plan; nowhere else will your strategic skills be so vigorously tested.)

We've tried to pick the cream of the crop—an entirely inclusive shopping guide to Hong Kong would require many lifetimes and even more volumes to compile. We've selected a cross section of goods that are the most sought after by travelers and have limited our parameters to Kowloon and Hong Kong, although for the intrepid, there are many factory outlets in the New Territories (contact the Hong Kong Tourist Association for information on those outlets). The following should, however, keep even the most voracious shopper busy for many trips.

ANTIQUES & CRAFTS

Since the 1950s, when mainland China began what could be termed a wholesale divestiture of every vestige of its imperial past, Hong Kong has been a fabulous clearing house for Chinese antiques and artifacts. While the former flood of antiques from across the border has slowed to a trickle, there are still some real finds around and about—but caveat emptor. If you aren't knowledgeable about antiques, try to find a dealer you trust and ask to see what he has that isn't on display (the good stuff is usually hidden away). And do embark on your antediluvian endeavor with a sense of fun rather than grim acquisitive determination. The greatest concentration of antiques shops is on Hollywood Road. And don't forget to bargain.

Altfield Gallery
42A Hollywood Rd.,
Central
• 5-422138
1 Hollywood Rd., Central
• 5-237852

Altfield carries primarily excellent reproductions of Ching and Ming Dynasty furniture as well as Chinese rugs, prints and Thai silks from the world-famous Bangkok store, Jim Thompson. (Another branch is located in Central, at 10 Upper Lascar Row, 5-445688.)
Open Mon.-Sat. 10 a.m.-6 p.m.

Ancient Chinese Antiques
199 Hollywood Rd.,
Central
• 5-410183

This shop stocks a stunning collection of breathtaking Tang and Han pottery horses—all of which come with certificates of authenticity. These ponies don't come cheap, but even if you can't afford them, at least take a look at them—they're beautiful.
Open Mon.-Sat. 9:30 a.m.-5:30 p.m.

Helene Bennett Antiques
7 Hollywood Rd., Central
• 5-253333

Porcelain lovers wouldn't dare make a trip to Hong Kong and neglect to visit Helene Bennett. There's a wonderful selection of beautiful blue-and-white ceramics as well as antique furniture, ivory carvings, fine embroidery and Ching Dynasty paintings. The staff here is a crack one, knowing whereof they speak (and sell).
Open Mon.-Sat. 10 a.m.-5 p.m.

Cat Street Galleries
38 Lok Ku Rd., Sheung Wan
• 5-431609

A collective of dealers under one roof in the Cat Street area (once a trove of purloined and fenced artifacts), these shops offer antique furniture, paintings, jade, lacquerware, carpets and screens in a wide range of prices. The selection of porcelains is quite good.
Open Mon.-Sat. 10 a.m.-6 p.m.

China Resources Artland Centre and Department Store
China Resources Bldg.,
Low Block, 26 Harbour
Rd., Wanchai
• 5-8317988

Down the block from the Museum of Chinese Historical Relics, this center, which encompasses two floors, is a fine resource for both the novice and the expert. Goods range from inexpensive figurines and trinkets to very costly, very fine antique screens and sculptures.
Open Mon.-Sat. 10 a.m.-5:30 p.m.

Hanart Gallery
140 Hollywood Rd.,
Central
• 5-410941
28-30 Braga Circuit,
Kowloon
• 3-7118850

Old and contemporary Chinese scroll paintings are the specialty at the Hanart Gallery, Hong Kong's number-one gallery for these pieces. You can also find calligraphy dating back to the thirteenth century. Hanart is quite pricey, but it publishes a beautiful catalog, available for HK$200, so you won't have to go home empty-handed.
Open daily 10 a.m.-6 p.m.

Honeychurch Antiques
29 Hollywood Rd., Central
• 5-432433

This shop represents a great crash course in just about every aspect of antique chinoiserie: beautifully selected prints and books, jewelry, silver, furniture and porcelain. Prices range from reasonable to quite expensive, but Honeychurch's reputation is impeccable.
Open Mon.-Sat. 10 a.m.-5:30 p.m.

Jade House
1-D Mody Rd.,
Tsimshatsui, Kowloon
• 3-680491

An emporium of all things jade, Jade House has a voluminous collection of antique and reproduction carvings, jewelry, snuff bottles and figurines, some of which can be purchased quite inexpensively.
Open Mon.-Sat. 9 a.m.-6 p.m.

Kander's
56A-58 Hollywood Rd.,
Central
• 5-442215

Kander's isn't for the faint of pocketbook, but it is well established and reputable. A veritable department store of antiques specializing in Chinese paintings, Ming and Qing porcelains, and Neolithic-painted pottery, Kander's also provides consultations for the serious buyer wishing to start a collection, and for the novice buying for investment.
Open Mon.-Sat. 10 a.m.-6 p.m.

Ian McLean
73 Wyndham St., Central
• 5-244542

Ian McLean is probably your best bet if you're looking for eighteenth- and nineteenth-century Chinese furniture. And this most attractive and reputable shop also sells paintings and other artifacts. Though prices aren't bargain basement, you can rest assured that you're not getting any bogus booty.
Open Mon.-Sat. 10 a.m.-5 p.m.

P. C. Lu
The Peninsula, Salisbury
Rd., Tsimshatsui, Kowloon
• 3-688436
Mandarin Oriental, 5
Connaught Rd., Central
• 5-243395

P. C. Lu specializes in the finest Chinese porcelains, and the prices befit the upscale-hotel locations. However, you can depend absolutely on the authenticity of anything purchased here—this really is the crème de la crème of Chinese ceramics.
Open Mon.-Sat. 9:30 a.m.-6 p.m.

Pok Art House
Chong Tak Bldg., 18
Granville Rd., Tsimshatsui,
Kowloon
• 3-685930

Hong Kong's most established China-controlled arts and crafts shop, Pok Art House features both old and new Chinese paintings, antique carving rubbings and various other artifacts.
Open Mon.-Sat. 9:30 a.m.-6 p.m.

T. Y. King
Swire House, 9 Connaught
Rd., Central
• 5-236434

T. Y. King specializes in gorgeous Tang Dynasty ceramics and powerful, early-Chinese bronzes. And you'd better be prepared to part with a pile of shekels here—but not to worry: you get what you pay for, and the staff is quite knowledgeable about the merchandise.
Open Mon.-Sat. 9:30 a.m.-5 p.m.

Tong-In Antiques Gallery
Hankow Centre, 5-15
Hankow Rd., Tsimshatsui,
Kowloon
• 3-691406

Located behind the YMCA, Tong-In carries an astounding number of Korean chests, both antiques and antique reproductions of very good quality—and at very good prices. Also in stock are various knickknacks and decorative items, which the shop will ship worldwide.
Open daily 9 a.m.-7 p.m.

Y. F. Yang
163 Ocean Terminal,
Tsimshatsui, Kowloon
• 3-679474

If you're in the market for snuff bottles, both antique and reproductions, this is the place. Y. F. Yang is known throughout the world, and you're bound to find something in your price range.
Open daily 10 a.m.-6 p.m.

Yin Chuan Tang
29 Hollywood Rd., Central
• 5-438466

Tony and pricey, Yin Chuan Tang deals in very fine Chinese art and sculpture, such as a gorgeous gilt bronze Buddha dated A.D. 594. This is the place to come after you've made a killing at the gaming tables in Macau. It's also a great place to browse and get an education in chinoiserie—the staff is extremely helpful and knowledgeable.
Open Mon.-Fri. 11 a.m.-5 p.m., or by appt.

BEAUTY

Elizabeth Arden
Hongkong Hotel, 3
Canton Rd., Tsimshatsui,
Kowloon
• 3-669368
The Peninsula, Salisbury
Rd., Tsimshatsui, Kowloon
• 3-7239911

The Elizabeth Arden salons have the art of pampering down pat, and the Hong Kong branches are no exception. The entire line of Arden cosmetics and perfumes are available here as well as beauty services: facials, massages, hair cutting and styling and manicures and pedicures. (Other branches are located in Central, at the Lane Crawford House, 5-231266; and at 109 Repulse Bay Road, Shop G107, 5-8126151.)
Open Mon.-Sat. 9 a.m.-7 p.m.

Beautymed
Century Square, 1-13
D'Aguilar St., Central
• 5-2260169

Beautymed not only sells the Glycel line of skin-care products, it also offers a complete program of electronic impulses, massage, beams of light and other voodoo to combat the terrors of cellulite and wrinkles. Discounting all the fountain-of-youth hyperbole, the Beautymed treatment is a vigorous one, and you really do leave feeling refreshed and younger—and hopeful that it will last.
Open Mon.-Sat. 8:30 a.m.-7 p.m.

Body Shop Skin and Hair Care Products
M Group, 96 Nathan Rd.,
Tsimshatsui, Kowloon
• 3-7238610
Landmark Bldg., Pedder
St., Central
• 5-8101052

Our favorite shampoos, conditioners and skin-care products are by Body Shop and made in England. Generically packaged à la Kiehl's (at a fraction of the cost), Body Shop products are made from fruits, vegetables and herbs with very little in the way of chemicals and dyes, and they aren't tested on laboratory animals. While Body Shop goods are available in the United States via mail order or from the Body Shop boutique in New York, they're cheaper in Hong Kong (at various locations throughout the region), so you may want to stock up here.
Open daily 10 a.m.-7 p.m.

Erno Laszlo Skincare
Swire House, 9 Connaught
Rd., Central
• 5-213291
Park Lane Square, Shop
AR1010, 132-134 Nathan
Rd., Tsimshatsui, Kowloon
• 3-6811552

Although you don't really save money buying Laszlo products here, as opposed to in the States, at least you don't have to panic if you run out of pHELITYL lotion midtrip. And the Laszlo staffers in Hong Kong are particularly sweet and helpful.
Open Mon.-Sat. 9:30 a.m.-6:30 p.m.

Watson's
Melbourne Plaza, Central
• 5-230666
18 Carnarvon Rd.,
Tsimshatsui
• 3-8233802

This popular chain of discount chemist's shops, with branches all over Hong Kong Island and Kowloon, houses cosmetics and perfumes ranging from Max Factor to Chanel and Guerlain. There's always some sort of promotional deal going on. (We bought a 3.5-ounce spray bottle of Guerlain's L'Heure Bleu for HK$96—a steal.) And often, if you buy more than one of a certain item, the staff will discount them even further for you.
Hours vary according to branch location.

BOOKSTORES & NEWSSTANDS

Bookazine
Prince's Bldg., Shop 249, 3
Des Voeux Rd., Central
• 5-221785

A good selection of American and European fiction and nonfiction, periodicals and Hong Kong guidebooks.
Open Mon.-Sat. 9:15 a.m.-6:15 p.m.

Chung Hwa Book Company
450-452 Nathan Rd.,
Kowloon
• 3-856588

This large bookstore stocks both Western and Asian-language books (the English-language book section is on the third floor), as well as a gallery housing excellent reproductions of Chinese paintings from various national museums.
Open Mon.-Sat. 9 a.m.-6 p.m.

Commercial Press
9-15 Yee Wo St., Causeway
Bay
• 5-7908028

There's a lot to browse through in this three-story shop: English- and foreign-language fiction, nonfiction and children's books, stamps and stationery, a gallery featuring paintings by Chinese artists, and art books in English and Chinese.
Open Mon.-Sat. 9 a.m.-6 p.m.

Family Book Shop
313 Ocean Centre, Canton
Rd., Tsimshatsui, Kowloon
• 3-7227695
232 Harbour City, Phase
IV, Tsimshatsui, Kowloon
• 3-668308

The Family Book Shop chain offers the most comprehensive selection of English-language books, periodicals and guides to be found in Hong Kong. The best-seller list is inclusively represented, and there are also beautiful art and travel books as well as a wide selection of American and European magazines. Keep in mind that many new American hardcover books are published only in paperback in foreign markets, so you can get current *New York Times*–list tomes at quite a discount, both money-wise and weight-wise. (Other branches are located in the Prince Hotel lobby in

Harbour City, 3-7234008; the Star Ferry Concourse, 5-221012; the lobby of the Furama Inter-Continental Hotel, 1 Connaught Road, 5-8450563.)
Open daily 8 a.m.-9 p.m.

Government Publication Centre
General Postal Bldg., Central
• 5-235377

The publications housed in this rather scholarly bookstore have more information on seemingly every aspect of Hong Kong than you could possibly assimilate in a lifetime. Books, pamphlets, guidebooks and dissertations on art, customs, ethos, botanica and geography are available as well as material on Canton and Macau. This shop will hold great appeal for the serious traveler who digs into the deeper gestalt of a country, and if you're truly fascinated with Hong Kong (and how can one fail to be?), this shop is a real find.
Open Mon.-Fri. 9 a.m.-6 p.m., Sat. 9 a.m.-1 p.m.

Harris Books
Prince's Bldg., Shop 110, 3 Des Voeux Rd., Central
• 5-239498

This well-stocked, rambling bookstore carries a full complement of American and European fiction and nonfiction, and art and historical books on Hong Kong and China as well as Western magazines and newspapers. It also sells stationery and greeting cards, and the adjacent shop (Shop 114-115, 5-230243) is dedicated to children's literature.
Open Mon.-Sat. 9 a.m.-8 p.m.

Kwong's Magazines & Newspapers
Star Ferry Pier, Tsimshatsui, Kowloon
• 3-690893

Located near the entrance to Star Ferry Pier, Kwong's carries just about every major—and not so major—American and European publication available. There's barely a lag between publication dates and arrival in Hong Kong, even for daily newspapers, and if you can't live a week without the *National Enquirer* or the *Star*, you'll find those harbingers of hearsay here.
Open daily 8 a.m.-11 p.m.

Swindon Book Company
13-15 Lock Rd., Tsimshatsui, Kowloon
• 3-668033
Lantao Gallery, 249 Deck 2, Ocean Terminal, Tsimshatsui, Kowloon
• 3-673242

The Swindon chain covers much the same ground as the Family Book Shops, with a bit of an accent on nineteenth-century European literature. The additional location, 64 Nathan Road (3-662046), is heavy on stationery and periodicals, and the Ocean Centre shops (Shop 346 and 358) specialize in stationery and art materials (at Shop 358) and business, law and medical books (at Shop 346).
Open daily 9 a.m.-7 p.m.

Theatre Lane Stall
Theatre Ln., Central
• No phone

This outdoor stall (located parallel to Pedder Street, between Des Voeux Road Central and Queen's Road Central on Theatre Lane) has Hong Kong's best selection of magazines from around the globe.
Open daily 9 a.m.-6 p.m.

CARPETS & RUGS

As everyone knows, for centuries the Chinese have been famous the world over for their intricate, sumptuous rugs. When shopping for Oriental rugs in Hong Kong, as always it's best to know your stuff and not buy blindly. Do some research beforehand, and check prices at home so you'll be able to judge whether or not you're actually getting a good deal. Though there certainly are rug dealers in Hong Kong who'll try to pass off poorly made new rugs as priceless antiques, there are many highly reputable dealers as well. The following comprises a list of some of these:

Aristocrat Rug Co. Ltd., Star House, Room 624-626, Tsimshatsui, Kowloon, 3-671153; Banyan Tree, 311 World Finance Centre, Harbour City, Canton Road, Tsimshatsui, Kowloon, 3-7397425; Carpet House, Ocean Terminal, Shop 2168, Harbour City, Tsimshatsui, Kowloon, 3-673329; Carpet World, 31 Leighton Road, Causeway Bay, 5-8930202; Chinese Carpet Centre, 49-51 Hollywood Road, Central, 5-8153315; Chinese Rugs Co., New World Centre, Shop 77, Tsimshatsui, Kowloon, 3-7227713; Hwa Yee Carpet Co., 31-33 King's Road, North Point, 5-710597; Sunny Rug Co., 102 Austin Road, Tsimshatsui, Kowloon, 3-684938; Tai Ping Carpet Salon, Mody Road, Wing On Plaza, Tsimshatsui East, Kowloon, 3-694061; Tribal Arts & Crafts, 41 Wyndham Street, Central, 5-222682.

CLOTHING

CHILDREN'S CLOTHING

Ba Ba
Mainslit Bldg., Stanley St.,
Central
• 5-248889

This shop's a bit difficult to find but well worth the search. (To get there, walk up Stanley Street away from D'Aguilar Street until you get to the ladder-like stairs on the left, near 42 Stanley Street. Go up the stairs, and the Mainslit Building is the first office building on the left.) Small and located in an office building, Ba Ba carries darling cotton dresses, blue jeans, colorful separates as well as gift items and accessories, all at quite reasonable prices.
Open Mon.-Sat. 10 a.m.-6 p.m.

Children's Clothing Company
Landmark Bldg., Pedder
St., Central
• 5-8101094
MTR Station, Central
• 5-8450514

Very cute boys' and girls' clothing and shoes at painless prices (although some of the dressier items get a little pricey). There's another location in Kowloon's Ocean Centre.
Open daily 9:30 a.m.-7 p.m.

Junior
The Peninsula, Salisbury
Rd., Tsimshatsui, Kowloon
• 3-3117048

If nothing is too good for your kids, and money's no object, this is the place to outfit them—never will your progeny be more sartorially splendid. Carrying only the best in imported children's clothing (including très expensive togs by très chic Trussardi), the togs here are to regular kids' clothes what Armani is to The Gap. The dressy outfits are absolutely exquisite and sophisticated, while the casual things resemble Lilliputian versions of Kenzo and Yohji Yamamoto. This shop is a potential hazard to the pocketbooks of indulgent grandparents.
Open Mon.-Sat. 9:30 a.m.-6:30 p.m.

Kinder Kind
Swire House, Shop 111, 9
Connaught Rd., Central
• 5-8452942

Adorable—and expensive—clothes for babies and children. The styling here is ultra-hip/Japanese, and the shoes and accessories are irresistible. A must for the au courant child.
Open Mon.-Sat. 9:30 a.m.-7 p.m.

Milk Mary
Swire House, Shop 9, 9
Connaught Rd., Central
• 5-2126023
Kowloon Hotel, 19-21
Nathan Rd., Tsimshatsui,
Kowloon
• 3-686050

Though this shop sells adorable casual clothing for kids, the formalwear here is showstopping (and the prices heartstopping). It's quite possible to drop a couple of C notes on a frock—oh, but what a frock! Givenchy would weep with joy over some of these dresses and suits (including a little boy's cutaway out of white gabardine trimmed in gold braid); the workmanship and fabrics are first class.
Open Mon.-Sat. 9:30 a.m.-6:30 p.m.

CUSTOM-MADE CLOTHING

Having clothing custom made in Hong Kong can be either a source of great pleasure or terrible disappointment. Given the plethora of custom-made clothing shops for both men and women in Hong Kong, making a decision as to which tailor to use can be a daunting one. Some guidelines to go by include: the number of fittings the tailor requires (you should have at least two for a properly fitted garment, and we prefer three); ask to see some of his work (any reputable tailor will be happy to show it to you); and check to see how the seams are finished and what kind of linings and buttons are used. Don't be afraid to ask questions.

Also, beware of cut-rate, sidestreet tailors. We've found through personal experience that you really do get what you pay for. Your best bet are tailors in the big hotels: The Regent and The Peninsula, for example, or the tailors mentioned around town who are established and revered. You may pay a bit more than you would to someone in an alleyway, but the cost will prove to be well worth the result. These tailors generally speak excellent English, and they're also better versed in contemporary Western fashion and have a wider selection of fabrics to offer. And even though you won't get a three-piece suit for US$99, you'll be getting exactly what you want.

A word of advice: If you'll only be in Hong Kong a short time, make the visit to your tailor of choice first on your list. That way you'll allow enough time for the several fittings required. As a general rule, you should allow three to four days for the shop to complete the clothing or shoes you order.

A. Man Hing Cheong
Mandarin Oriental, 5 Connaught Rd., Central
• 5-223336

This one's been around for a long, long time, and has a well-deserved reputation for excellence. One can be fitted for a bespoke suit here that will rival anything on Savile Row.
Open Mon.-Sat. 9:30 a.m.-6:30 p.m.

Ascot Chang Co.
The Peninsula, Shop 6, Salisbury Rd., Tsimshatsui, Kowloon
• 3-662398
The Regent Arcade, Shop 107, Salisbury Rd., Tsimshatsui, Kowloon
• 3-678319

One of the best-known shirtmakers in the world, Ascot Chang (which recently opened a branch in New York) more than deserves its reputation for beautiful hand-made shirts produced from the highest-grade European shirtings available. It's too easy to blow one's clothing budget here.
Open Mon.-Sat. 9:30 a.m.-6:30 p.m.

Ash Samtani
Burlington Arcade, 92-94 Nathan Rd., Shop 1, Tsimshatsui, Kowloon
• 3-674285

Specializing in men's and women's suits, shirts and blouses, Ash Samtani offers excellent fabrics and workmanship at very reasonable prices.
Open Mon.-Sat. 9:30 a.m.-6 p.m.

Jimmy Chen
Hongkong Hotel Shopping Arcade, 3 Canton Rd., Room 208, Tsimshatsui, Kowloon
• 3-665045

This well-known, first-rate Shanghainese tailor excels in menswear, and has a voluminous selection of fabrics from which to choose.
Open Mon.-Sat. 9:30 a.m.-6 p.m.

David's Shirts
Wing Lee Bldg., 33 Kimberley Rd., Tsimshatsui, Kowloon
• 3-684368
Mandarin Oriental, Shop M-7, 5 Connaught Rd., Central
• 5-242979

David's is right up there with Ascot Chang: gorgeous, luxurious men's and women's shirts that would have caused Daisy Buchanan to forget Jay Gatsby's closet in a trice. (Another David's branch is located in the Royal Garden Hotel Arcade, Shop 108, 3-667092.)
Open Mon.-Sat. 9:30 a.m.-6 p.m.

Four Seasons Garments

Kaiser Estate, G1, 51 Man Yue St., Tsimshatsui, Kowloon
• 3-632218

This terrific shop never fails: It offers an exte[...] handsomely crafted wardrobe.
Open Mon.-Sat. 9:30 a.m.-6:30 p.m.

Shanghai Custom Tailor

Sheraton Hotel, Shop D8-9, Tsimshatsui, Kowloon
• 3-686980

We had a couple of skirts and a wool jacket made up here, and they turned out beautifully. While the tailoring isn't quite as refined as that of Ying Tai, it's excellent nonetheless.
Open Mon.-Sat. 9:30 a.m.-6:30 p.m.

W. W. Chan & Sons Tailor

Burlington Arcade, Shop 2F, 92-94 Nathan Rd., Tsimshatsui, Kowloon
• 3-669738

This shop caters to the businessman—if you're looking for a conservatively styled suit constructed of the handsomest, finest-quality European fabrics, you will do very well here. (There's an adjacent shop that specializes in shirts and womenswear.) Prices are high, but you get what you pay for; the workmanship and quality are impeccable.
Open Mon.-Sat. 9:30 a.m.-6:30 p.m.

Ying Tai

The Peninsula, Shop MW1-2, Salisbury Rd., Tsimshatsui, Kowloon
• 3-7230404

For our money, Ying Tai is the best tailor we've found in Hong Kong. It was recommended to us by a high-fashion model in New York whose husband does business in Hong Kong, so we knew whereof she spoke. We took a photograph of a Chanel blazer that retailed for US$2,800 and asked to have it copied. Our tailor took us to the Chanel boutique downstairs, where we surreptitiously studied that very same blazer—and he told us of the improvements he'd make on it. Five days and three fittings later, we had our blazer—made of cashmere instead of wool, lined in silk and fitted perfectly. The only missing elements were the trademark Chanel buttons—and about US$2,300 off the price. We were ecstatic, to say the least. We also had an Armani jacket copied from a photo, and it was practically indistinguishable from the original. Ying Tai also keeps your measurements and specifications on file (as most good tailors do); when you're back home, you can mail or fax photos or drawings of garments you'd like made, and

the finished product will be sent back to you. You can't go wrong here.
Open Mon.-Sat. 9:30 a.m.-6 p.m.

CUSTOM-MADE SHOES

Lee Kee Boot & Shoe Maker
65 Peking Rd.,
Tsimshatsui, Kowloon
• 3-674903
19-21B Hankow Rd.,
Tsimshatsui, Kowloon
• 3-666389

Although Lee Kee makes shoes for both men and women, it's in the men's department that it really shines (no pun intended).
Open Mon.-Sat. 10 a.m.-6 p.m.

Lily Shoes
Kowloon Hotel, Shop
B203, 19-21 Nathan Rd.,
Tsimshatsui, Kowloon
• 3-7396111

Hong Kong's best-known shoemaker, Lily can copy just about any shoe (don't let the tacky designs on display turn you off) you've been pining for at surprisingly low prices. Lily also makes handbags.
Open Mon.-Sat. 10 a.m.-6 p.m.

MEN'S CLOTHING

L'Atelier 36
82-36 New World Centre,
Tsimshatsui, Kowloon
• 3-697965

The well-priced trendy menswear at L'Atelier includes an excellent selection of Mandarina Duck's durable and whimsical portfolios, briefcases and carry-alls.
Open Mon.-Sat. 10 a.m.-6:30 p.m.

The Bohemian Shop
Prince's Bldg., Shop
101-102, 3 Des Voeux Rd.,
Central
• 5-268266

An excellent selection of Italian menswear, including Versace, Canali, Bagutta and Armani ties.
Open Mon.-Sat. 10 a.m.-6 p.m.

Cerruti 1881
The Peninsula, Shop
BW14, Salisbury Rd.,
Tsimshatsui, Kowloon
• 3-7392421
Prince's Bldg., Shop 3A, 3
Des Voeux Rd., Central
• 5-8106249

Paris-based Cerruti's menswear is drop-dead elegant—impeccably styled and executed. Sure it's pricey, but the tags read a little less than they do in the States. (Another Cerruti branch is located in the Landmark Building, Shop B19, Pedder Street.)
Open Mon.-Sat. 10 a.m.-6 p.m.

Comme Ça du Monde
New World Centre, B2-56,
Tsimshatsui, Kowloon
• 3-7212505

Going into the basement of the New World Centre is an experience somewhat akin to a journey to the center of the earth. But there's a slew of terrifically hip shops down there, and Comme Ça du Monde is one of them. This menswear is spiritually related to that of Commes des Garçons—definitely not corporate looking. Prices are quite reasonable for the quality you get, and there are also some nice sleek-chic accessories.
Open Mon.-Sat. 10 a.m.-6:30 p.m.

Emporio Armani
New World Tower, 16
Queen's Rd., Central
• 5-244407

The store's as great looking as the clothes. Armani's lower-priced "younger" line features excellent men's separates.
Open Mon.-Sat. 10 a.m.-6 p.m.

Jean-Paul Gaultier
Prince's Bldg., Shop G35,
3 Des Voeux Rd., Central
• 5-241688

If you're not the Matsuda type, then you're definitely not the Gaultier type. His womenswear, for all it's radicalism, is much more accessible.
Open Mon.-Sat. 10 a.m.-6 p.m.

Gieves & Hawkes
Prince's Bldg., 1 Statue
Square, Central
• 5-8451564
The Peninsula, Shop BE1,
Salisbury Rd., Tsimshatsui,
Kowloon
• 3-114362

Just about the next best thing to bespoke, this venerable Savile Row–based shop is known for its conservative, handsome suits, sports jackets, trousers and men's furnishings. Its 200-year-old heritage is strongly felt—these are solid clothes.
Open Mon.-Sat. 10 a.m.-6:30 p.m.

Givenchy Gentlemen
Landmark Bldg.,
Gloucester Tower, Shop
102A, Pedder St., Central
• 5-8100659

Trop gentil, mais trop cher. The shirts are worth splurging on, however.
Open Mon.-Sat. 9:30 a.m.-6:30 p.m.

He & She Boutique
Ocean Terminal, Shop
3251A, Tsimshatsui,
Kowloon
• 3-690780

A good selection of Italian menswear by names both familiar and unfamiliar, along with Versace accessories for men and women.
Open Mon.-Sat. 10 a.m.-6 p.m.

Daniel Hechter
Ocean Centre, Canton Rd.,
Tsimshatsui, Kowloon
• 3-7309882
Prince's Bldg., 3 Des
Voeux Rd., Central
• 5-8450281

Hechter's menswear, with it's swingy yet classical styling, great colors and easy look, has long been one of our favorites. These shops offer a good selection—and the prices are a bit lower than those in the States.
Open Mon.-Sat. 10 a.m.-6 p.m.

Jenlini
The Peninsula, Shop ML8,
Salisbury Rd., Tsimshatsui,
Kowloon
• 3-683613

Jenlini sells beautiful Italian menswear (with the focus on Brioni and Missoni) and one of the wildest collections of ties we've ever seen.
Open Mon.-Sat. 10 a.m.-6:30 p.m.

Kent & Curwen
Prince's Bldg., 3 Des
Voeux Rd., Central
• 5-8452782
The Peninsula, Salisbury
Rd., Tsimshatsui, Kowloon
• 3-697901

While not quite as grave as Gieves & Hawkes, Kent & Curwen also specializes in beautifully made British suits, cricket sweaters and the kind of loud, striped sports jackets that only career WASPs can get away with wearing. It also stocks, of course, a fabulous collection of regimental and school badges for blazers. And we musn't neglect to mention that both Kent & Curwen shops have amazingly delightful staffs: friendly, helpful and personable. Once you've been a customer, they'll remember you forever.
Open Mon.-Sat. 10 a.m.-6 p.m.

Kenzo
The Peninsula, Shop G4,
Salisbury Rd., Tsimshatsui,
Kowloon
• 3-7231694
Swire House, Shop
10A-11A, 9 Connaught
Rd., Central
• 5-236994

Kenzo's menswear isn't for wallflowers. It's graphic and bold and makes a definite statement. We prefer his womenswear.
Open Mon.-Sat. 10 a.m.-6 p.m.

Krizia Uomo
Landmark Bldg., Shop
242, Pedder St., Central
• 5-253655

Krizia's menswear is as rich-looking and gorgeously tailored as her women's clothes are: all soft lines and casual elegance. And, of course, the sweaters are fabulous.
Open Mon.-Sat. 10 a.m.-6 p.m.

Matsuda
Swire House, Shop 10, 9
Connaught Rd., Central
• 5-255686
The Peninsula, Shop 8,
Salisbury Rd., Tsimshatsui,
Kowloon
• 3-7238180

These fashions are for rich rock 'n' rollers and too-hip celebs and their adjuncts—you really have to be a certain type to get away with wearing Matsuda's menswear. If you have to wonder if you can, you probably can't.
Open Mon.-Sat. 10 a.m.-6:30 p.m.

Montana
Kowloon Hotel, Shop
B113, 19-21 Nathan Rd.,
Tsimshatsui, Kowloon
• 3-3113029
Edinburgh Tower, Shop
117, Queen's Rd., Central
• 5-2401467

If you're a banker or attorney, Claude Montana's stylized designs may not be for you (unless you ply your trade in the music or show business worlds). But for the adventurous guy who wants to make a bold fashion statement, you can't do much better than this. The fabrics and colors are rich and sumptuous; the tailoring

beautifully finished. Sorry, you're not going to save much of anything buying Montana in Hong Kong.
Open Mon.-Sat. 10 a.m.-6 p.m.

Pace
Landmark Bldg., Shop
212, Pedder St., Central
• 5-8612417
The Peninsula, Shop BL8,
Salisbury Rd., Tsimshatsui,
Kowloon
• 3-698640

Well-executed Armani knockoffs are sold here at very reasonable prices.
Open Mon.-Sat. 10 a.m.-7 p.m.

Polo/Ralph Lauren
Hotel Nikko, Shop E, 72
Mody Rd., Tsimshatsui
East, Kowloon
• 3-663912
Repulse Bay Shopping
Arcade, Shop G125-126,
Central
• 5-8126086

As contrived and derivative as we feel Ralph Lauren's womenswear is, that's how much we love his menswear. These shops are beautifully merchandised, and Lauren's shirts and ties are the most elegantly creative around. (Other branches can be found in the Hongkong Hotel, Shop G02, Harbour City, Kowloon, and The Peninsula's basement, Shop BW10, 3-7242833.)
Open Mon.-Sat. 10 a.m.-6:30 p.m.

The Swank Shop
The Peninsula, Shop W1,
Salisbury Rd., Tsimshatsui,
Kowloon
• 3-7215956
The Regent Arcade, Shop
R115, 118 & 119,
Salisbury Rd., Tsimshatsui,
Kowloon
• 3-7212793

Disregard the dated 1950s-sounding name; The Swank Shop is one of Hong Kong's most established and respected designer boutiques for men and women, though we think the men's department far outshines the women's. Hushed and plush, it contains the works of Ermenegildo Zegna, Valentino Uomo and Gianfranco Ferrè, among others. (Other locations throughout Hong Kong, including Ocean Terminal in Kowloon and The Landmark Building in Central.)
Open Mon.-Sat. 10 a.m.-6 p.m.

SHOES

See Leather Goods.

WOMEN'S CLOTHING

One of the first things that struck us about Hong Kong was how chicly the women dress. From teenagers in black, white and navy Yohji Yamamoto knockoffs to society women exiting The Peninsula at teatime in their Chanel and Armani, the collective effect is that of a colony in which sartorial style is carefully cultivated. Even if you don't want to spring for designer garb (and with the present state of the U.S. dollar, you very well may not be saving much by purchasing your Versace here), there are lots of local private-label and chain boutiques in Hong Kong in which you can be outfitted quite admirably, often for less than you'd pay at home.

Alma Boutique
The Regent Arcade,
Salisbury Rd., Tsimshatsui,
Kowloon
• 3-3115275

Falling stylistically somewhere between Versace and Escada, the Italian designs here are lovely—and pricey. *Open Mon.-Sat. 9:30 a.m.-6:30 p.m.*

Giorgio Armani
Landmark Bldg., Shop
202, Pedder St., Central
• 5-8456678

Yes, you pay a premium for Armani, but with Armani, you really do get what you pay for (not always the case with many other designers). Armani is a quality-control freak, and you won't find more beautiful fabrics, more beautifully cut and styled pieces and more well-thought-out lines in all of ready-to-wear. This shop carries a thorough sampling, and while you may not really be saving anything by shopping here as opposed to at home, perhaps you'll be more willing to indulge yourself as a traveler than as a citizen. If so, this is the place to do it.
Open Mon.-Sat. 9 a.m.-6 p.m.

Laura Ashley
29C Wyndham St., Central
• 5-245041

This shop houses the full panoply of Laura Ashley chintzes, ruffles and frills—clothes, home furnishings and fabrics—and the prices are a bit lower than they are in the States.
Open Mon.-Sat. 10 a.m.-6 p.m.

The Ballantyne Boutique
Landmark Bldg., Pedder
St., Central
• 5-235826

Gorgeous, and expensive, Scottish-made cashmere sweaters and accessory pieces by this world-famous knitter are displayed here. Prices are a tad lower than they are in the West, but be prepared to part with some serious dough nevertheless.
Open Mon.-Sat. 10 a.m.-6:30 p.m.

Billy Jealousy Boutique

Landmark Bldg.,
Edinburgh Tower, Shop
222, Pedder St., Central
• 5-250812
Prince's Bldg., Shop M12,
3 Des Voeux Rd., Central
• 5-237807

This small chain features a wide selection of midpriced sportswear, separates and dressy dresses, though its main draw is the extensive selection of Il Bisonte's hip Florentine leather goods, which are among our favorites. (Another branch is located in the Ocean Terminal, Deck 2, Shop 3251, 3-685844.)
Open Mon.-Sat. 10 a.m.-7 p.m.

Bogner

Ocean Centre, Shop
207A-B, 5 Canton Rd.,
Tsimshatsui, Kowloon
• 3-7236160
New Henry House, Shop
2, 8B Des Voeux Rd.,
Central
• 5-245333

For those of you who thought that Bogner just made ultra-posh, ultra-expensive, ultra-trendy ski and après-ski clothing, guess again. Bogner also has a line of ultra-all-the-above sportswear. Amusingly, the clothes here are as conservative and classic as the skiwear is wild.
Open Mon.-Sat. 10 a.m.-6 p.m.

Cashmere House

Swire House, Shop 110, 9
Connaught Rd., Central
• 5-221910

For those who luxuriate in cashmere but can't stand the stratospheric prices for this fine wool, the Cashmere House is a must. We may never forget the gorgeous cardigan we saw there for about HK$2,000 (US$250) comparable to the one we saw at Henri Bendel for about US$600. Styles are simple and elegant, and the wool is of excellent quality.
Open Mon.-Sat. 10 a.m.-6 p.m.

Chanel

The Peninsula, Shop E11,
Salisbury Rd., Tsimshatsui,
Kowloon
• 3-686879
Prince's Bldg., Shop 6, 3
Des Voeux Rd., Central
• 5-8100978

While the prices are slightly lower here than they are in the States, it's not by enough to induce you to purchase a US$5,000 evening gown if you wouldn't buy it at home. However, for smaller items, such as earrings, belts and the smaller handbags, it's another story—and, after all, you only live once. Isn't that why you're in Hong Kong?
Open Mon.-Sat. 10 a.m.-6 p.m.

Lily Chao

Landmark Bldg.,
Gloucester Tower, Shop
116, Pedder St., Central
• 5-8101579
Tsimshatsui Centre, Shop
168-170, 66 Mody Rd.,
Tsimshatsui, Kowloon
• 3-686762

Lily Chao is a popular local designer whose clothes are the antithesis of austere simplicity. You'll find lots of appliqués, leathers and feathers festooning the colorful fashions, which range in price from moderate to expensive. (Another Lily Chao can be found at the Focal Centre, Block A, 21 Man Lok Street, Shop 906-7, in Kowloon, 3-346769.)
Open Mon.-Sat. 10 a.m.-6:30 p.m.

Comme Ça du Monde
New World Centre, Shop
B2-56, Salisbury Rd.,
Tsimshatsui, Kowloon
• 3-7212505

This is one impressive shop. It resembles a miniversion of Los Angeles's hyper-hip Maxfield boutique, and features austere Japanese-made clothing and shoes, very much in the Matsuda/Commes des Garçons mode, at lower prices: beautifully made and styled suits, jackets and dresses.
Open Mon.-Sat. 10 a.m.-6 p.m.

Courrèges
54A Nathan Rd.,
Tsimshatsui, Kowloon
• 3-683433
Landmark Bldg.,
Gloucester Tower, Shop
G15, Pedder St., Central
• 5-233776

While Courrèges has lost the considerable cachet he had in the '60s among Americans, his name—and designs—are still to be reckoned with in European and Oriental circles. These spare, chic boutiques feature Courrèges' spare, chic, trademark styles, which remain quite innovative and handsome.
Open Mon.-Sat. 10 a.m.-6 p.m.

Les Copains
The Peninsula, Salisbury
Rd., Tsimshatsui, Kowloon
• 3-7233116

This conservative (and expensive) private-label sportswear and businesswear is extremely well made.
Open Mon.-Sat. 10 a.m.-6 p.m.

Christian Dior
The Peninsula, Lobby
Arcade, Salisbury Rd.,
Tsimshatsui, Kowloon
• 3-7237800
Landmark Bldg., Atrium,
Pedder St., Central
• 5-263964

While it is rather small and cramped, this shop does stock a little bit of everything Dior (except the couture line), up to and including an excellent selection of hosiery.
Open Mon.-Sat. 10 a.m.-6 p.m.

Emporio Armani
New World Tower, 16
Queen's Rd., Central
• 5-244407

We're big fans of Giorgio Armani's less expensive, more youthful line of separates and dresses—and this shop stocks quite a selection. The shop is gorgeous, the shopping fun and the personnel thankfully helpful.
Open Mon.-Sat. 10 a.m.-6 p.m.

Louis Feraud Boutique
Prince's Bldg., Shop 3A, 3
Des Voeux Rd., Central
• 5-248326
Ocean Centre, Shop 206,
Canton Rd., Tsimshatsui,
Kowloon
• 3-687323

A beautiful shop with beautifully elegant clothes. The showing of the line is extremely representative.
Open Mon.-Sat. 10 a.m.-6 p.m.

Diane Freis

Lamma Gallery, Shop
259D, Ocean Terminal,
Kowloon
• 3-7214342
The Regent Arcade, Shop
R109, Salisbury Rd.,
Tsimshatsui, Kowloon
• 3-7244190

A California transplant and current Hong Kong native, Diane Freis is without question Hong Kong's hottest designer, as evidenced by the proliferation of her frothy synthetic signature prints all over the territory, not to mention the cottage industry that has been carved out by her numerous imitators. If you love the Freis look, stock up here; the prices are quite a bit lower than they are in the States. (Among the many other locations throughout Kowloon and Hong Kong are: Prince's Building, Shop UG25, 3 Des Voeux Road, Central; and at the Connaught Centre, Shop 2B, Central.) *Open Mon.-Sat. 10 a.m.-6 p.m.*

Jean-Paul Gaultier

Prince's Bldg., Shop G35,
3 Des Voeux Rd., Central
• 5-241688

Along with Franco Moschino, the bleached-blond Gaultier is fashion's premier bad boy. His clothes are nothing if not extreme, although once in a while an elegant statement sneaks through his almost cruel (yet whimsical) bondage-inspired styles. You'll find everything Gaultier here, including sunglasses, valises and other small accessories. Beware of the major attitude that pervades this shop: we were received so frostily on more than one occasion that we vowed never to purchase anything from this place again. *Open Mon.-Sat. 10 a.m.-6:30 p.m.*

Genny

Landmark Bldg., 232
Edinburgh Tower, Pedder
St., Central
• 5-8454606
The Peninsula, Shop
BW2A, Salisbury Rd.,
Tsimshatsui, Kowloon
• 3-7244138

While we prefer Gianni Versace's eponymous line to the allegedly younger and slightly less expensive one he designs for the Genny label, you will find a fine selection of clothes and accessories here. *Open Mon.-Sat. 10 a.m.-6 p.m.*

Green & Found

The Peninsula, Shop W3,
Salisbury Rd., Tsimshatsui,
Kowloon
• 3-7215851
Swire House, Shop 11A, 9
Connaught Rd., Central
• 5-8104939

Green & Found specializes in up-and-coming European and Japanese designers, with an accent on original, iconoclastic clothes. You'll find Romeo Gigli (represented by both his own and the line he designs for Callaghan), Dolce & Gabbana and Martine Sitbon as well as shoes by El Vaquero and belts and accessories by Barry Kieselstein-Cord. Green & Found also carries a limited selection of Gianni Versace pieces. *Open Mon.-Sat. 10 a.m.-6 p.m.*

Joseph Ho

Landmark Bldg., Shop
101, Pedder St., Central
• 5-8612437

This is the main branch of a chain of shops that carry Byblos-esque private-label ready-to-wear. Though not cheap, the clothes here are extremely well made and

highly fashionable. The Landmark Building shop also stocks Yves Saint Laurent shoes. (Other locations throughout Kowloon and Hong Kong.)
Open daily 9:30 a.m.-6:30 p.m.

Yoshie Inaba
Prince's Bldg., Shop 5A, 3 Des Voeux Rd., Central
• 5-256613

Yet another shop in the Yamamoto/Matsuda mode, though not as extreme as either, Yoshie Inaba lists prices in somewhat the same range.
Open Mon.-Sat. 10 a.m.-6 p.m.

Joyce Boutique
Landmark Bldg., Shop 214, Pedder St., Central
• 5-253655
The Peninsula, Shop BW1-5, Salisbury Rd., Tsimshatsui, Kowloon
• 3-687649

Joyce seems to have a stranglehold on fashion in Hong Kong. Her empire includes not only these two shops (and the one mentioned below), but she's also the licensee for the Armani, Krizia, Genny, Missoni and Miyake boutiques, among others. If you're into fashion, these quietly opulent shops are a must. Among the lines represented here are Lacroix, Donna Karan, Mary McFadden, Vicky Tiel and Alaia for clothes, and Maud Frizon, Philippe Model, Judith Leiber, and Butler and Wilson for shoes and accessories. On our last visit we found prices to be about the same as in the States, but we did find some pieces (especially from Alaia) that weren't carried at home.
Open Mon.-Sat. 10 a.m.-6:30 p.m.

Joyce for Men & Women
New World Tower, 16 Queen's Rd., Central
• 5-270002

This is Joyce's shop for avant-garde fashion: Commes des Garçons, Romeo Gigli, Sybilla, John Galliano, Franco Moschino as well as other pioneers in the trade.
Open Mon.-Sat. 10 a.m.-6 p.m.

Kenzo
The Peninsula, Shop G4, Salisbury Rd., Tsimshatsui, Kowloon
• 3-7231694
Swire House, Shop 10A-11A, 9 Connaught Rd., Central
• 5-236994

If you're a Kenzo fan, Hong Kong's a great place to shop for his beautifully crafted, imaginative wares. These shops are almost miniature department stores, carrying everything Kenzo from hose and accessory pieces to coats and umbrellas. The Landmark Building shop (Shop B31, 5-8680274) in Central features the younger, less-expensive Kenzo Jungle line.
Open Mon.-Sat. 10 a.m.-6:30 p.m.

Krizia
Landmark Bldg., Shop 242, Pedder St., Central
• 5-253655

We're big Krizia fans, but we found this small shop disappointing due to a surprisingly limited selection of stock. You will, however, find a number of Krizia's distinctive sweaters here.
Open Mon.-Sat. 10 a.m.-6 p.m.

Matsuda

Swire House, Shop 10, 9
Connaught Rd., Central
• 5-255686
The Peninsula, Shop 8,
Salisbury Rd., Tsimshatsui,
Kowloon
• 3-7238180

These very beautiful, very Japanese-moderne boutiques are the exclusive enclaves of Matsuda's gorgeous clothes, which take their cues from feudal Japan, Edwardian England and 1940s Hollywood.
Open Mon.-Sat. 10 a.m.-6 p.m.

Issey Miyake

Swire House, Shop
107-108, 9 Connaught
Rd., Central
• 5-8101972

This minimalist boutique is home to an excellent selection of Miyake's wildly creative, retro-futuristic clothing and shoes for men and women. The merchandise may not be to everyone's taste, but if you're into Miyake, this is the ultimate showcase.
Open Mon.-Sat. 10 a.m.-6 p.m.

Montana

Kowloon Hotel, Shop
B113, 19-21 Nathan Rd.,
Tsimshatsui, Kowloon
• 3-3113029

This shop carries Claude Montana's elegantly contemporary– -and expensive—designs for men and women as well as some accessories.
Open Mon.-Sat. 9:30 a.m.-6 p.m.

Mosaic

Star Ferry Pier,
Tsimshatsui, Kowloon
• 3-7215279
Star Ferry Pier, Central
• 5-230733

There are probably more knockoffs of Diane Freis designs in Hong Kong than there are people to wear them; Mosaic is yet another purveyor of them. While some of the dresses and separates here have, shall we say, a decidedly cheap look to them, some are pretty difficult to distinguish from the originals, and they're sold at a fraction of the price. In addition, Mosaic seems have nearly perpetual sales. (Another branch is located in the Silvercord Building, Shop 203, 30 Canton Road, 3-696483.)
Open 9:30 a.m.-6:30 p.m.

Plantation

Swire House, Shop 3, 9
Connaught Rd., Central
• 5-237243

Plantation represents Issey Miyake's less pricey, sportier line. However, over the last couple of seasons, his designs for this line have grown increasingly quirky and idiosyncratic, which only narrowed the market for them.
Open Mon.-Sat. 9:30 a.m.-10 p.m.

Mila Schoen

The Peninsula, Shop E10,
Salisbury Rd., Tsimshatsui,
Kowloon
• 3-7231442

A great-looking shop with friendly help and an excellent selection of Schoen's sophisticated line of womenswear.
Open Mon.-Sat. 10 a.m.-6 p.m.

Sparkle
573 Nathan Rd.,
Tsimshatsui, Kowloon
• 3-849398

Sparkle was a real find: sort of a cross between Benetton and Esprit. The youthful sportswear here (and at the many other Hong Kong locations) is stylish and sinfully cheap. We bought a miniwardrobe (fitted cotton-jersey jacket, pants, skirt and rayon baseball jacket) for about HK$400. Such a deal! (Many, many other locations; call for further information.)
Open daily 10 a.m.-6 p.m.

The Swank Shop
The Peninsula, Shop W1,
Salisbury Rd., Tsimshatsui,
Kowloon
• 3-7215956
The Regent Arcade, Shop
R115, 118 & 119,
Salisbury Rd., Tsimshatsui,
Kowloon
• 3-7212793

This shop certainly lives up to its name. Among the designers you'll find are Ungaro, Ferrè, Soprani, Yves Saint Laurent, Valentino and Walter Steiger. But beware: Service can be too snooty here. (Look for other Swanks in the Landmark Building and in Ocean Terminal.)
Open Mon.-Sat. 10 a.m.-6 p.m.

Theme
Park Lane Square, Shop
AR1003, 132-134 Nathan
Rd., Tsimshatsui, Kowloon
• 3-7393986
Prince's Bldg., Shop M37,
3 Des Voeux Rd., Central
• 5-8106700

The predominant style here is young sportswear, most of it looking like Gaultier knockoffs. Both prices and quality are quite good. (Other Theme locations can be found throughout Kowloon and Hong Kong.)
Open Mon.-Sat. 10 a.m.-7 p.m.

Tokio Kumagai
The Peninsula, Shop BL9,
Salisbury Rd., Tsimshatsui,
Kowloon
• 3-7239633

For fans of modern Japanese attire, this spare shop sells Yohji Yamamoto–inspired clothes and shoes, which, while pricey, aren't as costly as the originals.
Open Mon.-Sat. 10 a.m.-6 p.m.

Toppy
New World Centre, Shop
G9, Salisbury Rd.,
Tsimshatsui, Kowloon
• 3-7218413
Ocean Galleries, Shop 287,
Harbour City, Tsimshatsui,
Kowloon
• 3-699185

Toppy features fairly inexpensive cotton-knit separates, à la C.P. Shades. There's lots of great colors, along with a good selection of accessories.
Open Mon.-Sat. 10 a.m.-6 p.m.

Twiggy
Ocean Terminal, Shop
015A, Harbour City,
Kowloon
• 3-7360568
Landmark Bldg., Shop
112A, Pedder St., Central
• 5-2576888

If you happen to be *enceinte* while visiting Hong Kong, or plan to be anytime in the near future, Twiggy has some of the most attractive and chic maternity clothes, at reasonable prices. The stock here runs the gamut from casual to dressy, in only the most current styles.
Open Mon.-Sat. 10 a.m.-6:45 p.m.

Gianni Versace
Landmark Bldg., Shop
G19, Pedder St., Central
• 5-215437

If you love Versace, that Italian master of elegantly sexy womenswear, you'll love this undeniably pretty boutique. And if you're lucky enough to happen to hit it during a sale, you'll be extremely pleased with the generous markdowns.
Open Mon.-Sat. 10 a.m.-6 p.m.

Yohji Yamamoto
Swire House, Shop 21, 9
Connaught Rd., Central
• 5-238423

For the adventurous and hip, Yamamoto's austere, almost somber sculptural styles don't have the whimsy of Miyake or the playfulness of Commes des Garçons— they're almost a pared-down Japanese version of Edwardian clothing. Yamamoto has a real feel for fabric textures and colors as well as draping; if the movie *Blade Runner* had been produced by MGM in the '30s, Yamamoto would've been the perfect costumer.
Open Mon.-Sat. 10 a.m.-6 p.m.

LINGERIE

Marguerite
The Peninsula, Shop ML6,
Salisbury Rd., Tsimshatsui,
Kowloon
• 3-7219021
Prince's Bldg., Shop
G31A, 3 Des Voeux Rd.,
Central
• 5-221738

These frothy boutiques carry several lingerie lines, but lean heavily in favor of the elegantly sexy stuff by Italy's La Perla. They also house a terrific selection of hosiery, swimwear and coverups as well as some accessories. (There are several other Marguerite locations throughout Kowloon and Hong Kong.)
Open Mon.-Sat. 10 a.m.-6:30 p.m.

DEPARTMENT STORES

Hong Kong has a wealth of department stores that cover many ethnic bases, including Chinese, Japanese and European. The selections in most of these (particularly the Japanese ones) make the selections in our native emporiums seem almost pitiable.

Chinese Arts and Crafts
Silvercord Bldg., Canton
Rd., Tsimshatsui, Kowloon
• 3-7311333

This chain of Chinese department stores presents an array of goods to satisfy both the tourist looking for inexpensive trinkets to bring back home and the serious connoisseur of antiques. There's also a large clothing department with a huge selection of silk and cotton garments, a wealth of artifacts, hundreds of bolts of

textiles and both Oriental and Western jewelry. Prices are reasonable, and you can be assured of the authenticity of items bought here. (There are various other Chinese Arts and Crafts locations throughout Kowloon and Hong Kong.)
Open daily 10 a.m.-5 p.m.

Daimaru
Fashion Square, Paterson
St., Causeway Bay
• 5-767321

Daimaru is actually two stores; one concentrates on furniture and household goods and appliances, the other on apparel. Trendy, throwaway Japanese fashions nestle near the haughtier European designers.
Open Mon.-Tues. & Thurs.-Sun. 10:30 a.m.-9:30 p.m.

Dragon Seed
39 Queen's Rd., Central
• 5-242016
2-6 Granville Rd.,
Tsimshatsui, Kowloon
• 3-7237201

Dragon Seed carries a good selection of Parisian clothes (including Emmanuelle Khahn and Claude Havrey) and all things European, including beautiful garden furniture, jewelry and personal furnishings.
Open Mon.-Sat. 10 a.m.-7 p.m., Sun. 10 a.m.-6 p.m.

Hong Kong Matsuzakaya
2-20 Paterson St.,
Causeway Bay
• 5-8906622

This isn't Hong Kong's most hotsy-totsy department store, but the housewares department is top-notch, with lots of imported china and silverware from Europe and the United States.
Open Mon.-Wed. & Fri.-Sun. 10:30 a.m.-9:30 p.m.

Isetan
20 Nathan Rd.,
Tsimshatsui, Kowloon
• 3-690111

Isetan doesn't take itself too seriously: it's a great store for those into forward fashion. But there's also a wealth of more traditional name brands here: Burberry's, Wedgwood, Aquascutum, Fendi, Kent & Curwen and Dunhill among them. Isetan is also a good place to buy Chanel makeup and perfume, since the prices are a tad lower than they are elsewhere in Hong Kong. This is the most eclectic and electric of the Japanese department stores.
Open daily 10 a.m.-9 p.m.

Lane Crawford
Queen's Rd., Central
• 5-266121
Mansion House, Nathan
Rd., Tsimshatsui, Kowloon
• 3-7219668

Posh and conservative, Lane Crawford has the air of one of the last bastions of British colonialism about it. While the atmosphere is stuffy and dull, you can get practically anything you'd find at Lane Crawford elsewhere—in fact, about all it really has going for it is an Elizabeth Arden salon and the convenient location. (Other Lane Crawfords: Ocean Terminal, Main Concourse, 3-7393393; and the Windsor House at Causeway Bay, 5-891052.)
Open Mon.-Sat. 10 a.m.-6 p.m.

Marks & Spencer
Ocean Centre, Canton Rd.,
Tsimshatsui, Kowloon
• 3-7303136

Or as the Brits call it, Marks & Sparks. As anyone familiar with London knows, this is really a low-rent department store. However, it does have a pretty good selection of inexpensive kids' clothes.
Open Mon.-Sat. 10 a.m.-8 p.m.

Mitsukoshi
Hennessey Centre, 500
Hennessey Rd., Causeway
Bay
• 5-765222

This is a beautiful store with beautiful goods. You'll find the top European designers here as well as a wealth of leather goods, jewelry (check out the watches in particular) and cosmetics.
Open Mon. & Wed.-Sun. 10:30 a.m.-9:30 p.m.

Shui Hing
23-25 Nathan Rd.,
Tsimshatsui, Kowloon
• 3-689181

The name may be Chinese, but the goods are strictly upper-crust European: Chanel, Aquascutum, Yves Saint Laurent, Gucci, Lanvin and more.
Open Mon.-Sat. 10 a.m.-7 p.m.

Sogo
545 Hennessey Rd.,
Causeway Bay
• 5-8338338

If you're staying on the Kowloon side, you can't miss Sogo's huge neon sign flashing across the harbor. Sogo is an upscale department store with a terrific selection of European designer fashions, shoes, electronics and cosmetics.
Open daily 10:30 a.m.-10 p.m.

Tokyu
Salisbury Rd., Tsimshatsui,
Kowloon
• 3-7220102

Tokyu's a lot of fun, and it boasts a great selection of women's clothes, including Kansai and Pinky and Dianne fashions. It also has a well-chosen housewares department stocked with lots of the modern Italian–style products by Alessi, along with an excellent European bakery and a specialty market.
Open Tues.-Sun. 10 a.m.-9 p.m.

Yue Hwa Chinese Products Emporium
301 Nathan Rd.,
Mongkok, Kowloon
• 3-840084

This is about as authentically Chinese as you're going to get: all manner of medicaments, acupuncture paraphernalia and herbal remedies are presented alongside traditional and contemporary Chinese garb and other goodies. Your dollar goes a long way here.
Open daily 10 a.m.-9:30 p.m.

ELECTRONICS & CAMERAS

God only knows what Hong Kong's collective electric bill is—outside of Tokyo, this is the most amp-intensive place in the world. The population here is obsessed with anything that plugs in, has batteries or carries an electrical current. Car phones are old hat; countless thousands walk around the streets with cordless phones. Heaven forbid anyone should be parted from a communications conduit for a single moment. Forget the old Polo Lounge trick of being paged or having a phone brought to you and plugged in at your table; in Hong Kong, folks bring their own phones to meals at even the swankiest restaurants. Add to that Hong Kong's long-lived and well-deserved reputation as the place to purchase electronics at a discount, and you begin to understand why it seems as though every other shop in Hong Kong carries more computers, cameras, Walkmans, stereos, video cameras and VCRs than was previously comprehensible to our Western brains. Needless to say, when shopping for electrifying elements in Hong Kong, patronize only stores that display the Hong Kong Tourist Association (HKTA) sticker. And make sure that what you buy is compatible with your country's current—don't wait until it's too late to attempt to rectify this type of mistake.

As is the case with Hong Kong's multitudinous jewelry shops, you could lose your mind trying to choose from the thousands of electronics and camera purveyors that pepper the streets of Hong Kong, most of which stock the same basic equipment (and if they don't, you'd better believe the salesperson will go out of his or her way to get you what you want). Here's an additional listing of noteworthy HKTA-approved shops:

Asia Photo, 5 Queen Victoria Street, Central; Brilliant Photo & Audio Supplies, 35C Cameron Road, Tsimshatsui, Kowloon, 3-7225055; Crown Photo Supplies, 14 Queen Victoria Street, Central, 5-245039; Kung Brothers Audio & Photo Supply Co., 117 Nathan Road, Park Lane Shopper's Boulevard, Tsimshatsui, Kowloon, 3-7237699; Realty Audio & Video Supplies, 71 Des Voeux Road, Wing On House, Shop E1, Central, 5-211620; Royal Hi-Fi & Photo Supplies, 30-32 Cameron Road, Tsimshatsui, Kowloon, 3-699137; System Technology (computers), 18 Harcourt Road, Admiralty

Centre, Shop 42, Central, 5-286669; TRP Consumer Electronics Ltd., 20 Des Voeux Road, Tak Shing House, Shop 902, Central, 5-223638; Union Laservision & Video Centre, Prince's Building, 10 Chater Road, Shop 239, Central, 5-216266.

A-1 Electronics
Hankow Centre, Shop
G20, 5-15 Hankow Rd.,
Tsimshatsui, Kowloon
• 3-666552

A-1 stocks an excellent selection of computers, printers and software (Toshiba, Apple, IBM, NEC, Maxell). Its choice of laptops is thankfully comprehensive.
Open Mon.-Sat. 10 a.m.-7:30 p.m.

Bang & Olufsen
20 Des Voeux Rd., Central
• 5-268800
Ocean Terminal, Shop
2120C, Tsimshatsui,
Kowloon
• 3-676844

These cool, high-techie shops carry Bang & Olufsen's state-of-the-art stereo equipment and the most modernistic, matte-black, angular televisions we've ever seen. B & O is a top-of-the-line product, and you're paying for its rep and quality—but you will save a bit by buying in Hong Kong.
Open Mon.-Sat. 10 a.m.-6 p.m.

Carlton Audio & Photo Supplies
80D Nathan Rd.,
Tsimshatsui, Kowloon
• 3-685097

We found the staff at Carlton to be particularly helpful. And it's a good thing, for the sheer amount and selection of goods here can be overwhelming. So just be patient and don't be afraid to ask questions. The good prices will make it worth the necessary effort.
Open Mon.-Sat. 10 a.m.-6 p.m.

Champagne Radio & Photo Supply
46 Carnarvon Rd.,
Tsimshatsui, Kowloon
• 3-679681

Champagne has a great selection of audio equipment, especially varieties of Walkman-type gizmos that seem to have come from a more advanced planet.
Open Mon.-Sat. 10 a.m.-7 p.m.

Delon Photo & HiFi Centre
Ocean Centre, Shop 323-4,
Canton Rd., Tsimshatsui,
Kowloon
• 3-7230528

Delon's forte is cameras and sound equipment: Hasselblad, Nikon, Canon, Aiwa, Sony . . . all the biggies. The more you buy, the more they'll bargain, but after the final outcome, this is a nice shop to do business with.
Open daily 10 a.m.-7 p.m.

East Asia Company
Tung Ying Bldg., 100
Nathan Rd., Tsimshatsui,
Kowloon
• 3-7234392

Another computer specialist: Casio, Commodore, IBM, Sharp and so on. The staff is knowledgeable, helpful and eager to make a deal.
Open Mon.-Sat. 10 a.m.-6 p.m.

Esquire
8 Cameron Rd.,
Tsimshatsui, Kowloon
• 3-685117
101 Chungking Mansion,
Nathan Rd., Tsimshatsui,
Kowloon
• 3-660018

Esquire carries all the latest audio, video and camera equipment by JVC, Panasonic, Sony, Technics, Minolta, Nikon—you're familiar with the litany. The staff can be brusque, but they are helpful and quite amenable to heated bargaining. (Another location at 216 Melbourne Plaza, 33 Queen's Road, Central, 5-233602.)
Open Mon.-Sat. 10 a.m.-7 p.m.

Fortress
Ocean Terminal, Shop
3281, Tsimshatsui,
Kowloon
• 3-7398628

This large, reputable store carries a wide range of small appliances, including TVs, stereos and telephones of every possible permutation. The staff is harried and hurried, but once you pin them down, they're quite helpful.
Open Mon.-Sat. 10 a.m.-6 p.m.

Francisco Camera Co.
Hyatt Regency Arcade, 53
Nathan Rd., Tsimshatsui,
Kowloon
• 3-671297

Nathan Road is chockablock with electronics and camera shops, and you really can't go wrong with any of the ones that sport the HKTA sticker; it simply boils down to a matter of personality rather than price or selection. The people in this shop were particularly pleasant to deal with, and the place stocks an amazing selection of lenses.
Open Mon.-Sat. 10 a.m.-7 p.m.

Golden Arcade Shopping Centre
44B Fuk Wah St., Sham
Shui Po, Kowloon
• No phone

This is off the beaten path for most tourists, but it's well worth the trip for the computer buff looking for a good deal. At this electronics bazaar, you can find rock-bottom prices here for IBM-compatible computers, software and printers. There are more than 100 shops here, none of which are much different from their counterparts—just buy from whichever one you feel most comfortable with.
Open Mon.-Sat. 10 a.m.-7 p.m.

Javys-Casio
Ocean Galleries, Shop 313,
Harbour City, Canton Rd.,
Tsimshatsui, Kowloon
• 3-665343

You'll find all things Casio here, from calculators to keyboards, at very good prices.
Open Mon.-Sat. 10 a.m.-6:30 p.m.

Mark's Photo Supplies
20 Des Voeux Rd., Central
• 5-235273

This shop has been around for nearly twenty years, during which time it has maintained a good reputation for selection, quality and service. There is an excellent variety of all things photographic, and the staff is just as helpful and friendly to those buying a roll of film as to those stocking up on Nikons.
Open Mon.-Sat. 10 a.m.-7:30 p.m.

Tung Shing Trading Co.
Houston Centre, Shop
279, 63 Mody Rd.,
Tsimshatsui East, Kowloon
• 3-680361

A great place to shop for personal computers, Tung Shing provides the opportunity to make a very good deal. If staff members may try to push you an off-brand, just stand firm on what you want.
Open Mon.-Sat. 10 a.m.-8 p.m.

FABRICS, SILKS & LINENS

There are a couple of streetside fabric bazaars in Hong Kong that are the finest places to shop for dry goods: the Lanes, which is just off the Lane Crawford department store on Queen's Road Central, and on Wing On Street, past the Central Market near Graham Street (just ask the concierge at your hotel, or contact the Hong Kong Tourist Association for more precise directions). The following are excellent shops as well.

Hang Kong Woolen
Cammer Commercial
Bldg., 30-32 Cameron
Rd., Tsimshatsui, Kowloon
• 3-7213560

This is an excellent source for men's suiting fabrics, offering everything from lightweight gabardines to tweeds.
Open Mon.-Sat. 9:30 a.m.-6:30 p.m.

Old Peking Silk Co.
219B Nathan Rd.,
Tsimshatsui, Kowloon
• 3-663037

This shop's been around for quite a while, and it carries a breathtaking rainbow of Chinese and European silks of every imaginable weight, texture and color.
Open Mon.-Sat. 9:30 a.m.-6 p.m.

Shing Fung Co.
11 On Lan St., Central
• 5-2300668

A dark, warehousey place on a quiet street, Shing Fung is an outstanding source for fine linen and embroidery. It claims its embroidery is hand done; we aren't completely sure of that, but we can say that the craftsmanship is exceptional and the prices eminently reasonable. A must for aficionados of high-quality bed, bath and kitchen linens.
Open Mon.-Sat. 10 a.m.-6 p.m.

Wah Sing Lace
7 On Lan St., Central
• 5-222981

Another good, reputable source for fine linens, lace and embroidery. The merchandise here doesn't stand out

as much as Shing Fung's, but it's still sure to have something you can't live without.
Open Mon.-Sat. 10 a.m.-6 p.m.

FACTORY OUTLETS

Shopping in Hong Kong's factory outlets can be either a joy or a headache, fraught with both bargains and rip-offs. While you can get some real steals in legitimate designer lines, such as Diane Freis and Krizia knits, there are vendors who pass off bogus goods and definitely subscribe to P. T. Barnum's dictum about suckers. But while there are outlets that have no compunctions about selling defective goods for more than you'd pay for them in a shop, there are quite a few worthy ones that merit a visit. For the definitive guide to Hong Kong's outlets, pick up a copy of Dana Goetz's *Hong Kong Factory Bargains.* And when you do buy in factory outlets, make sure to check your items closely—and try them on—before making your final decision, since there are no refunds or returns.

CHINA, CRYSTAL & GIFTS

Ah Chow Porcelain
Hong Kong Industrial Centre, Block B, 489 Castle Peak Rd., Lai Chi Kok, Kowloon
• 3-7450209

If you drool when you browse through the Horchow catalog, you'll be in seventh heaven here. Ah Chow's merchandise can be found in those very pages as well as in many tony U.S. department stores and china shops. While you'll find a plethora of china, ceramics, lamps and gifts done in Oriental motifs, you can have any china pattern you desire copied or designed. This really is a marvelous outlet, and you can buy gift items for as little as HK$20.
Open Mon.-Sat. 10 a.m.-7 p.m.

Overjoy Porcelain
Kwai Hing Industrial Bldg., 10-18 Chun Pin St., Kwai Chung, Kowloon
• 0-4870615

Quite similar to Ah Chow, Overjoy stocks thousands of items, from tiny knickknacks to entire dinner services and gigantic vases. As at Ah Chow, you can also design your own china pattern, and deliveries are made to anywhere in the United States. Prices range from about HK$30 to HK$2,000.
Open Mon.-Sat. 9 a.m.-6 p.m.

CLOTHING

A-Win
23 Granville Rd.,
Tsimshatsui, Kowloon
• 3-697070

A-Win can't be beat for fashionable, casual, inexpensive clothes. Most of the goods here, for adults and teenagers, are very Esprit-esque, ranging from dresses and separates to jeans and even some skiwear. Prices are blissfully low, running from about HK$50 to HK$200. *Open Mon.-Sat. 11 a.m.-8:30 p.m., Sun. 11 a.m.-7:30 p.m.*

Ça Va
Star House, 3 Salisbury
Rd., Tsimshatsui, Kowloon
• 3-7231922

Although the prices here aren't quite bargain-basement range (about HK$300 to HK$1,000), Ça Va's wide selection of women's designer linen and cotton separates, wool blazers, gabardine suits and sweaters is an excellent one. The fashions sell for less than what you'd pay in a boutique.
Open Mon.-Sat. 10 a.m.-6 p.m.

Camberley
Swire House, 9 Connaught
Rd., Central
• 5-246264

This outlet (a licensee of Anne Klein II), in the très chichi Swire House, is quite tony. You'll find the current Anne Klein line, instead of rejects from four seasons back. Prices are most reasonable, ranging from about HK$250 to HK$700. A must for fans of the line.
Open Mon.-Sat. 9 a.m.-6 p.m.

Lily Chao
Focal Industrial Centre,
Block A, 21 Man Lok St.,
Hung Hom, Kowloon
• 3-346769

Hong Kong's female shopping mavens are familiar with Lily Chao's elegant Hong Kong boutiques. But if you don't mind trekking to this decidedly bizarre location (on the ninth floor yet), you can get some great deals on some very fancy clothes. If you're into minimalists like Yohji Yamamoto or Romeo Gigli, Chao's designs will be anathema to you, because her dresses, suits, separates and eveningwear are of the ornate variety, adorned with embroidery, appliqués, sequins and suede rosettes—what Angelenos call the Encino Look. You'll spend some dough (prices start at about HK$300), but less than you'd spend in a Lily Chao boutique.
Open daily 9 a.m.-6 p.m.

Dorfit
Shui Hing House, 23-25
Nathan Rd., Tsimshatsui,
Kowloon
• 3-7390770

Yet another sweatermonger, Dorfit has a selection that isn't as voluminous as that of Oriental Pacific or Top Knitters, but what there is is choice. Great cashmere, lambswool and cotton sweaters for men, women and kids, as well as some women's separates and dresses. And you can't beat the prices: HK$80 to HK$600.
Open Mon.-Sat. 9 a.m.-6 p.m.

___e
Kaiser Estate, Block A1, 21
Man Yue St., Hung Hom,
Kowloon
• 3-344218

Don't be discouraged when you walk into this plain-wrap clothing outlet—you can find some real treasures here, though it's pretty hit-and-miss. Every once in a while, some ladies' designer sportswear goodies pop up that are oh-so au courant, but you really have to dig and be discerning.
Open Mon.-Sat. 9:30 a.m.-6:30 p.m.

Fashions of Seventh Avenue
Kaiser Estate, Block M,
Hok Yuen St., Hung Hom,
Kowloon
• 3-659061

If you're a fan of Donna Karan, run, don't walk, to this outlet. Prices are dirt cheap (about HK$700 to HK$1,000), but savvy shoppers patrol this place regularly, stripping it clean after each shipment arrival. Stock up here on knit body suits, skirts, cardigans and trousers.
Open Mon.-Sat. 9 a.m.-5 p.m.

Leslie Fay
Wing On Plaza, Shop 207,
62 Mody Rd., Tsimshatsui
East, Kowloon
• 3-685787

Located next to the Shangri-La Hotel, Leslie Fay stocks reasonably priced women's designerwear (Leslie Fay and Head among them). The well-made garments here include lingerie, knitwear, silk dresses and blouses, sleepwear and some eveningwear. Since prices start at just HK$150 and top out at approximately HK$700, you can do some real damage here—but for a lot less than you'd pay for a wardrobe elsewhere.
Open Mon.-Sat. 10 a.m.-7 p.m., Sun. 11 a.m.-5:30 p.m.

Diane Freis
Chung Nam Centre, 414
Kwun Tong Rd., Kwun
Tong, Kowloon
• 3-436275

There are almost as many Diane Freis boutiques in Hong Kong as there are Benettons in Rome, but if you're among her legion of acolytes, you can sate yourself with her georgette print dresses and separates here, for about HK$700 to HK$1,000 per item.
Open Mon.-Fri. 9:30 a.m.-1 p.m. & 2 p.m.-5 p.m., Sat. 9:30 a.m.-12:30 p.m.

Geis & Tijan
Taurus Bldg., 21A
Granville Rd., Tsimshatsui,
Kowloon
• 3-7226287

This outlet flaunts the very hip and chic womenswear of the type you'd find in the trendy sportswear department of upscale department stores. Whatever the hot current styles are, you'll find them here, at prices (HK$80 to HK$500) that will induce you to buy by the bushelful.
Open Mon.-Fri. 9:30 a.m.-1 p.m. & 2 p.m.-6 p.m.

Jennie
Cheong Sun Bldg., 52-54
Wellington St., Central
• 5-253820

This really is Bargain City. Lots of very chic and current women's knit, cotton and silk separates are sold at flea-market prices (HK$70 to HK$400). Definitely worth a visit.
Open Mon.-Sat. 10 a.m.-5 p.m.

Jumbo Knitters
Kai It Bldg., 58 Pak Tai
St., To Kwa Wan, Kowloon
• 3-7118707

Though it's more often famine than feast here, Jumbo is one of Hong Kong's biggest outlets for men's and women's knits, and it's worth taking a chance look. Cashmere, fisherman's and lambswool sweaters, both plain and fancy, are among the discoveries awaiting you here at extremely reasonable (HK$150 to HK$500) prices.
Open Mon.-Sat. 10 a.m.-5 p.m.

Kam Doo
Wong King Industrial
Bldg., E & H, 2 Tai Yau
St., San Po Kong, Kowloon
• 3-211742

This is a terrific outlet for gorgeous lingerie and women's sleepwear at prices that make you wish you could wear this sort of apparel around the clock (well, we suppose some do). There's a wealth of silk pajamas and robes, but for the Jean Harlow in you, there are slinky, sexy teddies, bustiers and bra-and-panty sets. Prices range from about HK$75 to HK$600, so you can go wild here without making too much of a dent in your wallet.
Open Mon.-Sat. 10 a.m.-5 p.m.

Le Baron
Yeung Yiu Chung No. 6
Industrial Bldg., 19
Cheung Shun St., Lai Chi
Kok, Kowloon
• 3-7418591

Cashmere, cashmere and more cashmere for men and women at amazingly fine prices (HK$400 to HK$800). Sweaters come in just about every style imaginable, and there are also some women's pants.
Open Mon.-Fri. 9:30 a.m.-5:30 p.m., Sat. 9:30 a.m.-12:30 p.m.

Miss O
Sands Bldg., 17 Hankow
Rd., Tsimshatsui, Kowloon
• 3-672575

This is the outlet for Oscar de la Renta's subcouture line (done through a licensing agreement with the designer; this one's definitely on the up-and-up), and it features lovely afternoon dresses and feminine blouses in bold silk prints. You can usually find some chic eveningwear as well. Prices are in the neighborhood of HK$400 to HK$1,000.
Open Mon.-Sat. 9:30 a.m.-5:30 p.m.

Mosaic
Sino Industrial Plaza, Shop
13, Kai Cheung Rd.,
Kowloon Bay, Kowloon
• 3-7969373

Run by a renegade cadre of former Diane Freis employees, Mosaic sells darn-close copies of the originals for about HK$650 to HK$800.
Open Mon.-Fri. 9:30 a.m.-6 p.m., Sat. 9:30 a.m.-1 p.m.

Oriental Pacific
Star House, 3 Salisbury
Rd., Tsimshatsui, Kowloon
• 3-7242633

Extremely reputable, and probably Hong Kong's hottest outlet for knitwear, the well-stocked Oriental Pacific carries beautiful angora, cashmere, cotton and lambswool sweaters for men, women and children at eminently reasonable prices (starting at about HK$80). *Open Mon.-Sat. 9 a.m.-6 p.m.*

Shopper's World Safari
Jade Mansion, 40 Waterloo Rd., Yau Tsim, Kowloon
• 3-845585

Give yourself plenty of time to safari-shop here, be patient and diligent weeding through the crowded racks, and ye shall be rewarded. Shopper's World may look like an intractable jumble of garments, but among those tangles, you're likely to find Alexander Julian men's shirts, designer ties, knitwear separates by Adrienne Vittadini, a Chantal Thomass dress or two (remember, in factory outlets, the stock is constantly changing from season to season)—and even some flannel jammies. Prices here are unbelievably low (about HK$50 to HK$300); you may need to hire a cargo plane for the flight home.
Open daily 9:30 a.m.-6:30 p.m.

Top Knitters
Sands Bldg., 17 Hankow Rd., Tsimshatsui, Kowloon
• 3-7244821

One of Hong Kong's best-known outlets, Top Knitters is famous for it's off-price Krizia "Mirrors" line of knits, Armani knockoffs and other knit separates for both men and women. Goods are handsomely displayed, and prices are handsomely low (HK$125 to HK$1,000), considering the quality of the goods and the haute-name designers represented.
Open Mon.-Fri. 9 a.m.-6 p.m., Sat. 9 a.m.-3 p.m.

Tungtex
112 How Ming St., Kwun Tong, Kowloon
• 3-897327

You'll beat a creepy, Byzantine path to get here, but it's worth it: lots of silk goods, many by major-name designers (Issey Miyake, Calvin Klein). This is a great place for fashionable women's separates at worthwhile prices (about HK$80 to HK$600).
Open Mon.-Sat. 9 a.m.-12:30 p.m. & 1:30 p.m.-6 p.m.

Vica Moda
Kaiser Estate, 30 Man Yue St., Hung Hom, Kowloon
• 3-348363

Vica Moda carries a good selection of knits, silk dresses and linen sportswear for women. Though the names on the labels may not be familiar to you, the price is right—we found sweaters for about HK$80. (There are another locations in Kaiser Estate Phase II and in Central, but this is the best-stocked branch.)
Open Mon.-Sat. 9:30 a.m.-6:30 a.m.

LEATHER

Leather Concepts
Union Hing Yip Bldg., 20
Hing Yip St., Kwun Tong,
Kowloon
• 3-899338

You may have a devil of a time getting here (ask the concierge at your hotel for explicit instructions; even better, have them written out in Chinese as well as in English), but you will be well rewarded and happy you went to the trouble. Leather Concepts is the jobber of leather goods to many top designers, Calvin Klein and Yves Saint Laurent among them. Prices are fantastic, considering the quality (HK$700 to HK$2,500). What you'll find are primarily jackets for men and women, but there are also dresses, skirts and a smattering of purses and children's clothing.
Open Mon.-Sat. 9 a.m.-5 p.m.

Venice
Po Lung Centre, Wang
Chiu Rd., Kowloon Bay,
Kowloon
• 3-7962123

The surroundings are a tad, shall we say, industrial, but you can get some excellent buys on women's and men's leather jackets, most of which are quite au courant. The variety of styles and materials (pigskin, suede, embossed leather) is excellent; prices range from HK$600 to HK$2,000.
Open Mon.-Sat. 9:30 a.m.-7 p.m.

LINENS

Uluman
Kowloon Centre, 29
Ashley Rd., Tsimshatsui,
Kowloon
• 3-7219937

This is a terrific outlet for bed linens: 100 percent cotton, cotton-blend and cotton-flannel sheets, pillowcases and duvet covers for every size bed at rock-bottom prices (about HK$60 to HK$280).
Open Mon.-Fri. 9 a.m.-5 p.m., Sat. 9 a.m.-1 p.m.

SPORTING GOODS

Nag Trade
Star House Arcade, 3
Salisbury Rd., Tsimshatsui,
Kowloon
• 3-670123

With wagering on horseflesh such a popular Hong Kong pastime, it seems only appropriate that there should be an outlet for equestrian clothing and gear—and the aptly named Nag Trade is a terrific source for well-priced British- and Hong Kong–made riding clothes, boots and saddles for adults and children. Nag

Trade will even custom-make riding boots for you (this takes a few days) that cost in the lowly neighborhood of HK$850.
Open Mon.-Fri. 10 a.m.-6 p.m., Sat. 10 a.m.-4 p.m.

Overstock
218 Silvercord, 30 Canton Rd., Tsimshatsui, Kowloon
• 3-7238921

Hong Kong isn't exactly the first place that comes to mind when you think of skiwear, but this outlet, right across from The Marco Polo hotel, carries a great selection of men's and women's ski duds, quilted coats and sleeping bags, in both down and synthetic materials, at wonderfully low prices (ranging from HK$200 to HK$600).
Open daily noon-7 p.m.

MARKETS

PEDDER BUILDING

Give yourself a full day to wander through Central's Pedder Building, where there's an apparel bargain for just about everyone. We also like the terrific restaurant in the basement called The Bloom: very chic and modern with, appropriately, nouvelle-ish Chinese cuisine to match. Below are our favorite outlets in the building.

Boutique Bello
Pedder Bldg., 12 Pedder St., Central
• 5-8450383

A well-stocked shop featuring very stylish, youthful eveningwear at good prices (about HK$300 to HK$1,000).
Open Mon.-Sat. 9 a.m.-6 p.m.

Boutique Tommi
Pedder Bldg., 12 Pedder St., Central
• 5-8451180

This outlet is as chic as anything on Madison Avenue—and carries a lot of the same designers' pieces as well. We found Thierry Mugler suits, Bruce Oldfield dresses and Body Map separates at a fraction of their retail cost (from HK$400 to HK$2,000). This one you can't afford to miss.
Open Mon.-Fri. 9 a.m.-6 p.m., Sat. 9 a.m.-5 p.m.

Due Trio
Pedder Bldg., 12 Pedder St., Central
• 5-212648

For us, this shop was a designer-discount Valhalla. The focus is on women's clothes and housewares (admittedly a rather odd combo), with a smattering of menswear thrown in for good measure. We found a terrific selection of Chantal Thomass, Arlequin and Herve Bernard separates and dresses as well as Artech kitchen knick-

knacks and towels from Issey Miyake's Plantation line, all at rock-bottom prices.
Open Mon.-Sat. 10 a.m.-6 p.m.

Jomea
Pedder Bldg., 12 Pedder
St., Central
• 5-8453362

This well-merchandised outlet offers scads of trendy washed- silk separates and dresses for women as well as lots of Diane Freis–type knockoffs at good prices (about HK$300 to HK$900).
Open Mon.-Sat. 9 a.m.-6 p.m.

Piano
Pedder Bldg., 12 Pedder
St., Central
• 5-227227

Piano is knockoff heaven: Krizia-like sweaters, faux-Chanel belts and purses and lots of women's knits and contemporary sportswear. It's all quite fashionable, well made and priced, as they say in the trade, intelligently (about HK$200 to HK$800).
Open Mon.-Sat. 9 a.m.-6 p.m.

Shirt Stop
Pedder Bldg., 12 Pedder
St., Central
• 5-269178

For men and women who adore designer shirts, this outlet is indeed the shirt-stop heaven. Prices are unconscionably low (from HK$40 to HK$130) for shirts and blouses by Yves Saint Laurent, Calvin Klein and Nordstrom. Not to mention the sweaters, pants and jackets.
Open Mon.-Sat. 10 a.m.-7 p.m.

Wintex
Pedddder Bldg., 12 Pedder
St., Central
• 5-249943

Wintex is a top-notch outlet that features women's separates (often designer), beautiful cotton pajamas and some sweaters. The prices are fairly painless as well: in the neighborhood of about HK$300 to HK$1000.
Open Mon.-Fri. 9 a.m.-6 p.m., Sat. 9 a.m.-5 p.m.

STANLEY MARKET

We hate to be spoilsports, but as far as we're concerned, Stanley Market really isn't such a must. (Should you decide to visit it, however, it's located on Hong Kong Island's south side; just tell the cab driver you wish to go to Stanley Market or Stanley Village, or ask your concierge for information regarding bus routes.) We'd heard so much about Stanley Market over the years—that it was a fabulous outdoor bazaar—that it had acquired almost mythic status in our must-shop pantheon. But what a disappointment! Stanley Market is merely a couple of blocks' worth—a couple of tourist-infested blocks, may we add—of stalls brimming with all manner of schlock. Though we did find, and purchase, a couple of darling baby T-shirts emblazoned with pandas and Chinese characters (which were featured at several different stalls, the merchant at each one promising he had hand-painted his shirts himself), the bulk of the clothing, handbags, jackets, lingerie, blouses and shirts we saw here were entirely unappealing. And there was no shortage of bogus Fila, Polo, Louis Vuitton, Cartier and Gucci goods—the customary gang of suspects—most of which looked as though they would fall apart before you got them back to your hotel to try on. Sorry to be such sourpusses, but should you decide to make this trek, caveat emptor.

FURS

Hong Kong may not be the first place that springs to mind when it comes to purchasing furs, but you can get some excellent buys on these luxury garments. Though we prefer fakes to the real thing for moral reasons, we've listed below several highly reputable shops at which to buy the real thing. Once again, and we can't stress this enough, as with jewelry (or any high-ticket item), it is critical that you do a little research before you buy.

All World Fur Co.
Tung Ying Bldg., Shop
120, 100 Nathan Rd.,
Tsimshatsui, Kowloon
• 3-684540

There's a good selection of midprice furs here, and if you like your furs in wacky colors, this is the place. Quality varies, though, so examine your prospective purchase carefully.
Open Mon.-Sat. 9:30 a.m.-6 p.m.

East Asia Fur Co.
Tsimshatsui Centre, Shop
119, 66 Mody Rd.,
Tsimshatsui, Kowloon
• 3-7221618

This is a good bet for cute, casual fur jackets and parkas—don't try for anything too serious here. Prices are quite reasonable—and bargainable.
Open Mon.-Sat. 10 a.m.-6:30 p.m.

Jindo Furs
Kowloon Hotel Arcade,
Shop B101, Nathan Rd.,
Tsimshatsui, Kowloon
• 3-73910334
Harbour City, Shop
308-309, Canton Rd.,
Tsimshatsui, Kowloon
• 3-699208

The Jindo shops are best characterized as supermarkets of furs; if you're looking for very fine furs, you may do better elsewhere. But if you want a coat, jacket, stroller (or anything trimmed in fur, including accessories), but don't want to spend too much money, the inventory is factory direct and the prices reflect it, so you'll probably do well. The selection is mind-boggling, so do some Zen breathing exercises before you attempt to ferret

your way through the racks. (Another location in Causeway Bay at 17-19 Percival Street, 5-729577.)
Open Mon.-Sat. 10 a.m.-6 p.m.

Siberian Fur Store
29 Des Voeux Rd., Central
• 5-221380
21 Chatham Rd. South,
Tsimshatsui, Kowloon
• 3-667039

When you're ready to splurge on a designer fur, you'll be amazed at how much you can get for your money at Siberian. Prices are easily one-third to one-half less than you'd pay in Europe or the States. You'll find a wide price and style range of furs by major American and European designers, and you can absolutely trust the quality here. (The factory, where the furs are even less expensive, is located at 6 Shing Yip St., in Kwun Tong.)
Open Mon.-Sat. 10 a.m.-6 p.m.

Yick Fung
William Industrial Bldg.,
23-25 Ng Fong St., San Po
Kong, Kowloon
• 3-225555

If you happen to be in Hong Kong between Christmas and Chinese New Year and you're looking for a fur, you might find what you want at Yick Fung during its annual sale. Mink, fox, rabbit and yak are the featured representatives, but, as with buying jewelry in Hong Kong, do some research before you invest. Prices range from HK$500 to HK$25,000.
Open Mon.-Sat. 9 a.m.-1 p.m. & 2 p.m.-5 p.m.

GIFTS & MISCELLANY

The Black Shop
Kowloon Hotel Shopping
Arcade, Kowloon
• 3-7243129

As the name implies, this small, very Milanesque shop carries only black items, most of them of the high-tech, anodized variety. We found some starkly beautiful matte ceramic vases, anodized-steel candlesticks and rubberized place mats. For the nihilistic minimalist in your life.
Open Mon.-Sat. 10:30 a.m.-6 p.m.

**Candy &
Company**
Ocean Galleries, Shop 274,
Harbour City, Kowloon
• 3-7242432
Park Hotel, Shop 1, 61-65
Chatham Rd., Tsimshatsui,
Kowloon
• 3-660168

If you've got a serious sweet tooth, these shops are a must. It's a little like being inside a pinball machine, but for kids and older nostalgia fiends alike, Candy & Company has the best selection of penny candies we've ever seen, including silver and gold M & M–type pastilles. Though we nearly lapsed into a diabetic coma after one trip here, it was worth it—the candies are fresh and the young staffers adorable. (Look for other

branches throughout Kowloon, Hong Kong and the New Territories.)
Open daily 10 a.m.-6 p.m.

Christofle
Landmark Bldg., Shop
G18, Pedder St., Central
• 5-264740
Kowloon Hotel, Shop
B103, 19-21 Nathan Rd.,
Kowloon
• 3-7225423

Though the service can be chilly initially, this shop is quite pleasant. It carries Christofle's line of jewelry as well as handsome silver tableware.
Open Mon.-Sat. 10 a.m.-6 p.m.

Davidoff
The Peninsula, Shop EL3,
Salisbury Rd., Tsimshatsui,
Kowloon
• 3-685774
Landmark Bldg., Shop G2,
Gloucester Tower, Pedder
St., Central
• 5-255428

As recovering smokers, we get a vicarious thrill by stepping into one of Davidoff's clubby, masculine shops. Reminiscent of a time when men used to retire to the library after dinner for brandy and cigars, Davidoff's old-world Russian heritage remains to this day. Reputed to make the world's finest tobacco goods and humidors, Davidoff also carries all sorts of beautiful accessories for this deadly habit: cigar trimmers and cases, cigarette boxes and lighters. Breathe deep! (Other locations in The Regent Arcade, the Mandarin Oriental and the Hong Kong Hilton.)
Open Mon.-Sat. 10 a.m.-6 p.m.

Eileen Kershaw
The Peninsula, Lobby,
West Wing, Salisbury Rd.,
Tsimshatsui, Kowloon
• 3-664083
Landmark Bldg., Shop
G44, Pedder St., Central

Kershaw is Hong Kong's only authorized Lalique dealer, and its prices are lower here than they are in the States. The gallery-shops also carry gorgeous and might-as-well-be-priceless-for-what-they-cost Chinese antiquities and artifacts.
Open Mon.-Sat. 10 a.m.-6 p.m.

H & A Sock Shop
World Shopping Centre,
Shop 268A, Harbour City,
Kowloon
• 3-7300109
Cityplaza, Unit 227-229,
Tai Koo Shing
• 5-8853169

Don't miss this shop if you're a foot fetishist (or if your washing machine regularly eats one sock per pair). H & A's wealth of inexpensive socks, stockings and tights for men, women and kids ranges from conservative to things even Michael Jackson might balk at wearing.
Open Mon.-Sat. 10 a.m.-6 p.m.

Habitat
Ocean Terminal, Shop
3281A, Harbour City,
Tsimshatsui, Kowloon
• 3-666391

This spacious Conran's branch features Sir Terence's customary bag of inexpensive housewares and other goodies from bath towels to furniture, though there's really not much point in shopping here if there's a

Conran's in your neighborhood. It does make for a fun browse, though.
Open daily 10 a.m.-6 p.m.

Hunter's
The Peninsula, Shop
BE14, Salisbury Rd.,
Tsimshatsui, Kowloon
• 3-7221169
Kowloon Hotel, Shop
B216, 19-21 Nathan Rd.,
Tsimshatsui, Kowloon
• 3-690716

Hunter's is one of Hong Kong's best-known purveyors of china and crystal. Though we feel the service here could be improved, the selection is pretty good. You'll find the ubiquitous Lladro, Boehm, Ginori, Herend, Meissen and Saint Louis—and staff is quite prompt about shipping. (There's another branch at the Ocean Terminal, Shop 2122, in Harbour City, 3-7230155.)
Open Mon.-Sat. 10 a.m.-6 p.m.

New Bowling Ivory Co.
Hyatt Regency Arcade, 43
Nathan Rd., Tsimshatsui,
Kowloon
• 3-7214359

Though we're morally opposed to the means by which most ivory is acquired, if you must have it, this shop carries a wide selection of jewelry, new and antique carvings and netsukes. The prices seem quite reasonable, as long as you bargain.
Open Mon.-Sat. 10 a.m.-7 p.m.

Scandinavia Arts
Ocean Centre, Shop 253,
Canton Rd., Tsimshatsui,
Kowloon
• 3-7360386

This small, rather plain shop carries a terrific stock of reasonably priced English, Scandinavian and Italian glassware and china, including Kosta Boda, Arabia Finland and Rorstrand. A good place for gift buying.
Open Mon.-Sat. 10 a.m.-6 p.m.

Startram Gift Shops
Star Ferry Pier, Shop
KP9C & KP40,
Tsimshatsui, Kowloon
• 3-3112610
Star Ferry Pier, Shop
EP9A, Central
• 5-8450772

These shops are as touristy as they get, but they do carry two very sweet items that make great gifts: Rice Paddy Dolls, the Chinese equivalent to the now-passé Cabbage Patch variety (these cuties wear traditional Chinese outfits, coolie hats and carry Hong Kong passports and resident cards with their photos) and Dim Sum shirts, simple cotton T-shirts with various well-done graphic scenes of Hong Kong. And the shops couldn't be more convenient, located as they are at the ferry terminals. (There are also various other locations in Kowloon and Hong Kong.)
Open daily 9:30 a.m.-11 p.m.

Town House
Ocean Terminal, Shop
2116C & 3268, Harbour
City, Kowloon
• 3-670332
Prince's Bldg., Shop 210,
3 Des Voeux Rd., Central
• 5-8450633

Town House specializes in crystal and china and cheerfulness—your Royal Doulton, Sèvres, Waterford and Daum are happily packed up for travel—and the selection is excellent.
Open Mon.-Sat. 10 a.m.-6 p.m.

JADE

Chinese Arts and Crafts
Silvercord Bldg., Canton Rd., Tsimshatsui, Kowloon
• 3-7311333

This chain of department stores (see Department Stores above) is an excellent and reputable source for jade jewelry and carvings (to test jade's authenticity, drop a bit of water on it—it should bead up). (Other links in Shell House, in Central, and the New World Centre and Silvercord Building in Kowloon.)
Open Mon.-Sat. 10 a.m.-6 p.m. (Nathan Road & New World Centre branches also open Sun. noon-6 p.m.).

The Jade Market
Canton Rd., near Kansu St., Kowloon
• No phone

This loose arrangement of street vendors and bona-fide shops is probably the best place to purchase jade in all of Hong Kong. Most of the vendors are licensed and belong to an association of jade merchants, proof of which is on a prominently displayed sticker. Bargaining is a way of life here: counteroffer whatever price you're told by nearly half, and bargain civilly and calmly—just don't insult the merchant.
Open daily 10 a.m.-4 p.m.

Kwong Tai Jade Co.
23 Man Yee Bldg., Central
• 5-227983

Very reputable, with a good selection of jewelry that ranges from inexpensive, simple pendant charms to elaborate carvings.
Open Mon.-Sat. 10 a.m.-6 p.m.

JEWELRY

Demographically, it seems like there's one jewelry shop for every two people in Hong Kong. Walking down Nathan Road, one is absolutely poleaxed by the sheer number of shops featuring glittering goodies in their windows, some with displays so casual that it strains the brain to believe that this is the real thing, not costume junk.

Try not to get carried away by the treasure troves, though. Make sure you patronize only those shops that display the Hong Kong Tourist Association sticker (a decal depicting a red junk that reads "Hong Kong TA"), and make sure you get a written certificate describing the exact content of what you've purchased and a detailed gemological appraisal of any set or unset stones you walk away with. If you're buying a watch, you should get the manufacturer's guarantee, serial number and warranty. Yes, you certainly can get amazing buys on jewelry here, plus just about anything made to order, whether it's an original design or a copy of something Cartier once whipped up for the Duchess of Windsor. And don't forget to bargain.

The number of jewelry stores in Hong Kong is truly staggering —and after a while, they all begin to look the same. We've elaborated on the shops that are notably outstanding and/or carry the most unique items, but there are scores of stores carrying very similar merchandise on both sides of the harbor that are sanctioned by the Hong Kong Tourist Association and are, therefore, highly reputable. The only difference among most of these shops may be your feelings about them as far as attitude and salesmanship. The following is a listing of our selection:

Anglo Tex Ltd. (specializes in pearls), Wing On Life Building, Shop 801, 22 Des Voeux Road, Central, Hong Kong, 5-226181; Flawless Jewelers (specializes in pearls), Star House, Shop 1812, Tsimshatsui, 3-7211811; Fook Hoi Jewellery Co., Guangdong Building, 77 Connaught Road, Central, Hong Kong, 5-430839; Gem Lau Company (specializes in colored gemstones), 615-616 Houston Centre, 63 Mody Road, Tsimshatsui East, Kowloon, 3-691638; Heng Ngai Jewelry, Heng Ngai Jewelry Centre, Hok Yuen Street, Hunghom, Kowloon, 3-6462217; Made in Hong Kong, Kaiser Estate, Block J, 51 Man Yue Street, Hunghom, Kowloon, 3-344415; Merit Jewellery, Merit Industrial Centre, Block B, 94 ToKwawan Road, Tsimshatsui, Kowloon, 3-76422006; Philip Jewellery & Co., Empire Centre, Shop G4, 68 Mody Road, Tsimshatsui, Kowloon, 3-686759; Star Gems (specializes in opals), 14 Peking Road (main entrance at 1 Lock Road), Block A, Tsimshatsui, Kowloon, 3-667099; Way Shun Gems & Jewellery, Austin Tower, Room 1411-2, 22-26A Austin Avenue, Tsimshatsui, Kowloon, 3-690053.

Ronald Abram Jewellers
Prince's Bldg., Shop 128-129, 3 Des Voeux Rd., Central
• 5-8452279

This gorgeous, elegant shop (very eighteenth-century British) specializes in gorgeous, elegant estate jewelry, especially art deco and signed pieces by Van Cleef, Bulgari, Maubussin, Cartier and Tiffany. Prices are high, but the quality and selection are unparalleled. At the very least, worth just a look.
Open Mon.-Sat. 10 a.m.-6 p.m.

Gianmaria Buccellati
Landmark Bldg., Shop 113B, Pedder St., Central
• 5-269828

Ah, Buccellati. If you can't afford it at home, you can't afford it here. But don't lose heart. You can always take advantage of its presence and incorporate some design ideas from the pieces here into ones you can have cobbled up at one of the less pricey jewelers mentioned in this section.
Open Mon.-Sat. 10 a.m.-6 p.m.

Bulgari
The Peninsula, Mezzanine Arcade, Salisbury Rd., Tsimshatsui, Kowloon
• 3-683223
Landmark Bldg., Pedder St., Central
• 5-238057

Again, you're not going to get away with any bargains here, but the tax saving alone on Bulgari's seriously pricey bijoux is quite a saving indeed.
Open Mon.-Sat. 10 a.m.-6 p.m.

Cartier
The Peninsula, Lobby, Salisbury Rd., Tsimshatsui, Kowloon
• 3-688036
Prince's Bldg., 3 Des Voeux Rd., Central
• 5-222963

Though many jewelers in Hong Kong are authorized Cartier dealers, the eponymous shops feature the entire line of Cartier goods, including perfume, eyewear, leather goods, pens—and, oh yes, jewelry. (Other Cartier shops in several other locations throughout Kowloon.)
Open Mon.-Sat. 10 a.m.-6:30 p.m.

Dabera
Admiralty Centre, Tower 1, Central
• 5-277722

Dabera boasts a master Swiss jeweler overseeing its workshop as well as qualified gemologists who issue diamond certificates, gem-identification reports and evaluations for insurance purposes, and who adhere strictly to international GIA (Gemological Institute of America) standards, so you can be sure of the quality of your purchase. And the prices are quite competitive.
Open Mon.-Sat. 10 a.m.-6 p.m.

Dickson Watch & Jewellery Co.
The Peninsula, Salisbury Rd., Tsimshatsui, Kowloon
• 3-698264
Landmark Bldg., Pedder St., Central
• 5-214245

Though Dickson has a well-deserved reputation as a diamond specialist, the array of watches here is mind-boggling. Although you can find lower prices elsewhere, the selection here is truly fabulous: Piaget, Cartier, Patek Philippe, Rolex and Chopard, among many others. You're sure to find the watch you're looking for.
Open Mon.-Sat. 10 a.m.-6 p.m.

Divya Jewellery
35D Cameron Rd., Tsimshatsui, Kowloon
• 3-7390730

As long as you're not looking for important jewels, Divya can satisfy your craving for ropes of seed pearls, strings of cultured pearls and gold jewelry. Prices are astoundingly low.
Open Mon.-Sat. 10 a.m.-6 p.m.

Emperor Watch & Jewellery Co.
81 Nathan Rd.,
Tsimshatsui, Kowloon
• 3-7216121

Emperor has an excellent selection of watches: Patek Philippe, Cartier, Rolex, you name it. And if it isn't in stock, the staff can probably get it for you in short order. *Open Mon.-Sat. 10 a.m.-6:30 p.m.*

Gebo
Landmark Bldg., Pedder St., Central
• 5-226672

This shop features fine avant-garde jewelry (among more traditional pieces), including anodized silver and gold coiled rings and bracelets, whimsically dotted with diamonds and set in unusual ways. *Open Mon.-Sat. 10 a.m.-6 p.m.*

Henry
29 Nathan Rd.,
Tsimshatsui, Kowloon
• 3-683101
43-45 Queen's Rd., Central
• 5-265233

Henry's forte is gemstones (particularly rubies and emeralds) crafted into custom designs. You can't haggle here, but quality is assured. (Look for another branch at the Hilton Hotel Arcade, Shop 40, 5-252511.) *Open Mon.-Sat. 10 a.m.-6 p.m.*

House of Shen
The Peninsula, Shop 20, Salisbury Rd., Tsimshatsui, Kowloon
• 3-7215483

The prices are high here (though less than you'd pay in the States), but the quality of the stones and pearls—not to mention the workmanship—is even higher. This is a good place to have your custom designs made up. *Open daily 9:30 a.m.-6 p.m.*

Kai-Yin Lo
The Peninsula, Shop ML1, Salisbury Rd., Tsimshatsui, Kowloon
• 3-7219693
Mandarin Oriental, Shop M1, 5 Connaught Rd., Central
• 5-248238

If you shop at Neiman-Marcus, Saks or Harrod's, you may be familiar with Kai-Yin Lo's jewelry. Though a little too fussy for our tastes, her work is undeniably beautiful. The designs revolve around semiprecious stones and variously colored pearls. Though you'll save by buying here rather than in the States or London, these baubles don't come cheap. *Open Mon.-Sat. 10 a.m.-6:30 p.m.*

Ilias Lalaounis
The Regent Arcade, Shop R123, Salisbury Rd., Tsimshatsui, Kowloon
• 3-7212811
Landmark Bldg., Shop 137, Pedder St., Central
• 5-243328

You may not save any more than tax by buying this world-renowned Greek jeweler's wares in Hong Kong (although that amount can be quite considerable), but these shops do fulfill a promise of a good selection of beautifully handcrafted jewels—and, once again, you're sure to gather some design ideas here. *Open Mon.-Sat. 10 a.m.-6 p.m.*

Larry Jewelry
33 Nathan Rd.,
Tsimshatsui, Kowloon
• 3-7218133
Landmark Bldg., Shop G49, Pedder St., Central
• 5-211268

Even though Larry Jewelry has only three branches in Hong Kong, because of the amount of advertising it does, it seems far more ubiquitous. Larry has reputable stones, does good custom work and carries a massive selection of name watches. (Another Larry is located in

the third-floor Shop 3239 of the Ocean Terminal, 3-7398081.)
Open Mon.-Sat. 10 a.m.-6 p.m.

Mercury Centre
The Regent Arcade, Shop
RO21, Salisbury Rd.,
Tsimshatsui, Kowloon
• 3-690570

Though the service here can be a bit brusque, there are good deals to be made. We had a 24-inch string of seven-and-a-half-millimeter pearls made up for HK$4,000; they weren't perfect, but for that price, they were close enough.
Open Mon.-Sat. 10 a.m.-6 p.m.

Myrna Jewellery Co.
Sheraton Hong Kong
Hotel and Towers, Shop
D1, 20 Nathan Rd.,
Tsimshatsui, Kowloon
• 3-677249

If you've come to Hong Kong in search of pearls, stop in here and have Sammy show you his wares. His pearls boast excellent quality and equally excellent prices; we bought a beautiful jade-clasped strand that was appraised back home in the U.S. for well more than twice the purchase price. He'll also do a crack job of restringing in short order. An honest, reputable jeweler.
Open Mon.-Sat. 10 a.m.-6 p.m.

Opal Creations
Burlington House Arcade,
92 Nathan Rd.,
Tsimshatsui, Kowloon
• 3-7219933

Admittedly, opals really aren't our thing (our mother told us they were bad luck). But this shop, featuring Australian opals, carries every type of the stone imaginable, in settings that veer from simple to outlandish. Be forewarned: it's somewhat of a tourist trap, there's even a clumsy, Disneylandish mine replica, an opal museum and more information available on opals than you really want to know (it's a good place to drag the kids along for the kitschy, amusement-park ambience). While the prices aren't exactly of the bargain variety, everything you purchase is certified.
Open Mon.-Sat. 9:30 a.m.-7 p.m., Sun. 9:30 a.m.-3:30 p.m.

Treasurement Jewellery & Watch Co.
Hongkong Hotel, Shop
103-104, Tsimshatsui,
Kowloon
• 3-31112112

If you're into intricate jewelry designs, make a beeline for Treasurement; the staff here is particularly adept at copying Cartier pieces, especially those from the Panther line.
Open Mon.-Sat. 10 a.m.-6 p.m.

Trio Pearl
The Peninsula, Shop ME8,
Salisbury Rd., Tsimshatsui,
Kowloon
• 3-679171

The pearls here are pricey yet perfect. This is the place to come if you're looking for large-millimeter and black pearls—the quality and selection can't be beat.
Open Mon.-Sat. 10 a.m.-6 p.m.

**Tse Sui Luen
Jewellery Co.**
Summit Bldg., 21 Tai Wan
Rd., Tsimshatsui, Kowloon
• 3-7640753

This shop has a crackerjack staff and a very good selection of quality gemstones.
Open Mon.-Sat. 10 a.m.-6 p.m.

**Wing Sum
Jewellery Co.**
The Regent Arcade, Shop
RO11, Salisbury Rd.,
Tsimshatsui, Kowloon
• 3-7230116

This handsome shop has a friendly, knowledgeable staff who is eager to please—and deal. They're also very accommodating about copying pieces.
Open Mon.-Sat. 10 a.m.-6 p.m.

COSTUME JEWELRY

Blunco
Hanley House, 68-80
Canton Rd., Tsimshatsui,
Kowloon
• 3-7211489

Despite the unfortunate, though oddly appropriate choice of moniker (Blunco = Bunco?), Blunco's specialty is simulated gemstones—rubies, sapphires, emeralds, aquamarines—and pearls, in fourteen- or eighteen-carat-gold settings. The stone quality, especially that of the diamonds, is excellent, as is the craftsmanship. Prices are strikingly reasonable, and just about anything can be copied here.
Open Mon.-Sat. 9:30 a.m.-6:30 p.m.

Zoe
Shell House, Queen's Rd.,
Central
• 5-234454

Yes, this is the same Zoe as the one in Manhattan (and various other locations around the world). This small, whimsical shop sells adorable, modern-baroque costume jewelry and hair ornaments similar to those carried by Ylang-Ylang, yet at lower prices. Fun, young and cheap.
Open Mon.-Sat. 10 a.m.-7 p.m.

LEATHER GOODS

Accessoire
Prince's Bldg., Shop G37,
3 Des Voeux Rd., Central
• 5-268991

This shop concentrates on shoes made by two of our favorite footwear designers: Stephane Kelian and Diego della Valle. Terrific selection of handbags as well, with a most gracious and helpful staff.
Open Mon.-Sat. 10 a.m.-6:30 p.m.

Camhon Co.
29 Hankow Rd.,
Tsimshatsui, Kowloon
• 3-689720

This low-key, unprepossessing shop carries a surprisingly large selection of wallets, belts, handbags and luggage by Cartier, Dior, Lancel, Gucci, Ralph Lauren and Longchamp, all at bargainable prices.
Open Mon.-Sat. 9:30 a.m.-6:30 p.m.

Church's
Prince's Bldg., Shop 5A2,
3 Des Voeux Rd., Central
• 5-243848

British-based Church's has long been known for its handsome, expertly cobbled men's shoes. This shop offers a great selection, though you save only a little by shopping here.
Open Mon.-Sat. 10 a.m.-6:30 p.m.

Dunhill
Prince's Bldg., 3 Des
Voeux Rd., Central
• 5-243663
The Peninsula, East Wing,
Salisbury Rd., Tsimshatsui,
Kowloon
• 3-687721

Though we personally feel that this British line of leather goods and assorted sartorial accessories should be renamed *Dull* hill, we're in the minority. Okay, we will grudgingly admit that despite the stuffiness of style, it is unthinkable to quibble with the quality.
Open Mon.-Sat. 10 a.m.-6 p.m.

Etro
The Peninsula, Shop G1,
Salisbury Rd., Tsimshatsui,
Kowloon
• 3-7215474

Etro's Italian leather goods are just plain luxuriously gorgeous. All the designs of the rich leather handbags, briefcases, luggage and wallets revolve around subtle paisleys. Etro also makes beautiful silk ties, scarves and pocket squares. We think Prince must have named his record label Paisley Park after a successful Etro shopping excursion (well, it's as good a reason as any).
Open Mon.-Sat. 10 a.m.-6 p.m.

Carlos Falchi
Hyatt Regency Hotel,
Shop G17B, 67 Nathan
Rd., Tsimshatsui, Kowloon
• 3-3111027

Though Falchi's rich-hippie designs aren't for everyone, his handbags, wallets and accessories are wildly popular, and this shop in particular offers a very good selection.
Open Mon.-Sat. 10 a.m.-6 p.m.

Joan & David
Ocean Terminal, Shop
2122A-C, Tsimshatsui,
Kowloon
• 3-7360081

This is Joan & David's first foray into Hong Kong, and it's a hit. This good-looking, well-merchandised store carries Joan & David shoes and accessories for both men and women.
Open Mon.-Sat. 10 a.m.-6 p.m.

Lancel
The Peninsula, Shop E3B,
Salisbury Rd., Tsimshatsui,
Kowloon
• 3-695509

The styles here may not be the most imaginative, but the wildly expensive leather handbags, carry-alls, satchels, wallets and other hidebound items are wonderful looking and well crafted. (Additional Lancel

branches are locations throughout Kowloon and Hong Kong.)
Open Mon.-Sat. 10 a.m.-6:30 p.m.

The Leather Concept
Pedder Bldg., Shop 406,
12 Pedder St., Central
• 5-8455055

Leather Concept merchandise runs the gamut of leather goods for men, women and children, including some fine Bottega Veneta knockoffs. (There's also a factory outlet at 20 Hing Yip Street in the Union Hing Yip Building, Kwun Tong, 3-899338.)
Open Mon.-Sat. 9 a.m.-6 p.m.

Loewe
Landmark Bldg.,
Gloucester Tower, Pedder
St., Central
• 5-220996
The Peninsula, Salisbury
Rd., Tsimshatsui, Kowloon
• 3-683350

The Spaniards really do have a way with leather—witness Loewe's tailored designs for handbags, wallets, belts and other accessories. Expensive but well-crafted out of the best materials. (Yet another Loewe branch is located at 109 Repulse Bay in Central, 5-8126363.)
Open Mon.-Sat. 10 a.m.-6 p.m.

Orange-Room
New World Centre, Shop
B1-66, Tsimshatsui,
Kowloon
• 3-688051

Orange-Room is a real find. It stocks a great selection of midprice Japanese-designed shoes for men and women, both knockoff and original designs, at pleasingly low prices. There's also an array of ties by Versace and Moschino as well as small leather goods.
Open Mon.-Sat. 10 a.m.-7 p.m.

Prada
The Peninsula, Shop BL6,
Salisbury Rd., Tsimshatsui,
Kowloon
• 3-7245101

Prada of Milan is our favorite purveyor of leather goods—the hides are so buttery, the styles classic yet contemporary. From wallets to shoes, this shop is the greatest, with a crackerjack staff, to boot.
Open Mon.-Sat. 10 a.m.-6 p.m.

Louis Vuitton
The Peninsula, Salisbury
Rd., Tsimshatsui, Kowloon
• 3-663731

If we ruled the world, one of our first missions would be to purge anything with an "LV" imprint from the face of the earth. With the exception of Vuitton's grand old steamer trunks of yesteryear, this stuff has to be (along with Gucci) the most overexposed, overpriced line of luxury goods on the planet. From the LV-crazed crowds who clog these shops, you'd think they were giving the stuff away. And with so much bogus Vuitton flooding the universe, why bother? Anyway, if you're not to be dissuaded, there's more Vuitton in Hong Kong (and Kowloon) than you can poke a stick at—but don't poke too hard, you may damage the "leather-like" canvas.
Open Mon.-Sat. 10 a.m.-6 p.m.

SHOPPING CENTERS

To the casual visitor, Hong Kong may at first seem like one gigantic network of malls. But the experienced traveler knows that Hong Kong *is* one gigantic network of malls—almost life forces in and of themselves, tunneling under hotels, sprawling along the harborside. Massive and ubiquitous, they remind us of the gargantuan sand worms in *Dune*. Unless you've been to the Brobingdian, acres-large mall in Edmonton, Canada, there is little to prepare you for the sheer expanse of Ocean Terminal or Harbour City (a mall that publishes its own expensive, glossy give-away magazine). Even the "smaller" malls are far more all-encompassing than anything Westerners are used to. While some of these cathedrals of consumerism are fun to just meander aimlessly through for the sheer visual effect, the larger ones can be initially discouraging without a game plan; it's best to tackle them categorically or sectionally. Wear comfortable shoes, bring plenty of bucks—and don't forget to take regular lunch and coffee breaks. Working the malls of Hong Kong is a full-time job.

Landmark Bldg.
Pedder St., Central

Landmark is Hong Kong's most upscale mall. It houses Joyce's comprehensive boutique, Krizia, Ungaro, The Swank Shop, Davidoff's, Christofle—even a Pizza Hut. A dazzlingly sumptuous center, complete with atrium cafés, fountains and all manner of marble, terrazzo and tile, it provides plenty of opportunity to rest your tootsies as you're emptying your wallet.

New World Centre
Salisbury Rd., adjacent to
the New World Hotel,
Tsimshatsui, Kowloon

Though a great deal of the shops in this center are tacky and repetitive, don't get discouraged until you venture down to the basement level where you'll find a handful of shops specializing in avant-garde French and Japanese designs—at least a couple of seasons *before* you'll see them in Europe or the States. There's L'Atelier 36 and Comme Ça du Monde. There's also a terrific Japanese department store called Tokyu, where you can get some excellent buys. Not only does it carry clothes by Pinky and Dianne, but we found a pair of darling Kansai shoes on sale for US$15!

Ocean Terminal, Harbour City, Ocean Galleries & Ocean Centre
Tsimshatsui, Kowloon

Tsimshatsui, Kowloon's Ocean Terminal, Hong Kong's first megamall, begat Harbour City, which begat Ocean Centre. We've lumped these four indoor malls together, since they're all interconnected—shops as far as the eye can see. These malls form practically a city within the city. They encompass hotels, full-service restaurants, various entertainment edifices, information booths as well as hundreds and hundreds of retail shops. The sanest way to deal with this seemingly endless maze is to pick up copies of the various pamphlets and magazines (which are gratis) that serve as guides at an information booth, and map out your game plan from those. Or, conversely, you can just wander about. You'll find everything in these malls from a branch of Britain's Lane Crawford department store to a huge, two-floor arm of Toys "R" Us and Habitat, featuring Terence Conran's well-priced contemporary home furnishings. Clothing boutiques range from the divine (Louis Feraud) to the banally casual (Benetton). There are also a number of eateries at which to make refueling stops (Sara's, Ocean Centre, Shop 248, is good for cappuccino)—you'll need them. We personally prefer the smaller (and in the case of the New World Centre, that term is relative) hotel shopping arcades—you could literally spend days down here without coming up for air.

Swire House
9 Connaught Rd., Central

Swire House is home to an eclectic mix of upscale shops ranging from Miyake to Matsuda to Magli.

SIGHTS

INTRODUCTION

Although when most people think of Hong Kong, they think first of dining, shopping, custom tailors and fine hotels, the city and its environs are also blessed with some eminently worthy sights, from art museums to a time-warp Chinese village. For more information about the places described below, and for details on fine organized tours, contact the Hong Kong Tourist Association (HKTA), Jardine House, 35th Floor, 1 Connaught Road, Central, Hong Kong, 5-244191. The HKTA also has another information number: 3-7225555.

SIGHTS FROM A TO Z

Aberdeen
Southwest Hong Kong Island (accessible via bus and taxi)

Aberdeen is a former fishing village that has become famous as the home of Hong Kong's floating Cantonese restaurants (including Jumbo and Tai Pak, both of which are reviewed in Restaurants). Though none of them are very good, they're definitely worth visiting for their garish decor and many thousand points of light. Until redevelopment sends the last boat person packing, this is also an excellent place to take a leisurely sampan ride though the floating city of Aberdeen, where squid dry from clotheslines like so many pairs of socks, and old residents watch you float by like a bug on a leaf. Once there, sampans are easy to catch (in fact, they'll catch you), but for those who like things neat and planned, guided sampan tours are available; call 3-3116111 for information.

Bird Market
Hong Lok St., Mong Kok, Kowloon

This is the street of the teahouses to which men bring their birds; it is also the street of the shops in which the men buy those birds and their sundry accessories. The noise in the teahouses is remarkable, an astounding cacophony of birds hanging above their masters in ornate cages, some of which are fashioned of pure silver. Much is made of the perfection of each bird and its song. Sadly, this is also one of the dying rituals of Hong

Kong (and Chinese) life. The next generation prefers the songs of Bon Jovi to the sweet lilt of budgies. Hong Lok Street can be found near the intersection of Argyle Street and Nathan Road, not far from the Mong Kok MTR station.

Cat Street Centre
Lok Ku Rd., Western District

A former sailors' district known for its houses of easy virtue, opium dens and generally unsavory characters, Cat Street has been gentrified into a fine area for shopping for art and antiques, which are sold at prices that would have shocked the old pirates. Bargaining is decidedly called for, but only rarely is a real deal found. Still, the selection is admirable, though the setting has lost much of its cachet from former times.

Causeway Bay Typhoon Shelter
Causeway Bay

The shelter is home to several thousand boats, moored there for protection against Hong Kong's fierce typhoons. At night (from April through November), sampans take interested parties out to the middle of the shelter, where they can buy fresh fish from seafood boats, have it cooked on wok boats (beer is available from drink boats) and be serenaded by women on sing-song boats, with all of Hong Kong glowing about you. We must say that this can be one of those experiences you'll remember for the rest of your life.

Central Market
Queen's Rd., Central

We were unpleasantly surprised by this rather nasty, blocky warehouse of a building, the largest of the more than 50 public markets operated by the Crown Colony. Though we are uncommonly fond of markets—for within them you truly find the soul of a city—this one leaves us cold. Among other things, the smell is truly ghastly, and this is not a comment that comes from those who are easily repulsed by the charnel house. Relating the squalor of the Central Market to the food on our plates is a less-than-edifying experience. Trust us—you'll enjoy your meals more if you have not spent a morning gagging your way through the Central Market.

Cheung Chau Island

See The Outlying Islands section of the Out of Hong Kong chapter.

City Hall
Edinburgh Pl., Central
• 5-739595

City Hall is a proud structure just off the Star Ferry terminal, notable for its good Chinese restaurant (called, of course, City Hall Chinese), its museum (the

Hong Kong Museum of Art; see below), its gardens and its Marriage Registry, which a friend discovered was not quite as easy to use as those in Las Vegas. Though foreigners can be married in Hong Kong, the residual British bureaucracy means it entails numerous forms, waiting periods and documents proving that you are who you are. If wedding your beloved in Hong Kong seems like a fun idea, contact your nearest Hong Kong Tourist Association as early as possible, and plan to have lots of time to think it over.

Food Street
Between Kingston St. &
Gloucester Rd., Causeway
Bay

Here, one block west of Cleveland Street, we found a sort of culinary mini-mall with more than three dozen restaurants in a setting that's as devoid of charm as any modern shopping center. The good news is that you can find just about anything you want here, food-wise: from seafood and Szechuan to Vietnamese and vegetarian. The concept seems to be to make eating easier for tourists; the result is a street that's all food, but no flash at all. See the Food Street entry in the Cafés & Coffee Shops section of the Quick Bites chapter for more details.

Fung Ping Shan Museum
University of Hong Kong,
94 Bonham Rd., Western
District
• 5-8592114

Best appreciated by those with a strong commitment to Oriental art and artifacts, this smallish museum run by the university is worth seeing for its vast assortment of Chinese works, some of which date back 2,500 years and more. The Shang Dynasty (1600 to 1027 B.C.) and the Zhou Dynasty (1027 to 256 B.C.) are represented with ritual vessels; the Han (206 B.C. to A.D. 220) and Tang (A.D. 618 to 907) dynasties, by bronze mirrors. The bronze and early pottery works are particularly impressive. We are told the museum houses the world's largest collection of Nestorian crosses from the Yuan Dynasty. Oh.
Open Mon.-Sat. 9:30 a.m.-6 p.m., Sun. 2 p.m.-6 p.m.

Happy Valley Racetrack
Happy Valley
• 5-8378345

Dating back to 1845, this venerable (though surprisingly modern-looking) track attracts as many as 50,000 racing fans every Wednesday evening and all day Saturday during its September-through-May season. Since Hong Kong residents adore gambling, and partake with gusto, the energy and tension can be quite a remarkable thing to experience. You'll also be as aware of the social stratification here as at Ascot; it is clear who the members of the right set are (i.e., those who belong to the

Royal Hong Kong Jockey Club), and then there's everyone else. The HKTA puts together helpful guided tours of the track; call 5-7225555 for information.

Hollywood Road
Central

Hollywood Road is the primary shopping street for antiques and various bric-a-brac in Hong Kong. Though much of its character has disappeared as a result of urban renewal, its many hills and alleyways make this western section of the Central district a jolly place to spend an afternoon, though we've rarely found much in the way of merchandise that we like. Perhaps that's because the idea of carrying a suit of armor home seems a bit bothersome. The mix of antiques leans toward chinoiserie, though interesting items from England's colonial rule are also well scattered about. See the Antiques & Crafts section of the Shops chapter for more details.

Hong Kong Museum of Art
City Hall High Block, 10th & 11th Fl., Connaught Rd., Central
• 5-224127

Scheduled to move soon to the Cultural Centre next to Kowloon's soccer ball–like Space Museum (thereby further destroying the view from The Peninsula), this museum, whose scope is limited due to limited floor area, is not the sort of place you go to see a rare Picasso or Rembrandt. The art is mostly Chinese and is not up to the collection at the National Museum in Taiwan (though nothing in the world is). It's nice to know it's there, but visiting art museums is far from our primary (or even secondary) reason for being in Hong Kong. *Open Mon.-Wed. & Fri.-Sat. 10 a.m.-6 p.m., Sun. 1 p.m.-6 p.m.*

Hong Kong Space Museum
Salisbury Rd., Tsimshatsui, Kowloon
• 3-7212361

Say what you will, but the Space Museum looks like a dirty soccer ball carelessly left lying across the street from The Peninsula hotel, thereby obliterating the hotel's once-fabulous view. Probably the most experientially exciting of Hong Kong's four centrally located museums, the Space Museum includes such exhibits as Scott Carpenter's *Aurora 7* space capsule. Once again, a space museum is not one of the reasons we go to Hong Kong, but for science/space buffs, and for families, this isn't a bad choice. There's the Space Theatre (its 75-foot- diameter domed roof acts as screen for grand-scale films); the Hall of Solar Sciences (which houses a solar telescope to provide a closer look at the star that gives us life); the Exhibition Hall (home

to the *Aurora 7*); and an astronomy bookshop and a snack bar.
Open Mon. & Wed.-Sun. 2 p.m.-9:30 p.m.

Hong Kong Stock Exchange
Exchange Sq., Central
• 5-221122

Designed by Remo Riva, the exchange sits inside a massive structure that boasts waterfalls, a computer-controlled environment and talking elevators. Along with architect I. M. Pei's Bank of China building and the incredible Hong Kong & Shanghai Banking Corporation building (supposedly the most expensive building in the world, constructed at a cost of HK$8 billion), these make up Hong Kong's newly created Central financial district. Together they make an awesome sight as you cross the harbor from Kowloon.
Open Mon.-Fri. 10 a.m.-12:30 p.m. & 2:30 p.m.-3:30 p.m.

Jade Market
Kansu & Reclamation sts., Yaumatei, Kowloon

For those who like jade, that initial trip to the Jade Market is like dying and going to heaven. Three blocks of jade merchants, working from small stalls on the street, endlessly haggle and compare prices. You'll feel as if they knocked down the Emerald City to create all this jade. Most of it's real; some of it isn't. Bargaining, as a rule, is easier as the hour gets later—early in the day, tourists don't have much leverage at all. See the Jade section of the Shops chapter for more details.
Open daily 10 a.m.-4 p.m.

Kam Tin Walled Villages
New Territories

Actually, there are three walled villages here—Kat Hing Wai, Wing Lung Wai and Shui Tau Tsuen (and there's another called Tsang Tai Uk near the Lion Rock Tunnel)—that date back four or five centuries (the earliest residents, the Tangs, settled the most fertile land, and to ward off the advances of bandits, they constructed walls). All are colorful, scenic and just made for tourists on bus tours. Kat Hing Wai is the most touristy of the three; the ancestral hall and Hung Shing Temple make Shui Tau Tsuen the most interesting.

Ladder Street
Near Hollywood Rd., Central

This "street" is really a long staircase that climbs 213 feet as it wends its way up the side of old Hong Kong, past many small merchants and alleys. Squint a little and it looks just like it did 100 years ago, when the population wore pigtails and pulled rickshaws through the narrow lanes.

Lamma Island

See The Outlying Islands section of the Out of Hong Kong chapter.

Lantau Island

See The Outlying Islands section of the Out of Hong Kong chapter.

Man Mo Temple
126 Hollywood Rd.,
Central
• 5-400350

If you visit only one temple in Hong Kong, Man Mo must be it. This traditional Taoist temple is actually half temple and half museum, with its collection of altars and sedan chairs. Its two fierce gods are Man Cheong (the patron god of literature and civil servants) and Kwan Tung (patron god of war and antiques sellers). Incense fills the air, and joss sticks can be thrown to predict your future—the feeling of being in the presence of the mystic is undeniable.
Open daily 7 a.m.-5 p.m.

Nathan Road
Kowloon

Hong Kong's proverbial Golden Mile, a seemingly endless stretch of shops and neon, begins next to The Peninsula hotel and continues all the way to the New Territories (though most of the action is within the first ten blocks or so). Nathan Road, with its many side streets and alleyways, and the myriad pleasures of Tsim-shatsui can be so engrossing that one can easily forget that Hong Kong Island is just across the harbor. For many, Nathan Road is Hong Kong.

New Territories

See the Out of Hong Kong chapter.

Noonday Gun
Opposite the World Trade
Centre, Causeway Bay

At the turn of the century, the noonday gun was the equivalent of the lunch whistle for employees of the great trading company of Jardine, Matheson (the prototype for James Clavell's *Noble House*). These days, it's nothing more than a nostalgic tradition, to which Noël Coward paid tribute in his song "Mad Dogs and Englishmen," writing: "In Hong Kong/They strike a gong/And fire a noonday gun/To reprimand each inmate/Who's in late." These days, mad dogs and tourists gather gladly to hear the noonday gun.

**Ocean Centre/
Ocean Terminal/
Harbour City**
Tsimshatsui, Kowloon

In a city of monstrous shopping malls, the Ocean/Harbour complex stands out as the modern-day equivalent of the Seven Wonders of the World—all rolled into one. So vast is this overlapping series of complexes that the chances are better than ever that you'll never find your way back to any given store once you've headed off in another direction. There are shops we've seen here that we've never managed to find again. In fact, there are whole floors we've somehow lost for good. See the Shopping Centers section of the Shops chapter for more details.

Ocean Park & Water World
Wong Chuk Hang Rd., Aberdeen
• 5-550947

Proof that Americans do not have a monopoly on tawdry amusement parks, this 160-acre complex houses, among myriad other aquatic diversions, the Ocean Theatre (presenting leaping dolphins and killer whales), an amusement park with a roller coaster, and an aquatic park with water slides. We even saw a fellow selling hot dogs. A very popular day's outing for Hong Kong families (buses leave regularly from the Admiralty MTR station), the park draws two million visitors a year. *Open Mon.-Sat. 10 a.m.-6 p.m., Sun. & holidays 9 a.m.-6 p.m. Adults HK$100, children HK$50.*

Ohel Leah Synagogue
70 Robinson Rd., Midlevel
• 5-594872

This hard-to-find temple (it's down a small street below Robinson Road) dates back to 1902, when it was built by the Sassoons, one of Hong Kong's most famous trading families. The simplicity of the synagogue and the contrast between its serenity and the noise of the world outside can be a remarkable experience. A good place to go for a few moments of quiet reflection.

Peak Tram
Victoria Peak, Central
• 5-220922

A funicular of astounding steepness climbs Victoria Peak from upper Central. As you ascend the hill, you'll find yourself looking at the world from a breathtaking angle; the high-rises built along the Peak appear to be off their axis like the Leaning Tower of Pisa. Though actually at an incline of 45 degrees, the ride feels much steeper, nearly vertical, as it sweeps up the 1,000 feet to Victoria Peak in eight minutes (not to worry: the tram has a perfect safety record). At the top, you'll find souvenir shops and restaurants. Our favorite gambit once on top is to follow the paths that travel around the Peak and offer a 360-degree view of Hong Kong Harbour and a rather nosy view of some of the great houses that sit atop Hong Kong's highest point. *Tram runs 6 a.m.-midnight. HK$10 per person.*

Poor Man's Nightclub
Hong Kong Ferry, Macau Ferry Pier, Western District
• 5-432081

Every evening starting at sunset, this area fills up with hawkers of every description peddling their wares and their services, providing an excellent taste of authentic Hong Kong. The bazaar, which usually stays open until about 1 a.m., pulses with energy and vitality—and with quite a few pickpockets, so do watch yourself. Thanks to the many food stands, this is also a great place to try Chinese street food, which is safer than you might think (just exercise some common sense). Watch for the hawkers selling birds and tropical fish, which we assume are bought as pets, though one never knows.

Shanghai Street
Yaumatei, Kowloon

This street is home to the Night Market, another of the several "poor man's nightclubs" that sprout around Hong Kong every evening as the sun vanishes over China. Less frequented by tourists, this market area looks and feels like the Hong Kong one imagines: filled with noise and excitement, scribes and street-corner barbers, paper shops and fortune tellers. In the midst of it all is the Tin Hau Temple, and nearby, on weekends, open-air Chinese operas are often performed.

Stanley Market
Stanley

Actually, this market was rather a disappointment; in fact, it was a great disappointment. This former fishing village, dating back to 1841, is less well known for its fine residences than for its tacky market street, a strip of stalls selling one of the largest collections we've ever seen of T-shirts with slogans on them. There is some sort of sewage-processing facility at the ocean end of the town that makes standing downwind a decidedly gamey experience. On the up side, the bus ride there from Central is fun, especially for roller coaster fans.

Star Ferry
Kowloon & Hong Kong
Island
• 3-662576

The Star Ferry is the best known of the ferries that service Hong Kong. Quite possibly it is the most famous ferry in the world outside of New York's Staten Island line. The green-and-white boats have been traveling between Central and Tsimshatsui since the end of the last century. The cross-harbor ride (daily, from 6:30 a.m. to 11:30 p.m.) leaves about every ten minutes (every twenty minutes during the very early-morning and late-night hours and on Sunday), costs next to nothing and is one of the great joys of Hong Kong. First class, which is upstairs, costs only slightly more than second class. We once asked a fellow what the difference was between the classes. He told us that when the people in first class spit, it lands on the heads of the people in second class, and when the people in second class spit, it only lands in the sea.
Open daily 6:30 a.m.-11:30 p.m.

Sung Dynasty Village

Kau Wa Keng, Kai Chi Kok, Kowloon
• 3-7415111

In America there's Williamsburg, a painstaking re-creation of a colonial town. In Hong Kong there's the Sung Dynasty Village, a slightly less painstaking re-creation (just ten years old) of the way life was between A.D. 960 and 1279. This 60,000-square-foot tourist attraction makes such a life seem rather jolly, with lots of musicians, acrobats, jugglers, bakers and pagodas. For some reason, we suspect that life was actually just a little bit harder than what's displayed here. There's a wax museum as well. The village is reached from Kowloon via the Kowloon Canton Railway.
Open Sat.-Sun. & holidays 12:30 p.m.-5 p.m.; group tours available weekdays. Admission HK$50.

Tiger Balm Gardens

Aw Boon Haw Villa, Tai Hang Rd., Happy Valley
• 5-8107576

Quite possibly the most garish creation this side of California's ghastly Madonna Inn, this monument to bad taste (and Chinese mythology) is the creation of the brothers who first marketed Tiger Balm, a liniment of many uses known best for its colorful containers. The bizarre eight acres of gardens were built in 1935 and are a wonderland of lions and tigers and bears, along with dragons and creatures of less explicable demeanor, most of which have fallen on slightly bad times. Incredibly, there's a duplicate garden in Singapore.
Open daily 10 a.m.-4 p.m.

Walled City

Kowloon City, North Kowloon

The Walled City is one of the more run-down sections of Hong Kong, largely because it's not actually part of the Crown Colony but rather a part of China. It was constructed in the 1840s by a group of Chinese to protect themselves from the "barbarians" (the British). The wall running around the area was destroyed during World War II by the Japanese, who needed the stones to build Kai Tak Airport's runway.

Zoological and Botanical Gardens

Garden Rd. (near Government House), Central

Though this is not an exceptional zoo, it is an opportunity to see how zoos were built back in 1871. It's also a good chance to experience the native flora of the Orient—in season the gardens are vivid with color—and, in the wee hours of the morning, to see elderly t'ai chi enthusiasts do their thing. We recommend a pleasant stroll through the twelve acres that make up this small sanctuary in the heart of Hong Kong.
Open daily 6 a.m.-7 p.m.

OUT OF HONG KONG

MACAU

INTRODUCTION

You can lose your heart (and probably a good part of your shopping budget for the next decade) with ease in Hong Kong. Loving Macau—even liking Macau—takes a good deal more work. We haven't yet managed it, though we are intrigued by the place. In a way, leaving the glitz and glitter of Hong Kong for the scruffiness of Macau is a bit like leaving Manhattan for the Bronx; you're fascinated by where you've gone, but you're not entirely sure why you've gone there. Though Macau is just 40 miles (by water) from Hong Kong, it seems both worlds and centuries apart. It's a crumbling colony of waterfronts and back alleys, the sort of place you'd almost expect to find pirates still swaggering about, and for romantics like us who have seen Marlene Dietrich in *Shanghai Express* far too many times, Macau has the air of a strangely exotic city filled with gimlet eyes that have seen much and forgotten little.

The reality is probably considerably less interesting, for despite its reputation as the Las Vegas of the East, Macau is actually more like the Atlantic City of the Orient—a place filled with smoky gambling halls in which men half crazed with gambling fever risk their last pataca (there are 100 avos to the pataca, by the way, which sounds more like something from Li'l Abner or Pogo than a world currency) on a throw of the dice, a turn of the card or a lucky combination of the mah-jongg tiles.

The casinos are large and garish, with no real sense of joy to them; the overriding atmosphere is one of frenzy and desperation. Out in the streets, which are cracked and poorly swept, you have a sense of past glories fading and buildings moldering away among increasingly invasive foliage and flora. Where Hong Kong seems to re-create itself with embarrassing rapidity, and Singapore has turned into a full-blown American-style city complete with an urban-renewal plan that's stripped away virtually every vestige of its colonial charm, Macau is still (and no doubt will be until it crumbles into the sea) a reminder of colonialism, an expatriate outpost where gambling and drinking are the lingua franca and life just moves along, with no real purpose at all. Actually, we're rather fond of that idea, and we look forward to getting to know the soul of Macau a bit better. But since, like most, you'll probably be there for no more than a day or two, some basic facts are in order.

HISTORY

Appropriately enough, Macau—a mere 90 miles downriver from Canton—was founded in 1557 as a trading post center for less-than-legal exchanges of goods and services between China and Japan, with Portuguese traders acting as middlemen. Since trade was banned between the two countries, the Portuguese (in the style of modern-day arms dealers who sell weapons of one country to another by filtering them through a variety of intermediaries) profited greatly from their position on the fence. They grew rich and fat, building grand cathedrals, fortified embankments and wholly excessive mansions, some of which have been transformed into hotels. Indeed, so thankful were the Portuguese to the God who gave them this golden goose of a colony that at one time Macau was reputed to have more churches per square mile than any other city in the world.

Unfortunately, Macau's glory days were short-lived. The blows came one after another: Japan was closed to Western influence; Portugal—a small country that had spread itself too thin protecting its worldwide colonial interests—began to lose its grip on trade, eventually being replaced by the somewhat more pragmatic (that is, less religiously driven) Dutch and English; and with the founding of Hong Kong in the nineteenth century, Macau's influence on the region came to an end, though it remained a powerful center for missionary work—the missionary doorway into heathen China.

Since the nineteenth century, not a whole lot has happened in Macau. It developed quite a reputation as a city of myriad sins, thanks to the legalization of gambling and the sundry evils that accompany such an industry (ranging in general from opium sales to prostitution). It was also noted for being a hotbed of spies and for hosting one of the last vestiges of the slave trade. You hear many stories about Macau, though those who know the place well say most of them are hogwash, that compared to Hong Kong and Shanghai, Macau was just a walk in the park; it just happens, thanks to its incipient decay, to look a lot more sinful.

Macau is surprisingly tiny—and, not so surprisingly, tightly packed with people. Most of its population of 500,000 live on the Macau Peninsula, a two-and-a-half-square-mile thumb of land jutting out from China; a few live on the nearby islands of Taipa and Coloane. More than 95 percent of the population is Chinese, but in true colonial style, most of the signs are in Portuguese, a language understood by an estimated 7,000 Macanese. Despite this confusion, it's easy to get around. In fact, aside from walking, the best way to travel is via a Mini Moke (Macau Mokes; call 5-434190 in Hong Kong to reserve one), a funny little open-air vehicle that looks like an overpowered golf cart. If you arrange it in advance, you can even take your Mini Moke into China proper. Border relations have long been fairly relaxed between China and Macau, which is officially a Chinese territory under Portuguese administration, a status it's worn comfortably since 1974. What that means is that Macau's governor and his cabinet are appointed in Lisbon, while the legislative assembly is elected locally. As with Hong Kong, Portugal will return Macau to China in 1999, though the current economic system is guaranteed for at least 50 years after that.

GETTING THERE

Residents of most Western countries, Japan or Hong Kong, don't have to worry about getting a Macanese visa, as long as you don't stay longer than six months (twenty days for Hong Kong residents).

Getting there from Hong Kong is eminently simple. Jetfoil and hydrofoil tickets can be reserved through most hotels and travel agents, or at any of the computerized Ticketmate booking outlets around Hong Kong (several of them are found in MTR stations). You can also order tickets by phone (5-8593288) if you have a major credit card. Both the jetfoils (which take 45 minutes) and the pokier hydrofoils (75 minutes) depart from the Macau Ferry Pier in the Western District on Hong Kong Island, a short walk from the Star Ferry Pier. At the Macau end, it's a short taxi ride from the pier to the middle of town.

RESTAURANTS

After days (weeks, months or even a lifetime) of eating Chinese food in Hong Kong, sampling the Portuguese food, and its various hybrids, found on Macau is lots of fun. It's a cuisine of seafood and wine, both of which are consumed in excessive amounts. The essential local cuisine is called Macanese, which comprises an astounding mixture of ingredients, herbs, spices and cooking techniques drawn from the kitchens of Portugal, China and sundry Portuguese colonies: Brazil, Goa, Mozambique and so forth. A typical dish might be a chicken stew made with potatoes (from South America), tomatoes (from Latin America), curry spices (from India), olive oil and olives (from Southern Europe), with coconut and saffron thrown in for good measure. Pork and potatoes are cooked with soy and with tamarind; bacalhau, that multipurpose Portuguese dish of dried salted cod that can be cooked any of a hundred ways, is ubiquitous. Colonial cuisine persists in an assortment of dishes from all over the world, many of which haven't changed in the past four centuries. And the seafood, the local waters' contribution to this culinary mix, can be some of the best in the world—prawns in Macau are bigger than most lobsters. And whatever you eat will inevitably be washed down with a bottle of vinho verde, which has the slightest fizz to it and costs close to nothing.

Any culinary tour of Macau would have to include such favorites as the venerable (circa 1903) Fat Siu Lau (64 Rua da Felicidade, 573585), which is no relation to the restaurant of the same name in Hong Kong. In this House of the Smiling Buddha situated in the midst of a long-gone red-light district, you'll eat some of the best bacalhau in town, along with cooked game birds of great renown, in a setting of long-lost elegance, just a stroll from the Inner Harbour.

Alfonso's (Hyatt Regency Macau, Taipa Island, 27000) provides the opportunity to sit around a small lake, in colonial rattan chairs, eating grilled Macanese sole, a fine seafood stew called caldeirada and that classic Brazilian pork-and-red-bean dish with the lilting name of feijoada. At the high end, good Macanese cooking can be found at A Galera Grill (Hotel Lisboa, 77666), though the dining rooms are as slapdash tacky as the rest of the hotel; at the Grill (The Oriental Hotel, 567888); and at the Restaurante Grill Fortaleza (Pousada de Sao Tiago, 78111), where African baked chicken and braised rabbit in red wine sauce are revered, and the bacalhau is a longtime favorite.

Though dining is not very expensive in Macau, even at the high end, those on a budget might consider dinner at Estrela do Mar (11 Travessa do Paiva, 81270), which may serve the most reasonably priced Portuguese chicken in town, or the absolutely wonderful Pinocchio's (4 Rua do Sol, Taipa Island, 27128), a madcap place just off the main street in funky old Taipa Village, where customers consume immense portions of steamed shrimp, chili crab and baked quail. Other good Macanese restaurants include Henri's Galley (4 Avenida da Republica, 76207); Portugues (16 Rua do Camp, 75445); and the marvelous little Riquexo (69 Sidonio Pais, 76294), a bargain lunch-only place that serves food prepared in nearby homes—perhaps the truest home cooking in the world.

HOTELS

Much ado has been made about the new Hyatt Regency Macau on Taipa Island (on the Taipa Island end of the Macau-Taipa Bridge, 27000). Prefabricated in the American South and shipped to Macau in modules, which were then assembled into the hotel, it looks, unfortunately, like a prefab place. The rooms are unpleasant boxes, with dreadfully noisy air conditioning and a startling lack of amenities (though one gets spoiled by Hong Kong's superb hotels). There's a free shuttle service to town, though we found it a bit inconvenient. If you're going to Macau, we suggest you stay in Macau, not a bridge away in a pile of shoe boxes that someone's nailed together.

More to our liking are the grand hotels situated between the wharf and the casinos, specifically the Oriental Hotel (Avenida da Amizade, 567888), which is built over the bones of the venerable Pan Am seaplane terminal on the edge of the Pearl River; it offers marble bathrooms and teak furniture. The nearby Hotel Presidente (Avenida da Amizade, 553888) is several steps below in luxury but nevertheless well located, and it's popular with business people on their way in and out of Macau. And the Hotel Royal (Estrada da Vitoria, 552222; managed by the Japanese Dai-Ichi chain) is quite fine for those who want to experience the pleasures of staying at the foot of Guia Hill near some of the finest old residences in Macau, adjacent to the wonderfully overgrown Vasco da Gama Garden.

Those who insist on staying in the casino in which they'll be throwing away their money will want to know about Hotel Lisboa (Avenida da Amizade, 77666), probably the most famous (and with its distinctly Chinese roof, the most visual) casino in town. Its two floors of casinos are open 24 hours a day, every day, a fact that guarantees a certain manic energy in the halls, including a noise level that is sure to interrupt your sleep. Somewhat more appealing is the Sintra (Avenido Dom Joao IV, 85111), which is owned by the

Lisboa—it apparently sends its good customers there when they finally need some sleep. Down the bay a bit, it's located on the Praia Grande, close enough to the action but far enough away to have some pleasant quiet. In deference to the Lisboa, its dining room is open 24 hours. Less recommended is the Metropole (63 Rua da Praia Grande, 88166), managed by the China Travel Service, which means it's a convenient place for booking a trip into China. We found it a less-than-convenient place for sleeping comfortably.

Those intrigued by the idea of slumbering in the midst of fallen colonial splendor can try the shabby (yet genteel) Bela Vista (Rua Comendador Kou Ho Neng, 573821), more than a century old and looking every minute of it. There are also a number of rather fine Portuguese inns (*pousadas*), most notably the Pousada de Sao Tiago (Avenida da Republica, 78111), a marvelously restored place that was built over the ruins of the seventeenth-century Barra Fort. Another is reached by car: the Pousada de Coloane (Praia de Cheoc Van, Coloane Island, 28144), which overlooks a beach and serves exceptional Portuguese food. Still, as we've said, if we're going to Macau, we'd rather be in Macau.

SIGHTS

There is gambling, of course, which has none of the chic overtones found at the far more elegant casinos of Las Vegas and Monte Carlo. Gambling in Macau is simply the act of throwing money on a table and either losing it or making more—that's all there is to it. Except that, thanks to the incredibly superstitious nature of Chinese in general, and Chinese gamblers in particular, there's actually much more to it.

The main casinos are those in the Lisboa and Oriental hotels, in the Jai Alai Stadium and on the Palacio de Macau (a floating casino), with the Lisboa being the busiest—though certainly not because of an excess of class or luxury. The games run from such American favorites as blackjack, craps and roulette, through such European games as baccarat (ah, such images of James Bond!) and boule, to such Chinese games as fan tan and dai siu. Slot machines, known quite aptly as "hungry tigers," fill side rooms.

Of the various so-called Macau Rules, the most notable is that any number of side bets can be made on your hand in a card game—and if one of those side bets is higher than the bet of the person playing the hand, the side bettor has the right to dictate when the hand is called. This can be a decidedly disconcerting experience, especially for those of us who thought that, at least when playing blackjack, we hold at least a bit of our destiny in our own hands. Another Macau Rule is that the dealer automatically takes a cut of the winnings as a tip. Trying to argue the point can be an ugly experience.

Aside from gambling, Macau offers a pleasant day of walking around its ruins and near-ruins. After departing the ferry, you head down the Guia, the road used every November during the Grand Prix of Macau. The Guia leads directly (after a few blocks) into the center of town. If you turn down Rua da Praia Grande, you can stroll past the antediluvian pile called the Hotel Bela Vista, the elegantly restored Pousada de Sao Tiago, the still-formal Government House and the A-Ma Temple, citadel of Macau's patron goddess.

Meandering into the side streets, you can lose yourself (and you will get lost, have no doubt of that) among church after church: St. Paul's, St. Augustine's, St. Joseph's and many more. Ascending the hills at the center of Macau, you can look out across the harbor from Monte Fort, wander through the old Protestant Cemetery, explore the Camoes Museum (a superb example of colonial architecture) and the garden in the Camoes Grotto, and contemplate the Lou Lim Loc Garden, modeled on the gardens of Soochow, which will give you an idea of how the wealthy Chinese maintained their identity in the midst of so many affluent Europeans.

Harness racing can be found at the Macau Trotting Club on Taipa Island; greyhound races at the Canidrome on Avenida General Castelo Branco; jai alai in the Jai Alai Stadium opposite the ferry wharf; and cricket fights at private homes, where the crickets are inspired to fight by trainers who tickle their abdomens with mouse whiskers. We've never been to one, but we're told they last longer and are harder fought than most of Mike Tyson's matches; sadly, no one, to the best of our knowledge, has ever suggested matching Tyson with a world-class cricket.

NEW TERRITORIES

INTRODUCTION

Most visitors to Hong Kong see only a small part of the colony—they believe that by visiting Central and an outlying island or two they've seen all there is to see. But the more curious and adventurous travelers should spend at least one day exploring the New Territories, a region still trying to hold fast to the pace of an earlier time, not yet completely conquered by the twentieth century. Between Tsuen Wan and Castle Peak you'll find yourself in a countryside rich in farmland (about one-third of the vegetables consumed in Hong Kong are grown in this area), where paddy fields are still sown by hand and plows are pulled by buffalo, where agricultural villages that date back several centuries rub shoulders with towering new housing structures, where ancient conventions are still honored and forefathers revered (however dilapidated the shrines and ancestral halls may appear), and where tower blocks cast shadows on ancient markets selling vegetables, fruit, fish, herbs and ducks from the local farms.

The eve of the twentieth century was the heyday of imperialism in the British Empire, and, with several other powers grabbing parts of China for themselves, the British acquired the rest of the Kowloon Peninsula and its immediate hinterland—the New Territories—together with all the rocks and islands of the archipelago that lies immediately around Hong Kong. The strategic importance of the New Territories was the hue and cry, but a certain amount of land speculation can also account for the lease of the New Territory (later called the New Territories) by the Chinese Empire to the British government in 1898 for a period of 99 years—an eternity. The total land area of Hong Kong thus increased from 32 to 390 square miles.

Today many of Hong Kong's 5.6 million people live in the New Territories. As modern times are beginning to encroach on the region, seven new towns, the first planned urban centers outside of Hong Kong, are linked by new roads and support industries that have grown up and prospered around them.

In the mix of ethnic cultures existing in the New Territories, the population is made up of three main peoples: Hakkas, Cantonese and

Tankas, each originating from a different part of China and Asia and each maintaining customs quite different from their neighbors.

The Tankas are thought to have been the earliest inhabitants, originating from Vietnam. They are the famous "boat people" of Hong Kong, and though many have moved to terra firma, there are still sizable colonies living in junks and sampans on the water.

The Hakkas, especially the women, with their black pajama-like attire and conical hats decorated with a short black curtain, are always of interest to the tourists; however, these mysterious women do not like having their pictures taken and will not hesitate to give chase to anyone who does not respect the rules.

By far the most populous group is the Cantonese, who, unlike the Tankas, are a land-based people and were quick to dominate the region. There are still a number of ancient Cantonese settlements, the oldest of which belong to the Tang clan in the Yen Long area.

The fish market at Lau Fau Shan is a must. Here you will find a restaurant whose walls are decorated with thousands of oyster shells, a street too narrow for cars (good for the dozens of open-air eateries and stalls selling wares there). Buy your fresh fish and the restaurant of your choice will cook it for you.

Perhaps the best known of the walled villages is Kat Hing Wai, whose 400 inhabitants all bear the clan name Tang. It was built in the 1600s and fortified with sixteen-foot-thick walls and watchtowers on every angle. Even if the TV antennae and modern buildings within detract somewhat from the authenticity of the village, tourists (on payment of an entrance fee) can visit, passing through the one and only entrance to the village, and collect (again for a small fee) snapshots of the old people hanging around the gate. Next to the Lok Ma Chau police station atop a hill, you can admire the magnificent countryside traversed by the Shum Chun River, the demarcation line of the Chinese border.

GETTING THERE

The New Territories are connected with Kowloon via the Kowloon-Canton Railway (KCR), which runs straight to the Chinese border, where it connects with other trains bound for various points Chinese. The KCR is base station is in Hung Hom, not far from Tsimshatsui; the trains are quick and cheap, taking you deep into the New Territories for about HK$22 (round-trip, first-class). This train will take you directly to Shatin, the Shatin Racecourse and Fanling, among other stops. For more information, call the KCR at 0-6069606.

RESTAURANTS

See New Territories & Outlying Islands in the Restaurants chapter.

SIGHTS

Aside from the spots mentioned in the Introduction, the New Territories are home to several places worth seeing. In bustling Shatin, one of the area's largest towns, is the Shatin Racecourse, which, along with Happy Valley on Hong Kong Island, is the center of Hong Kong's thriving horse-racing industry (as we've noted earlier, the Chinese adore gambling). Shatin Racecourse comprises three tracks and a public park on 250 acres of reclaimed land next to the impressive Jubilee Sport Centre; call 0-6956603 for racing information. The track can be reached directly via the KCR train.

Also on the KCR train route is Sung Dynasty Village, a re-creation of a 1,000-year-old Chinese village; see Sights for more information. Just outside of Shatin, crowning a steep hill, is the Ten Thousand Buddhas Monastery, whose name modestly underestimates the number of Buddhas here: there are 12,800 of them, in every size imaginable, along with the embalmed—and still sitting upright—Reverend Yuet Kai, the monastery's founder. The monastery is reached by a half-hour climb through a pine and bamboo wood; it's marked by a hexagonal pink pagoda.

Bird watchers won't want to miss the area around the fast-growing town of Taipo. And golfers should arrange a tee time at the Royal Hong Kong Golf Club at Fanling (0-901211), where clubs, carts or caddies are available for play and hire on any of the *three* eighteen-hole courses. Yet more golfing, and other sports as well, are offered at the exclusive, plush Clearwater Bay Golf and Country Club (3-7191595). For more information on any of the New Territories sights, contact the HKTA at 3-722555.

THE OUTLYING ISLANDS

INTRODUCTION

Victoria Harbour is a sensational backdrop for one of the world's most dramatic flight paths. If you take a look below well before touching down, you will have a bird's-eye view of Hong Kong's loveliest attractions: its islands.

Officially, there are 235 of them, not counting the one on which Britain's navy (and Chinese opium traders) set up camp in 1841—Hong Kong Island. Like Manhattan, Hong Kong Island is sui generis. Nearly all the other islands entered the colonial embrace in 1898, being South China Sea mountaintops that happened to lie inside the rectangle of the New Territories lease. Apart from a measly vein of silver, they held no natural resources. The British, stepping clumsily but effectively into the shoes of Imperial China's magistrates and evacuated garrisons, subdued the islands' pirates and smugglers, codified local laws and subjected the islanders to decades of generally benign neglect.

In this century, some island communities vanished after all their young people emigrated to Hong Kong, and a few islands were entirely swallowed up in reclamation projects. Others became dumping grounds for the unwanted (drug addicts, prisoners, refugees) or the unsightly and dangerous (power stations, gas tanks, explosives). But while the islands have entered the modern age (some just a little bit), most remain traffic-free and places of true natural beauty.

The ferry sailings to these islands can be a noisy proposition on a weekend or public holiday, when all of Hong Kong's younger generation seems to be ghetto-blasting its way back to its insular roots. Avoid, too, the waves of 300,000 outlying islanders commuting to work on the mainland and Hong Kong Island; the cattle-pen ferry piers are bad enough at the best of times (between rush hours on weekdays: after 10 a.m. and before 5 p.m.). And do not expect any of Hong Kong & Yaumatei Ferry Company's 76 vessels—be it high-speed hovercraft or triple-decked craft with a purportedly deluxe air-conditioned partially nonsmoking deck—to provide marine comforts.

The obstinately old-fashioned Hong Kong & Yaumatei Ferry Company, one of Hong Kong's (and the world's) first major Chinese-owned enterprises, is staffed by gruff, long-serving crewmen, who run a profitable sideline of atrocious on-board noodle shops. We can only say: avoid these and look on the bright side, which is wonderfully easy from the sun terrace on the stern of the so-called deluxe deck. You're sailing through the scenic South China Sea, after all, in scheduled safety (the company's record is remarkable), for most likely no more than HK$12 per person (per one-hour one-way journey), to discover islands still soaked in the ancient character of South China. Scruffy ferries and piers, and noisily festive fellow passengers, are all just part and parcel of the character. For more information on island ferry transportation, call the ferry company at 5-423081 or the Hong Kong Tourist Association (HKTA) at 3-7225555.

CHEUNG CHAU ISLAND

The Cheung Chau ferry glides through the island harbor's ranks of bunting-clad deep-sea-fishing junks. From its sun deck, you can see why scores of Caucasians choose to live on dumbbell-shape Cheung Chau (Long Island): it looks and feels Mediterranean, almost Aegean (if you can manage to overlook the government housing estate plunked on a low cliff).

Fiercely insular, tiny twelve-square-kilometer Cheung Chau is Hong Kong's most densely developed isle, with a population (over 20,000) bigger than Lantau's. Its pirate bands ruled the roost, slaughtering seafarers, until early in this century, but the signposted Cheung Po Tsai pirate's cave isn't even worth visiting; it is a poor memorial for an antihero claimed to have ruled a fleet of 40,000 followers and 250 war junks.

To really get a sense of the vibrant yet unhurried mood of this quintessential Chinese maritime community, wander along the Praya (harborside promenade). Narrow lanes intersecting it crisscross the crowded sandbar, which is cheek-by-jowl home for thousands of Hakka, Cantonese and Tanka families. Though many islanders now commute to Central, Cheung Chau is still a thriving market-town community and fishing port.

If you stroll through the area, you'll wind up at the playground in front of two-centuries-old Pak Tai Temple, which was built to honor the "supreme emperor of the dark heaven" whose image saved the islanders from the plague. Cheung Chau's annual Bun Festival commemorates this miracle with parades of "floating" children and the construction of three 70-feet-high towers of pink and white buns (whose good luck is eaten at festival end). Unfortunately, the annual challenge race to climb the towers has been banned—local clan and triad rivalries resulted in bloodthirsty bun fights.

On the other side of the sandbar, facing Hong Kong, are two beaches (Kun Iam, to the south, is the superior one). The lumpen mass of the Warwick Hotel looms over a Bronze Age rock carving unceremoniously preserved in a cage near a windsurfing club. Backtrack, inland and upward, to discover the island's sylvan side, on and off a hilltop road whose social pretensions were modeled on those of Hong Kong Island's own mansion-topped Peak.

RESTAURANTS

Because it's so heavily populated, Cheung Chau has a good selection of eating places, though none are worth a special trip to the island. The island's best Cantonese restaurant, known locally as The Hole in the Wall, recently closed. Many resident Caucasians frequent the East Lake restaurant, opposite the post office on the path leading to the main (Tung Wan) beach, behind which the Warwick Hotel operates a coffee shop. The Bor Kee restaurant, a crowded, popular eating place for Chinese residents, fills two connected shop sites near the post office, flanking the site of the Village Tree, a former expatriate hangout scheduled to become—in a sign of changing island times—a sushi bar. Down the side lane next to it, the grandly titled Cheung Chau Country Club offers low views of the bay and mediocre Cantonese cuisine. Across the sandbar settlement, flanking the ferry pier, is the Praya, the most popular eating area in town. You can sit outside and watch the world bustle past. Fisherfolk and vegetable growers display their stocks, a score of cafés and restaurants turn out passable meals, and there are a couple of Western-style cafés to make visitors feel at least welcomed. The mood of the Praya, and Cheung Chau's individuality, is best savored after dark, when commuters have returned home and day-trippers have gone for the day.

LAMMA ISLAND

Facing Aberdeen, to the southwest of Hong Kong Island, Lamma is the territory's third-largest island. Ferry services make the one-hour trip from Central to the fishing harbors of Yung Shue Wan (Banyan Tree Bay) and Sok Kwu Wan (Hand Net). *Kaido* ferries also serve Sok Kwu Wan from Aberdeen.

Though industrial eyesores have literally disfigured Lamma—Yung Shue Wan's 7,000 inhabitants are overwhelmed by a power station, and Sok Kwu Wan's 2,000 quarried cliffs—it remains a pleasant spot for island walks, swimming and, best of all, seafood. The 90-minute island-crossing walk from one harbor to the other (via a concrete pathway) presents grand panoramas of the South China Sea as well as insights into contrasting island lifestyles: farmers have settled the land around Yung Shue Wan, while fishing remains the major livelihood for Sok Kwu Wan residents. Sea turtles were once caught at Lo So Shing beach, a half-hour shoreline stroll from Sok Kwu Wan, but humans will be happiest swimming at Hung Shing Ye, a small inlet about a 30-minute walk from Yung Shue Wan.

RESTAURANTS

More than any other island, Lamma is a place to go to eat. Yung Shue Wan's lanes are dotted with unpretentious Chinese restaurants, Western-style bars and noodle shops. The Lancombe and Man Fung seafood restaurants on Main Street are both well-established places; their club-like neighbor, the Capital Restaurant, attracts a mixed clientele of residents for its ethnically mixed menu. For a more memorable seafood experience, we suggest you go to Sok Kwu Wan and pay a visit to one of the harbor's waterfront restaurants. A favorite destination for Sunday sailors, Sok Kwu Wan's dozen or so stilt-terraced restaurants display well-stocked fish tanks and wine cabinets. The three-unit Peach Garden Seafood (see Restaurants, New Territories & Outlying Islands) and others vie for a market that is composed of predominantly Caucasian and repeat customers. On weekdays and weeknights, when tablefuls of wine-flushed Caucasians are less in evidence. Sok Kwu Wan is an English-speaking haven.

Fresh-seafood prices (quoted per tael, or Chinese ounce) are below those of Hong Kong restaurants, the staff is shyly attentive, and the stillness is only rarely disturbed by a harbor fish farm's yapping dog or the occasional arrival of a ferry or *kaido*. (Romantics ignore the quarry workings on the other side of the harbor.)

LANTAU ISLAND

To the delight of today's hill climbers, beach-goers and monks, the British rejected Lantau as a colonial base, despite its size and height (nearly twice that of Hong Kong Island). Its mountain range's Sunset and Lantau peaks dwarf Victoria Peak by 1,300 feet. Dotted with monasteries (Island of Prayer is just one of its local names), splendidly underpopulated (at 16,000, the population comprises about 1 percent of Hong Kong Island's mass) and conserved primarily within two country parks, Lantau (alias Tai Yue Shan or Big Island Mountain), could be a tourist destination in its own right. But it isn't. On the entire island, there is only one biggish hotel (run by the ferry company, so enough said). Privileged Hong Kong residents take their R & R breaks in company-house compounds, while congregations of local youths gather, ten to a "Spanish-villa" bedroom, around the altar of their ghetto blasters.

Camping is possible; many backpackers hike along the Lantau Trail to youth hostels or Po Lin Monastery's basic accommodations (of hard boards). But it appears to be a worthwhile adventure: they rise early for the climb to watch the sun rise over Lantau Peak.

Founded by three hermits in 1905, the Po Lin (Precious Lotus) retreat on 2,400-foot-high Ngong Ping (Lofty Plateau) is now a florid, flower-bedecked operation, entering the record books with its 110-foot-high open-air statue of Lord Buddha. Below him lies a serenely successful commercial operation, whose main temple is a riot of color. Vegetarian lunch sittings are a HK$25 penance (see Restaurants, New Territories & Outlying Islands). The monastery's scruffy neighbor, the Lantau Tea Gardens, is Hong Kong's only tea plantation. Visit its tea terrace to try the local wan mo ("cloud and mist") tea. Horseback riding and roller skating are added attractions.

The single-decker bus, which hairpin-bends its way uphill to Po Lin, is a sight-seeing treat in and of itself; it can be boarded at the Silvermine Bay ferry pier. In fact, as soon as you arrive on Lantau, board any red-and-orange Lantau bus or blue taxi (Lantau is color-fully different than Hong Kong) and head out of Silvermine Bay. Its mines, in the hinterland behind Mui Wo village, were closed up years ago, and its scenic bay's polluted waters are unsafe for swimmers.

Bus schedules are keyed to ferry arrivals, so disembark quickly to line up for a bumpily scenic 45-minute ride to far-off Tai O, the market-town capital of Lantau. Its historical economic might rested on its now-abandoned salt-panning fields. A small island of stilt houses, Tai O is connected to Lantau's mainland by a unique rope-drawn creek ferry. For 20 cents, the Tanka ferrywoman will allow you to squeeze onto the standing-room-only sampan raft and haul you into a prehistoric atmosphere.

Life on land never appealed to Tai O's thousands of Tanka fisher-folk, descended from Hong Kong's aborigines. So they built a mini-Venice around their creeks, only recently erecting one primitive net-sided drawbridge. Wander at will—Tai O is exceptionally neat, friendly and charming; a map near the bus stop outlines the routes to three ancient temples. Don't miss the picturesque Hau Wong temple at the end of a small causeway.

The bus stop with fewest tourists, and the most overwhelming sense of South China Sea antiquity, is at Tung Chung. A north-coast farming and fishing community, it is reached via a single-track lane that soars through country parkland and the twin peaks of cloud and mist. We suggest you leave the bus when the lane begins to run parallel to Tung Chung's sandy bay and breathe in the history: the last of the Sung Dynasty emperors (two young brothers) and their loyal retinue stayed for a time in this coastal valley during their flight from China's Mongol conquerors.

Follow the signposts to Tung Chung Fort, whose preserved Qing Dynasty walls and rusty Chinese cannons now guard a primary school. After studying the historical plaque, head coastward past ruminative cows (a roadside feature throughout undeveloped Lan-tau) until you reach a maze of elevated footpaths crisscrossing the wetlands behind the bay. Amid a clump of trees, another Hau Wong temple (probably founded during the Ming Dynasty) adorns a grassy beachside knoll. Here, as in all the island's isolated communities, festival days are celebrated in massive mat sheds and with enough noise to keep evil spirits away for another year.

It is important to schedule your Lantau day trip carefully (using the Hong Kong Tourist Association's Information Centres for transpor-tation information). On your return route, you can board a scheduled local ferry (*kaido*) in Tung Chung and chug across the Lantau Channel, via the barely populated island of Chek Lap Kok, to Castle Peak Bay, on the outskirts of Tuen Mun New Town. From its ferry pier, hovercrafts zip back to Central in 35 minutes, past mountainous north Lantau's unspoiled coastline. The Hovercrafts also spurt past rustic Ma Wan Island (see below).

Beach lovers may well abandon all of the above sight-seeing bus rides when they set eyes on the virtually unexploited beaches of Cheung Sha, twenty minutes west of Silvermine Bay. Running alongside South Lantau Road (Lantau's only main road) for over three kilometers, Cheung Sha's "Long Sand" stretch of beach is among Hong Kong's whitest. In the swimming season, for safety, stay within sight of the lifeguards.

Beyond Cheung Sha, buses cross the high dam of the forest-flanked Shek Pik reservoir (you can look down to see the private beach belonging to the island's prison). Beside the dam is one of Lantau's rock carvings (probably Bronze Age), and on the other side, the lowland sections of the 70-kilometer, twelve-stage Lantau Trail streak past magnificent beaches and the ruins of another Imperial Chinese fort. Hikers wishing to follow these trail stages should come equipped with maps and sturdy shoes.

Lantau is ideal for independent travelers (study the HKTA's free "Outlying Islands" leaflet), though guided tours are available (the Information Centres—see Basics—have contact numbers for whole-day or afternoon Lantau Island monastery tours, as well as visits to Cheung Sha, Tai O and the Po Lin Monastery).

Town planners and estate developers are, of course, very interested in Discovery Bay, a huge Hawaii-style private-housing estate to the east of Silvermine Bay, accessible only by sea. A 24-hour hovercraft service ferries the residents of Disco Bay (many of whom are British expatriates) to and from Central's Blake Pier (the HK$20 one-way fare for nonresidents is intended to keep out the riffraff). Initially developed by an entrepreneur who went bankrupt, Disco Bay is actually home to dull restaurants, a big beach whose shallows are a quagmire and an excellent hilltop championship golf course (Discovery Bay Golf Club, 5-9877271).

RESTAURANTS

Unfortunately, Lantau boasts of no eating places of distinction, though the vegetarian refectories at the Po Lin Monastery can be soul-cleansing. Hong Kong expats, mostly those with a penchant for french fries and Mateus Rosé, make a beeline for the Tong Fuk Provision Store, which, confusingly, is not in Tong Fuk village but on the western side of Pui O village, about fifteen minutes from Silvermine Bay along the South Lantau Road. Also known as Charlie's or the Lantau Hilton (its chef/owner worked at the Hilton in Central), the roadside grocery-cum-café occupies a converted village house and a patio-garden. It lacks views, but its bilingual menu includes inexpensive Chinese, Western and curry platters (chilled brand-label wine can be purchased in the grocery); you'll spend about HK$70 per person.

PENG CHAU ISLAND

A busy little commuter island, Peng Chau is the first port of call for most ferries and Hovercraft bound for Lantau's Silvermine Bay. Caucasians live here, too, or own weekend apartments, enjoying an island that is a microcosm of the South Chinese lifestyle. Small enough to stroll around in half a day, Peng Chau has a little bit of everything (fishing boats, porcelain painters, rattanware and furniture makers, temples and terraced fields). There isn't a good beach, but the main town and outlying hamlets are bonded by a strong sense of community.

Avoid Peng Chau on summer weekends; at any other time, you may want to plan to end a trip at an outdoor table of the restaurant near the old ferry pier. Seafood can be bought directly from old-timers (on the pier or bobbing about in the shallows beneath it) and brought to the restaurant, which will see that it is cooked up for a small charge.

For a full day trip, combine your visit to Peng Chau with a trip to Lantau Island. You can take the *kaido* from Peng Chau's old pier to the jetty of Lantau's Trappist Monastery, whose spire rises above a forest of fir trees. A climb up the hillside road, past the Stations of the Cross, will deliver you into serene silence: the monks belong to an order that urges visitors to whisper quietly. The noisiest residents are cows, whose milk is the monastery's claim to worldly fame (as well as its major money-making interest).

Hilltop paths lead from the monastery to Lantau's Silvermine Bay, or around to the golf course and residential estate of Discovery Bay, which also can be reached via the ancient Lantau coastal settlement of Nim Shue Wan—the *kaido* docks there after leaving the monastery's jetty. The *kaido* then returns to Peng Chau. It's helpful to study the *kaido* schedule carefully to avoid being stranded: overnight visitors can be accommodated at the monastery only by prior arrangement.

OTHER ISLANDS

Many other islands and island communities are accessible by *kaido* or excursion ferry services. Anyone planning a lengthy stay in Hong Kong, or return visitors wanting to explore rarely visited scenic spots, can obtain transportation information from HKTA Information Centres (see Basics).

MA WAN, a well-wooded small island off the northeast tip of Lantau, has a fine, sandy beach with extraordinary panoramas of distant Hong Kong Island (and, less attractively, of nearby industrially scarred Tsing Yi Island). Many islanders commute across the Lantau channel to the mainland's Castle Peak Road, using a busy *kaido* service that shuttles back and forth all day and whose jetty, at Sham Tseng, is an ugly semi-industrial coastal settlement worth visiting if only for the roast goose dishes at its roadside Chiu Chow restaurants.

PING CHAU, the most outlying of all Hong Kong's Outlying Islands, lies hours of ferry travel out in Mirs Bay; now largely unoccupied, it is famed for its multicolored rock strata. Since the ferry arrives on Saturdays and leaves on Sundays, overnighting is obligatory (in a tent or primitive village housing).

PO TOI, way down in the south, is accessible by public transportation only on Sundays, when *kaido* services chug out of Aberdeen and Stanley, bearing island-goers off to a grand beach littered with ad hoc seafood cafés.

TAP MUN, or Grass Island, off the northeast coast of the Sai Kung peninsula, is a major offbeat attraction and one of Hong Kong's finer day-tripping experiences. The ferry company's afternoon Tolo Harbor service (itself a delightful marine sight-seeing tour of New Territories mountains and bays) docks at Tap Mun and returns an hour later, allowing enough time for visitors to scamper through a virtually undeveloped offshore fishing community and its handsome Tin Hau temple. The alternate route to Tap Mun is to go overland to Sai Kung and board the bus to Wong Shek pier; it is met by a *kaido* that plies in and out of superbly scenic, fjord-like Long Harbor en route to Tap Mun.

CITYLORE

After rampaging through the brand-name boutiques of The Landmark and witnessing Club Volvo's hundreds of hostesses at work, Kubla Khan might swear that his decreed Xanadu of stately pleasure domes had indeed come to pass in Hong Kong. Colony, territory or "accident of history"—call it what you will, Hong Kong is indisputably grand. If it did not rest on volcanic outcrops, it might well sink into the South China Sea under the weight of all the imported marble with which it has decked its halls.

Beneath its shimmering surface, however, Hong Kong is, at heart, the child of its environment—even if its foster parents were British traders. Part of the South China coast, both rural and maritime, Hong Kong is a 1,070-square-kilometer (664-square-mile) parvenu whose marble facades and Gucci culture cannot mask its ancient superstitions and peasantry past.

While China tried to expunge millennia of domestic imperialism, social taboos and religious rites, little capitalist Hong Kong maintained its faith in a system of ancient beliefs structured around family loyalty and supernatural forces. Accounting for Hong Kong's success more than capitalism per se, this ancient system can be seen everywhere in contemporary Hong Kong.

Those who regularly flick spilt salt over their shoulders or refuse to walk under ladders will feel right at home in superstitious Hong Kong, once they recognize some of the ground rules that control the Chinese game of life. Belief in *chi*, or the spiritual balance of yin and yang (male- female, active-passive, day-night, hot-cold and so forth), is fundamental. No local needs a fortune cookie (which you will never find here) to know how to gain health, wealth and happiness (the Chinese holy trinity); these are attained by balancing one's yin and yang, if necessary nudging nature and the gods in the right direction.

THE SCIENCE OF FUNG SHUI

One set of shortcuts is *fung shui* ("wind water"), an ancient system of geomancy officially scorned in the People's Republic but practiced devoutly in Hong Kong. A complex form of celestial town planning, it accounts for many of the physical oddities visitors note in Hong Kong. Why are Hang Seng Bank entrances always situated diagonally to the road? To stop money flowing out. Why is it you can never walk straight into a building, but must turn left or right? To keep out evil spirits who, fortunately for the living, are not bright enough to handle corners. Why do major buildings facing the water often have open spaces or walls of windows at their back (like The Regent hotel and the Hong Kong Bank headquarters)? So the dragons who inhabit the hills behind the building can enjoy unimpeded access to their favorite swimming waters.

Western-trained architects rarely ignore such *fung shui* considerations; their own criteria (security, ventilation, natural lighting) often justify them. Consultant *fung shui* masters are paid small fortunes to advise how best to enhance a building site's natural advantages (or overcome its disadvantages). They are called in as well at the interior-decoration stage or, like exorcists, to correct a building's bad-luck streak. Harmony-seeking suggestions may include moving desks (they should never face a doorway) and erecting baffles (in case evil spirits should get past the main entrance). Installing aquariums is a favorite—if your window does not face luck-bringing water, you can create a symbolic monetary flow with an aquarium. Sometimes a disaster-prone main entrance is simply sealed up permanently (as at Radio Television Hong Kong's Broadcasting House).

A visit to a Hong Kong home, particularly one in a rural village, reveals how *fung shui* principles and related superstitions stem from climatic and geotechnical concerns. In the ideal Chinese home, the building generally faces south, and northern back walls have no windows. A fortune-bringing stream flows beside the home, but never too swiftly. Heads of beds never face doorways, and mirrors are carefully positioned (they can double one's luck or steal one's soul, depending on their locations). Green plants, especially "money trees," are nurtured in "money corners." Big-leaf plants are favored symbols, implying that good fortune will arrive in large doses; lots of small leaves signify much hard labor.

To outsiders, such meticulous avoidance of bad *fung shui* may appear to be a tedious household chore. We can only respond: In Hong Kong, ignore it at your peril. Even the British colonial authorities play the ancient game—whenever excavation work for a new road or tunnel endangers the health of a dragon living in the hills, elaborate propitiatory ceremonies are organized to placate the creatures. Of course, in reality, these reassure the dragons' human neighbors, whose supernatural anxieties often are most effectively eased by other means: money.

If superstitions are the seeds of religions, then China's merry mix of religions has produced a bountiful harvest of additional superstitions. In fact, few temples in Hong Kong are devoted exclusively to one religion or god. Whether the temple is as old as the colony (like Hong Kong Island's Man Mo) or much, much older, it offers multiple spiritual insurance. Worshippers can have prayerful words with the whole heavenly host of ancestral spirits and Buddhist and Taoist gods.

SOOTHING THE SPIRITS

There are myriad ways to a spirit or divinity's heart. In temples, smoke signals are sent via burnt offerings or smoldering incense coils. The heavenly answers are revealed by shaking canisters of numbered bamboo sticks or tossing up a pair of wooden shapes (whose landing positions indicate the divine answer: Yes, No or Ask the Question Another Way). Worshippers pay fees for such services; temple-keeping is a family business, whose rights are bid for just like any concession. And like grocers, Hong Kong's temple-keepers keep their surveillance moniters switched on all the time, warily eyeing non-Chinese interlopers.

A visitor need not go to a temple to see Hong Kong's religious devotions. There are shrines everywhere, even in marbled downtown office blocks and pleasure domes. Many Chinese homes boast ancestral altars with ever-burning red lights and joss sticks. Some have a shrine for the kitchen god (each family has its own), and other traditionalist homes have external, door-side shrines. Trees have shrines as well, set at the base of venerable spirit-inhabited trunks. Banyans, in particular, are favored; the preservation of the banyan tree inside Queensway's Pacific Place complex cost the site's developers tens of millions of dollars (highways had to be rerouted).

Each community has additional shrines dedicated to local city or earth gods. Even in Central, just a cobblestone's throw from the trendy Lan Kwai Fong nightlife district, an unusually large pink-walled neighborhood shrine decorates the far end of Wo On Lane.

Throughout Hong Kong, heavenly smoke-signaling is strongest during the midsummer Hungry Ghosts Festival, when the roadside gutters of such older-fashioned districts as Western are littered with small pyres of burning paper. Every little tribute helps to soothe the troubled souls of the ghostly spirits, who, much like the French in August, get a month's freedom in which to wander the world and wreak havoc. We joke, but we shouldn't: Hungry Ghosts is the equivalent of a month of Friday the thirteenths.

Which brings us to numerology, a Chinese science cheerily exploited by the Cantonese, whose multitoned dialect (more complex than Mandarin) is a punster's playground. Each number's sound is akin to another word's character, which is why you won't find a fourth floor in some buildings: "four" can be aurally associated with "death." That is why the territory's major television station, which congratulates itself shamelessly on every anniversary of its profitable birth, never had a fourth or fourteenth birthday. Eight is Hong Kong's favorite number; it sounds like "prosperity." August 8, 1988, was a day so magical that even the Bank of China turned a blind eye and allowed the contractors for its new headquarters building to plan celebratory events. Hong Kong telephone numbers rich with eights are coveted; vehicle registration numbers with juicy combinations of eights are held back by the licensing authorities and sold to the highest bidders at fund-raising charity auctions. Other desirable numbers at such auctions are three (which sounds similar to "life") and nine ("eternity"). Walk down any street, glance at shop and restaurant signs, and you will see countless examples of numbers intended to bring luck to businesses.

You'll also notice door gods guarding businesses (The Peninsula hotel has a particularly handsome pair) in the same way they protect temples and village houses. A supernatural pride of lions often holds bad luck and evil spirits at bay. Hong Kong's best-known lions are the ancient, war-wounded, bronze pair that can outstare anyone planning a holdup at the Hong Kong & Shanghai Bank Corporation's headquarters on Queen's Road in Central. The duo was very carefully relocated when the bank opened its high-rise, high-tech new building (which, of course, was scheduled for the auspicious moment specified by *fung shui* masters).

THE OLD WAYS ARE STILL THE BEST

Remarkably low-tech, on the other hand, is the construction industry's scaffolding system: bamboo strung together by aerial acrobats with sheaths of dampened reeds hanging from their waists. Tubular steel scaffolding has never caught on here, as a web of unbreakable bamboo bends better during typhoons. Bamboo, like all of nature's gifts, is fully exploited by the Chinese; its shoots and pith are prized ingredients in cooking. Bamboo can also be found in old-fashioned apothecary stores, where the pith and outer skin are two common ingredients in herbal and natural medicines.

If the prescription charge is toted up the old-style way, you will experience the mesmerizing music of the abacus. Its clicks are rarely heard now in the computerized downtown offices, but family-store old-timers still scorn calculating machines. So do some cashiers in the Chinese-owned department stores. Though most of these stores are modernized (and accept credit cards and stock Taiwanese products), they still employ three staff members to handle one sale.

Yes, some things in Hong Kong are still done the old-fashioned way. And, of course, there are still signs of the British, though they appear to have been a modest lot, erecting few monuments to themselves. In fact, there is only one "colonial" statue in Central Hong Kong. It stands, logically enough, in Statue Square, and commemorates neither a king nor a governor. It is a black, bigger-than-man-size farewell tribute to Sir Thomas Jackson, who, as the statue's plaque reveals, was the sterling chap who managed the Hong Kong & Shanghai Bank at the end of the nineteenth century.

In a city where money talks, this remembrance makes sense. The statue of King George V is hidden away inside the Zoological and Botanical Gardens. As for his mum, Queen Victoria, Hong Kong's colonial mistress for 60 years, her statue was carted off during the Japanese occupation and never returned to the city center that once bore her name (the City of Victoria). One spot in particular cries out for a statuesque memorial: the Western District hillside where a British naval officer first planted the Union Jack. But all it ever got was a street name—Possession Street.

What's in a name? Much in Hong Kong, which, you will quickly realize, is no longer called a possession, and *never* a "colony." Tactfully, these are "territories" (just as Macau is an "enclave").

It is nineteenth-century spite, rather than modern diplomacy, that accounts for the lack of any visible tribute to the buccaneering boldness of Hong Kong's first British administrator and de facto governor, Captain Charles Elliott. (Poor old Elliott was the black sheep of the colonial family: he exceeded London's orders in the first place by annexing Hong Kong without permission, and then angered Hong Kong's opium traders by being an even craftier capitalist than they were and auctioning off land leases.) All his successors have been allowed to leave their names on Hong Kong's map, usually for roads and in the recent past for a hospital, a university building and a country-park walking trail. It is possible to stroll around the north end of Hong Kong Island and rarely step off a governor, other than to walk down streets named for nineteenth-century members of the British Royal Family.

On Sundays, over in Kowloon, a regiment of Filipino *amahs* (maids) makes its way to mass in Hong Kong's century-old Roman Catholic cathedral, Rosary. Then they flock to Statue Square to spend their off-duty day visiting with one another. There are now at least 35,000 Filipino *amahs* in Hong Kong, and each costs her employers a steep government-fixed rate of pay. These imported servants verify the phenomenal growth of Hong Kong's middle class.

Few young Hong Kong Chinese women now choose to go into domestic service, but aging Chinese *amahs* can be seen at their old-style best in the early mornings at any public garden (Chater Garden in Central, Victoria Park in Causeway Bay, Kowloon Park off Nathan Road). There they join their uniformed "sisters" and other older citizens in slow-motion, soul-soothing, body-tuning t'ai chi ch'uan exercises.

Early morning is also the time to catch another old-style human Hong Kong species in the act: the bird lover. Rising early, these men troop off to their regular teahouse accompanied by their pampered pet bird. Taking their regular seats, the men gossip over dim sum and newspapers, while the birds, their cages set high on hooks, chirp in competitive crescendoes. No greater love hath a Chinese man, it appears, than that for his bird.

Well, not really. For many Hong Kong gentlemen, gambling is a grander passion, consummated at the Royal Hong Kong Jockey Club's two high-tech race courses (Happy Valley and Shatin), in the Club's enormous chain of off-course betting centers, in mah-jongg parlors, over in Macau's casinos or down in Central's biggest temple

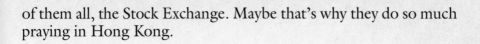

of them all, the Stock Exchange. Maybe that's why they do so much praying in Hong Kong.

BASICS

AT YOUR SERVICE

ADDRESSES & TELEPHONE NUMBERS

Ambulance—St. John's Ambulance Service (free), Hong Kong: 5-766555; Kowloon: 3-7135555; New Territories: 0-437543.

American Express—New World Tower, 16-18 Queen's Rd., Central, Hong Kong, 5-8431888.

Arts Centre box office—5-8230230.

Cable and Wireless—3-7324336.

Chambers of Commerce—American, 5-260165; Hong Kong General Chamber of Commerce—5-299229.

City Hall—5-739595.

Consulate Offices—American, 26 Garden Rd., Hong Kong, 5-239011; Australian, 5-731881; British, Overseas Visa Section, Hong Kong Immigration Department, Mirror Tower, 61 Mody Rd., Tsim-shatsui East, Kowloon, 3-7333111; Canadian, 5-81014321; Japanese Consulate, Bank of America Tower, 12 Harbour Rd., Central, Hong Kong, 5-221184.

Department of Immigration—3-7333111.

Emergency Services (Police, Fire, Ambulance)—999.

Ferries—Star Ferry, 3-662576; Hong Kong Ferry, 5-423081.

Hong Kong Tourist Association (HKTA)—Jardine House, 35th Fl., 1 Connaught Rd., Central, Hong Kong, 5-244191; Information Number, 3-7225555.

Hospitals—Queen Mary Hospital, Pokfulam Rd., Hong Kong, 5-8192111; Hong Kong Adventist Hospital, 40 Stubbs Rd., Hong Kong, 5-746211; Queen Elizabeth Hospital, Wylie Rd., Kowloon, 3-7102111.

Kai Tak International Airport—3-7697531.

Police—Crime Hotline and Taxi Complaints, 5-277177; Information, 5-284284 ext. 231; Japanese Hotline, 3-290000.

Post Office—Hong Kong: 2 Connaught Pl., Central, 5-231071; Kowloon: 405 Nathan Rd., Tsimshatsui, 3-884111.

Railways: Kowloon-Canton Railway, 0-6069606; Mass Transit Railway (MTR), 3-7500170.

Tramways: Peak Tramway, 5-220922; Hong Kong Tramway, 5-8918765.

CRIME

As the signs along Nathan Road attest, pickpockets generally congregate in areas frequented by tourists. Beyond that, all the standard bits of common wisdom will be sufficient to keep you from turning into an American Express commercial: make sure your wallet is secure in your pocket or your purse; don't walk along with an open purse; never flash large amounts of money in public places. And keep in mind that while the gangs described in *Noble House* may exist, the tourist trade is not their primary interest.

ELECTRICITY

You'll need adapters to match your blow dryers and travel irons to Hong Kong's 220 volts 50 cycles AC, with three-pin plugs—but take note that many hotels also offer American-style outlets.

ENGLISH-LANGUAGE BOOKSTORES

Besides the books sold in most hotel lobbies, English bookstores abound. Some of the best of these are Times Books (Hutchison House, Central, Hong Kong), Hong Kong Book Centre (25 Des Voeux Road, Central, Hong Kong), Swindons (Ocean Terminal, Tsimshatsui, Kowloon) and the exceptional Family Book Shop on the Hong Kong side of the Star Ferry. See the Bookstores & Newsstands section of Shops for details.

FOREIGN EXCHANGE

Hong Kong is one of the shopping capitals of the modern world, and, appropriately, changing money there is never a problem. Most banks are open from 9 a.m. to 5 p.m. on weekdays and from 9 a.m. to noon (or 1 p.m.) on Saturday. In addition, hotels generally change money 24 hours a day; storefront money changers abound along Nathan Road and throughout Central; and we've found that even most small stores and restaurants are happy to change foreign currency. In this money-obsessed city, few will turn down cash or traveler's checks of any type.

At this writing, one U.S. dollar will buy you almost eight Hong Kong dollars.

LANGUAGE

English is usually spoken, particularly in hotels, shops and the more elegant restaurants. Most street signs are in English, which makes getting around quite easy for the most part. (By comparison, in nearby Taiwan, most street signs and maps are in Chinese, so one spends a lot of time trying to match the characters on the signs with those on the map.) But English can be surprisingly rare among taxi drivers, and English-language menus are not readily found in many of the Chinese restaurants less frequented by Westerners. We've found that one useful strategy is to simply point at dishes on other people's plates that look good.

TIME

To sort out the time change between your home town and Hong Kong, a degree in metaphysics wouldn't hurt (or one of those convenient watches that tells you the time in Dubai, Dacca and Denver at a glance). But the official line is that Hong Kong is sixteen hours ahead of the United States' West Coast, thirteen hours ahead of the East Coast, eight hours ahead of England and France and one hour behind Japan. However, Daylight Savings Time is not followed, so you'll have to subtract one hour during that period. Or buy one of those watches.

TIPPING

Many hotels and restaurants add an automatic service charge of between 10 and 15 percent. But because this sort of enforced tipping isn't uniformly practiced, and since it's not always easy to figure out on a bill written entirely in Chinese, one should always check to see if the tip is indeed included. An additional modest gratuity is usually appropriate, assuming the service has not been utterly disastrous. Bad service, by the way, is fairly rare in Hong Kong, especially at such hotels as The Regent and The Peninsula, where the staff bends over backward to please the customers. And though service in many restaurants may be brusque, that doesn't make it bad—often you'll find the grumpier the service, the faster the food arrives. (And what would you rather have: quick, efficient service or a fawning waiter who pretends to be your new best friend?)

WATER

Hong Kong's tap water is drinkable, though we have noticed that many people prefer bottled water. You'll find yourself drinking most of your water boiled anyway, simply because of the British and Chinese penchant for tea at all hours. Still, in our many trips to Hong Kong, we've never suffered from any stomach ailment, other than those self-induced by too much eating and drinking. The harbor is, unfortunately, rather polluted; though there are beaches around

Hong Kong, care should be exercised before swimming in the waters off any of them. Posted signs will list the restrictions and options available.

BEFORE YOU GO

VISAS

U.S. and French citizens can visit Hong Kong for one month without a visa (as can citizens of most European, South American, Asian and other non-Communist countries). British citizens can stay for up to six months. And citizens of countries in the British Commonwealth can visit for three months without obtaining further documents. Others should contact the Hong Kong Tourist Association (see Addresses & Telephone Numbers above) or the Hong Kong Immigration Department (Mirror Tower, 61 Mody Road, Tsimshatsui East, Kowloon, Hong Kong) for additional information. Be advised that visas can take up to six weeks to obtain.

OTHER DOCUMENTS

Proof of vaccinations and inoculations are only necessary for visitors from countries that have problems with infectious diseases, so Americans, Canadians and Europeans don't have to worry about shots. Foreign driver's licenses are valid for one year, making international driver's licenses unnecessary.

CLOTHING

Weather during the fall and early winter is mild and comfortable, similar to that found on the United States' West Coast, so sportswear and light sweaters will be satisfactory. Later-winter weather can grow chillier, though not for very long, and never dauntingly so. Spring heralds the arrival of summer, with rising temperatures and, more importantly, increasing humidity. Summer is generally horrific—hot, muggy, thoroughly enervating weather, punctuated by the occasional subtropical rainstorm. *Typhoon* is a Chinese word . . . and remember the climactic rainstorms in both *Tai-pan* and *Noble House*. As far as dressing for restaurants, most are casual, though the few upscale Chinese restaurants and the more expensive Western restaurants deserve (and often demand) ties and jackets for men.

GETTING AROUND

ARRIVAL

The majority of visitors to Hong Kong arrive by plane. A wide assortment of international carriers passes through Kai Tak International Airport, which is one of the more dramatic airports in the world, built as it is on a spit of land that extends out from what seems like the center of town. As your plane descends into the maelstrom of lights that is Hong Kong, you'll notice that you can actually look directly into the windows of apartment houses surrounding the airport. Kai Tak is an incredibly efficient airport; you can expect to go from touchdown to customs in a remarkably short period of time. Customs itself is quite efficient as well, and an army of cabs is always waiting outside the airport's front doors.

Those arriving by sea will dock at the Kowloon Ocean Terminal, one of the largest shopping centers in Hong Kong (which is saying something), so you can hit the stores as soon as your ship has tied up.

Those arriving by train from China arrive at the Hung Hom Railway Station in Kowloon, on the edge of Tsimshatsui East—also convenient to shopping and a number of Cantonese seafood restaurants.

TRANSPORTATION

Hong Kong offers a marvelous variety of transportation options. Most of the top hotels have limousine services, which means you can take a Daimler-Benz from The Regent or a Rolls-Royce from The

Peninsula, as you wish. On a more prosaic level, inexpensive cabs (at this writing, HK$6.50 to start and 80 cents each additional quarter kilometer), carefully metered for honesty, abound. If a cab is available for hire, a red flag will be visible through the windshield; after dark, the "Taxi" sign on the roof will be lit up. Along with the basic fare, you'll have to pay appropriate tunnel tolls (including the driver's return toll), should you go to Aberdeen or cross the harbor. Be forewarned that cab drivers usually know only "their" side of the harbor—Hong Kong or Kowloon—and are more likely to get lost if you cab it to the other side. We prefer to take the Star Ferry anyway (see below), and just pick up a new cab on the other side. If you do cab it to the other side, carry a good map with you, in case you need to help with directions.

Along with all those taxis, quaint trams roll up and down Nathan Road (Tram Company, 5-8918765), double-decker buses wheeze their way over the Peak on Hong Kong Island (China Motor Bus, 5-658556), and the Mass Transit Railway (MTR) subway carries commuters back and forth beneath the harbor. The subway system is wonderfully fast and efficient, but since it's a major means of transportation for Hong Kong's commuters, traveling the MTR at rush hour can be a claustrophobe's worst nightmare. Fully automated and electronic, the subway runs from 6 a.m. to 1 a.m. daily. Tickets vary in price depending on your destination; the best bet for visitors is to pick up a $20 Tourist Ticket at one of the HKTA's Information Centres or an MTR station.

Our favorite mode of transportation, though, aside from foot, is the wonderful ferry system, which crosses the harbor with clockwork regularity from a variety of points, heading for a variety of destinations. The Star Ferry, dating back to 1898, departs from its site next to the Ocean Terminal on the Kowloon side and from in front of the HKTA building on Connaught Road on the Hong Kong side. It's as classic a ride as New York's Staten Island Ferry, and it's dirt cheap: 80 cents (Hong Kong) for a first-class one-way ticket. The ten ferry boats start running at 6:30 a.m. and quit at 11:30 p.m., and during the peak travel times they depart as frequently as every three minutes. Call 3-662576 for more information.

Finally, we mustn't forget to mention the funicular tram that climbs the view-rich Peak on Hong Kong Island, a virtually vertical eight-minute ride that's as much fun as any Disneyland ride. The base station is on Garden Road behind the Hilton. A round-trip ticket on the 101-year-old (but perfectly safe) tram is HK$10; call 5-220922 for information.

GOINGS-ON

Below is a list of our favorites of the many events, occasions and festivals that go on annually in Hong Kong. Many of the dates we give are approximations, since all the Chinese holidays and festivals are keyed to the Chinese calendar, which is not quite in sync with the Western calendar. For more details on exact dates, locations and other information, contact the Hong Kong Tourist Association, 3-7225555.

JANUARY

Jan. 1–New Year's Day: Open House at The Peninsula, featuring bagpipers and eggnog.

Third week: Hong Kong Arts Festival. This respected performing arts festival brings music, opera, dance and theater to Hong Kong's better theaters.

Fourth week: Hong Kong International Marathon.

FEBRUARY

First two weeks: Chinese New Year. *The* Chinese festival, sort of like Christmas and New Year's rolled into one big extravaganza. It's a time of family gatherings, colorful parades and dances, and cheerful lights and decorations. It's also a time for the Chinese to pay off old debts and buy new clothes. Be aware that most shops close for two or three days during the New Year celebration, and the week before the festivities start can be chaotic: frenzied tailors won't accept new work, shops are extremely busy, and hairdressers double their rates.

MARCH

First week: Yuen Siu (Lantern) Festival. Lanterns are hung all over town in commemoration of the end of Chinese New Year.

First week: Hong Kong Open Golf Championship.

Last week: Cathay Pacific–Hong Kong Bank Invitational International Seven-a-Side Rugby Championship.
Last week: Coast of China Marathon.

APRIL

First week: Ching Ming Festival. Chinese families visit the grave sites of family members and ancestors, honoring them via traditional rites.

Second week: Hong Kong International Film Festival.

MAY

May 8: Birth of Tin Hau, "Queen of Heaven," the patron deity of fishermen and seafarers. The Tin Hau Festival is held in late April or early May; notable celebrations are held at Joss House Bay.

May 23: Birth of Buddha. Religious ceremonies are held throughout Hong Kong in honor of Buddha's birth.

May 23: Tam Kung Festival. A festival honoring Tam Kung, the patron saint of boat people.

Last week: Cheung Chau Bun Festival. Also called the Festival of the Bun Hills, this week-long religious festival takes over Cheung Chau Island, with elaborate parades, Chinese opera, religious rites and the collecting of good-luck buns.

JUNE

June 11: Birth of Queen Elizabeth.

June 18: Tuen Ng (Dragon Boat) Festival. An important festival honoring Ch'u Yuen, who drowned himself to protest a corrupt government. It is celebrated with the eating of special dumplings, water-oriented festivities and boat races (see below for the largest of these races).

Last week: Hong Kong Dragon Boat Festival International Races. Teams from around the world race long, narrow dragon boats as part of the Dragon Boat Festival.

JULY

July 26: Birth of Lu Pan. Those in the building trade (an important trade in this heavily developed city) celebrate China's "Master Builder."

AUGUST

Mid month: Maiden's Festival. Also called the Seven Sisters Festival, this celebration honoring girls and young lovers dates back more than 1,500 years.

Late Aug.-early Sept.: Hong Kong Food Festival. A food-tasting extravaganza sponsored by the Hong Kong Tourist Association.

Aug. 25: Start of Yue Lan (Hungry Ghosts) Festival, a month-long period of offering tributes to ghostly spirits.

Last Mon.: Liberation Day.

SEPTEMBER

Late month: Mid-Autumn Moon Festival. An important festival akin to harvest festivals in the western world, celebrated in part with the eating of special cakes.

Sept. 26: Horse Racing Season Begins. Festivities at the Happy Valley and Shatin racecourses.

OCTOBER

Early month: Birth of Confucius. Religious ceremonies are held at the Confucius Temple in Causeway Bay.

Mid-month: Chung Yeung Festival. The Chinese head for the hills in this celebration that dates back to the Han Dynasty, when legend has it that a soothsayer told a man to take his family to a high place on the ninth day of the ninth moon. The man did as advised, and returned home the next day to find all living things dead. Don't plan on visiting the Peak on this busy day.

Late month: Festival of Asian Arts.

Late month: Hong Kong Open Squash Championship.

NOVEMBER

Mid-month: Hong Kong International Kart Grand Prix.

Mid-month: Lawn Bowls Classic.

DECEMBER

Early month: Christmas Light Festival at New World Centre and Hong Kong Harbor.

MAPS

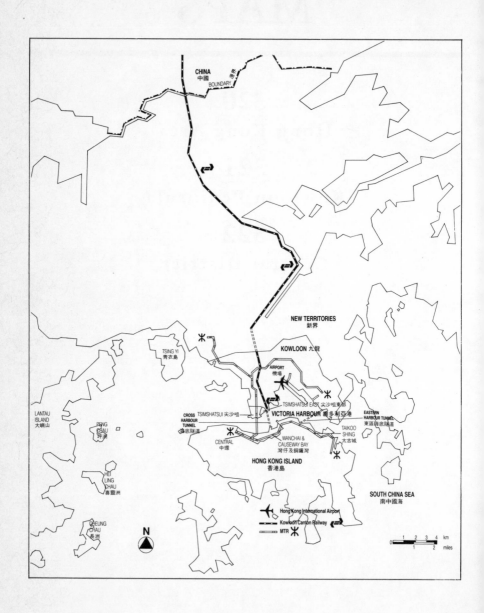

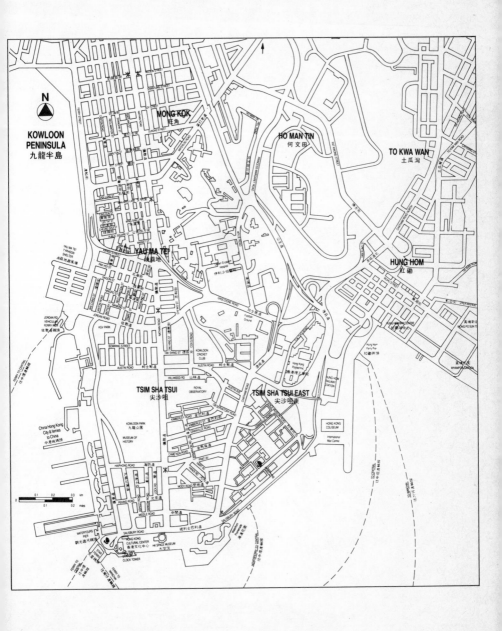

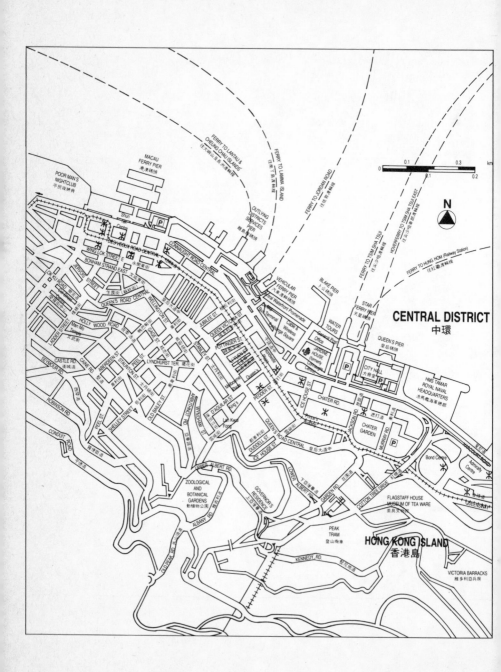

CENTRAL DISTRICT
中環

HONG KONG ISLAND
香港島

INDEX

MORE GAULT MILLAU "BEST" GUIDES

Now the series known throughout Europe for its wit and savvy reveals the best of major U.S. and European areas—New York, Washington, D.C., Los Angeles, San Francisco, Chicago, New England, France and Italy. Following the guidelines established by the world-class French food critics Henri Gault and Christian Millau, local teams of writers directed by André Gayot, partner of Gault Millau, have gathered inside information about where to stay, what to do, where to shop, and where to dine or catch a quick bite in these key locales. Each volume sparkles with the wit, wisdom and panache that readers have come to expect from Gault Millau, whose distinctive style makes them favorites among travelers bored with the neutral, impersonal style of other guides. There are full details on the best of everything that makes these cities special places to visit, including restaurants, destinations, quick bites, nightlife, hotels, shops, the arts—all the unique sights and sounds of each city. These guides offer practical information on getting around and coping with each city. Filled with provocative, entertaining, and frank reviews, they are helpful as well as fun to read. Perfect for visitiors and residents alike.

Please send me the books checked below.

☐ The Best of Chicago $15.95
☐ The Best of Hong Kong $16.95
☐ The Best of Los Angeles $14.95
☐ The Best of New England $15.95
☐ The Best of New York $14.95
☐ The Best of San Francisco $14.95
☐ The Best of Washington, D. C. $14.95
☐ The Best of France $16.95
☐ The Best of Italy $16.95

PRENTICE HALL TRADE DIVISION
Order Department—Travel Books
200 Old Tappan Road
Old Tappan, New Jersey 07675

In U.S. include $2 shipping UPS for 1st book, $1 each additional book. Outside U.S., $3 and $1 respectively.

Enclosed is my check or money order for $ _____

NAME _____

ADDRESS _____

CITY_____ STATE _____ ZIP_____